MICROSOFT
VISUAL C++ 5

No experience required.

MICROSOFT®
VISUAL C++®5

No experience required.™

Steven Holzner

SYBEX®

San Francisco • Paris • Düsseldorf • Soest

Associate Publisher: Gary Masters
Acquisitions Manager: Kristine Plachy
Acquisitions & Developmental Editor: Suzanne Rotondo
Editor: Ben Miller
Technical Editor: Don Hergert
Book Designers: Patrick Dintino, Catalin Dulfu
Electronic Publishing Specialist: Nathan Johanson
Production Coordinator: Alexa Riggs
Proofreaders: Theresa Gonzalez, Charles Mathews
Indexer: Ted Laux
Cover Designer: Ingalls + Associates

Screen reproductions produced with Collage Complete.

Collage Complete is a trademark of Inner Media Inc.

Library of Congress Card Number: 97-67413
ISBN: 0-7821-2120-9

Manufactured in the United States of America

10 9 8 7 6 5 4 3 2

*To my sweetie, Nancy, the cutest
editor ever*

Acknowledgments

A book like this is a collaborative effort, and many people have helped me in producing this one. I would especially like to thank Ben Miller for his excellent, detailed edit, and Don Hergert for his thorough and helpful technical edit. I would also like to thank Suzanne Rotondo, Alexa Riggs, Theresa Gonzalez, Charles Mathews, Andrew Freeman, Nancy Conner, Nathan Johanson, and Ted Laux. These people all contributed to this book, from the concept to the finished pages. Many thanks for all your hours of work!

Contents at a Glance

Table of Contents

Introduction

Visual C++ 5 is the premiere Windows programming product today. If it can be done in Windows, you can do it in Visual C++, and this book will be your guided tour of Visual C++ 5.

Over the years, Visual C++ has evolved into a set of incredibly powerful Windows programming tools, and if you started Windows programming back in the early days of the only product available then—Windows Software Development Kit, or SDK—you can appreciate what Visual C++ has to offer us with its wealth of editors, tools, test containers, class libraries, debugging techniques, and more.

VisualC++ is really an immense package, and sometimes it seems *too* big. Just when you think you've gotten someplace, whole new vistas appear that were hidden before, and you realize it'll take a long time to incorporate these new skills into what you already know. And just when you've done that, a new vista opens up and you have to go through the whole learning process all over again.

This book can make that process a lot easier by taking us on a guided tour of Visual C++. We'll see how to use the many tools, Wizards, editors, and resources of Visual C++ in a clear, careful way. We'll tour through the many regions of Visual C++, and finally tame it—seeing how we can make it work for us, not the other way around.

What's in This Book?

This book's goal is to present Visual C++ 5 at work and give you the skills you need to use it effectively. There's nothing like seeing working code if you want to get something from it. Many books start off with abstractions, programming constructs, and theory, but here we will consider Visual C++ as a set of tools (and very fine tools at that) that the programmer uses to create programs they are interested in, and not as an end in itself.

Often, programming is taught from programming's point of view—that is, in terms of programming constructs like loops and conditionals and class inheritance and so on; that makes for very dry reading. In this book, we will look at things from a different point of view—that of the programmer. Instead of chapters named "If Statements," "Access Modifiers," or "Abstract C++ Classes," our chapters are actually called *skills* and are named for the experience you gain as you work through them, such as "Getting the Most Out of File Handling," "Graphics—and a Complete Mouse-Driven Paint Program," "Creating Check Boxes and Radio Buttons," and more.

The skills are organized from simple to more advanced, so that you will build on the expertise you gain in early skills as you progress through the book. After starting with the basics, such as how to read keystrokes from the keyboard, you will learn how to create menus, toolbar buttons, and shortcut keys. In Skills 6 and 7 you will learn how to design submenus, check boxes, and dialog boxes. Skill 8 will show you how to use list boxes, combo boxes, and sliders. At this point you will have advanced enough to be able to create a full mouse-driven paint program that saves files to disk, and a full word processing program. In the later skills, this book will show you how to connect a database to a Visual C++ program, how to create Internet programs, including a full Web browser, and how to create ActiveX controls. Finally (anticipating the inevitable), we'll show you how to fix things that go wrong in the final skill on debugging.

You will also see plenty of bite-sized examples, because trying to learn Visual C++ without running it is like trying to learn to fly by reading an airplane parts manual. The examples will be short and to the point, without too many extraneous details. We will put Visual C++ to work for you, using all its Wizards and editors in the process of creating working programs.

The Visual C++ package provides you with many tools, and you will use them fully as we create our programs. In addition, we'll include Notes, Tips, and Warnings throughout the book to add more power and expertise.

This is a note, and we'll use notes to indicate points of special concern. For example, why working with the mouse one way instead of another is important at a particular time.

Tips look like this; they are written to save you some time, and they may point out additional information that can be of help. In either case, they were created to provide you with something extra, and hopefully you'll find them worthwhile.

Warnings look like this, and are included to prepare you for common pitfalls you might encounter.

We will build the examples in this book incrementally, so when we add a new line or lines of code, we'll indicate which lines are new with arrows, like this:

```
  void CWelcomeView::OnDraw(CDC* pDC)
  {
➜     CString welcome_string = "Welcome to Visual C++";
      CWelcomeDoc* pDoc = GetDocument();
      ASSERT_VALID(pDoc);

➜     pDC->TextOut(0, 0, welcome_string);
  }
```

There are times when long lines of program code will have to be broken to fit on the page. When code wraps down like this, we will indicate that it represents continuous program code with a carriage return, like this:

```
#endif // !defined(AFX_COMBOSDLG_H__ED674083_9309_11D0_8860_444553540000__
➜INCLUDED_)
```

Visit the No experience required Web Site

In addition, the code we write in this book will also appear on the No experience required Web site, and can be accessed from `http://www.sybex.com`. Each example program has its own subdirectory, which means you don't have to type anything in as we develop our examples. It's all there on the Web site, ready to run. You'll also find other related links to Visual C++ Web resources, links to top technology job sites, and information about other No experience required books.

What You'll Need

Although Visual C++ is an object-oriented language, you don't need to have object-oriented programming experience to read this book. We'll cover how object-oriented programming works in Skill 1. If you have some experience with C++, you already have a leg up here, because you know about object-oriented programming already.

To use this book, you'll need Microsoft Visual C++, of course, and we'll use Visual C++ 5 in this book. Visual C++ provides all the tools you'll need to complete the examples in this book. In addition, note that if you want to execute our Internet-oriented programs, you should have some way to connect to the Internet, such as an Internet Service Provider (ISP). But that's all you'll need.

You can also find more help on Visual C++ on the Internet at: `http://www.microsoft.com/visualc` and in the online documentation that comes with Visual C++.

That's it—we've gotten an overview of our guided tour of Visual C++, and we're ready to begin. Let's start with our first C++ programs now, as we turn to Skill 1.

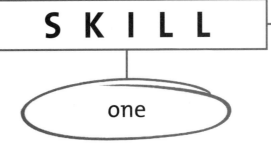

SKILL

one

Welcome to C++

1

Welcome to Visual C++! Visual C++ is an extremely powerful tool for Windows programming—in fact, many programmers consider it *the* most powerful Windows programming tool today. Visual C++ is actually not one tool—it's a collection of many tools, all wrapped together into one dynamic, ready-to-use package.

In this book, we're going to examine those tools and put them to work creating professional Windows programs, from displaying graphics to using menus, from working with buttons and text boxes to handling files, from tapping into the Internet to creating our own ActiveX controls. Among other things, we'll see how to create a fully functional Web browser, including hyperlinks, graphics, and more, and a word processor that includes cut and paste, print, save text to disk, word wrap, and other functions. We'll also develop a powerful paint program that lets us draw graphic figures by "stretching" them with the mouse, filling them in, saving them to disk, and a great deal more. We're going to see a lot in this book, and we'll get started in this skill.

There are really three major topics in this book: C++ programming itself (how to use classes, objects, and other object-oriented programming techniques); Visual C++ itself (especially the built-in resources that Visual C++ includes in the Microsoft Foundation Classes, or MFC); and Windows programming (how to work in Windows programs: the fundamentals of using windows, menus, buttons, and other features). In this skill, we'll get an introduction to the fundamentals of C++ programming: classes, objects, overriding functions, and more.

To keep things simple, our first programs will not create windows themselves; rather, they will use a window that Visual C++ creates for them. These first programs will show us how to work with C++ and give us the vital knowledge we need to continue on to Windows programming itself. In the next skill, we'll use Visual C++ to work with and create windows in the Windows environment. Let's dig into our first skill now with a quick overview of the package we'll be using and get started with Visual C++.

NOTE   If you are already familiar with C++ concepts like inheritance, overriding, overloading, classes, and objects, you can skip on to the next skill and start using our programs that work with and create windows. If these topics are new to you, however, please continue with this skill—we'll need a firm foundation in all of these topics to work with the code in the rest of this book. Note that we are assuming you have a little programming skill already, such as understanding what variables and functions are. If you are entirely new to programming, you might want to spend a little time on the basics, such as what variables and functions are, before you proceed.

Getting an Overview of Visual C++

If you've ever done any Windows programming before Visual C++ came out, you probably have bad memories of the experience. The first way to create Windows programs was to use C, not C++, and to create large, complex programs. In fact, many of the official ways of doing things in original Windows programming were very bad, including stretching a single statement (a C switch statement) over many pages of code. It took five pages of difficult and mysterious code to simply put a blank window on the screen.

Times have changed. C++ was introduced, and C++ is perfect for Windows programming. As we'll see, you can wrap large parts of your code into self-contained C++ objects, which unclutters long programs. (C++ was first developed to work with large programs and make them more manageable.) This meant that it became a great deal easier to handle Windows programming, and the original bad programming practices were replaced with good ones (which made the C++ programs much easier to debug as well). Instead of one long monolithic program, Windows programs were now divided up into neat, manageable chunks.

In addition, Microsoft introduced the Microsoft Foundation Class library, and although you might not expect it, introducing the MFC was just as important as introducing C++ to Windows. The MFC is an extraordinary package of *prewritten*, ready-to-use code. For example, instead of having to write all the code to support a new window (and that's a considerable amount of code), we can just rely on the MFC CWnd code package, which handles all the details for us. Using the standard C++ techniques we'll see in this skill, we'll be able to customize the MFC packages like CWnd the way we want them (for example, we might want to change the text in a window's title bar).

Visual C++ not only makes use of the MFC, but makes Windows programming far easier by introducing many programming tools, such as the menu editor for designing menus, and the dialog editor for designing dialog boxes. Visual C++ provides us with one integrated design *environment* in which we can write our programs and run them. In addition, Visual C++ organizes the many files a Windows program needs into projects, as we'll see very soon, handling a lot of the work for us. In fact, the Visual C++ Wizards (special programming tools) will even write a good part of our programs for us, as we'll see in the next skill.

That's enough of an overview of Visual C++ to get us started. Now we'll begin putting the many parts of this diverse and robust programming package to work.

In this first skill, we will use Visual C++, but not to create programs that support their own windows. Instead, we'll use Visual C++ in the simplest possible way so that we don't clutter up our C++ programming examples with numerous, needless details. Trying to learn C++ programming from a Visual C++ program that supports and creates its own window would be a very difficult task indeed, so we'll take Visual C++ programming in stages.

In the rest of this skill, we'll concentrate on getting the basics of C++ down, letting Visual C++ create windows for our programs and letting them run in the simplest way. In the next skill, we'll see how to start working in the windowing environment of Windows itself.

Our First Example at Work

Visual C++ programs can become very involved and lengthy before you even notice it, so we will be very careful about keeping them simple while we work with and explore C++ programming ideas like classes and objects.

Not many programmers are aware of this, but you can use Visual C++ to create non-windowed (i.e., "console") programs, and we'll do that now. These programs run in windows that look like DOS windows, and our first program will be quite simple, just putting a message on the screen: "Welcome to C++":

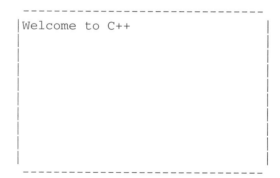

```
-------------------------------
|Welcome to C++                |
|                              |
|                              |
|                              |
|                              |
|                              |
|                              |
|                              |
|                              |
|                              |
-------------------------------
```

Let's see how to do this now. Start Visual C++ itself, as shown in Figure 1.1. This environment is actually the Microsoft Developer Studio, an Integrated Development Environment (IDE) that hosts Visual C++ and other packages like Visual J++ (for Java programming).

The menus and toolbars you see in Figure 1.1 are part of the Developer Studio, but since we'll never see Visual C++ apart from the Developer Studio, we'll treat them as synonymous in this book (for example, when we say, "select the New item in the Visual C++ File menu," we actually mean, "select the New item in the Developer Studio File menu").

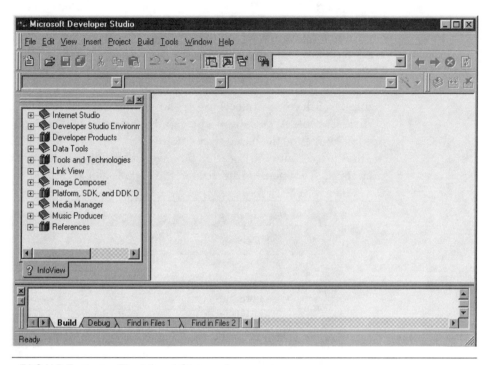

FIGURE 1.1: The Visual C++ environment

In most of this book, we'll create Visual C++ programs that handle their own windows, but not in this skill. We'll create *Win32 console* programs here—these programs run in their own windows, which Visual C++ sets up for them. All we have to worry about is the C++ programming, and that's perfect for us now.

Visual C++ Workspaces and Projects

Our first program will simply be named "first," and we'll create that program as a new Visual C++ project. Visual C++ organizes programming tasks into projects, and usually each separate program gets its own project. A project is a collection of files that are all used to create one working, runnable program.

In addition, projects themselves are placed in *workspaces*, and a workspace can have several projects in it (you set the "active" project with the Set Active Project item in Visual C++'s Project menu). Each project we develop will have its own workspace, but we'll deal with workspaces very little in this book: Visual C++ creates a default workspace each time we start an entirely new program, so we'll concentrate on projects, not workspaces. Even so, we should realize that the main environment we are working in is a Visual C++ workspace, and that our project is a project inside that workspace.

Let's create and run our first project now. We do that by selecting the New item in Visual C++'s File menu; this opens the New dialog box, as shown in Figure 1.2. Select the Projects tab as shown in Figure 1.2 now, and select the "Win32 Console Application" entry in the New dialog box, as shown in Figure 1.2. Now type the name **first** into the Project name box and the path for the first project into the Location box; we will use the directory c:\vcpp for our projects, so we type **c:\vjpp\first** in the Location box.

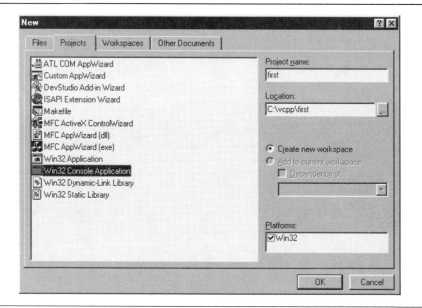

FIGURE 1.2: Creating a new Visual C++ project

Now click the OK button in the New dialog box. This creates our new program, named "first", including two important files: first.dsw to handle our new workspace and first.dsp to handle our new project.

 TIP   When you open a program you've worked on before to work on it again, you use the "Open Workspaces... item" in Visual C++'s File menu and open the program's .dsw workspace file.

So far, we have a new workspace and a new project named "first" in that workspace. We will add the actual code for this program next; here we just want to print out the message "Welcome to C++".

Creating a Source Code File

To add programming code to our project, we will need a new file: first.cpp. The extension .cpp is used with C++ source files.

 NOTE   Besides source files, C++ programs often have header files, which use the extension .h. Header files can hold the declarations of variables and functions in them, as we'll see in the next skill.

Now let's create `first.cpp` and add it to our project. We create `first.cpp` with the New item in the Visual C++ File menu. This time, however, click the Files tab, as shown in Figure 1.3.

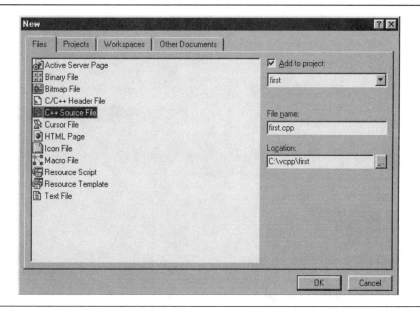

FIGURE 1.3: Creating a new Visual C++ source code file

Now select the C++ Source File entry, as shown in Figure 1.3, give this file the name first.cpp in the File name box, and make sure the box marked "Add to project" is clicked, as shown in Figure 1.3. Then click the button marked OK.

This creates the file first.cpp, and opens it in the Visual C++ environment, as shown in Figure 1.4. There are three main windows you can see in Visual C++ now: the viewer window at left, which has three tabs at the bottom (ClassView, FileView, and InfoView); the Editor window at right, in which we edit our documents (you can see the empty first.cpp file opened there now); and the Results window at bottom, with tabs like Build, Debug, and Find in Files.

The Viewer window shows us overviews of our projects, and how those overviews are organized depends on the tab we click—ClassView, FileView, and InfoView. The ClassView tab shows us our workspace organized by C++ *classes*, and we'll see all about classes soon. The FileView tab shows us how our workspace is organized by files, and you can see our workspace, project, and first.cpp file displayed there in Figure 1.4. The InfoView tab shows all the online documentation that comes with Visual C++, organized into online books.

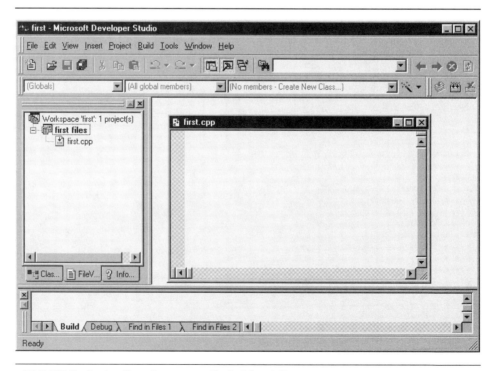

FIGURE 1.4: Opening a new file in Visual C++

> **NOTE** When we start working with fully windowed Visual C++ programs in the next skill, we'll see another tab in the viewer window, the Resources tab. Items like menus, dialog boxes, and toolbars are considered *resources* in Windows programming.

The editor window shows us all the documents we have open. We'll see the text editor in this window, as well as other editors like the menu editor and the dialog editor.

The last window, the Results window at the bottom of Figure 1.4, shows the results of asking Visual C++ to compile our programs, meaning to convert them into the binary code that the computer can run. It also handles debugging and more, as we'll see.

Adding C++ Code to a Program

Now we'll add our source code to the program, in the file first.cpp, which is open in the Visual C++ editor window. To create our first C++ program, just type in this C++ code:

```
#include <iostream.h>

void main()
{
    cout << "Welcome to C++ \n";
}
```

This is our first C++ program. Here, we are using standard C++ techniques to display our message "Welcome to C++".

In particular, we *include* the file iostream.h, which lets us use the standard C++ techniques of writing to the screen. (Including a file like this inserts the contents of that file into our main file.)

Next, we set up a function named main(). This is the actual function that is called when the program starts. That is, when you run an executable file like first.exe, Windows looks for the main() function in the .exe file and starts executing the code there first, so we'll place the code we want executed in this function. We'll see more about main() in a minute.

Now that we know where the program starts, let's look into what it actually does—it displays a message on the screen using C++ input/output techniques.

What Are C++ Streams?

In our program, we write to the C++ *stream* named cout using the << operator like this: cout << "Welcome to C++ \n";:

```
#include <iostream.h>

void main()
{
→    cout << "Welcome to C++ \n";
}
```

What this means is that we send the text "Welcome to C++ \n" to the C++ output stream, which goes directly to the screen. You can think of a C++ stream as a data conduit, sending data to various destinations; the cout stream sends text to the screen.

The "\n" at the end of the message is a *newline* code, which ends our text with a carriage return. With this simple line, we will display our message on the screen by sending it to the cout stream.

We won't dwell on the specifics of the cout stream, because you don't use that stream when displaying text in standard Windows programs; we use it here just to make things easier for the moment. In fact, we're only using the cout stream to let our program display output on the screen so we can see what the classes and objects we develop in this skill are doing when we run programs. After this skill, we won't use cout at all.

That completes our discussion of the code in first.cpp. After typing the code in to Visual C++, that file appears as shown in Figure 1.5. Now we have our project and our source code set up and we're ready to see the program at work—it's ready to run.

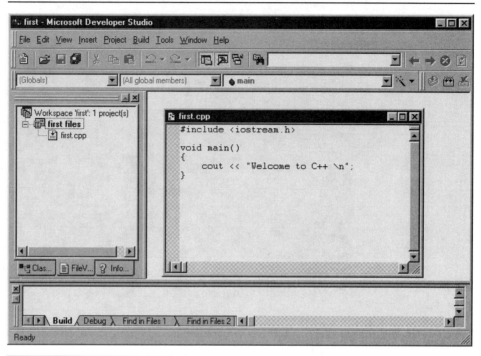

FIGURE 1.5: Adding code to a program in Visual C++

Running Our First Program

To run our first program, we need to create the actual runnable program that the computer can use: first.exe. We do this by compiling the source code first.cpp into first.exe, and we do that by selecting the "Build first.exe" item in the Visual C++ Build menu.

Compiling our program displays the following text in the Visual C++ Results window, at the bottom of the Developer Studio:

```
--------Configuration: first - Win32 Debug--------
Compiling...
first.cpp
Linking...

first.exe - 0 error(s), 0 warning(s)
```

Next, we run the program by selecting the "Execute first.exe" item in the Visual C++ Build menu. Running the program gives us the results shown in Figure 1.6.

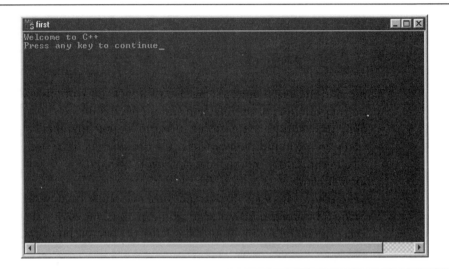

FIGURE 1.6: Running our first program

In Figure 1.6, we see our message, "Welcome to C++", and a prompt, "Press any key to continue", which is placed there by Visual C++. When you press any key, the first window disappears from the screen.

We've created and run our first Win32 console program successfully—we're already using C++. The code for this program appears in first.cpp below.

 **first.cpp**

```
#include <iostream.h>

void main()
{
    cout << "Welcome to C++ \n";
}
```

This tiny program was just to get us started with Visual C++ projects, workspaces, compiling programs, and the text editor. Now we're ready to launch ourselves into C++ programming itself. In particular, C++ programming is *object-oriented* programming, and we'll see what that—the backbone of C++—is all about now.

All About C++ Classes and Objects

Objects and *classes* are two fundamental concepts in object-oriented languages like C++, and because they're important concepts, we'll take a minute to examine them. Doing so now will save us time and confusion later. There's been a lot of hype about object-oriented programming (OOP), and that often makes the whole topic seem mysterious and unapproachable, but it's not. In fact, OOP was really introduced to make longer programs *easier* to create. We'll start our mini-survey of object-oriented programming by looking at objects.

What Is an Object?

In long, involved programs, variables and functions can become quite profuse, sometimes with hundreds of each. This makes creating and maintaining the program code a very cluttered task, because you have to keep so many things in mind. There may also be unwanted interaction if various functions use variables of the same name. To break such large programs up, object-oriented programming was invented.

The idea behind objects is quite simple—you just break up the program into the various parts, each of which you can easily conceptualize as performing a discrete task, and those are your objects. For example, you may put all the screen-handling parts of a program together into an object named screen. Objects are more powerful than simply functions or sets of variables, because an object can hold both functions and variables wrapped up together in a way that makes it easy to use. Our screen object may hold not only all the data displayed on the screen, but also the functions needed to handle that data, like drawString() or drawLine(). This means that all the screen handling is hidden from the rest of the program in a convenient way, making the rest of the program easier to handle.

As another example, think of a refrigerator. A refrigerator would be far less useful if you had to regulate all the temperatures and pumps and so forth by hand at all times. Making all those functions internal and automatic to the refrigerator makes it both useful and a much easier object to deal with. Wrapping up code and data this way into objects is the basis of object-oriented programming.

What Is a Class?

But how do we create objects? That's where *classes* come in. A class is to an object what a cookie cutter is to a cookie—that is, a class acts like a template or blueprint for an object. In terms of programming, you might think of the relationship between a data type, like an integer, and the actual variable itself the same way, as in this example, where we set up an integer named the_data:

```
int the_data;
```

This is the actual way we create an integer variable in C++. Here, int is the type of variable we are declaring and the_data is the variable itself. This is the same relationship that a class has to an object, and informally we may think of a class as an object's type.

 TIP   As we'll see, C++ supports all the standard programming data types like int, double, long, float, and so forth.

For example, if we had set up a class named screenclass, we can create an object of that class named screen this way:

```
screenclass screen;
```

What's important to remember is this: the object itself is what holds the data we want to work with; the class itself holds no data, it only describes how the object should be set up.

Object-oriented programming at root is nothing more than a way of grouping functions and data together to make your program less cluttered. We'll see more about object-oriented programming throughout this book, including how to create a class, how to create an object of that class, and how to reach the functions and data in that object when we want to.

That completes our mini-overview of classes and objects for the moment. To sum up, a class is just a programming construct that groups together (a process called *encapsulating*) functions and data, and an object may be thought of as a variable of that class's type, as our object screen is to the class screenclass.

Visual C++ comes complete with a whole library of pre-defined classes— the Microsoft Foundation Class (MFC) library—which saves us a great deal of work. Using those predefined classes, we'll create objects needed to handle buttons, text fields, scroll bars, and much more. Microsoft has already done much of the programming for us, which we will use later on.

Next we'll look at an example program that uses both classes and objects.

Our First C++ Classes and Objects Example

In our next example, we'll see how to set up a class, which we'll name `DataClass`, and an object of that class, which we'll name `DataObject`. Neither this class nor the object will do much, but this example will make it clear how classes and objects work.

Using Visual C++, start a new project named classes, as we did in the previous example. Now add a new file to that project named `classes.cpp`. We're ready to add code to that file now, and we begin by including `iostream.h` as we did before in `classes.cpp`:

```
    #include <iostream.h>
➜           .
            .
            .
```

Next, we set up the declaration of our new class, `DataClass`:

```
    #include <iostream.h>

➜class DataClass
➜{

➜};
```

This is how you declare a new class—with the `class` keyword. The rest of the class's declaration will go between the curly braces, { and }.

A big part of C++ objects is storing data, and we can set up some data storage in our `DataClass` class. A data item in a class is stored in a variable known as a *data member*. For example, we can set up a new integer variable—(that is, an integer data member)—called `PrivateDataMember` this way:

```
    #include <iostream.h>

    class DataClass
    {
➜private:
➜       int PrivateDataMember;
             .
             .
             .
    };
```

This new data member is an integer, and so it can store integer values. Note the private keyword here—this means that only objects of our DataClass have access to this data member. This keyword, private, is called an *access modifier*.

 TIP   If you omit the access modifier in a class declaration, the default is private.

What Are Access Modifiers?

Besides the private access modifier, you can also use the *public* access modifier, which means that the data member is available to all other parts of the program freely. We'll see more about the third access modifier—*protected*—later; this restricts access to a data member to objects of our class and objects *derived* from our class (we'll see what this means soon).

We can put the public keyword to use now, declaring a new data member named PublicDataMember:

```
#include <iostream.h>

class DataClass
{
private:
    int PrivateDataMember;
public:
➜    int PublicDataMember;
         .
         .
         .
```

This data member will be available to all other parts of the program, as we're about to see.

Next, let's add a function to our DataClass class. Functions that are members of a class are named *methods*. In this case, we'll add a new method named PublicMethod():

```
#include <iostream.h>

class DataClass
{
private:
    int PrivateDataMember;
public:
    int PublicDataMember;
➜    int PublicMethod(void);
};
```

> **NOTE**   **The methods of a class usually work with the data internal to the class in a way that hides the details from the rest of the program. This is very useful, because it helps divide the program up into manageable sections, and in fact, doing this was the original idea behind the use of objects.**

We pass data as variables named *parameters* this way: add(variable1, variable2). Methods can take data passed to them and those parameters become available for use in the method, just as in other programming languages.

Here, however, we indicate that our method takes no parameters by declaring it using the void keyword this way: int PublicMethod(void) (using void in the parentheses is optional here—we could have declared the PublicMethod() method this way: int PublicMethod();). We also indicate that this method returns an integer value in the above declaration by prefacing the declaration with the keyword int. This means that this method takes no parameters, and it returns an integer.

We've declared our PublicMethod() method now, but how do we write the code for this method? We do that by setting up the definition of this method separately from the class declaration, and we preface that definition with DataClass::, indicating which class this method is part of (in this way, Visual C++ will know to which class the method we're defining belongs).

```
#include <iostream.h>

class DataClass
{
private:
    int PrivateDataMember;
public:
    int PublicDataMember;
    int PublicMethod(void);
};

int DataClass::PublicMethod(void)
{

}
```

Now we're ready to add some code to this method. The method takes no parameters, but it returns an integer value. What value should we return? Because our PrivateDataMember member cannot be reached by the rest of the program directly, let's return that data member in PublicMethod() so the rest of the program can gain access to it.

We can return the value in `PrivateDataMember` this way in `PublicMethod()` (note that since `PublicMethod()` is part of the `DataClass` class, we have no problem getting access to the private data member `PrivateDatamember`):

```
#include <iostream.h>

class DataClass
{
private:
    int PrivateDataMember;
public:
    int PublicDataMember;
    int PublicMethod(void);
};

int DataClass::PublicMethod(void)
{
    return PrivateDataMember;
}
```

Now we've set up `PublicMethod()` to return `PrivateDataMember`—but what value does our `PrivateDataMember` hold? We haven't initialized that variable to hold any data, so when we call `PublicMethod()`, the value it returns will be meaningless. We'll look into initializing our `PrivateDataMember` next.

Initializing Data in a Class Using Constructors

It's often the case that we need to initialize the data in an object; for example, in our `DataClass` class, we need to initialize the data member `PrivateDataMember`. We can do that in the class's *constructor*.

A class's constructor is a special method that the program runs automatically when an object of that class is created. You perform initialization in that method, as we'll see. You declare a constructor in a class by declaring a method with the same name as the class itself, with no return value. A constructor can have as many parameters passed to it as you like, however. Here, we'll take one parameter in the constructor—the value we should place in the `PrivateDataMember` variable when the object is first created.

Declaring this new constructor looks like this:

```
#include <iostream.h>

class DataClass
{
private:
    int PrivateDataMember;
public:
➡    DataClass(int Value);
     int PublicDataMember;
     int PublicMethod(void);
};
Now we set up the constructor's definition:
#include <iostream.h>

class DataClass
{
private:
    int PrivateDataMember;
public:
    DataClass(int Value);
    int PublicDataMember;
    int PublicMethod(void);
};

➡DataClass::DataClass(int Value)
➡{

➡}
```

In this case, we'll just store the value passed to us in `PrivateDataMember`:

```
#include <iostream.h>

class DataClass
{
private:
    int PrivateDataMember;
public:
    DataClass(int Value);
    int PublicDataMember;
    int PublicMethod(void);
};

DataClass::DataClass(int Value)
{
➡    PrivateDataMember = Value;
}
```

Now we're set. We've set up a class with public and private data members, and a method that we can call. The only thing left is to make use of this new class, and we do that in the main() function.

Using Our DataClass Class

Add the main() function to the classes.cpp file now:

```
#include <iostream.h>

class DataClass
{
private:
     int PrivateDataMember;
public:
     DataClass(int Value);
     int PublicDataMember;
     int PublicMethod(void);
};

DataClass::DataClass(int Value)
{
     PrivateDataMember = Value;
}

int DataClass::PublicMethod(void)
{
     return PrivateDataMember;
}

➡void main()
➡{

➡}
```

The main() function holds the code that will be executed first when the program runs. We start this new function by declaring an object of our DataClass class. At the same time, we pass a value to the class's constructor (this value will be placed in the PrivateDataMember data member). Let's just pass a value of 1, which looks like this, where we create an object named DataObject of our DataClass class:

```
void main()
{
```

```
→       DataClass DataObject(1);
                .
                .
                .
        }
```

Now we have an object named `DataObject`. This object stores the data we've put into it, and it also supports the `PublicMethod()` method.

We can set the value in the public data member, `PublicDataMember`, using the C++ dot operator (".") this way, where we set it to 2:

```
void main()
{
        DataClass DataObject(1);

→       DataObject.PublicDataMember = 2;
                .
                .
                .
        }
```

The general way we refer to the members of an object is by using the dot operator. For example, we can display the value in the `PublicDataMember` this way, sending it to the cout stream:

```
void main()
{
        DataClass DataObject(1);

        DataObject.PublicDataMember = 2;

→       cout << "DataObject.PublicDataMember = " << DataObject
      ↪.PublicDataMember << "\n";
                .
                .
                .
        }
```

But how do we read the value set in `PrivateDataMember`? Because the code in the `main()` function is not part of `DataObject`, we can't reach that data member directly. To read the value in that member, we can call `PublicMethod()` here, where we display that value:

```
void main()
{
```

```
DataClass DataObject(1);

DataObject.PublicDataMember = 2;

    cout << "DataObject.PublicDataMember = " << DataObject
➥.PublicDataMember << "\n";
    cout << "DataObject.PrivateDataMember = " << DataObject
➥.PublicMethod() << "\n";

}
```

Now our classes program is complete; run it now, as shown in Figure 1.7. As you can see in that figure, we're able to display the values in both the public and private data members in our DataClass object. We've gotten a good start with C++ classes and objects.

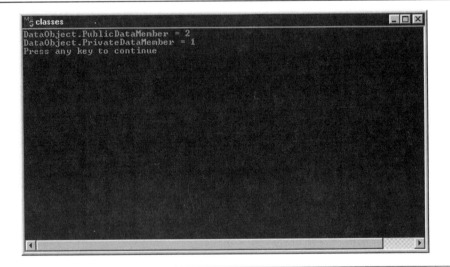

FIGURE 1.7: Running our classes program

The code for this program appears in classes.cpp.

classes.cpp

```
#include <iostream.h>

class DataClass
{
private:
    int PrivateDataMember;
public:
    DataClass(int Value);
    int PublicDataMember;
    int PublicMethod(void);
};

DataClass::DataClass(int Value)
{
    PrivateDataMember = Value;
}

int DataClass::PublicMethod(void)
{
    return PrivateDataMember;
}

void main()
{
    DataClass DataObject(1);

    DataObject.PublicDataMember = 2;

    cout << "DataObject.PublicDataMember = " << DataObject
➡.PublicDataMember << "\n";
    cout << "DataObject.PrivateDataMember = " << DataObject
➡.PublicMethod() << "\n";

}
```

This first example was very rudimentary; it really does nothing more than show how to set up a C++ program with a class and an object. This example doesn't point out what objects are really good for—holding and working on data internally. We'll take a look at an example with more meat on it now to make it clearer how objects work and why they are useful.

A True C++ Example: SchoolRoom

Let's see a more real-life C++ example now, pointing out the kinds of internal data-management and manipulations that objects are good for.

In this example, we will assume that we have to manage the test scores of two sets of students—a history class and an English class. In particular, we can create an object that handles all the details of storing those scores internally, and can also figure out the average score for the students in each class. Let's put this to work now in an example named "schoolroom."

Create the schoolroom project now and add a new file named `schoolroom.cpp` to it. We set up a new class named `SchoolClass` to store the student's scores and manipulate them:

```
#include <iostream.h>

→class SchoolClass {

→};
```

Now we'll set up storage for the students' scores as a section of memory named `ClassData`. We will make the actual variable named `ClassData` a pointer to the beginning of the data we're storing in memory. We'll allocate the memory at that location only when we know how many students there are in the class—a number that will be passed to us in the class's constructor—so we can set aside the appropriate amount of space.

 NOTE   A pointer is just a variable that holds an address of a memory location. In C and C++, array names are pointers to the beginning of the array's data in memory. To declare a pointer in C and C++, you preface the variable's name with an asterisk, "*".

We also set up an integer index, `ClassDataIndex`, into our data storage area so we know where we are in memory when we add new student's scores:

```
#include <iostream.h>

class SchoolClass {
→     int *ClassData;
→     int ClassDataIndex;

};
```

We can allocate the actual data storage for the students' scores in the class constructor. We'll pass the number of students to allocate space for the constructor and set up the new data storage this way. Note that we also initialize the data storage index, ClassDataIndex to 0:

```
#include <iostream.h>

class SchoolClass {
    int *ClassData;
    int ClassDataIndex;
public:
    SchoolClass(int NumberStudents);
        .
        .
        .
};

SchoolClass::SchoolClass(int NumberStudents)
{
    ClassData = new int[NumberStudents];
    ClassDataIndex = 0;
}
```

Here, we use the C++ *new* operator to allocate the new data storage. In this case, we allocate space for NumberStudents integers. The new operator is actually a built-in part of C++ (and replaces C functions like malloc() and calloc()). We'll see more about new throughout this book.

We can treat this new data storage space as an array if we like (the names of arrays and pointers are practically interchangeable in C and C++), and we can reference the first integer in it as ClassData[0], the next integer as ClassData[1], and so on.

At this point, then, we have set up a data space that we will treat as an array, with space enough to hold NumberStudents integer scores.

But how do we get rid of this allocated memory when we want to now that we've allocated it in our new object? Besides constructors, C++ also supports *destructors*, called when an object is destroyed, and we can put clean-up code there—in this case, we'll just deallocate the memory we allocated earlier.

C++ Destructors

A destructor is just like a constructor, except that it's automatically called when the object is destroyed. We set up a destructor just like a constructor, except we use a tilde ("~") to preface its name:

```
#include <iostream.h>

class SchoolClass {
    int *ClassData;
    int ClassDataIndex;
public:
    SchoolClass(int NumberStudents);
➜   ~SchoolClass(void);
        .
        .
        .
};

SchoolClass::SchoolClass(int NumberStudents)
{
    ClassData = new int[NumberStudents];
    ClassDataIndex = 0;
}

➜SchoolClass::~SchoolClass(void)
➜{

➜}
```

In the destructor, we simply deallocate the memory we allocated with the new operator. The opposite of the new operator is the delete operator, and we use it like this to remove our array:

```
SchoolClass::~SchoolClass(void)
{
➜   delete ClassData;
}
```

Now we have our constructor and destructor, but there's a new concern: this new class can't exist in a vacuum. We'll need some methods to store and retrieve students' scores in our new class.

That is, when a new object of the SchoolClass class is created, we'll have to load it with data and provide some means of working with that data. This is fundamental to objects—their whole purpose is usually to store and work on internal data.

Storing, Retrieving, and Averaging Data

To execute our data-handling tasks, we will add three methods to our SchoolClass class:

> AddScore() to add a new student score to the object's internal array.
>
> GetScore() to retrieve a score from the object's internal (private) data array.
>
> AverageScore() to return the average score of all students in this class.

These three methods point out the standard methods of data-handling: saving data, retrieving data, and manipulating data.

The AddScore() and GetScore()methods are easy to write, so we'll add them now.

Storing the Data with AddScore()

When we call AddScore(), we just want to add a new score to the object's internal data storage of scores, so we write AddScore() like this:

```
#include <iostream.h>

class SchoolClass {
    int *ClassData;
    int ClassDataIndex;
public:
    SchoolClass(int NumberStudents);
    ~SchoolClass(void);
→   void AddScore(int Score);
};
            .
            .
            .
→void SchoolClass::AddScore(int Score)
→{
→   ClassData[ClassDataIndex++] = Score;
→}
```

In AddScore(), we just store the new score, passed to us as a parameter, to the internal array of scores, and increment the array index. Note how we increment the array index ClassDataIndex like this: ClassDataIndex++.

This is the famous ++ operator of C++, and it increments its argument. When used as a *postfix* operator like this, it increments the value of its argument *after* the present statement is executed. When used as a prefix operator: ++ClassDataIndex, it increments its argument, ClassDataIndex, *before* the rest of the statement executes.

 TIP   **Besides ++, C++ also has the - - operator, which decrements its argument and can also be used as a prefix or postfix operator.**

Now we will write GetScore(), in which we get the score at a certain index in the internal data storage and return it.

Retrieving the Data with GetScore()

When we call GetScore() with an index value, we want to get the score at that index in the internal data storage. Let's write GetScore() now.

First in GetScore(), we check to make sure the index we're supposed to use does not exceed the total number of scores we've saved so far. If we are being asked for a valid score, we return that score this way:

```
#include <iostream.h>

class SchoolClass {
    int *ClassData;
    int ClassDataIndex;
public:
    SchoolClass(int NumberStudents);
    ~SchoolClass(void);
    void AddScore(int Score);
    int GetScore(int Index);

            .
            .
            .

};

int SchoolClass::GetScore(int Index)
{
    if(Index <= ClassDataIndex)
    {
        return ClassData[Index];
    }

            .
            .
            .

}
```

Otherwise, we are being asked for a score that we haven't even stored yet, so we return a value of -1 in the if statement's else clause (executed when the conditional for the if clause was false):

```
#include <iostream.h>

class SchoolClass {
    int *ClassData;
    int ClassDataIndex;
public:
    SchoolClass(int NumberStudents);
    ~SchoolClass(void);
    void AddScore(int Score);
    int GetScore(int Index);
        .
        .
        .
};

int SchoolClass::GetScore(int Index)
{
    if(Index <= ClassDataIndex)
    {
        return ClassData[Index];
    }
    else
    {
        return -1;
    }
}
```

That completes our methods for storing and retrieving data, AddScore() and GetScore().

All that's left to write is AverageScore(), which manipulates the stored data by returning the average score of all the students for whom we've saved scores so far.

Averaging the Data with AverageScore()

In AverageScore(), we will sum all the scores in a floating point variable named Sum, then we will divide that value by the total number of students to get the average score, which we will return to the rest of the program.

To work with the floating point variable Sum, we have to temporarily treat the integer scores as floating point numbers, which we do with a *cast*, like this: (float) ClassData[loop_index]. This lets us treat the integer value at ClassData[loop_index] as a floating point temporarily, so we can add it to our running total (note that we also return a value of -1 if there is no data to average):

```
#include <iostream.h>

class SchoolClass {
    int *ClassData;
    int ClassDataIndex;
public:
    SchoolClass(int NumberStudents);
    ~SchoolClass(void);
    void AddScore(int Score);
    int GetScore(int Index);
➜   float AverageScore(void);
};
        .
        .
        .
➜float SchoolClass::AverageScore(void)
➜{
➜   float Sum = 0;

➜   if(ClassDataIndex == 0)
➜   {
➜       return -1;
➜   }

➜   for(int loop_index = 0; loop_index < ClassDataIndex; loop_index++)
➜   {
➜       Sum += (float) ClassData[loop_index];
➜   }
        .
        .
        .
}
```

NOTE   We use the C++ for loop here, which has the general form:

```
for(init; end; perform)
{
    [loop body]
}
```

Here, the `init` statement is executed first, then the `end` condition is tested, and the code in the loop body is executed. After the loop is executed, the `perform` statement is executed, which usually increments a loop index.

You might note one thing here—we declare our loop index variable loop_index right in the for loop itself (as int loop_index = 0):

➜
```
        for(int loop_index = 0; loop_index < ClassDataIndex; loop_index++)
        {
            Sum += (float) ClassData[loop_index];
        }
```

This points out a very nice feature of C++: you can declare variables as you need them throughout your code; you don't have to declare them all at the beginning of a function as you do in languages like C.

At this point, we've stored the sum of the student's scores in the variable named Sum, and we can divide that by the total number of scores to find the average, which we return as the AverageScore() method's return value:

```
    #include <iostream.h>

    class SchoolClass {
        int *ClassData;
        int ClassDataIndex;
    public:
        SchoolClass(int NumberStudents);
        ~SchoolClass(void);
        void AddScore(int Score);
        int GetScore(int Index);
```
➜
```
        float AverageScore(void);
    };
            .
            .
            .
```
➜
```
float SchoolClass::AverageScore(void)
```
➜
```
{
```
➜
```
    float Sum = 0;
```

➜
```
    if(ClassDataIndex == 0)
```
➜
```
    {
```
➜
```
        return -1;
```
➜
```
    }
```

➜
```
    for(int loop_index = 0; loop_index < ClassDataIndex; loop_index++)
```
➜
```
    {
```
➜
```
        Sum += (float) ClassData[loop_index];
```
➜
```
    }
```

➜
```
    return Sum / (float) ClassDataIndex;
}
```

That's it—we've completed our SchoolClass class now, complete with data storage, retrieval, and handling methods. It's time to put this class to work.

Using SchoolClass in Our Program

We will put the SchoolClass class to work in a main() function, which we add to schoolroom.cpp:

```
void main()
{

}
```

We start by declaring two SchoolClass objects: HistoryClass to keep track of history students, and EnglishClass to keep track of an English class:

```
void main()
{
    SchoolClass HistoryClass(9);
    SchoolClass EnglishClass(10);
            .
            .
            .
}
```

Next, we fill up the internal arrays in these objects with data, using our AddScore() method:

```
void main()
{
    SchoolClass HistoryClass(9);
    SchoolClass EnglishClass(10);

➜    HistoryClass.AddScore(80);
    HistoryClass.AddScore(81);
    HistoryClass.AddScore(82);
    HistoryClass.AddScore(83);
    HistoryClass.AddScore(84);
    HistoryClass.AddScore(85);
    HistoryClass.AddScore(86);
    HistoryClass.AddScore(87);
    HistoryClass.AddScore(88);

➜    EnglishClass.AddScore(91);
    EnglishClass.AddScore(92);
    EnglishClass.AddScore(93);
    EnglishClass.AddScore(94);
```

```
        EnglishClass.AddScore(95);
        EnglishClass.AddScore(96);
        EnglishClass.AddScore(97);
        EnglishClass.AddScore(98);
        EnglishClass.AddScore(99);
        EnglishClass.AddScore(100);
                .
                .
                .
}
```

Finally, we print out the average scores for the two classes of students:

```
void main()
{
        SchoolClass HistoryClass(9);
        SchoolClass EnglishClass(10);

        HistoryClass.AddScore(80);
        HistoryClass.AddScore(81);
        HistoryClass.AddScore(82);
        HistoryClass.AddScore(83);
        HistoryClass.AddScore(84);
        HistoryClass.AddScore(85);
        HistoryClass.AddScore(86);
        HistoryClass.AddScore(87);
        HistoryClass.AddScore(88);

        EnglishClass.AddScore(91);
        EnglishClass.AddScore(92);
        EnglishClass.AddScore(93);
        EnglishClass.AddScore(94);
        EnglishClass.AddScore(95);
        EnglishClass.AddScore(96);
        EnglishClass.AddScore(97);
        EnglishClass.AddScore(98);
        EnglishClass.AddScore(99);
        EnglishClass.AddScore(100);

➡       cout << "Average score for History class: " << HistoryClass
➥.AverageScore() << "\n";
➡       cout << "Average score for English class: " << EnglishClass
➥.AverageScore() << "\n";

}
```

The schoolroom program is ready to run.

Run it now, as shown in Figure 1.8. As you can see there, we've loaded our SchoolClass objects with data and found the average value of that data—our objects were successful in manipulating their data.

Using objects, we were able to break the program up into smaller, more easily managed units, and that's their whole point. In this way, we've gotten some insights into what objects do best. Our program is a success. The code for this program appears in schoolroom.cpp.

FIGURE 1.8: Running our classes program

schoolroom.cpp

```cpp
#include <iostream.h>

class SchoolClass {
    int *ClassData;
    int ClassDataIndex;
public:
    SchoolClass(int NumberStudents);
    ~SchoolClass(void);
    void AddScore(int Score);
    int GetScore(int Index);
    float AverageScore(void);
};
```

```
SchoolClass::SchoolClass(int NumberStudents)
{
    ClassData = new int[NumberStudents];
    ClassDataIndex = 0;
}

SchoolClass::~SchoolClass(void)
{
    delete ClassData;
}

void SchoolClass::AddScore(int Score)
{
    ClassData[ClassDataIndex++] = Score;
}

int SchoolClass::GetScore(int Index)
{
    if(Index <= ClassDataIndex)
    {
        return ClassData[Index];
    }
    else
    {
        return -1;
    }
}

float SchoolClass::AverageScore(void)
{
    float Sum = 0;

    if(ClassDataIndex == 0)
    {
        return -1;
    }

    for(int loop_index = 0; loop_index < ClassDataIndex; loop_index++)
    {
        Sum += (float) ClassData[loop_index];
    }

    return Sum / (float) ClassDataIndex;
}

void main()
{
    SchoolClass HistoryClass(9);
```

```
    SchoolClass EnglishClass(10);

    HistoryClass.AddScore(80);
    HistoryClass.AddScore(81);
    HistoryClass.AddScore(82);
    HistoryClass.AddScore(83);
    HistoryClass.AddScore(84);
    HistoryClass.AddScore(85);
    HistoryClass.AddScore(86);
    HistoryClass.AddScore(87);
    HistoryClass.AddScore(88);

    EnglishClass.AddScore(91);
    EnglishClass.AddScore(92);
    EnglishClass.AddScore(93);
    EnglishClass.AddScore(94);
    EnglishClass.AddScore(95);
    EnglishClass.AddScore(96);
    EnglishClass.AddScore(97);
    EnglishClass.AddScore(98);
    EnglishClass.AddScore(99);
    EnglishClass.AddScore(100);

        cout << "Average score for History class: " << HistoryClass
➥.AverageScore() << "\n";
        cout << "Average score for English class: " << EnglishClass
➥.AverageScore() << "\n";

    }
```

We've gotten a good start with C++, but there are several more concepts that we'll dig into before going on to the next skill: C++ inheritance, overriding, and overloading.

What Are Inheritance and Overriding?

An important part of object-oriented programming, is called *inheritance*. Using inheritance, a *derived* class inherits the functionality of its *base* class, and adds more on top of it. For example, we may have a base class called vehicle. We can derive various classes from this base class called truck and helicopter. In this way, two derived classes can share the same base class—and all the methods in that base class—which saves us time and effort when we write our program.

Although our helicopter and truck classes share the same base class, vehicle, they added different items to the base class, ending up as two quite different classes.

 TIP   Remember the distinctions between private, protected, and public access modifiers. You can reach a class's public members from anywhere in the program, its private members only in objects of that class, and its protected members only in objects of that class or objects derived from that class.

Both of our new derived classes can use the built-in methods of the vehicle class, such as, say, start(), and move(). But a helicopter moves in a different way from a truck. How do we make additions and even alterations to the vehicle class to customize our own class? One way is by overriding the base class's built-in functions (overriding is an important part of object-oriented programming). When we redefine a base class's method in a derived class, the new version of the method is the one that takes over. In this way, we can customize the functions from the base class as we like them in the derived class.

Let's see both inheritance and overriding at work. Create a new project named inheritance. We can declare the vehicle class now, giving it two methods, start() and move():

```
#include <iostream.h>

class vehicle {
public: void start();
    void move();
};
```

The start() method just prints out "Starting..." and the move() method just prints out "Driving...":

```
#include <iostream.h>

class vehicle {
public: void start();
    void move();
};

void vehicle::start() { cout << "Starting...\n";}
void vehicle::move() { cout << "Driving...\n";}
            .
            .
            .
```

Now we'll create a new class, helicopter, and derive this new class from the vehicle class.

Deriving a New Class: Inheritance

We derive the helicopter class from its base class, vehicle, like this:

```
#include <iostream.h>

class vehicle {
public: void start();
     void move();
};
```
→`class helicopter : public vehicle {`

→`};`

Note that we indicate we are deriving helicopter from the class vehicle by placing a colon and the name of the base class, vehicle, after the declaration of the helicopter class:

→`class helicopter : public vehicle {`
```
          .
          .
          .
     }
```

Because the helicopter class is derived from the vehicle class, the helicopter class already has built-in the methods of the vehicle class: start() and move().

Changing a Method: Overriding

But the vehicle class's move() method prints out "Driving...", which is not appropriate for a helicopter. So we override the vehicle class's move() method in helicopter to print out "Flying..." instead by simply redefining the method:

```
#include <iostream.h>

class vehicle {
public: void start();
     void move();
};

class helicopter : public vehicle {
```

```
➜public: void move();
 };

 void vehicle::start() { cout << "Starting...\n";}
 void vehicle::move() { cout << "Driving...\n";}

➜void helicopter::move() { cout << "Flying...\n";}
            .
            .
            .
```

Now we can call the helicopter class's start() and move() methods like this in a main() function:

```
 #include <iostream.h>

 class vehicle {
 public: void start();
        void move();
 };

 class helicopter : public vehicle {
 public: void move();
 };

 void vehicle::start() { cout << "Starting...\n";}
 void vehicle::move() { cout << "Driving...\n";}

 void helicopter::move() { cout << "Flying...\n";}

➜void main()
➜{
➜       helicopter whirly;

➜       whirly.start();
➜       whirly.move();
➜}
```

The inheritance program is complete—run it now, as shown in Figure 1.9. As you can see in that figure, we've overridden the move() method successfully, so that move() displays the text "Flying...", not "Driving...". Now we're using C++ inheritance and overriding. The code for this program appears in inheritance.cpp.

FIGURE 1.9: Overriding a C++ method

inheritance.cpp

```cpp
#include <iostream.h>

class vehicle {
public: void start();
    void move();
};

class helicopter : public vehicle {
public: void move();
};

void vehicle::start() { cout << "Starting...\n";}
void vehicle::move() { cout << "Driving...\n";}

void helicopter::move() { cout << "Flying...\n";}

void main()
{
    helicopter whirly;

    whirly.start();
    whirly.move();
}
```

Our last topic in this skill will be function overloading, and we'll turn to that now.

C++ Function Overloading

C++ also allows you to call the same method with different types of parameters, or even different numbers of parameters. For example, we might have a method named display() that can display either a single character, using the C++ char type, or a string of characters, which are handled as arrays of characters in standard C++. In other words, we can call display() with either a single character or an array of characters. Let's see how this works now in a new program named overloading. Create that program and the file overloading.cpp now.

For this example, we will create a new object named DisplayObject in the main() function:

```
void main()
{
→      DisplayClass DisplayObject;
            .
            .
            .
}
```

This is the object that will support our display() method, and we'll call it with a single character to display, 'h':

```
void main()
{
       DisplayClass DisplayObject;

→      DisplayObject.display('h');
            .
            .
            .
}
```

We'll also call it with a string (that is, an array of characters) which holds just one letter, "i" (in C++, double quotes indicate a character string, not a character):

```
void main()
{
       DisplayClass DisplayObject;

       DisplayObject.display('h');
```

```
➜        DisplayObject.display("i");
         cout << "\n";
  }
```

We're calling this same method with two different types of arguments, a character and a string. How can we do that? In C++ it's easy, we just define the method twice, once for each type of parameter it's supposed to have. That looks like this, where we define display() twice to accept both character and string parameters:

```
#include <iostream.h>

class DisplayClass
{
public:
➜     void display(char character);
➜     void display(char* string);
};

➜void DisplayClass::display(char character)
➜{
➜     cout << character;
➜}

➜void DisplayClass::display(char* string)
➜{
➜     cout << string;
➜}
```

How will C++ know which version of display() to use when you call that method? It knows by the type of parameter you pass to it. For example, if that parameter is a character, it will use the version of display() that we set up to take a character parameter. If you call it with a string, it will use the string parameter version.

Run the program now, as shown in Figure 1.10. As you can see in that figure, we've overloaded the display() method successfully. That's how overloading works, and it's going to be a common feature throughout this book.

The code for this program appears in overloading.cpp.

FIGURE 1 . 1 0 : We overload a C++ method.

overloading.cpp

```cpp
#include <iostream.h>

class DisplayClass
{
public:
    void display(char character);
    void display(char* string);
};

void DisplayClass::display(char character)
{
    cout << character;
}

void DisplayClass::display(char* string)
{
    cout << string;
}

void main()
{
```

```
DisplayClass DisplayObject;

DisplayObject.display('h');
DisplayObject.display("i");
cout << "\n";
}
```

We've come far in this skill, seeing the basics of C++ such as classes and objects, inheritance, overloading, overriding, and more. In the next skill, we'll see how to put all these concepts to work as we start creating our own true Windows programs.

If you feel comfortable with the above material, turn to Skill Two now. Otherwise, it's a good idea to do some brushing up on programming topics before continuing: we're going to jump right in to Visual C++ in the next skill.

Are You Experienced?

Now You Can...

☑ **Understand the ideas of C++ classes and C++ objects**

☑ **Understand how to use C++ inheritance**

☑ **Use C++ constructors and destructors**

☑ **Use C++ overloading to let a method take different types of parameters**

☑ **Use C++ overriding to redefine a base class's methods**

Getting Started in Visual C++

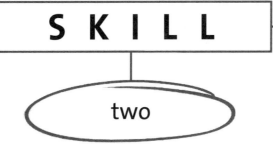

- ❏ Our first windowing program

- ❏ Using AppWizard to create programs

- ❏ Visual C++ documents

- ❏ Visual C++ views

- ❏ Dissecting a Visual C++ program

In the last skill, we started working with Visual C++, and we saw how to create Win32 console applications. In this skill, we're going to create our first true windowing example program. We'll see how to use Visual C++ tools to write our first real Windows program, and how to run the program.

Next, we'll dissect the example program we've created. A Visual C++ program usually involves quite a bit of C++ code—fortunately, Visual C++ itself writes this code for the most part. It's important that we understand the various parts of a standard Visual C++ program before we continue on, because such a program will form the basis of our programs throughout the book.

When you create a Visual C++ program, you usually use a *Wizard* like the Visual C++ AppWizard that we'll use in this skill. After it generates the code that it needs, we will modify that code to customize the program the way we want it. To do that, we have to know what goes where in a Visual C++ program, and we'll explore that in this skill. Let's get started at once.

Our First True Windows Visual C++ Program

Our first true (that is, windowing) Visual C++ example will be a simple one for clarity. All we'll do is create a window that displays the text "Welcome to Visual C++":

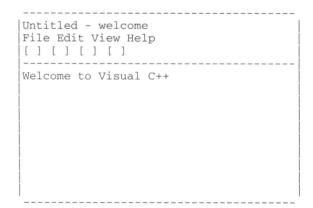

```
----------------------------------------
|Untitled - welcome                     |
|File Edit View Help                    |
|[ ] [ ] [ ] [ ]                        |
|---------------------------------------|
|Welcome to Visual C++                  |
|                                       |
|                                       |
|                                       |
|                                       |
|                                       |
|                                       |
|                                       |
|                                       |
|                                       |
----------------------------------------
```

In fact, our first program will have a great deal more built into it than this simple message. Visual C++ will build menus and a toolbar into the program for us, although those items won't do anything (we'll see how to work with those items later).

Let's start this program now; it will give us our welcome to true Windows Visual C++ programming. Open Visual C++ and click the New item in the File menu, opening the New dialog box, as shown in Figure 2.1. Now select the "MFC AppWizard(exe)" entry in the New dialog box, as shown in Figure 2.1, and give the new program the name "welcome" in the Project name box, as also shown in Figure 2.1. Next, click OK.

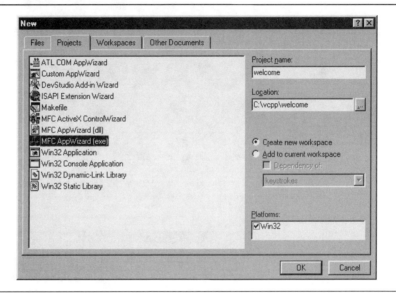

FIGURE 2.1: Starting a new program with the MFC AppWizard

Clicking OK starts the Visual C++ AppWizard, as shown in Figure 2.2.

The AppWizard will write a great deal of the code in our program for us. We see Step 1, the first of six steps in the AppWizard, in Figure 2.2. We will accept all the defaults in the AppWizard except one—by default, the AppWizard creates multi-windowed programs, and we'll change that so that it creates a single-windowed program. This will keep things simple and clear in the beginning. Click the option marked "Single Document" in the AppWizard, as shown in Figure 2.2 and click the button marked Next. This moves us to Step 2 of the AppWizard, as shown in Figure 2.3.

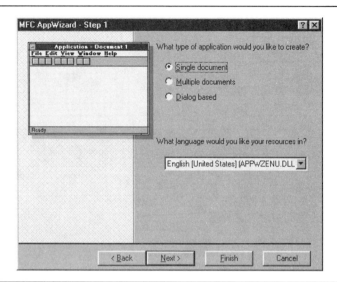

FIGURE 2.2: The MFC AppWizard lets us create Visual C++ programs

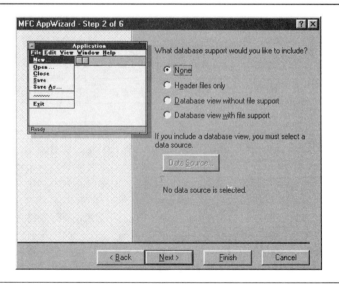

FIGURE 2.3: Step 2 of the MFC AppWizard

In Figure 2.3, the AppWizard is asking what database support we want in our program; we'll leave the None option selected. Keep pressing Next until you reach Step 6 in the AppWizard, as shown in Figure 2.4.

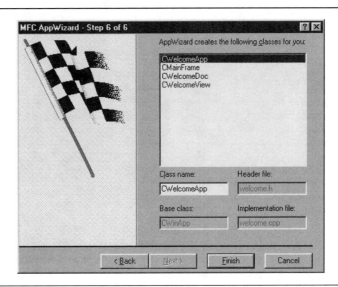

FIGURE 2.4: Step 6 of the MFC AppWizard

Here, the AppWizard indicates what classes it will create for us in the new program: CWelcomeApp, CMainFrame, CWelcomeDoc, and CWelcomeView. These are the classes that we will explore in this skill. Click the AppWizard Finish button now. This opens the New Project Information box, as shown in Figure 2.5.

Click the OK button in the New Project Information box now to create the project. This creates the following files in the directory you've specified:

```
welcome.clw        ClassWizard file
welcome.dsw        Main workspace file
welcome.h          Application header file
welcome.cpp        Application code file
StdAfx.h           Standard application framework header
StdAfx.cpp         Standard application framework code
MainFrm.h          Main window header
MainFrm.cpp        Main window code
welcomeDoc.h       Document header
welcomeDoc.cpp     Document code
welcomeView.h      View header
welcomeView.cpp    View code
```

```
Resource.h              Resource constants file
welcome.rc              Resource file
welcome.ncb             Layout and dependencies file
welcome.dsp             Project file
res                     Resource directory
```

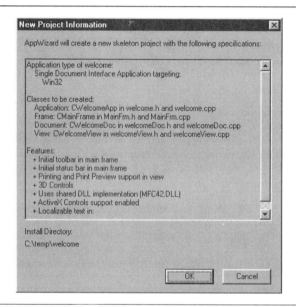

FIGURE 2.5: The MFC AppWizard New Project Information box

The AppWizard has also created a file named ReadMe.txt, which explains more about some of the files the AppWizard has written for us:

```
=============================================================================
        MICROSOFT FOUNDATION CLASS LIBRARY : welcome
=============================================================================


AppWizard has created this welcome application for you.  This application
not only demonstrates the basics of using the Microsoft Foundation classes
but is also a starting point for writing your application.

This file contains a summary of what you will find in each of the files that
make up your welcome application.

welcome.h
```

This is the main header file for the application. It includes other
project specific headers (including Resource.h) and declares the
CWelcomeApp application class.

welcome.cpp
This is the main application source file that contains the application
class CWelcomeApp.

welcome.rc
This is a listing of all of the Microsoft Windows resources that the
program uses. It includes the icons, bitmaps, and cursors that are stored
in the RES subdirectory. This file can be directly edited in Microsoft
Developer Studio.

res\welcome.ico
This is an icon file, which is used as the application's icon. This
icon is included by the main resource file welcome.rc.

res\welcome.rc2
This file contains resources that are not edited by Microsoft
Developer Studio. You should place all resources not
editable by the resource editor in this file.

welcome.clw
This file contains information used by ClassWizard to edit existing
classes or add new classes. ClassWizard also uses this file to store
information needed to create and edit message maps and dialog data
maps and to create prototype member functions.

///

For the main frame window:

MainFrm.h, MainFrm.cpp
These files contain the frame class CMainFrame, which is derived from
CFrameWnd and controls all SDI frame features.

res\Toolbar.bmp
This bitmap file is used to create tiled images for the toolbar.
The initial toolbar and status bar are constructed in the
CMainFrame class. Edit this toolbar bitmap along with the
array in MainFrm.cpp to add more toolbar buttons.

///

AppWizard creates one document type and one view:

```
welcomeDoc.h, welcomeDoc.cpp - the document
    These files contain your CWelcomeDoc class.  Edit these files to
    add your special document data and to implement file saving and loading
    (via CWelcomeDoc::Serialize).

welcomeView.h, welcomeView.cpp - the view of the document
    These files contain your CWelcomeView class.
    CWelcomeView objects are used to view CWelcomeDoc objects.



/////////////////////////////////////////////////////////////////////////////
Other standard files:

StdAfx.h, StdAfx.cpp
    These files are used to build a precompiled header (PCH) file
    named welcome.pch and a precompiled types file named StdAfx.obj.

Resource.h
    This is the standard header file, which defines new resource IDs.
    Microsoft Developer Studio reads and updates this file.

/////////////////////////////////////////////////////////////////////////////
Other notes:

AppWizard uses "TODO:" to indicate parts of the source code you
should add to or customize.

If your application uses MFC in a shared DLL, and your application is
in a language other than the operating system's current language, you
will need to copy the corresponding localized resources MFC40XXX.DLL
from the Microsoft Visual C++ CD-ROM onto the system or system32 directory,
and rename it to be MFCLOC.DLL.  ("XXX" stands for the language abbreviation.
For example, MFC40DEU.DLL contains resources translated to German.)  If you
don't do this, some of the UI elements of your application will remain in the
language of the operating system.

/////////////////////////////////////////////////////////////////////////////
```

Now that we've actually created our program, let's take a minute to get an overview of it.

The Parts of a Visual C++ Program

There are four major parts of a Visual C++ AppWizard program: the application object, the main window object, the document object, and the view object. These objects will become very familiar to us in this book.

The Application Object

The application object, supported in `welcome.h` and `welcome.cpp` (the `.h` file holds the definitions of constants and the declarations of variables and methods in this class), is what Windows actually runs first. When this object is started, it places the main window on the screen.

The Main Window Object

The main window object displays the program itself, and this is where we find the menu bar, the title bar of the window, and the tool bar. The main window object is responsible for everything that surrounds the area where the action—the drawing, text, and other graphics—goes on in our window. That area is called the *client area* in a window; for example, the text that you edit in a word processor appears in the word processor's client area. The view object is responsible for handling the client area itself.

The View Object

The view object handles the client area—this is where we'll format and display the data in our program, such as the text we're editing if we're creating a word processing program. In fact, the view object is really a window itself that appears on top of the client area. The data we display in the view object is stored in the document object.

The Document Object

In the document object, we store the data for our program. You may wonder why we don't store it in the view object—the reason is that we may have a great deal of data, more than will fit into our client area at once. Visual C++ makes it easier for us by allowing us to store all that data in the document object, then handle the display of the data that will fit into the client area in the view object. In fact, we'll see that you can have several different views open in the same document at once later in this book.

Overall, the four parts of our Visual C++ program look like this:

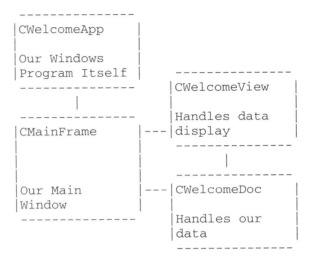

```
---------------
|CWelcomeApp   |
|              |
|Our Windows   |
|Program Itself |          ---------------
---------------            |CWelcomeView  |
       |                   |              |
---------------            |Handles data  |
|CMainFrame    |   ---     |display       |
|              |           ---------------
|              |                  |
|              |           ---------------
|Our Main      |   ---     |CWelcomeDoc   |
|Window        |           |              |
---------------            |Handles our   |
                           |data          |
                           ---------------
```

Now let's make our program *do* something.

Displaying Our Welcome Message

So far we've had an overview of our program as AppWizard has written it; now let's modify it so that it prints out the "Welcome to Visual C++" message. To do that, we will add some code to the OnDraw() method of the CWelcomeView class (recall that this class handles the display of our data). The program calls the OnDraw() method when it wants to display the program's client area (such as when our program first starts, or when its window is closed and then reopened, or when a window that covers the client area is moved). Currently, that method looks like this (in the file welcomeView.cpp):

```
void CWelcomeView::OnDraw(CDC* pDC)
{
    CWelcomeDoc* pDoc = GetDocument();
    ASSERT_VALID(pDoc);

    // TODO: add draw code for native data here
}
```

We will add the code to display our message in this method. To open this method for editing, click the ClassView tab in Visual C++ and find the entry for the CWelcomeView class, as shown in Figure 2.6. Click the small "+" next to that entry to open it. This displays the methods in this class, as shown in Figure 2.6.

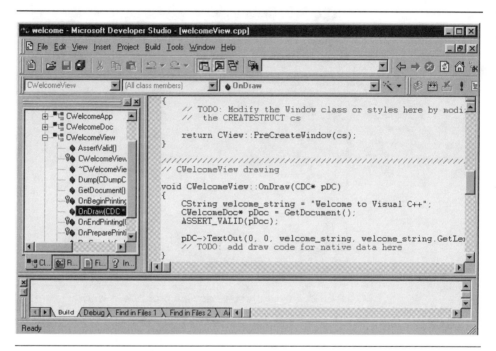

FIGURE 2.6: Editing the OnDraw() method

Find the entry for the OnDraw() method, and double-click it. This opens OnDraw() in the text editor, as also shown in Figure 2.6. To customize our program, add this one line of code:

```
void CWelcomeView::OnDraw(CDC* pDC)
{
➜       CString welcome_string = "Welcome to Visual C++";
        CWelcomeDoc* pDoc = GetDocument();
        ASSERT_VALID(pDoc);

➜       pDC->TextOut(0, 0, welcome_string);
}
```

Now our program is ready. Run it by choosing the Build welcome.exe item in the Build menu, followed by Execute welcome.exe in the same menu (as shown in Figure 2.7).

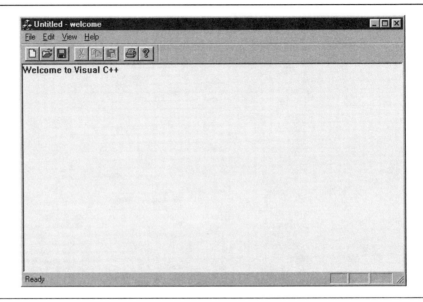

F I G U R E 2 . 7 :   Our first windowing program at work

As you can see, our welcome program is working; our message appears in the window. Now it's time to take it apart piece by piece and understand just how it works. We'll start with the application object.

Dissecting the Application Object

Windows calls the `WinMain()` method in the application object to get our program started, so we'll look at the application object first. From our point of view, the application object really has three tasks: to start the program, to launch our main window, and to pass *Windows messages* on from Windows to our main window.

What are Windows messages? They are special codes sent between various objects in Windows to communicate. For example, when the user quits our program, Windows sends the application object the `WM_QUIT` message. When the user resizes our program's window, we get the `WM_SIZE` message. Some of the more interesting Windows messages appear in Table 2.1.

TABLE 2.1: Some Windows Messages

Windows Message	Means
WM_ACTIVATE	Window becoming active or inactive
WM_ACTIVATEAPP	Window being activated belongs to a different app
WM_CANCELMODE	Cancel system mode
WM_CHILDACTIVATE	Window moved
WM_CLOSE	Window was closed
WM_CREATE	Create function was called
WM_DESTROY	Destroy function was called
WM_ENABLE	Window was enabled or disabled
WM_ENDSESSION	Session is ending
WM_ENTERIDLE	Idle for user action
WM_ERASEBKGND	Background needs to be erased
WM_GETMINMAXINFO	Get size info about the window
WM_GETTEXT	Get text corresponding to window
WM_GETTEXTLENGTH	Get length of text associated with window
WM_ICONERASEBKGND	Window background needs to be erased
WM_KILLFOCUS	Window is losing the input focus
WM_MENUCHAR	User pressed char not in current menu
WM_MENUSELECT	Menu item selected
WM_MOVE	Window was moved
WM_PAINT	Repaint a portion of window
WM_PAINTICON	Repaint a portion of icon
WM_PARENTNOTIFY	Window is created or destroyed
WM_QUERYENDSESSION	End Session command
WM_QUIT	Quit application
WM_SETFOCUS	Window received input focus
WM_SETFONT	Font was changed
WM_SETREDRAW	Clears redraw flag
WM_SETTEXT	Sets title of window
WM_SHOWWINDOW	Window is to be hidden or shown
WM_SIZE	Size of window changed

Skill 2

The application object sends most windows messages on to the main window object, except for WM_QUIT, which makes the application object finish up and exit.

In fact, there is a great deal of communication that takes place between the various objects in a Visual C++ program. Because such programs are divided up into four main objects, that's to be expected—you need to reach the other objects at times. Here's an overview of the way the four main objects in a Visual C++ program communicate; we'll see more about these methods throughout this book:

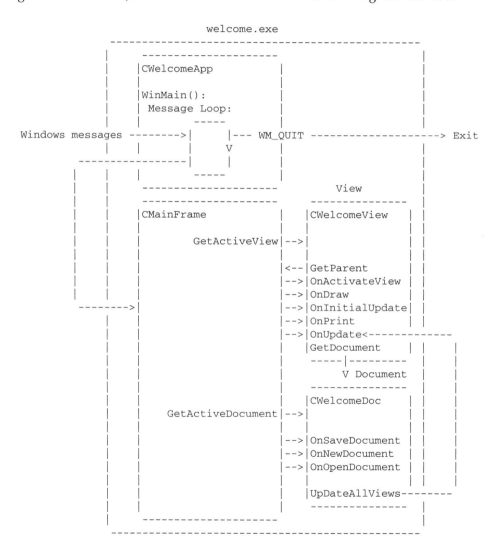

The application object's code appears in the file welcome.cpp. In that file, the InitInstance() method is of interest to us, because this is where the program assembles the other classes we'll need: the main window, document, and view classes, and puts them into a *document template*, which is a blueprint for how the application object will display the rest of the program:

```
BOOL CWelcomeApp::InitInstance()
{
    AfxEnableControlContainer();

    // Standard initialization
    // If you are not using these features and wish to reduce the size
    //  of your final executable, you should remove from the following
    //  the specific initialization routines you do not need.

#ifdef _AFXDLL
    Enable3dControls();            // Call this when using MFC in a shared DLL
#else
    Enable3dControlsStatic();      // Call this when linking to MFC statically
#endif

    // Change the registry key under which our settings are stored.
    // You should modify this string to be something appropriate,
    // such as the name of your company or organization.
    SetRegistryKey(_T("Local AppWizard-Generated Applications"));

    LoadStdProfileSettings();  // Load standard INI file options (including MRU)

    // Register the application's document templates.  Document templates
    //  serve as the connection between documents, frame windows and views.

➜    CSingleDocTemplate* pDocTemplate;
➜    pDocTemplate = new CSingleDocTemplate(
➜        IDR_MAINFRAME,
➜        RUNTIME_CLASS(CWelcomeDoc),
➜        RUNTIME_CLASS(CMainFrame),        // main SDI frame window
➜        RUNTIME_CLASS(CWelcomeView));
➜    AddDocTemplate(pDocTemplate);

    // Parse command line for standard shell commands, DDE, file open
    CCommandLineInfo cmdInfo;
    ParseCommandLine(cmdInfo);

    // Dispatch commands specified on the command line
    if (!ProcessShellCommand(cmdInfo))
        return FALSE;
```

```
       // The one and only window has been initialized, so show and update it.
➡      m_pMainWnd->ShowWindow(SW_SHOW);
       m_pMainWnd->UpdateWindow();

       return TRUE;
}
```

Note also the line at the end of the `InitInstance()` method: `m_pMainWnd->ShowWindow(SW_SHOW);`. This is where the application object actually displays the main window of our program, using the main window object's `ShowWindow()` method. The m_pMainWnd variable holds a pointer to the main window object, and the -> operator functions just like the dot (".") operator when used with a pointer to an object. That is, it lets us reach the member data and methods of the object we are pointing to.

Using "m_" to preface a member variable is standard in Visual C++. In fact, Visual C++ uses this kind of notation, called Hungarian Notation, to preface most variables that it uses. This helps us by indicating what type a variable is in its preface; for example, the preface `c` is used for characters, so we know the variable `cInput` is a character variable. The common Hungarian Notation prefixes appear in Table 2.2.

T A B L E 2 . 2 : Hungarian Notation Prefixes

Prefix	Means
a	array
b	bool (int)
by	unsigned char (byte)
c	char
cb	count of bytes
cr	color reference value
cx, cy	short (count of x, y length)
dw	unsigned long (dword)
fn	function
h	handle
I	integer
m_	data member of a class
n	short or int

TABLE 2.2 CONTINUED: Hungarian Notation Prefixes

Prefix	Means
np	near pointer
p	pointer
l	long
lp	long pointer
s	string
sz	string terminated with a zero
tm	text metric
w	unsigned int (word)
x, y	short (x or y coordinate)

Now that we've displayed the main window on the screen, we're done with the application object for the moment, so let's turn to the main window object next. The code for the application object appears in welcome.h/welcome.cpp.

welcome.h and welcome.cpp

```
// welcome.h : main header file for the WELCOME application
//

#if !defined(AFX_WELCOME_H__AF072C83_900A_11D0_8860_444553540000__INCLUDED_)
#define AFX_WELCOME_H__AF072C83_900A_11D0_8860_444553540000__INCLUDED_

#if _MSC_VER >= 1000
#pragma once
#endif // _MSC_VER >= 1000

#ifndef __AFXWIN_H__
    #error include 'stdafx.h' before including this file for PCH
#endif

#include "resource.h"        // main symbols

/////////////////////////////////////////////////////////////////////
// CWelcomeApp:
// See welcome.cpp for the implementation of this class
//
```

```
class CWelcomeApp : public CWinApp
{
public:
    CWelcomeApp();

// Overrides
    // ClassWizard generated virtual function overrides
    //{{AFX_VIRTUAL(CWelcomeApp)
    public:
    virtual BOOL InitInstance();
    //}}AFX_VIRTUAL

// Implementation

    //{{AFX_MSG(CWelcomeApp)
    afx_msg void OnAppAbout();
        // NOTE - the ClassWizard will add and remove member functions here.
        //    DO NOT EDIT what you see in these blocks of generated code !
    //}}AFX_MSG
    DECLARE_MESSAGE_MAP()
};


/////////////////////////////////////////////////////////////////////////////

//{{AFX_INSERT_LOCATION}}
// Microsoft Developer Studio will insert additional declarations immediately
// before the previous line.

#endif // !defined(AFX_WELCOME_H__AF072C83_900A_11D0_8860_444553540000__
➥INCLUDED_)



// welcome.cpp : Defines the class behaviors for the application.
//

#include "stdafx.h"
#include "welcome.h"

#include "MainFrm.h"
#include "welcomeDoc.h"
#include "welcomeView.h"

#ifdef _DEBUG
#define new DEBUG_NEW
#undef THIS_FILE
static char THIS_FILE[] = __FILE__;
```

```
#endif

/////////////////////////////////////////////////////////////////////////
// CWelcomeApp

BEGIN_MESSAGE_MAP(CWelcomeApp, CWinApp)
    //{{AFX_MSG_MAP(CWelcomeApp)
    ON_COMMAND(ID_APP_ABOUT, OnAppAbout)
        // NOTE - the ClassWizard will add and remove mapping macros here.
        //      DO NOT EDIT what you see in these blocks of generated code!
    //}}AFX_MSG_MAP
    // Standard file based document commands
    ON_COMMAND(ID_FILE_NEW, CWinApp::OnFileNew)
    ON_COMMAND(ID_FILE_OPEN, CWinApp::OnFileOpen)
    // Standard print setup command
    ON_COMMAND(ID_FILE_PRINT_SETUP, CWinApp::OnFilePrintSetup)
END_MESSAGE_MAP()

/////////////////////////////////////////////////////////////////////////
// CWelcomeApp construction

CWelcomeApp::CWelcomeApp()
{
    // TODO: add construction code here,
    // Place all significant initialization in InitInstance
}

/////////////////////////////////////////////////////////////////////////
// The one and only CWelcomeApp object

CWelcomeApp theApp;

/////////////////////////////////////////////////////////////////////////
// CWelcomeApp initialization

BOOL CWelcomeApp::InitInstance()
{
    AfxEnableControlContainer();

    // Standard initialization
    // If you are not using these features and wish to reduce the size
    //  of your final executable, you should remove from the following
    //  the specific initialization routines you do not need.

#ifdef _AFXDLL
    Enable3dControls();        // Call this when using MFC in a shared DLL
#else
    Enable3dControlsStatic();     // Call this when linking to MFC statically
```

```
#endif

    // Change the registry key under which our settings are stored.
    // You should modify this string to be something appropriate
    // such as the name of your company or organization.
    SetRegistryKey(_T("Local AppWizard-Generated Applications"));

    LoadStdProfileSettings();  // Load standard INI file options (including MRU)

    // Register the application's document templates.  Document templates
    //  serve as the connection between documents, frame windows and views.

    CSingleDocTemplate* pDocTemplate;
    pDocTemplate = new CSingleDocTemplate(
        IDR_MAINFRAME,
        RUNTIME_CLASS(CWelcomeDoc),
        RUNTIME_CLASS(CMainFrame),         // main SDI frame window
        RUNTIME_CLASS(CWelcomeView));
    AddDocTemplate(pDocTemplate);

    // Parse command line for standard shell commands, DDE, file open
    CCommandLineInfo cmdInfo;
    ParseCommandLine(cmdInfo);

    // Dispatch commands specified on the command line
    if (!ProcessShellCommand(cmdInfo))
        return FALSE;

    // The one and only window has been initialized, so show and update it.
    m_pMainWnd->ShowWindow(SW_SHOW);
    m_pMainWnd->UpdateWindow();

    return TRUE;
}

/////////////////////////////////////////////////////////////////////////////
// CAboutDlg dialog used for App About

class CAboutDlg : public CDialog
{
public:
    CAboutDlg();

// Dialog Data
    //{{AFX_DATA(CAboutDlg)
    enum { IDD = IDD_ABOUTBOX };
    //}}AFX_DATA
```

```
    // ClassWizard generated virtual function overrides
    //{{AFX_VIRTUAL(CAboutDlg)
    protected:
    virtual void DoDataExchange(CDataExchange* pDX);     // DDX/DDV support
    //}}AFX_VIRTUAL

// Implementation
protected:
    //{{AFX_MSG(CAboutDlg)
        // No message handlers
    //}}AFX_MSG
    DECLARE_MESSAGE_MAP()
};

CAboutDlg::CAboutDlg() : CDialog(CAboutDlg::IDD)
{
    //{{AFX_DATA_INIT(CAboutDlg)
    //}}AFX_DATA_INIT
}

void CAboutDlg::DoDataExchange(CDataExchange* pDX)
{
    CDialog::DoDataExchange(pDX);
    //{{AFX_DATA_MAP(CAboutDlg)
    //}}AFX_DATA_MAP
}

BEGIN_MESSAGE_MAP(CAboutDlg, CDialog)
    //{{AFX_MSG_MAP(CAboutDlg)
        // No message handlers
    //}}AFX_MSG_MAP
END_MESSAGE_MAP()

// App command to run the dialog
void CWelcomeApp::OnAppAbout()
{
    CAboutDlg aboutDlg;
    aboutDlg.DoModal();
}

/////////////////////////////////////////////////////////////////////////////
// CWelcomeApp commands
```

Now that we've explored the application object in our program, we'll turn to the main window object next, because one of the application object's main tasks is to place that window on the screen.

Dissecting the Main Window Object

The program's main window object is responsible for all of our program's window except for the client area:

```
 ----------------------------------------
|Untitled - welcome                      |
|File Edit View Help                     |
|[ ]  [ ]  [ ]  [ ]                      |
|----------------------------------------|
|Welcome to Visual C++                   |
|                                        |
|                                        |
|                                        |
 client area ------>                     |
|                                        |
|                                        |
|                                        |
|                                        |
|                                        |
 ----------------------------------------
```

That is, the main window object is responsible for the title bar, the menu bar, the tool bar, and the status bar at the bottom of our window. The title bar and menu bar are automatically created when the window is created, but we add the tool bar and status bar in the OnCreate() method. That looks like this, from the file MainFrm.cpp:

```
    int CMainFrame::OnCreate(LPCREATESTRUCT lpCreateStruct)
    {
        if (CFrameWnd::OnCreate(lpCreateStruct) == -1)
            return -1;

➡        if (!m_wndToolBar.Create(this) || !m_wndToolBar
    ➡.LoadToolBar(IDR_MAINFRAME))
        {
            TRACE0("Failed to create toolbar\n");
            return -1;      // fail to create
        }

➡        if (!m_wndStatusBar.Create(this) || !m_wndStatusBar
    ➡.SetIndicators(indicators,
                sizeof(indicators)/sizeof(UINT)))
```

```
        {
            TRACE0("Failed to create status bar\n");
            return -1;      // fail to create
        }

        // TODO: Remove this if you don't want tool tips or a resizeable
➥toolbar
        m_wndToolBar.SetBarStyle(m_wndToolBar.GetBarStyle() |
➥CBRS_TOOLTIPS | CBRS_FLYBY | CBRS_SIZE_DYNAMIC);

        // TODO: Delete these three lines if you don't want the toolbar to
        //   be dockable
        m_wndToolBar.EnableDocking(CBRS_ALIGN_ANY);
        EnableDocking(CBRS_ALIGN_ANY);
        DockControlBar(&m_wndToolBar);

        return 0;
    }
```

Our menus and toolbars will be displayed by the main window, but we won't
write much code here. We'll connect most of the code in the program's view
object, which is the window that covers the client area. The main window displays the view object, so now that we've gotten a glimpse at the main window
object, we will examine the view object itself next. The code for the main window
object is in MainFrm.h/MainFrm.cpp.

MainFrm.h and *MainFrm.cpp*

```
// MainFrm.h : interface of the CMainFrame class
//
/////////////////////////////////////////////////////////////////////////////

#if !defined(AFX_MAINFRM_H__AF072C87_900A_11D0_8860_444553540000__INCLUDED_)
#define AFX_MAINFRM_H__AF072C87_900A_11D0_8860_444553540000__INCLUDED_

#if _MSC_VER >= 1000
#pragma once
#endif // _MSC_VER >= 1000

class CMainFrame : public CFrameWnd
{
protected: // create from serialization only
    CMainFrame();
    DECLARE_DYNCREATE(CMainFrame)

// Attributes
```

```
public:

// Operations
public:

// Overrides
    // ClassWizard generated virtual function overrides
    //{{AFX_VIRTUAL(CMainFrame)
    virtual BOOL PreCreateWindow(CREATESTRUCT& cs);
    //}}AFX_VIRTUAL

// Implementation
public:
    virtual ~CMainFrame();
#ifdef _DEBUG
    virtual void AssertValid() const;
    virtual void Dump(CDumpContext& dc) const;
#endif

protected:  // control bar embedded members
    CStatusBar  m_wndStatusBar;
    CToolBar    m_wndToolBar;

// Generated message map functions
protected:
    //{{AFX_MSG(CMainFrame)
    afx_msg int OnCreate(LPCREATESTRUCT lpCreateStruct);
        // NOTE - the ClassWizard will add and remove member functions here.
        //    DO NOT EDIT what you see in these blocks of generated code!
    //}}AFX_MSG
    DECLARE_MESSAGE_MAP()
};

/////////////////////////////////////////////////////////////////////////

//{{AFX_INSERT_LOCATION}}
// Microsoft Developer Studio will insert additional declarations immediately
// before the previous line.

#endif // !defined(AFX_MAINFRM_H__AF072C87_900A_11D0_8860_444553540000__
➥INCLUDED_)




// MainFrm.cpp : implementation of the CMainFrame class
//
```

```
#include "stdafx.h"
#include "welcome.h"

#include "MainFrm.h"

#ifdef _DEBUG
#define new DEBUG_NEW
#undef THIS_FILE
static char THIS_FILE[] = __FILE__;
#endif

//////////////////////////////////////////////////////////////////////
// CMainFrame

IMPLEMENT_DYNCREATE(CMainFrame, CFrameWnd)

BEGIN_MESSAGE_MAP(CMainFrame, CFrameWnd)
    //{{AFX_MSG_MAP(CMainFrame)
        // NOTE - the ClassWizard will add and remove mapping macros here.
        //     DO NOT EDIT what you see in these blocks of generated code !
    ON_WM_CREATE()
    //}}AFX_MSG_MAP
END_MESSAGE_MAP()

static UINT indicators[] =
{
    ID_SEPARATOR,           // status line indicator
    ID_INDICATOR_CAPS,
    ID_INDICATOR_NUM,
    ID_INDICATOR_SCRL,
};

//////////////////////////////////////////////////////////////////////
// CMainFrame construction/destruction

CMainFrame::CMainFrame()
{
    // TODO: add member initialization code here

}

CMainFrame::~CMainFrame()
{
}

int CMainFrame::OnCreate(LPCREATESTRUCT lpCreateStruct)
{
    if (CFrameWnd::OnCreate(lpCreateStruct) == -1)
```

```
            return -1;

    if (!m_wndToolBar.Create(this) || !m_wndToolBar.LoadToolBar(IDR_MAINFRAME))
    {
        TRACE0("Failed to create toolbar\n");
        return -1;      // fail to create
    }

    if (!m_wndStatusBar.Create(this) || !m_wndStatusBar.SetIndicators
➡(indicators, sizeof(indicators)/sizeof(UINT)))
    {
        TRACE0("Failed to create status bar\n");
        return -1;      // fail to create
    }

    // TODO: Remove this if you don't want tool tips or a resizeable toolbar
    m_wndToolBar.SetBarStyle(m_wndToolBar.GetBarStyle() |
        CBRS_TOOLTIPS | CBRS_FLYBY | CBRS_SIZE_DYNAMIC);

    // TODO: Delete these three lines if you don't want the toolbar to
    //   be dockable
    m_wndToolBar.EnableDocking(CBRS_ALIGN_ANY);
    EnableDocking(CBRS_ALIGN_ANY);
    DockControlBar(&m_wndToolBar);

    return 0;
}

BOOL CMainFrame::PreCreateWindow(CREATESTRUCT& cs)
{
    // TODO: Modify the Window class or styles here by modifying
    //   the CREATESTRUCT cs

    return CFrameWnd::PreCreateWindow(cs);
}

/////////////////////////////////////////////////////////////////////////////
// CMainFrame diagnostics

#ifdef _DEBUG
void CMainFrame::AssertValid() const
{
    CFrameWnd::AssertValid();
}

void CMainFrame::Dump(CDumpContext& dc) const
{
```

```
        CFrameWnd::Dump(dc);
}

#endif //_DEBUG

/////////////////////////////////////////////////////////////////////////////
// CMainFrame message handlers
```

We'll turn to the view object now—this is the object responsible for displaying the data in the program's document in the program's client area. Most of the action goes on in the view.

Dissecting the View Object

Inside the view object is where we display our message, "Welcome to Visual C++". We do that in the OnDraw() method in the file welcomeView.cpp:

```
void CWelcomeView::OnDraw(CDC* pDC)
{
        CString welcome_string = "Welcome to Visual C++";
        CWelcomeDoc* pDoc = GetDocument();
        ASSERT_VALID(pDoc);

        pDC->TextOut(0, 0, welcome_string);
}
```

This method is called when the client area needs to be redrawn. In fact, that's the way our programs will work—they'll be broken up into many different methods, each designed to handle a different Windows *event*.

Windows Event-Oriented Programming

Windows programs are *event-driven*. This means that such programs respond to user actions—called *events*—such as clicking the mouse, striking a key, and so on. Each time such an event occurs, the corresponding method is called in our program. In this way, the whole program is broken up into bite-sized methods responding to various Windows events. The OnDraw() method, in particular, handles the case in which our client area needs to be redrawn, as when the window is first displayed, or when the user has moved a window that covered ours, or closed and then reopened our window.

Drawing Our Message in the View

What are we really doing in OnDraw() when we display our message? First, we set up a new object of the MFC CString class named welcome_string and we place our message in that object:

```
void CWelcomeView::OnDraw(CDC* pDC)
{
    CString welcome_string = "Welcome to Visual C++";
    CWelcomeDoc* pDoc = GetDocument();
    ASSERT_VALID(pDoc);

    pDC->TextOut(0, 0, welcome_string);
}
```

The MFC CString class handles text strings for us. This class is very useful, and a great improvement on the C technique of handling strings as character arrays. The Cstring Class's Methods are:

AllocSysString	AnsiToOem	Collate
Compare	CompareNoCase	Cstring
Empty	Find	FindOneOf
Format	FormatMessage	FreeExtra
GetAt	GetBuffer	GetBufferSetLength
GetLength	IsEmpty	Left
LoadString	LockBuffer	MakeLower
MakeReverse	MakeUpper	Mid
OemToAnsi	operator []	operator +
operator +=	operator <<	operator =
operator == <, etc.	operator >>	operator LPCTSTR
ReleaseBuffer	ReverseFind	Right
SetAt	SetSysString	SpanExcluding
SpanIncluding	TrimLeft	TrimRight
UnlockBuffer	Windows-Specific	

Next in OnDraw(), we display the text string using the pointer that was passed to us, pDC, which points to an object of the MFC CDC class. In particular, we use the TextOut() method of this object:

```
void CWelcomeView::OnDraw(CDC* pDC)
{
    CString welcome_string = "Welcome to Visual C++";
    CWelcomeDoc* pDoc = GetDocument();
```

```
        ASSERT_VALID(pDoc);

➜       pDC->TextOut(0, 0, welcome_string);
    }
```

The CDC class is a very important one for us, because it supports *device contexts*. All the drawing of graphics and text we do in Visual C++ will be done in a device context.

What Is a Device Context?

A device context takes a little bit of understanding. It's a special object that has a great number of built-in methods for us to use in drawing. All drawing you do in Windows takes place in a device context.

TIP   Device contexts may seem to make things more complex at first, but they are actually Windows' way of making things easier. A device context can correspond to all types of devices, like the screen or the printer. When you've set up your graphics to appear in a device context, your display can appear in many different types of devices, including the screen and the printer.

To draw in our view, we use a device context corresponding to the view. You can also get device contexts corresponding to the whole window, the whole screen, or the printer. To draw in a device context, you use the CDC class's methods that appear below; note how many of them there are.

AbortDoc	AbortPath	AddMetaFileComment
AngleArc	Arc	ArcTo
Attach	BeginPath	BitBlt
CDC	Chord	CloseFigure
CreateCompatibleDC	CreateDC	CreateIC
DeleteDC	DeleteTempMap	Detach
DPtoHIMETRIC	DPtoLP	Draw3dRect
DrawDragRect	DrawEdge	DrawEscape
DrawFocusRect	DrawFrameControl	DrawIcon
DrawState	DrawText	Ellipse
EndDoc	EndPage	EndPath
EnumObjects	Escape	ExcludeClipRect
ExcludeUpdateRgn	ExtFloodFill	ExtTextOut
FillPath	FillRect	FillRgn

FillSolidRect	FlattenPath	FloodFill
FrameRect	FrameRgn	FromHandle
GetArcDirection	GetAspectRatioFilter	GetBkColor
GetBkMode	GetBoundsRect	GetBrushOrg
GetCharABCWidths	GetCharWidth	GetClipBox
GetColorAdjustment	GetCurrentBitmap	GetCurrentBrush
GetCurrentFont	GetCurrentPalette	GetCurrentPen
GetCurrentPosition	GetDeviceCaps	GetFontData
GetGlyphOutline	GetHalftoneBrush	GetKerningPairs
GetMapMode	GetMiterLimit	GetNearestColor
GetOutlineText	GetOutputCharWidth	GetOutputTabbed
Metrics		TextExtent
GetOutputTextExtent	GetOutputText-	GetPath
	Metrics	
GetPixel	GetPolyFillMode	GetROP2
GetSafeHdc	GetStretchBltMode	GetTabbedTextExtent
GetTextAlign	GetTextCharacter-	GetTextColor
	Extra	
GetTextExtent	GetTextFace	GetTextMetrics
GetViewportExt	GetViewportOrg	GetWindow
GetWindowExt	GetWindowOrg	GrayString
HIMETRICtoDP	HIMETRICtoLP	IntersectClipRect
InvertRect	InvertRgn	IsPrinting
LineTo	LPtoDP	LPtoHIMETRIC
MaskBlt	MoveTo	OffsetClipRgn
OffsetViewportOrg	OffsetWindowOrg	PaintRgn
PatBlt	Pie	PlayMetaFile
PlgBlt	PolyBezier	PolyBezierTo
PolyDraw	Polygon	Polyline
Polyline	PolylineTo	PolyPolygon
PolyPolyline	PtVisible	QueryAbort
RealizePalette	Rectangle	RectVisible
ReleaseAttribDC	ReleaseOutputDC	ResetDC
RestoreDC	RoundRect	SaveDC
ScaleViewportExt	ScaleWindowExt	ScrollDC
SelectClipPath	SelectClipRgn	SelectObject

SelectPalette	SelectStockObject	SetAbortProc
SetArcDirection	SetAttribDC	SetBkColor
SetBkMode	SetBoundsRect	SetBrushOrg
SetColorAdjustment	SetMapMode	SetMapperFlags
SetMiterLimit	SetOutputDC	SetPixel
SetPixelV	SetPolyFillMode	SetROP2
SetStretchBltMode	SetTextAlign	SetTextCharacter-Extra
SetTextColor	SetTextJustification	SetViewportExt
SetViewportOrg	SetWindowExt	SetWindowOrg
StartDoc	StartPage	StretchBlt
StrokeAndFillPath	StrokePath	TabbedTextOut
TextOut	UpdateColors	WidenPath

In particular, we're using the CDC TextOut() method to print in the view (which corresponds to our window's client area). We are passed a pointer, pDC, in OnDraw(), which points to a device context for our view. To draw our welcome_string text in the client area, then, we just have to execute this line:

```
pDC->TextOut(0, 0, welcome_string);
```

We pass the location of the upper left of the text string as we want it to appear on the screen to the TextOut() method. In this case, we display the text starting at (0, 0), which is the upper-left corner of the client area. We next pass the string itself, welcome_string.

TIP   In our client area, (0, 0) is the upper left. The x coordinate increases to the right, and the y coordinate increases downward. You can think of this coordinate system like reading text on a page: you move downward and to the right as you read text.

Thus, executing the entire line of code displays our string on the screen. In this way, we are displaying the program's data in our view object.

We'll see a great deal more about the view object in skills to come, since the view object is where most of our programming will take place. The code for the welcome example's view object appears in welcomeView.h/welcomeView.cpp.

TIP   A program may pass different device contexts to the OnDraw() method at different times. For example, now that we've placed code in OnDraw(), our program already supports printing. When the user uses the Print menu item in the program's File menu, or presses the button with a printer icon in the tool bar, the program passes a device context to OnDraw(), which corresponds to the printer, and our text is printed out. If you want to take special steps to prepare for a printing job, such as specially formatting your document, you can place the necessary code in the program's OnPreparePrinting() method.

welcomeView.h and *welcomeView.cpp*

```
// welcomeView.h : interface of the CWelcomeView class
//
/////////////////////////////////////////////////////////////////////////////

#if !defined(AFX_WELCOMEVIEW_H__AF072C8B_900A_11D0_8860_444553540000__INCLUDED_)
#define AFX_WELCOMEVIEW_H__AF072C8B_900A_11D0_8860_444553540000__INCLUDED_

#if _MSC_VER >= 1000
#pragma once
#endif // _MSC_VER >= 1000

class CWelcomeView : public CView
{
protected: // create from serialization only
    CWelcomeView();
    DECLARE_DYNCREATE(CWelcomeView)

// Attributes
public:
    CWelcomeDoc* GetDocument();

// Operations
public:

// Overrides
    // ClassWizard generated virtual function overrides
    //{{AFX_VIRTUAL(CWelcomeView)
    public:
    virtual void OnDraw(CDC* pDC);  // overridden to draw this view
    virtual BOOL PreCreateWindow(CREATESTRUCT& cs);
    protected:
    virtual BOOL OnPreparePrinting(CPrintInfo* pInfo);
    virtual void OnBeginPrinting(CDC* pDC, CPrintInfo* pInfo);
```

```
        virtual void OnEndPrinting(CDC* pDC, CPrintInfo* pInfo);
        //}}AFX_VIRTUAL

// Implementation
public:
        virtual ~CWelcomeView();
#ifdef _DEBUG
        virtual void AssertValid() const;
        virtual void Dump(CDumpContext& dc) const;
#endif

protected:

// Generated message map functions
protected:
        //{{AFX_MSG(CWelcomeView)
                // NOTE - the ClassWizard will add and remove member functions here.
                //     DO NOT EDIT what you see in these blocks of generated code !
        //}}AFX_MSG
        DECLARE_MESSAGE_MAP()
};

#ifndef _DEBUG  // debug version in welcomeView.cpp
inline CWelcomeDoc* CWelcomeView::GetDocument()
   { return (CWelcomeDoc*)m_pDocument; }
#endif

/////////////////////////////////////////////////////////////////////////////

//{{AFX_INSERT_LOCATION}}
// Microsoft Developer Studio will insert additional declarations immediately
// before the previous line.

#endif //
!defined(AFX_WELCOMEVIEW_H__AF072C8B_900A_11D0_8860_444553540000__INCLUDED_)



// welcomeView.cpp : implementation of the CWelcomeView class
//

#include "stdafx.h"
#include "welcome.h"

#include "welcomeDoc.h"
#include "welcomeView.h"

#ifdef _DEBUG
```

```
#define new DEBUG_NEW
#undef THIS_FILE
static char THIS_FILE[] = __FILE__;
#endif

/////////////////////////////////////////////////////////////////////////////
// CWelcomeView

IMPLEMENT_DYNCREATE(CWelcomeView, CView)

BEGIN_MESSAGE_MAP(CWelcomeView, CView)
    //{{AFX_MSG_MAP(CWelcomeView)
        // NOTE - the ClassWizard will add and remove mapping macros here.
        //    DO NOT EDIT what you see in these blocks of generated code!
    //}}AFX_MSG_MAP
    // Standard printing commands
    ON_COMMAND(ID_FILE_PRINT, CView::OnFilePrint)
    ON_COMMAND(ID_FILE_PRINT_DIRECT, CView::OnFilePrint)
    ON_COMMAND(ID_FILE_PRINT_PREVIEW, CView::OnFilePrintPreview)
END_MESSAGE_MAP()

/////////////////////////////////////////////////////////////////////////////
// CWelcomeView construction/destruction

CWelcomeView::CWelcomeView()
{
    // TODO: add construction code here

}

CWelcomeView::~CWelcomeView()
{
}

BOOL CWelcomeView::PreCreateWindow(CREATESTRUCT& cs)
{
    // TODO: Modify the Window class or styles here by modifying
    //   the CREATESTRUCT cs

    return CView::PreCreateWindow(cs);
}

/////////////////////////////////////////////////////////////////////////////
// CWelcomeView drawing

void CWelcomeView::OnDraw(CDC* pDC)
{
    CString welcome_string = "Welcome to Visual C++";
    CWelcomeDoc* pDoc = GetDocument();
```

```
        ASSERT_VALID(pDoc);

        pDC->TextOut(0, 0, welcome_string);
        // TODO: add draw code for native data here
}

/////////////////////////////////////////////////////////////////////////
// CWelcomeView printing

BOOL CWelcomeView::OnPreparePrinting(CPrintInfo* pInfo)
{
        // default preparation
        return DoPreparePrinting(pInfo);
}

void CWelcomeView::OnBeginPrinting(CDC* /*pDC*/, CPrintInfo* /*pInfo*/)
{
        // TODO: add extra initialization before printing
}

void CWelcomeView::OnEndPrinting(CDC* /*pDC*/, CPrintInfo* /*pInfo*/)
{
        // TODO: add cleanup after printing
}

/////////////////////////////////////////////////////////////////////////
// CWelcomeView diagnostics

#ifdef _DEBUG
void CWelcomeView::AssertValid() const
{
        CView::AssertValid();
}

void CWelcomeView::Dump(CDumpContext& dc) const
{
        CView::Dump(dc);
}

CWelcomeDoc* CWelcomeView::GetDocument() // non-debug version is inline
{
        ASSERT(m_pDocument->IsKindOf(RUNTIME_CLASS(CWelcomeDoc)));
        return (CWelcomeDoc*)m_pDocument;
}
#endif //_DEBUG

/////////////////////////////////////////////////////////////////////////
// CWelcomeView message handlers
```

Skill 2

The view object displays the data in the program, and the data is usually stored in the document object. That's the last of the four major objects in our program, so we'll turn to that now.

Dissecting the Document Object

The document object is where we store the program's data. In our welcome program, we haven't stored any data, except for the `welcome_string object`. We placed that object in the view object to make this program simpler, but it should actually go into the document object.

How would we place `welcome_string` in the document object? We start by declaring `welcome_string` in the document's header file, `welcomeDoc.h` this way:

```
// welcomeDoc.h : interface of the CWelcomeDoc class
//
/////////////////////////////////////////////////////////////////////////////

#if !defined(AFX_WELCOMEDOC_H__AF072C89_900A_11D0_8860_444553540000__INCLUDED_)
#define AFX_WELCOMEDOC_H__AF072C89_900A_11D0_8860_444553540000__INCLUDED_

#if _MSC_VER >= 1000
#pragma once
#endif // _MSC_VER >= 1000


class CWelcomeDoc : public CDocument
{
protected: // create from serialization only
    CWelcomeDoc();
    DECLARE_DYNCREATE(CWelcomeDoc)
➜   Cstring welcome_string;
        .
        .
        .
}
```

Next, we initialize the `welcome_string` object in the document class's constructor in the file `welcomeDocument.cpp`:

```
CWelcomeDoc::CWelcomeDoc()
{
➜   welcome_string = "Welcome to Visual C++";
}
```

Now our data is stored in the document object and is ready to go—but how do we reach that data from the view object?

Reaching the Document from the View

If you take a look at the code that the AppWizard has written for our view class, you'll see that it has already added the code necessary for us to get a pointer to the document object using the View class's GetDocument() method. AppWizard has named this pointer pDoc:

```
void CWelcomeView::OnDraw(CDC* pDC)
{
→        CWelcomeDoc* pDoc = GetDocument();
         ASSERT_VALID(pDoc);
                .
                .
                .
}
```

NOTE   You might also notice the line ASSERT_VALID(pDoc) in the above code. This is a special Visual C++ test using the ASSERT_VALID macro to make sure that nothing has gone wrong and that the pointer to the document is correct (a *macro* is just a set of prewritten C++ instructions, and we'll see more about macros and what they do throughout the book).

To reach welcome_string in the document object, we can refer to it as: pDoc->welcome_string; so we display the text in welcome_string this way:

```
void CWelcomeView::OnDraw(CDC* pDC)
{
         CWelcomeDoc* pDoc = GetDocument();
         ASSERT_VALID(pDoc);

→        pDC->TextOut(0, 0, pDoc->welcome_string);
}
```

Now the document-enabled program works as expected, and displays our message. Of course, with such a small amount of data, it hardly seems worth moving that data from the view object to the document object. In fact, it is very useful for one reason in particular—saving data to disk and reading it back in. Let's take a look at how that works now.

Saving Data to Disk

We'll see more about saving and retrieving data from disk when we cover file handling, but we can take a look at one aspect of file-handling now. In the document's code file, welcomeDocument.cpp, you'll find the Serialize() method:

```
void CWelcomeDoc::Serialize(CArchive& ar)
{
    if (ar.IsStoring())
    {
        // TODO: add storing code here
    }
    else
    {
        // TODO: add loading code here
    }
}
```

Our program already has quite a few menu items built in that deal with file handling: Save, Save As, Open, and so on. The program itself handles almost all the details of saving our documents to disk, but in this case we have to customize it so it will save our welcome_string object as well.

We are passed an object named ar in the Serialize() method, and we can use that just as we used cout in the last skill. In particular, we can add this code to store the welcome_string object in case we are saving data to disk, and to read it back in case we are reading data from disk:

```
void CWelcomeDoc::Serialize(CArchive& ar)
{
    if (ar.IsStoring())
    {
➜       ar << welcome_string;
    }
    else
    {
➜       ar >> welcome_string;
    }
}
```

Now the user can store and retrieve our document to and from disk. We'll see more about this process later, but already we've gotten a good start. The code for the document object appears in welcomeDoc.h and welcomeDoc.cpp.

welcomeDoc.h and *welcomeDoc.cpp*

```
// welcomeDoc.h : interface of the CWelcomeDoc class
//
/////////////////////////////////////////////////////////////////////

#if !defined(AFX_WELCOMEDOC_H__AF072C89_900A_11D0_8860_444553540000__INCLUDED_)
#define AFX_WELCOMEDOC_H__AF072C89_900A_11D0_8860_444553540000__INCLUDED_

#if _MSC_VER >= 1000
#pragma once
#endif // _MSC_VER >= 1000


class CWelcomeDoc : public CDocument
{
protected: // create from serialization only
    CWelcomeDoc();
    DECLARE_DYNCREATE(CWelcomeDoc)

// Attributes
public:

// Operations
public:

// Overrides
    // ClassWizard generated virtual function overrides
    //{{AFX_VIRTUAL(CWelcomeDoc)
    public:
    virtual BOOL OnNewDocument();
    virtual void Serialize(CArchive& ar);
    //}}AFX_VIRTUAL

// Implementation
public:
    virtual ~CWelcomeDoc();
#ifdef _DEBUG
    virtual void AssertValid() const;
    virtual void Dump(CDumpContext& dc) const;
#endif

protected:

// Generated message map functions
protected:
```

```
    //{{AFX_MSG(CWelcomeDoc)
        // NOTE - the ClassWizard will add and remove member functions here.
        //    DO NOT EDIT what you see in these blocks of generated code !
    //}}AFX_MSG
    DECLARE_MESSAGE_MAP()
};

//////////////////////////////////////////////////////////////////////

//{{AFX_INSERT_LOCATION}}
// Microsoft Developer Studio will insert additional declarations immediately
// before the previous line.

#endif //
!defined(AFX_WELCOMEDOC_H__AF072C89_900A_11D0_8860_444553540000__INCLUDED_)




// welcomeDoc.cpp : implementation of the CWelcomeDoc class
//

#include "stdafx.h"
#include "welcome.h"

#include "welcomeDoc.h"

#ifdef _DEBUG
#define new DEBUG_NEW
#undef THIS_FILE
static char THIS_FILE[] = __FILE__;
#endif

//////////////////////////////////////////////////////////////////////
// CWelcomeDoc

IMPLEMENT_DYNCREATE(CWelcomeDoc, CDocument)

BEGIN_MESSAGE_MAP(CWelcomeDoc, CDocument)
    //{{AFX_MSG_MAP(CWelcomeDoc)
        // NOTE - the ClassWizard will add and remove mapping macros here.
        //    DO NOT EDIT what you see in these blocks of generated code!
    //}}AFX_MSG_MAP
END_MESSAGE_MAP()

//////////////////////////////////////////////////////////////////////
// CWelcomeDoc construction/destruction

CWelcomeDoc::CWelcomeDoc()
{
```

```
        // TODO: add one-time construction code here

}

CWelcomeDoc::~CWelcomeDoc()
{
}

BOOL CWelcomeDoc::OnNewDocument()
{
    if (!CDocument::OnNewDocument())
        return FALSE;

    // TODO: add reinitialization code here
    // (SDI documents will reuse this document)

    return TRUE;
}



////////////////////////////////////////////////////////////////////////
// CWelcomeDoc serialization

void CWelcomeDoc::Serialize(CArchive& ar)
{
    if (ar.IsStoring())
    {
        // TODO: add storing code here
    }
    else
    {
        // TODO: add loading code here
    }
}

////////////////////////////////////////////////////////////////////////
// CWelcomeDoc diagnostics

#ifdef _DEBUG
void CWelcomeDoc::AssertValid() const
{
    CDocument::AssertValid();
}

void CWelcomeDoc::Dump(CDumpContext& dc) const
{
    CDocument::Dump(dc);
}
```

```
#endif //_DEBUG

/////////////////////////////////////////////////////////////////////////////
// CWelcomeDoc commands
```

We've now explored our first AppWizard program, the type of program we'll be using throughout this book. We've seen that quite a lot of code is involved in such programs, but that it's divided up into many different bite-sized methods, which make it easier to handle. Now that we've seen how to display a message in a window, let's go on to the next skill, where we will see how to read input from the user.

Are You Experienced?

Now You Can...

- ☑ **Create a working Visual C++ program that creates its own window and displays data in that window**

- ☑ **Understand and modify the four basic parts of a Visual C++ program**

- ☑ **Use the view object to display data**

- ☑ **Use the document object to store data**

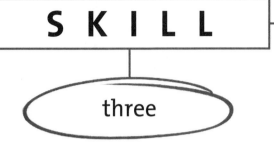

Reading Keystrokes from the Keyboard

- ❑ Handling Windows events
- ❑ Using the Visual C++ Class Wizard
- ❑ Reading from the keyboard
- ❑ Formatting displayed text
- ❑ Determining the dimensions of a window
- ❑ Determining the screen dimensions of a text string

In the last skill, we started working with Visual C++ and saw how to create a program that set up and displayed its own window, then displayed a message in that window. In other words, we were able to display some text output to the user. In this skill, we're going to focus on getting *input* from the user. The type of user input we'll get is keystrokes from the keyboard—as the user types keystrokes, we'll show how they appear in our window.

This is important not just because we are learning how to handle the keyboard; the more important aspect is that we will learn how to handle a Windows event— in this case, a keyboard event. Because our programs will be event-driven (that is, they will respond to mouse clicks, key strikes, menu selections, and so on), this is the first step on a long path that we will follow in this book: handling Windows events. We'll see how to use the Visual C++ ClassWizard to connect the Windows message sent to us to a method called an *event-handler*. In our case, we will handle the Windows WM_CHAR message, connecting it to the event-handler OnChar(), which means that when the user strikes a key, the program calls our OnChar() method.

In addition, we'll learn a little about displaying and formatting text in a window in this skill. We will see how to display the text that the user types as *centered* in our window. That is, it will appear in the middle of the window's client area—halfway up, halfway down, and centered between right and left. This involves determining the dimensions of our window's client area, as well as the size of the string of text as displayed on the screen, so we can position that string correctly.

We have a lot going on in this skill, so let's start at once by reading keys from the keyboard.

Using the Keyboard

In our first keyboard example, we will read keys from the keyboard and display them as the user types them in the client area (that is, the view) of our window.

```
-----------------------------------------------
|Untitled - keystrokes                          |
|File Edit View Help                            |
|[ ] [ ] [ ] [ ]                                |
|-----------------------------------------------|
|Here is text we have read from the keyboard.   |
|                                               |
|                                               |
|                                               |
|                                               |
|                                               |
|                                               |
|                                               |
|                                               |
-----------------------------------------------
```

This example will show us how to use the keyboard, and also how to start making use of Windows events.

We will call this example program "keystrokes." Create this program now using the MFC AppWizard to create a single window (select the Single Document Interface (SDI) option in AppWizard) program, giving this program the name **keystrokes**.

We will divide this program into two parts, setting up storage for the keystrokes we read, and actually reading the keystrokes themselves. We'll start by setting up a place to store the keys that the user types, as we assemble the individual keys into a string of text.

Setting Up Storage for Our Keyboard Data

As we know, a program's document is intended to hold the data that we display in the program's view. For that reason, we will set up storage for our keystrokes in the document now.

As the user types each key, we can add it to a string of text, which we store in an MFC Cstring object. In the view object, we can display this text string (in the OnDraw() method). We will call this string of text StringData, and we declare it with the declarations of the other variables in the document, in the document's header file, keystrokesDoc.h:

```
// keystrokesDoc.h : interface of the CKeystrokesDoc class
//
/////////////////////////////////////////////////////////////////////
```

```
          .
          .
          .
class CKeystrokesDoc : public CDocument
{
protected: // create from serialization only
     CKeystrokesDoc();
     DECLARE_DYNCREATE(CKeystrokesDoc)
➔    CString StringData;
          .
          .
          .

}
```

Next, we initialize that string to an empty string—""—in the document's con-structor, which we find in the file keystrokesDoc.cpp:

```
CKeystrokesDoc::CKeystrokesDoc()
{
     // TODO: add one-time construction code here
➔    StringData = "";

}
```

Now our data storage is set up—as the user types each key, we will add it to the StringData variable.

Reading Keystrokes

Now we've set up storage for the keys the user will type—but how do we read those keys in the first place? When the user types a key, Windows sends us a WM_CHAR message, and we want to connect that to a method in our view class named OnChar(). We'll do that with the Visual C++ ClassWizard.

 NOTE   There can be many windows open in a Windows session, and only one can get keyboard events at any one time. The window that is currently active and get-ting keyboard events is called the window with the *focus*.

To start ClassWizard, select the ClassWizard item in the View menu now. This opens ClassWizard, as shown in Figure 3.1. (Make sure the Message Maps tab is clicked in ClassWizard—the ClassWizard connects a Windows message to our program through what it calls a *message map*.)

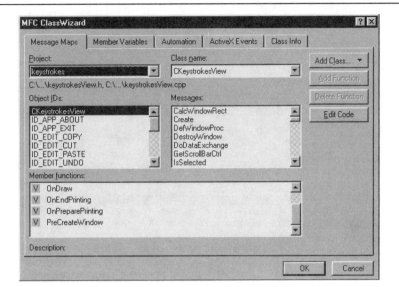

FIGURE 3.1: The Visual C++ ClassWizard

We will add a new event-handler—OnChar()—to our view class, CKeystrokes-View, so make sure that class is selected in the ClassWizard's Class name box. The Windows message we want to use is WM_CHAR, which is sent to our program when the user types a key. After connecting OnChar() to the WM_CHAR message, OnChar() will be called each time the user types a character. Find that message now in the ClassWizard Messages box now and double-click it.

This adds our OnChar() method at once, as shown in Figure 3.2, in the Class-Wizard Member functions box. That is, OnChar() is the default name ClassWizard gives to WM_CHAR event-handlers, just as OnMouseMove() is the name it gives the event-handler for the WM_MOUSEMOVE message.

> **TIP**   Besides the WM_CHAR message, Windows also sends our program WM_KEYDOWN messages when a key is pressed and WM_KEYUP when a key is released. These messages are handled in the event-handlers OnKeyDown() and OnKeyUp() by ClassWizard.

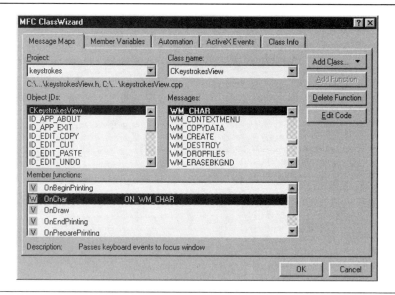

FIGURE 3.2: Creating the OnChar() method in ClassWizard

Find the OnChar() method now in the keystrokesView.cpp file:

```
void CKeystrokesView::OnChar(UINT nChar, UINT nRepCnt, UINT nFlags)
{
    // TODO: Add your message handler code here and/or call default

    CView::OnChar(nChar, nRepCnt, nFlags);
}
```

 TIP   After creating a new event-handler, you can go directly to it in code by double-clicking its entry in the ClassWizard Member functions box.

This is the method that is called when the user types a key. Note that the code the ClassWizard has placed here for us already calls the OnChar() method of the view's base class (our keystrokeView class's base class is the MFC CView class). This is typical of event-handlers the ClassWizard generates—it supplies us with a default call to the base class's event-handler for the event, in case we want the base class to handle the event instead of adding our own code.

The actual key is passed to us as the nChar parameter. If the user has held down the key, generating type-ahead (called *typematic*), the number of times the keystroke has been sent will be in the nRepCnt parameter. The nFlags parameter works like this, bit-by-bit:

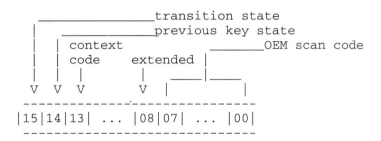

```
_____transition state
|     _____previous key state
|    |  context               _____OEM scan code
|    |  code      extended  |
|    |  |           |    ___|___
V    V  V           V    |       |
----------------------'-----------------
|15|14|13|  ...  |08|07|  ...  |00|
---------------------------------------
```

The transition state is 1 if the key has just been released and 0 if it's just been pressed. The previous key state parameter is 1 if the key was previously down and 0 if it was up. The context code parameter is 1 if the Alt key is down.

 TIP   **If the user is holding a key down, and the keyboard is sending repeated typematic keys to you, the previous state parameter will be 1 in** OnChar()**.**

The next step is to record the character the user typed.

Recording a Character in Our Document

The character the user typed is now in the nChar parameter, and we should store that character in our data string object, StringData. That object is in our document, so first we need a pointer to our document object. We get that pointer, pDoc, this way:

```
void CKeystrokesView::OnChar(UINT nChar, UINT nRepCnt, UINT nFlags)
{
    // TODO: Add your message handler code here and/or call default

→   CKeystrokesDoc* pDoc = GetDocument();
→   ASSERT_VALID(pDoc);
        .
        .
        .
}
```

Note the use of ASSERT_VALID() here. As before, this is just a Visual C++ technique for making sure we did in fact get a pointer to the document (if not, it generates an error).

Next, we add the character nChar to the string StringData. It's actually quite easy; we just add that character to the string this way (note that we use the -> operator to refer to the StringData object in the document pointed to by pDoc):

```
void CKeystrokesView::OnChar(UINT nChar, UINT nRepCnt, UINT nFlags)
{
    // TODO: Add your message handler code here and/or call default

    CKeystrokesDoc* pDoc = GetDocument();
    ASSERT_VALID(pDoc);
➜   pDoc->StringData += nChar;
            .
            .
            .
}
```

Here, we use the C++ shortcut operator +=. Using this shortcut operator, the above line of code is equal to this:

```
pDoc->StringData = pDoc->StringData + nChar;
```

> **TIP**   Besides the shortcut operator +=, C++ has other shortcut operators like *=, -=, /=, and so on.

Now we've stored the newly struck character in our string of text. The next job is to display that newly updated string in our client area.

Displaying Our Text

As is usual for AppWizard-generated programs, we'll handle the display of our data in the view's OnDraw() method.

> **TIP**   We could actually display the new text from the OnChar() method, but it is better to display it in OnDraw(), because when our window is redrawn or uncovered, the program will call OnDraw(), not OnChar(), to redraw and restore our window's display.

To make the program call OnDraw() and so draw the new text string (using code we will add to OnDraw() in a moment), we call the view's Invalidate() method:

```
void CKeystrokesView::OnChar(UINT nChar, UINT nRepCnt, UINT nFlags)
{
    // TODO: Add your message handler code here and/or call default

    CKeystrokesDoc* pDoc = GetDocument();
    ASSERT_VALID(pDoc);
    pDoc->StringData += nChar;
→   Invalidate();

    CView::OnChar(nChar, nRepCnt, nFlags);
}
```

This method forces the program to redraw the view by calling OnDraw(), so open OnDraw() now:

```
void CKeystrokesView::OnDraw(CDC* pDC)
{
    CKeystrokesDoc* pDoc = GetDocument();
    ASSERT_VALID(pDoc);

    // TODO: add draw code for native data here
}
```

TIP   You can also use Invalidate() to invalidate only a part of a view, causing the program to redraw only that part of the view.

All we need to do here is draw the text string, which we do with TextOut():

```
void CKeystrokesView::OnDraw(CDC* pDC)
{
    CKeystrokesDoc* pDoc = GetDocument();
    ASSERT_VALID(pDoc);

→   pDC->TextOut(0, 0, pDoc->StringData);
}
```

The program is ready. Run it now, as shown in Figure 3.2, and type some text. When you do, the text appears in the window, as you can see in Figure 3.2. Our program is a success; now we're reading keystrokes from the keyboard.

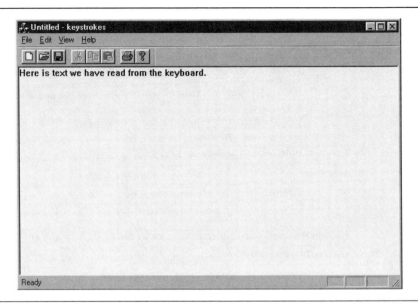

FIGURE 3.3: Reading keys from the keyboard

The code for this program appears in keystrokesView.h/keystrokesView.cpp.

keystrokesView.h and keystrokesView.cpp

```
// keystrokesView.h : interface of the CKeystrokesView class
//
/////////////////////////////////////////////////////////////////////////////

#if !defined(AFX_KEYSTROKESVIEW_H__8FABEF6D_9152_11D0_8860_444553540000__
➥INCLUDED_)
#define AFX_KEYSTROKESVIEW_H__8FABEF6D_9152_11D0_8860_444553540000__INCLUDED_

#if _MSC_VER >= 1000
#pragma once
#endif // _MSC_VER >= 1000

class CKeystrokesView : public CView
{
protected: // create from serialization only
    CKeystrokesView();
    DECLARE_DYNCREATE(CKeystrokesView)
```

```
// Attributes
public:
    CKeystrokesDoc* GetDocument();

// Operations
public:

// Overrides
    // ClassWizard generated virtual function overrides
    //{{AFX_VIRTUAL(CKeystrokesView)
    public:
    virtual void OnDraw(CDC* pDC);  // overridden to draw this view
    virtual BOOL PreCreateWindow(CREATESTRUCT& cs);
    protected:
    virtual BOOL OnPreparePrinting(CPrintInfo* pInfo);
    virtual void OnBeginPrinting(CDC* pDC, CPrintInfo* pInfo);
    virtual void OnEndPrinting(CDC* pDC, CPrintInfo* pInfo);
    //}}AFX_VIRTUAL

// Implementation
public:
    virtual ~CKeystrokesView();
#ifdef _DEBUG
    virtual void AssertValid() const;
    virtual void Dump(CDumpContext& dc) const;
#endif

protected:

// Generated message map functions
protected:
    //{{AFX_MSG(CKeystrokesView)
    afx_msg void OnChar(UINT nChar, UINT nRepCnt, UINT nFlags);
    //}}AFX_MSG
    DECLARE_MESSAGE_MAP()
};

#ifndef _DEBUG  // debug version in keystrokesView.cpp
inline CKeystrokesDoc* CKeystrokesView::GetDocument()
   { return (CKeystrokesDoc*)m_pDocument; }
#endif

/////////////////////////////////////////////////////////////////////////

//{{AFX_INSERT_LOCATION}}
// Microsoft Developer Studio will insert additional declarations immediately
// before the previous line.
```

```
#endif //
!defined(AFX_KEYSTROKESVIEW_H__8FABEF6D_9152_11D0_8860_444553540000__INCLUDED_)



// keystrokesView.cpp : implementation of the CKeystrokesView class
//

#include "stdafx.h"
#include "keystrokes.h"

#include "keystrokesDoc.h"
#include "keystrokesView.h"

#ifdef _DEBUG
#define new DEBUG_NEW
#undef THIS_FILE
static char THIS_FILE[] = __FILE__;
#endif

/////////////////////////////////////////////////////////////////////////////
// CKeystrokesView

IMPLEMENT_DYNCREATE(CKeystrokesView, CView)

BEGIN_MESSAGE_MAP(CKeystrokesView, CView)
    //{{AFX_MSG_MAP(CKeystrokesView)
    ON_WM_CHAR()
    //}}AFX_MSG_MAP
    // Standard printing commands
    ON_COMMAND(ID_FILE_PRINT, CView::OnFilePrint)
    ON_COMMAND(ID_FILE_PRINT_DIRECT, CView::OnFilePrint)
    ON_COMMAND(ID_FILE_PRINT_PREVIEW, CView::OnFilePrintPreview)
END_MESSAGE_MAP()

/////////////////////////////////////////////////////////////////////////////
// CKeystrokesView construction/destruction

CKeystrokesView::CKeystrokesView()
{
    // TODO: add construction code here

}

CKeystrokesView::~CKeystrokesView()
{
}
```

```
BOOL CKeystrokesView::PreCreateWindow(CREATESTRUCT& cs)
{
    // TODO: Modify the Window class or styles here by modifying
    //   the CREATESTRUCT cs

    return CView::PreCreateWindow(cs);
}

/////////////////////////////////////////////////////////////////////////////
// CKeystrokesView drawing

void CKeystrokesView::OnDraw(CDC* pDC)
{
    CKeystrokesDoc* pDoc = GetDocument();
    ASSERT_VALID(pDoc);

    pDC->TextOut(0, 0, pDoc->StringData);
    // TODO: add draw code for native data here
}

/////////////////////////////////////////////////////////////////////////////
// CKeystrokesView printing

BOOL CKeystrokesView::OnPreparePrinting(CPrintInfo* pInfo)
{
    // default preparation
    return DoPreparePrinting(pInfo);
}

void CKeystrokesView::OnBeginPrinting(CDC* /*pDC*/, CPrintInfo* /*pInfo*/)
{
    // TODO: add extra initialization before printing
}

void CKeystrokesView::OnEndPrinting(CDC* /*pDC*/, CPrintInfo* /*pInfo*/)
{
    // TODO: add cleanup after printing
}

/////////////////////////////////////////////////////////////////////////////
// CKeystrokesView diagnostics

#ifdef _DEBUG
void CKeystrokesView::AssertValid() const
{
    CView::AssertValid();
}
```

```
void CKeystrokesView::Dump(CDumpContext& dc) const
{
    CView::Dump(dc);
}

CKeystrokesDoc* CKeystrokesView::GetDocument() // non-debug version is inline
{
    ASSERT(m_pDocument->IsKindOf(RUNTIME_CLASS(CKeystrokesDoc)));
    return (CKeystrokesDoc*)m_pDocument;
}
#endif //_DEBUG

/////////////////////////////////////////////////////////////////////////////
// CKeystrokesView message handlers

void CKeystrokesView::OnChar(UINT nChar, UINT nRepCnt, UINT nFlags)
{
    // TODO: Add your message handler code here and/or call default

    CKeystrokesDoc* pDoc = GetDocument();
    ASSERT_VALID(pDoc);
    pDoc->StringData += nChar;
    Invalidate();

    CView::OnChar(nChar, nRepCnt, nFlags);
}
```

Now we've been able to read keys and display them, but we've only been able to display them in a rudimentary way, starting at the extreme upper left in our client area. We can do better than that; we'll see how to center text in the client area next.

Centering Text in a Window

Our next example will show more about displaying text in a window. In particular, we'll see how to present the text the user types as *centered* in our client area. In other words, the text will appear right in the middle of the client area.

```
-----------------------------------------------------
|Untitled - centered                                |
|File Edit View Help                                |
|[ ] [ ] [ ] [ ]                                    |
|---------------------------------------------------|
|                                                   |
|                                                   |
|                                                   |
|                                                   |
|                                                   |
|      Here is centered text we read from the keyboard. |
|                                                   |
|                                                   |
|                                                   |
|                                                   |
|                                                   |
-----------------------------------------------------
```

In order to center the text in the client area, we'll need to determine two things: the dimensions of our client area, and the dimensions of the text string as it appears on the screen.

First, create a new single-window (SDI) program named centered. We will read keys from the keyboard in this program just as we did in our previous example, keystrokes. That is, we will set up an object named StringData in the document:

```
// centeredDoc.h : interface of the CCenteredDoc class
//
/////////////////////////////////////////////////////////////////////////
          .
          .
          .
class CCenteredDoc : public CDocument
{
protected: // create from serialization only
     CCenteredDoc();
     DECLARE_DYNCREATE(CCenteredDoc)
➜    CString StringData;
          .
          .
          .
```

Next, we initialize the StringData object:

```
CCenteredDoc::CCenteredDoc()
{
```

```
→       StringData = "";
        // TODO: add one-time construction code here

}
```

We then use ClassWizard to add the OnChar() method to the centered program's view class, CCenteredView:

```
void CCenteredView::OnChar(UINT nChar, UINT nRepCnt, UINT nFlags)
{
    // TODO: Add your message handler code here and/or call default
    CCenteredDoc* pDoc = GetDocument();
    ASSERT_VALID(pDoc);

    CView::OnChar(nChar, nRepCnt, nFlags);
}
```

Then we add our key-storing code:

```
void CCenteredView::OnChar(UINT nChar, UINT nRepCnt, UINT nFlags)
{
    // TODO: Add your message handler code here and/or call default
    CCenteredDoc* pDoc = GetDocument();
    ASSERT_VALID(pDoc);

→   pDoc->StringData += nChar;
→   Invalidate();

    CView::OnChar(nChar, nRepCnt, nFlags);
}
```

After the user types a key and we store it, it's time to display the newly struck key. We'll turn to that now.

Finding the Size of a Window

We display our text in OnDraw(), which currently looks like this:

```
void CCenteredView::OnDraw(CDC* pDC)

{
    CCenteredDoc* pDoc = GetDocument();
    ASSERT_VALID(pDoc);

    // TODO: add draw code for native data here
}
```

Currently, we only have enough code to get a pointer to the document object. The next step is to determine the size of our client area, that is, our view, so that we can center the typed text in it.

We can use the `CWnd` `GetWindowRect()` method to get the size of the client area (that is, our view class, `CCenteredView`, is derived from the MFC class `CView`, which in turn is derived from the basic MFC window class, `CWnd`). We pass a pointer to a `CRect` object to `GetWindowRect()` to get the size of our view. The `CRect` class is used to hold the dimensions and size of a rectangle, and here that rectangle will be our client area.

In particular, we set up a `CRect` object named rect and pass a pointer to that object to `GetWindowRect()` using the C++ operator &:

```
void CCenteredView::OnDraw(CDC* pDC)
{
    CCenteredDoc* pDoc = GetDocument();
    ASSERT_VALID(pDoc);
➜    CRect rect;

➜    GetWindowRect(&rect);
        .
        .
        .

}
```

TIP

If you want to find the size of our main window, including title bar, status bar, and so on, call `GetParent()->GetWindowRect()` **in the view object. This works because the main window is the parent window of our view.**

Now the `rect` object holds the dimensions of our client area. We'll use the `CRect` class's `Width()` and `Height()` methods to get the client area's width and height. To start centering the text, find the exact center of the client area and store that location in two variables, x and y (i.e., a coordinate pair, (x, y)):

```
void CCenteredView::OnDraw(CDC* pDC)
{
    CCenteredDoc* pDoc = GetDocument();
    ASSERT_VALID(pDoc);
    CRect rect;

    GetWindowRect(&rect);
➜    int x = rect.Width()/2;
```

```
→       int y = rect.Height()/2;
                    .
                    .
                    .
    }
```

Now we have the exact center of the client area stored as (x, y). The next step is to determine the dimensions of the text string itself so we can center that string around this point.

Finding the Size of a Displayed Text String

To determine the size of our text string as it will appear in the client area, use the CDC class's GetTextExtent() method (recall that CDC is the device context class, and we draw our text in a device context).

To use the GetTextExtent() method, we just pass our text string to it and that method returns an object of the MFC CSize class that we'll call size:

```
void CCenteredView::OnDraw(CDC* pDC)
{
    CCenteredDoc* pDoc = GetDocument();
    ASSERT_VALID(pDoc);
    CRect rect;

    GetWindowRect(&rect);
    int x = rect.Width()/2;
    int y = rect.Height()/2;

→   CSize size = pDC->GetTextExtent(pDoc->StringData);
                    .
                    .
                    .
}
```

The CSize class has two important members, cx and cy, which hold the dimensions of our text string. Using those two members, we can center our text around the center of the client area this way:

```
void CCenteredView::OnDraw(CDC* pDC)
{
    CCenteredDoc* pDoc = GetDocument();
    ASSERT_VALID(pDoc);
    CRect rect;

    GetWindowRect(&rect);
```

```
        int x = rect.Width()/2;
        int y = rect.Height()/2;

        CSize size = pDC->GetTextExtent(pDoc->StringData);

➜       x -= size.cx/2;
➜       y -= size.cy/2;
                    .
                    .
                    .
        }
```

TIP   Now that you know how to find a text string's height when it's displayed on the screen, you can modify the key-reading programs to handle the <Enter> key. Just check if the struck key is a carriage return, '\r', and if so, move to the next line by adding the height of the text string to the y variable to skip to the next text line on the screen.

Now all that remains is to draw our text string at the new coordinates (x, y), and we do that with TextOut():

```
void CCenteredView::OnDraw(CDC* pDC)
{
        CCenteredDoc* pDoc = GetDocument();
        ASSERT_VALID(pDoc);
        CRect rect;

        GetWindowRect(&rect);
        int x = rect.Width()/2;
        int y = rect.Height()/2;

        CSize size = pDC->GetTextExtent(pDoc->StringData);

        x -= size.cx/2;
        y -= size.cy/2;

➜       pDC->TextOut(x, y, pDoc->StringData);

}
```

Now run the program and type some text. When you type text, it appears centered in our client area, as shown in Figure 3.4. You're now able to place text in a window as you want and where you want it.

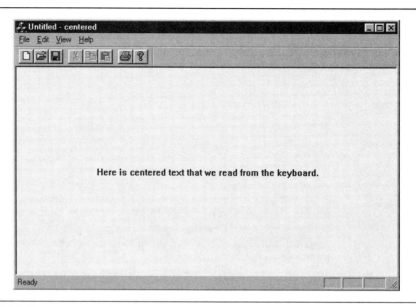

FIGURE 3.4: Reading keys from the keyboard and displaying them as centered text.

 TIP   You may note that we haven't supported the delete key in our keyboard-reading program. That's because text is drawn as graphics in Windows, and to delete a character on the screen, we have to draw over it with the background color of the view. You can do that by drawing the character again in the background color. To set the color of text, use `SetTextColor()`, and to get the view's background color, use `GetBkColor()`. We'll see more about using color this way later.

The code for this program appears in `centeredView.h/centeredView.cpp`.

centeredView.h and *centeredView.cpp*

```
// centeredView.h : interface of the CCenteredView class
//
/////////////////////////////////////////////////////////////////////////

#if !defined(AFX_CENTEREDVIEW_H__2B76F46F_917D_11D0_8860_444553540000__INCLUDED_)
#define AFX_CENTEREDVIEW_H__2B76F46F_917D_11D0_8860_444553540000__INCLUDED_

#if _MSC_VER >= 1000
```

```
#pragma once
#endif // _MSC_VER >= 1000

class CCenteredView : public CView
{
protected: // create from serialization only
    CCenteredView();
    DECLARE_DYNCREATE(CCenteredView)

// Attributes
public:
    CCenteredDoc* GetDocument();

// Operations
public:

// Overrides
    // ClassWizard generated virtual function overrides
    //{{AFX_VIRTUAL(CCenteredView)
    public:
    virtual void OnDraw(CDC* pDC);   // overridden to draw this view
    virtual BOOL PreCreateWindow(CREATESTRUCT& cs);
    protected:
    virtual BOOL OnPreparePrinting(CPrintInfo* pInfo);
    virtual void OnBeginPrinting(CDC* pDC, CPrintInfo* pInfo);
    virtual void OnEndPrinting(CDC* pDC, CPrintInfo* pInfo);
    //}}AFX_VIRTUAL

// Implementation
public:
    virtual ~CCenteredView();
#ifdef _DEBUG
    virtual void AssertValid() const;
    virtual void Dump(CDumpContext& dc) const;
#endif

protected:

// Generated message map functions
protected:
    //{{AFX_MSG(CCenteredView)
    afx_msg void OnChar(UINT nChar, UINT nRepCnt, UINT nFlags);
    //}}AFX_MSG
    DECLARE_MESSAGE_MAP()
};

#ifndef _DEBUG  // debug version in centeredView.cpp
inline CCenteredDoc* CCenteredView::GetDocument()
```

```
        { return (CCenteredDoc*)m_pDocument; }
#endif


//////////////////////////////////////////////////////////////////////////

//{{AFX_INSERT_LOCATION}}
// Microsoft Developer Studio will insert additional declarations immediately
// before the previous line.

#endif // !defined(AFX_CENTEREDVIEW_H__2B76F46F_917D_11D0_8860_444553540000__
➥INCLUDED_)




// centeredView.cpp : implementation of the CCenteredView class
//

#include "stdafx.h"
#include "centered.h"

#include "centeredDoc.h"
#include "centeredView.h"

#ifdef _DEBUG
#define new DEBUG_NEW
#undef THIS_FILE
static char THIS_FILE[] = __FILE__;
#endif

//////////////////////////////////////////////////////////////////////////
// CCenteredView

IMPLEMENT_DYNCREATE(CCenteredView, CView)

BEGIN_MESSAGE_MAP(CCenteredView, CView)
    //{{AFX_MSG_MAP(CCenteredView)
    ON_WM_CHAR()
    //}}AFX_MSG_MAP
    // Standard printing commands
    ON_COMMAND(ID_FILE_PRINT, CView::OnFilePrint)
    ON_COMMAND(ID_FILE_PRINT_DIRECT, CView::OnFilePrint)
    ON_COMMAND(ID_FILE_PRINT_PREVIEW, CView::OnFilePrintPreview)
END_MESSAGE_MAP()

//////////////////////////////////////////////////////////////////////////
// CCenteredView construction/destruction
```

```
CCenteredView::CCenteredView()
{
    // TODO: add construction code here

}

CCenteredView::~CCenteredView()
{
}

BOOL CCenteredView::PreCreateWindow(CREATESTRUCT& cs)
{
    // TODO: Modify the Window class or styles here by modifying
    //   the CREATESTRUCT cs

    return CView::PreCreateWindow(cs);
}

/////////////////////////////////////////////////////////////////////////
// CCenteredView drawing

void CCenteredView::OnDraw(CDC* pDC)
{
    CCenteredDoc* pDoc = GetDocument();
    ASSERT_VALID(pDoc);
    CRect rect;

    GetWindowRect(&rect);
    int x = rect.Width()/2;
    int y = rect.Height()/2;

    CSize size = pDC->GetTextExtent(pDoc->StringData);

    x -= size.cx/2;
    y -= size.cy/2;

    pDC->TextOut(x, y, pDoc->StringData);

    // TODO: add draw code for native data here
}

/////////////////////////////////////////////////////////////////////////
// CCenteredView printing

BOOL CCenteredView::OnPreparePrinting(CPrintInfo* pInfo)
{
    // default preparation
    return DoPreparePrinting(pInfo);
```

```
}

void CCenteredView::OnBeginPrinting(CDC* /*pDC*/, CPrintInfo* /*pInfo*/)
{
    // TODO: add extra initialization before printing
}

void CCenteredView::OnEndPrinting(CDC* /*pDC*/, CPrintInfo* /*pInfo*/)
{
    // TODO: add cleanup after printing
}

/////////////////////////////////////////////////////////////////////////////
// CCenteredView diagnostics

#ifdef _DEBUG
void CCenteredView::AssertValid() const
{
    CView::AssertValid();
}

void CCenteredView::Dump(CDumpContext& dc) const
{
    CView::Dump(dc);
}

CCenteredDoc* CCenteredView::GetDocument() // non-debug version is inline
{
    ASSERT(m_pDocument->IsKindOf(RUNTIME_CLASS(CCenteredDoc)));
    return (CCenteredDoc*)m_pDocument;
}
#endif //_DEBUG

/////////////////////////////////////////////////////////////////////////////
// CCenteredView message handlers

void CCenteredView::OnChar(UINT nChar, UINT nRepCnt, UINT nFlags)
{
    // TODO: Add your message handler code here and/or call default
    CCenteredDoc* pDoc = GetDocument();
    ASSERT_VALID(pDoc);

    pDoc->StringData += nChar;
    Invalidate();

    CView::OnChar(nChar, nRepCnt, nFlags);
}
```

That's it for our keyboard exercises for the moment. In this skill, we've seen how to read keys from the keyboard, store them in the document object, display them in the client area of our window, and display them as centered text in the client area. In the next skill, we're going to work on another input device—the mouse.

Are You Experienced?

Now You Can...

- ☑ Use the ClassWizard tool to connect Windows messages to event-handler methods
- ☑ Read keys from the keyboard as the user types them
- ☑ Store data in the program's document object
- ☑ Find a window's size
- ☑ Find a displayed text string's size
- ☑ Display centered text in a window

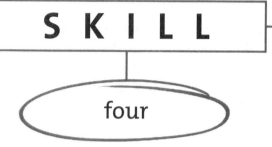

S K I L L

four

Handling the Mouse in Visual C++

- ❏ Handling Windows mouse events
- ❏ Creating and using an insertion-point caret
- ❏ Using the Windows TEXTMETRIC structure
- ❏ Connecting mouse events to code

In the last skill, we got our start handling Windows events when we connected the keyboard to a program. In this skill, we're going to continue working with Windows events, only from a different source this time—the mouse. The mouse can generate quite a number of events, from WM_LBUTTONDOWN, when the user presses the left button on the mouse, to WM_MOUSEMOVE, when the user moves the mouse.

In this skill, we'll augment our key-reading program from the last skill to include mouse events. In particular, we'll let the user select a location in our client area simply by clicking it. Then, when they type text, that text appears at the location they clicked. In this way, they can decide where they want the text to appear in our window.

On the other hand, this raises a new issue: when the user clicks a new location in the window, how do we mark that location so they'll know where the text will appear when they type it? This is usually handled in Windows with a *caret* (also called the insertion point), which is one of those blinking vertical lines you see that indicate where text will appear when you type it. Because we're going to let the user select where they will place the text they type in our window, we'll spend some time seeing how to create and use carets in windows.

Let's see how to support and draw a caret in a Visual C++ view now. We'll start with a program that simply lets us add a caret to a window and then move the caret as we type. After that, we'll start working with the mouse, allowing the user to place text where they want it in the view.

Adding a Caret to a Window

Our first example shows how to use carets. In particular, we'll place a blinking caret in our client area at the extreme upper left of the following graphic.

```
-----------------------------------------------------
|Untitled - carets                                  |
|File Edit View Help                                |
|[ ]  [ ]  [ ]  [ ]                                 |
|---------------------------------------------------|
||                                                  |
||                                                  |
|                                                   |
|                                                   |
|                                                   |
|                                                   |
|                                                   |
|                                                   |
|                                                   |
|                                                   |
|                                                   |
-----------------------------------------------------
```

Then, as the user types text, we'll display that text, starting at upper left, and move the caret to the end of the text, indicating where the next character will go:

```
-----------------------------------------------------
|Untitled - carets                                  |
|File Edit View Help                                |
|[ ]  [ ]  [ ]  [ ]                                 |
|---------------------------------------------------|
|Here is some text|                                 |
|                                                   |
|                                                   |
|                                                   |
|                                                   |
|                                                   |
|                                                   |
|                                                   |
|                                                   |
|                                                   |
-----------------------------------------------------
```

Let's see this at work. Use AppWizard to create a new single-window (SDI) program named carets. We begin by setting up storage for our text string's data, StringData, in the program's document header file:

```
class CCaretsDoc : public CDocument
{
protected: // create from serialization only
    CCaretsDoc();
    DECLARE_DYNCREATE(CCaretsDoc)
        .
        .
        .
// Implementation
public:
    virtual ~CCaretsDoc();
➜   CString StringData;
        .
        .
        .

}
```

We reset that string object to an empty string, "", in the document's constructor:
CCaretsDoc::CCaretsDoc()

```
{
➜   StringData = "";
    // TODO: add one-time construction code here

}
```

In addition, use ClassWizard now to connect the OnChar() method to the WM_CHAR Windows message in the view. As in the last skill, we add code to record the keys the user types this way:

```
void CCaretsView::OnChar(UINT nChar, UINT nRepCnt, UINT nFlags)
{
    CCaretsDoc* pDoc = GetDocument();
    ASSERT_VALID(pDoc);

➜   pDoc->StringData += nChar;
➜   Invalidate();

    CView::OnChar(nChar, nRepCnt, nFlags);
}
```

Now we are ready to create and use a new caret in the view.

To create a new caret, we'll have to decide what size that caret should be (a caret's size is not pre-set), and to decide that, we'll need to know something about the size of the text we're working with. A caret is usually made the same height as the current characters, and 1/8th the width of an average character. To determine the height and width of characters, we'll use the CDC method GetTextMetrics() (recall that CDC is the device context class).

Measuring Text Sizes with Textmetrics

Let's get down to the business of creating a new caret for our window now in the OnDraw() method. We'll set up a boolean variable named CaretCreated in the view object to keep track of whether or not we've already created the caret:

```
// caretsView.h : interface of the CCaretsView class
        .
        .
        .
class CCaretsView : public CView
{
protected: // create from serialization only
     CCaretsView();
     DECLARE_DYNCREATE(CCaretsView)
➜    boolean CaretCreated;
        .
        .
        .

}
```

> **TIP**
>
> In case you're not familiar with them, Boolean variables, also called Boolean flags, can take two values: true and false.

After setting CaretCreated to false in the view's constructor, we check to see if we've already created the caret in a previous call to OnDraw():

```
void CCaretsView::OnDraw(CDC* pDC)
{
     CCaretsDoc* pDoc = GetDocument();
     ASSERT_VALID(pDoc);

➜    if(!CaretCreated){
        .
        .
        .
➜    }
   }
```

If we haven't created the caret, it's time to do so now. We'll need to decide on a
size for the caret, and we'll get that size from a TEXTMETRIC structure by calling
GetTextMetrics(). The GetTextMetrics() method fills a structure of the TEXT-
METRIC type; that structure has these members:

```
typedef struct tagTEXTMETRIC { // tm
    LONG tmHeight;
    LONG tmAscent;
    LONG tmDescent;
    LONG tmInternalLeading;
    LONG tmExternalLeading;
    LONG tmAveCharWidth;
    LONG tmMaxCharWidth;
    LONG tmWeight;
    LONG tmOverhang;
    LONG tmDigitizedAspectX;
    LONG tmDigitizedAspectY;
    BCHAR tmFirstChar;
    BCHAR tmLastChar;
    BCHAR tmDefaultChar;
    BCHAR tmBreakChar;
    BYTE tmItalic;
    BYTE tmUnderlined;
    BYTE tmStruckOut;
    BYTE tmPitchAndFamily;
    BYTE tmCharSet;
} TEXTMETRIC;
```

We fill a TEXTMETRIC structure named textmetric this way in our program now:

```
void CCaretsView::OnDraw(CDC* pDC)
{
    CCaretsDoc* pDoc = GetDocument();
    ASSERT_VALID(pDoc);

    if(!CaretCreated){
➤        TEXTMETRIC textmetric;

➤        pDC->GetTextMetrics(&textmetric);
            .
            .
            .
    }
}
```

Now we're ready to create our new caret. We'll make the caret the same height as our text, using `textmetric.tmHeight`, and $1/8^{th}$ the width of an average character—`textmetric.tmAveCharWidth/8`. We call `CreateSolidCaret()` to actually create the caret:

```
void CCaretsView::OnDraw(CDC* pDC)
{
    CCaretsDoc* pDoc = GetDocument();
    ASSERT_VALID(pDoc);

    if(!CaretCreated){
        TEXTMETRIC textmetric;

        pDC->GetTextMetrics(&textmetric);

        CreateSolidCaret(textmetric.tmAveCharWidth/8,
    textmetric.tmHeight);
            .
            .
            .
    }
}
```

TIP   Besides `CreateSolidCaret()`, **you can also create a gray caret with** `CreateGrayCaret()`. **The caret methods also include** `ShowCaret()`, `SetCaretPos()`, **and** `HideCaret()`.

This creates the new caret and installs it in our view.

Before using this new caret, however, we also need to set the caret position, using `SetCaretPos()`.

Setting the Caret's Position

We'll store the caret's position in a new `CPoint` object named `CaretPosition`. The `CPoint` class has two data members, `x` and `y`, which will hold the position of the caret:

```
// caretsView.h : interface of the CCaretsView class
        .
        .
        .
class CCaretsView : public CView
{
```

```
       protected: // create from serialization only
           CCaretsView();
           DECLARE_DYNCREATE(CCaretsView)
   ➜       CPoint CaretPosition;
           boolean CaretCreated;
                   .
                   .
                   .
```

Initially, we set the caret's position to (0, 0) in OnDraw( ) this way:

```
       void CCaretsView::OnDraw(CDC* pDC)
       {
           CCaretsDoc* pDoc = GetDocument();
           ASSERT_VALID(pDoc);

           if(!CaretCreated){
               TEXTMETRIC textmetric;

               pDC->GetTextMetrics(&textmetric);

               CreateSolidCaret(textmetric.tmAveCharWidth/8,
       ➥textmetric.tmHeight);
   ➜           CaretPosition.x = CaretPosition.y = 0;
           }
                   .
                   .
                   .

       }
```

TIP   You might note the handy C++ shortcut method of setting several variables to the same value here: x = y = z = 1;.

Then we set the caret's position with SetCaretPos( ), show the caret on the screen with ShowCaret( ), and set the CaretCreated boolean flag to true:

```
       void CCaretsView::OnDraw(CDC* pDC)
       {
           CCaretsDoc* pDoc = GetDocument();
           ASSERT_VALID(pDoc);

           if(!CaretCreated){
               TEXTMETRIC textmetric;

               pDC->GetTextMetrics(&textmetric);
```

```
            CreateSolidCaret(textmetric.tmAveCharWidth/8,
    ➥textmetric.tmHeight);
            CaretPosition.x = CaretPosition.y = 0;

➜           SetCaretPos(CaretPosition);
➜           ShowCaret();
➜           CaretCreated = true;
        }
                .
                .
                .

    }
```

At this point, the caret appears on the screen, as shown in Figure 4.1. We've
created our own, blinking, functional caret.

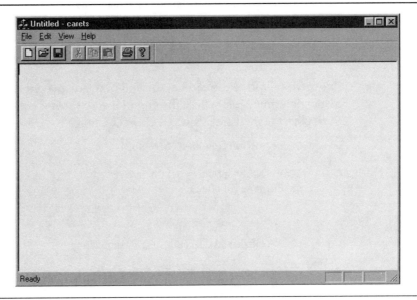

FIGURE 4.1: Displaying a new caret in our window

The next step is to move the caret as the user types text; the caret should always
indicate where typed text will appear. We first display the text that the user has
typed:

```
void CCaretsView::OnDraw(CDC* pDC)
{
    CCaretsDoc* pDoc = GetDocument();
```

```
        ASSERT_VALID(pDoc);

        if(!CaretCreated){
            TEXTMETRIC textmetric;

            pDC->GetTextMetrics(&textmetric);

            CreateSolidCaret(textmetric.tmAveCharWidth/8,
➥textmetric.tmHeight);
            CaretPosition.x = CaretPosition.y = 0;

            SetCaretPos(CaretPosition);
            ShowCaret();
            CaretCreated = true;
        }

➜       pDC->TextOut(0, 0, pDoc->StringData);
            .
            .
            .

    }
```

Now we can place the caret at the end of the displayed text string. First, we have to determine just where the end of the text string is, which we do by filling a CSize object named size using GetTextExtent():

```
void CCaretsView::OnDraw(CDC* pDC)
{
    CCaretsDoc* pDoc = GetDocument();
    ASSERT_VALID(pDoc);
        .
        .
        .
    pDC->TextOut(0, 0, pDoc->StringData);

➜   CSize size = pDC->GetTextExtent(pDoc->StringData);
        .
        .
        .
}
```

To display the caret at the end of the text string, we first hide it using HideCaret():

```
void CCaretsView::OnDraw(CDC* pDC)
{
```

```
        CCaretsDoc* pDoc = GetDocument();
        ASSERT_VALID(pDoc);
                .
                .
                .
        pDC->TextOut(0, 0, pDoc->StringData);

        CSize size = pDC->GetTextExtent(pDoc->StringData);

➜       HideCaret();
                .
                .
                .

    }
```

WARNING   If you don't hide the caret before moving it, you risk leaving an image of it on the screen in the old location.

Next, we set the x data member of the CaretPosition point to the end of the text string on the screen:

```
void CCaretsView::OnDraw(CDC* pDC)
{
        CCaretsDoc* pDoc = GetDocument();
        ASSERT_VALID(pDoc);
                .
                .
        pDC->TextOut(0, 0, pDoc->StringData);

        CSize size = pDC->GetTextExtent(pDoc->StringData);

        HideCaret();

➜       CaretPosition.x = size.cx;
                .
                .
                .

    }
```

Finally, we move the caret to its new location and show it again:

```
void CCaretsView::OnDraw(CDC* pDC)
{
        CCaretsDoc* pDoc = GetDocument();
        ASSERT_VALID(pDoc);
```

Skill 4

```
            .
            .
            .
        pDC->TextOut(0, 0, pDoc->StringData);

        CSize size = pDC->GetTextExtent(pDoc->StringData);

        HideCaret();

        CaretPosition.x = size.cx;
→       SetCaretPos(CaretPosition);

→       ShowCaret();
    }
```

And we're ready to run the program, as shown in Figure 4.2. As you can see, the caret appears at the end of the typed text. Our carets program is a success; now we're using a text-insertion caret.

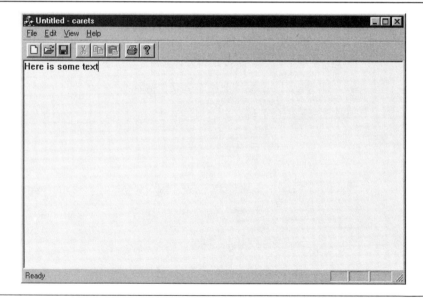

FIGURE 4.2: Displaying a caret after text

There's one more point to consider, however. When the user clicks another window, moving the focus to that window, we should hide our blinking caret, as is customary in Windows programs. We'll do that now.

Showing and Hiding a Caret When We Lose or Gain the Focus

When our program loses the focus, we get a WM_KILLFOCUS message, and when our program gains the focus, we get a WM_SETFOCUS message. Using ClassWizard, connect an event-handler method to the WM_KILLFOCUS message now. ClassWizard will call this method OnKillFocus():

```
void CCaretsView::OnKillFocus(CWnd* pNewWnd)
{
    CView::OnKillFocus(pNewWnd);

    // TODO: Add your message handler code here

}
```

Here, we've lost the focus, so we hide the caret this way:

```
void CCaretsView::OnKillFocus(CWnd* pNewWnd)
{
    CView::OnKillFocus(pNewWnd);
➜   HideCaret();

    // TODO: Add your message handler code here

}
```

Similarly, add the OnSetFocus() method to the WM_SETFOCUS message now, and place this code in that method to show the caret when we (re)gain the focus:

```
void CCaretsView::OnSetFocus(CWnd* pOldWnd)
{
    CView::OnSetFocus(pOldWnd);
➜   ShowCaret();

    // TODO: Add your message handler code here

}
```

That completes the program; now when we gain the focus, our caret will appear, and when we lose the focus, it will disappear. The code for the carets program appears in caretsView.h/caretsView.cpp.

Skill 4

caretsView.h and *caretsView.cpp*

```
// caretsView.h : interface of the CCaretsView class
//
/////////////////////////////////////////////////////////////////////

#if !defined(AFX_CARETSVIEW_H__AF4DCFCD_9222_11D0_8860_444553540000__INCLUDED_)
#define AFX_CARETSVIEW_H__AF4DCFCD_9222_11D0_8860_444553540000__INCLUDED_

#if _MSC_VER >= 1000
#pragma once
#endif // _MSC_VER >= 1000

class CCaretsView : public CView
{
protected: // create from serialization only
    CCaretsView();
    DECLARE_DYNCREATE(CCaretsView)
    CPoint CaretPosition;
    boolean CaretCreated;

// Attributes
public:
    CCaretsDoc* GetDocument();

// Operations
public:

// Overrides
    // ClassWizard generated virtual function overrides
    //{{AFX_VIRTUAL(CCaretsView)
    public:
    virtual void OnDraw(CDC* pDC);   // overridden to draw this view
    virtual BOOL PreCreateWindow(CREATESTRUCT& cs);
    protected:
    virtual BOOL OnPreparePrinting(CPrintInfo* pInfo);
    virtual void OnBeginPrinting(CDC* pDC, CPrintInfo* pInfo);
    virtual void OnEndPrinting(CDC* pDC, CPrintInfo* pInfo);
    //}}AFX_VIRTUAL

// Implementation
public:
    virtual ~CCaretsView();
#ifdef _DEBUG
    virtual void AssertValid() const;
    virtual void Dump(CDumpContext& dc) const;
#endif
```

```
protected:

// Generated message map functions
protected:
    //{{AFX_MSG(CCaretsView)
    afx_msg void OnChar(UINT nChar, UINT nRepCnt, UINT nFlags);
    //}}AFX_MSG
    DECLARE_MESSAGE_MAP()
};

#ifndef _DEBUG   // debug version in caretsView.cpp
inline CCaretsDoc* CCaretsView::GetDocument()
    { return (CCaretsDoc*)m_pDocument; }
#endif


/////////////////////////////////////////////////////////////////////////////

//{{AFX_INSERT_LOCATION}}
// Microsoft Developer Studio will insert additional declarations immediately
// before the previous line.

#endif // !defined(AFX_CARETSVIEW_H__AF4DCFCD_9222_11D0_8860_444553540000__
➥INCLUDED_)




// caretsView.cpp : implementation of the CCaretsView class
//

#include "stdafx.h"
#include "carets.h"

#include "caretsDoc.h"
#include "caretsView.h"

#ifdef _DEBUG
#define new DEBUG_NEW
#undef THIS_FILE
static char THIS_FILE[] = __FILE__;
#endif

/////////////////////////////////////////////////////////////////////////////
// CCaretsView

IMPLEMENT_DYNCREATE(CCaretsView, CView)

BEGIN_MESSAGE_MAP(CCaretsView, CView)
```

```
     //{{AFX_MSG_MAP(CCaretsView)
     ON_WM_CHAR()
     ON_WM_KILLFOCUS()
     ON_WM_SETFOCUS()
     //}}AFX_MSG_MAP
     // Standard printing commands
     ON_COMMAND(ID_FILE_PRINT, CView::OnFilePrint)
     ON_COMMAND(ID_FILE_PRINT_DIRECT, CView::OnFilePrint)
     ON_COMMAND(ID_FILE_PRINT_PREVIEW, CView::OnFilePrintPreview)
END_MESSAGE_MAP()

/////////////////////////////////////////////////////////////////////////
// CCaretsView construction/destruction

CCaretsView::CCaretsView()
{
     CaretCreated = false;
     // TODO: add construction code here

}

CCaretsView::~CCaretsView()
{
}

BOOL CCaretsView::PreCreateWindow(CREATESTRUCT& cs)
{
     // TODO: Modify the Window class or styles here by modifying
     //  the CREATESTRUCT cs

     return CView::PreCreateWindow(cs);
}

/////////////////////////////////////////////////////////////////////////
// CCaretsView drawing

void CCaretsView::OnDraw(CDC* pDC)
{
     CCaretsDoc* pDoc = GetDocument();
     ASSERT_VALID(pDoc);

     if(!CaretCreated){
         TEXTMETRIC textmetric;

         pDC->GetTextMetrics(&textmetric);

         CreateSolidCaret(textmetric.tmAveCharWidth/8, textmetric.tmHeight);
         CaretPosition.x = CaretPosition.y = 0;
```

```
        SetCaretPos(CaretPosition);
        ShowCaret();
        CaretCreated = true;
    }

    pDC->TextOut(0, 0, pDoc->StringData);

    CSize size = pDC->GetTextExtent(pDoc->StringData);

    HideCaret();

    CaretPosition.x = size.cx;
    SetCaretPos(CaretPosition);

    ShowCaret();

    // TODO: add draw code for native data here
}

/////////////////////////////////////////////////////////////////////////
// CCaretsView printing

BOOL CCaretsView::OnPreparePrinting(CPrintInfo* pInfo)
{
    // default preparation
    return DoPreparePrinting(pInfo);
}

void CCaretsView::OnBeginPrinting(CDC* /*pDC*/, CPrintInfo* /*pInfo*/)
{
    // TODO: add extra initialization before printing
}

void CCaretsView::OnEndPrinting(CDC* /*pDC*/, CPrintInfo* /*pInfo*/)
{
    // TODO: add cleanup after printing
}

/////////////////////////////////////////////////////////////////////////
// CCaretsView diagnostics

#ifdef _DEBUG
void CCaretsView::AssertValid() const
{
    CView::AssertValid();
}
```

Skill 4

```
void CCaretsView::Dump(CDumpContext& dc) const
{
    CView::Dump(dc);
}

CCaretsDoc* CCaretsView::GetDocument() // non-debug version is inline
{
    ASSERT(m_pDocument->IsKindOf(RUNTIME_CLASS(CCaretsDoc)));
    return (CCaretsDoc*)m_pDocument;
}
#endif //_DEBUG

/////////////////////////////////////////////////////////////////////////////
// CCaretsView message handlers

void CCaretsView::OnChar(UINT nChar, UINT nRepCnt, UINT nFlags)
{
    CCaretsDoc* pDoc = GetDocument();
    ASSERT_VALID(pDoc);

    pDoc->StringData += nChar;
    Invalidate();

    CView::OnChar(nChar, nRepCnt, nFlags);
}

void CCaretsView::OnKillFocus(CWnd* pNewWnd)
{
    CView::OnKillFocus(pNewWnd);
    HideCaret();

    // TODO: Add your message handler code here

}

void CCaretsView::OnSetFocus(CWnd* pOldWnd)
{
    CView::OnSetFocus(pOldWnd);
    ShowCaret();

    // TODO: Add your message handler code here

}
```

Now we've seen how to handle the caret, so we're ready to work with the mouse in our client area, displaying typed text at the location the user selects with the mouse.

Using the Mouse

In this next example, we'll let the user click the mouse somewhere in our client area. When they do, we'll display a caret at that location:

```
----------------------------------------------------
|Untitled - mouser                                 |
|File Edit View Help                               |
|[ ] [ ] [ ] [ ]                                   |
|--------------------------------------------------|
|                                                  |
|                                                  |
|                                                  |
|                                                  |
|                       |                          |
|                                                  |
|                                                  |
|                                                  |
|                                                  |
|                                                  |
|                                                  |
----------------------------------------------------
```

Then they can type the text they want starting at that location:

```
----------------------------------------------------
|Untitled - mouser                                 |
|File Edit View Help                               |
|[ ] [ ] [ ] [ ]                                   |
|--------------------------------------------------|
|                                                  |
|                                                  |
|                                                  |
|                 Here is some text|               |
|                                                  |
|                                                  |
|                                                  |
|                                                  |
|                                                  |
----------------------------------------------------
```

When they click another place in the client area, we'll clear the characters in the text string and let them type a new text string at the new location. Let's look into this now.

Using the ClassWizard Mouse Methods

Now we'll create a new SDI program named mouser. Give it the same key-reading capabilities as our previous program, carets; that is, when the user types, we store the keystrokes in a CString object named StringData in the document. We also add OnKillFocus() and OnSetFocus(), placing the HideCaret() and ShowCaret() calls in those methods, as we did in the carets program, placing the code from that program in those methods. Now we will display the data as the user types it.

Because the user has clicked a place on our client area, they want the text to appear starting at that clicked location. This means that we should use Class-Wizard to handle the left mouse down Windows message, WM_LBUTTONDOWN, in our code; specifically, to a method the ClassWizard will name OnLButtonDown().

Start ClassWizard now, as shown in Figure 4.3.

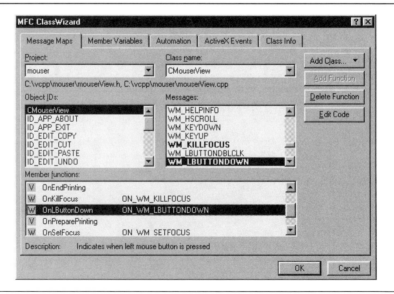

FIGURE 4.3: Using ClassWizard to handle the mouse down event

Make sure our view class, CMouserView, is selected in the Class name box, and find the WM_LBUTTONDOWN message in the Messages box. Double-click that message now, creating the new method OnLButtonDown(), as shown in the ClassWizard Member functions box. Double-click the OnLButtonDown() method's entry in that box now to open the code for that method:

```
void CMouserView::OnLButtonDown(UINT nFlags, CPoint point)
{
    // TODO: Add your message handler code here and/or call default

    CView::OnLButtonDown(nFlags, point);
}
```

Besides OnLButtonDown(), you can use methods like OnLButtonUp(), OnRButtonDown() for the right mouse button, OnLButtonDblClk() for double-clicks, and so on. You can find the mouse methods inTable 4.1.

TABLE 4.1: The ClassWizard Mouse Methods

Method	Does this
OnLButtonDblClk	Called when the user double-clicks the left mouse button.
OnLButtonDown	Called when the user presses the left mouse button.
OnLButtonUp	Called when the user releases the left mouse button.
OnMButtonDblClk	Called when the user double-clicks the middle mouse button.
OnMButtonDown	Called when the user presses the middle mouse button.
OnMButtonUp	Called when the user releases the middle mouse button.
OnMouseActivate	Called when the cursor is in an inactive window and the user presses a mouse button.
OnMouseMove	Called when the mouse cursor moves.
OnMouseWheel	Called when a user rotates the mouse wheel. Uses Windows NT 4.0 message handling.
OnRButtonDblClk	Called when the user double-clicks the right mouse button.
OnRButtonDown	Called when the user presses the right mouse button.
OnRButtonUp	Called when the user releases the right mouse button.
OnRegisteredMouseWheel	Called when a user rotates the mouse wheel. Uses Windows 95 and Windows NT 3.51 message-handling.
OnSetCursor	Called if mouse input is not captured and the mouse causes cursor movement within a window.

Skill 4

We are passed two parameters in OnLButtonDown(): nFlags and point. The nFlags parameter indicates the state of various keys on the keyboard, and can take these values:

```
MK_CONTROL      Control key was down
MK_LBUTTON      Left mouse button down
MK_MBUTTON      Middle mouse button down
MK_RBUTTON      Right mouse button down
MK_SHIFT        Shift key was down
```

The point parameter, an object of the CPoint class, holds the mouse's present location.

Now that the mouse has gone down, the first order of business is to store its location, and we'll store that location in the variables x and y as (x, y), which we get from the x and y members of the point object:

```
void CMouserView::OnLButtonDown(UINT nFlags, CPoint point)
{
    // TODO: Add your message handler code here and/or call default
➜   x = point.x;
➜   y = point.y;
        .
        .
        .

}
```

We also put aside space for the x and y values in the view's header file, mouserView.h:

```
// mouserView.h : interface of the CMouserView class
        .
        .
        .
protected: // create from serialization only
    CMouserView();
    DECLARE_DYNCREATE(CMouserView)
    CPoint CaretPosition;
    boolean CaretCreated;
➜   int x, y;
        .
        .
        .
```

Now that the user has moved the mouse to a new position, we will also empty the text string, using the CString class Empty() method:

```
void CMouserView::OnLButtonDown(UINT nFlags, CPoint point)
{
```

```
        // TODO: Add your message handler code here and/or call default
        x = point.x;
        y = point.y;

        CMouserDoc* pDoc = GetDocument();
        ASSERT_VALID(pDoc);
→       pDoc->StringData.Empty();
            .
            .
            .

    }
```

Finally, we invalidate the view so we will display the cursor in the view at its new location (using code we will add to the OnDraw() method):

```
    void CMouserView::OnLButtonDown(UINT nFlags, CPoint point)
    {
        // TODO: Add your message handler code here and/or call default
        x = point.x;
        y = point.y;

        CMouserDoc* pDoc = GetDocument();
        ASSERT_VALID(pDoc);
        pDoc->StringData.Empty();

→       Invalidate();

        CView::OnLButtonDown(nFlags, point);
    }
```

That will finish recording the location of the mouse. Now let's draw the text there as the user types it.

Drawing Text at the New Mouse Location

We handle the text drawing in OnDraw(). Start by creating a caret if you don't already have one, just as we did in the previous example, carets:

```
    void CMouserView::OnDraw(CDC* pDC)
    {
        CMouserDoc* pDoc = GetDocument();
        ASSERT_VALID(pDoc);

→           if(!CaretCreated){
→           TEXTMETRIC textmetric;

→           pDC->GetTextMetrics(&textmetric);
```

```
➜            CreateSolidCaret(textmetric.tmAveCharWidth/8,
  ➥textmetric.tmHeight);
➜            CaretPosition.x = CaretPosition.y = 0;

➜            SetCaretPos(CaretPosition);
➜            ShowCaret();
➜            CaretCreated = true;
        }
            .
            .
            .

    }
```

Now we display the string of text, StringData. Because the user clicked the mouse at the location we've recorded as (x, y), we display the text starting at that point:

```
void CMouserView::OnDraw(CDC* pDC)
{
    CMouserDoc* pDoc = GetDocument();
    ASSERT_VALID(pDoc);

        if(!CaretCreated){
            .
            .
            .

        }

➜        pDC->TextOut(x, y, pDoc->StringData);
            .
            .
            .

    }
```

We can place the caret at the end of the text string on the screen. First, we find out where the end of the string is and hide the caret:

```
void CMouserView::OnDraw(CDC* pDC)
{
    CMouserDoc* pDoc = GetDocument();
    ASSERT_VALID(pDoc);

        if(!CaretCreated){
            .
            .
            .
```

```
        }

        pDC->TextOut(x, y, pDoc->StringData);

→       CSize size = pDC->GetTextExtent(pDoc->StringData);

→       HideCaret();
                .
                .
                .

}
```

Then we move the caret to the end of the text string and show it again:

```
void CMouserView::OnDraw(CDC* pDC)
{
        CMouserDoc* pDoc = GetDocument();
        ASSERT_VALID(pDoc);

            if(!CaretCreated){
                .
                .
                .

        }

        pDC->TextOut(x, y, pDoc->StringData);

        CSize size = pDC->GetTextExtent(pDoc->StringData);

        HideCaret();

→       CaretPosition.x = x + size.cx;
→       CaretPosition.y = y;
→       SetCaretPos(CaretPosition);

→       ShowCaret();
}
```

And that finishes off our code for this example. Run mouser now, as shown in Figure 4.4. Click any place in the client window, and type some text. As you can see in Figure 4.4, the text appears where the user clicked, and the blinking caret indicates where the next character will appear. Our mouser program is a success.

The code for this program appears in mouserView.h/mouserView.cpp.

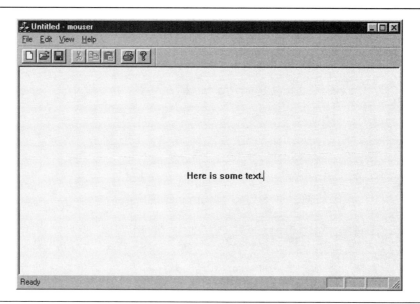

FIGURE 4.4: The user can click a location and type text there.

mouserView.h and *mouserView.cpp*

```
// mouserView.h : interface of the CMouserView class
//
/////////////////////////////////////////////////////////////////////////////

#if !defined(AFX_MOUSERVIEW_H__AF4DCFE1_9222_11D0_8860_444553540000__INCLUDED_)
#define AFX_MOUSERVIEW_H__AF4DCFE1_9222_11D0_8860_444553540000__INCLUDED_

#if _MSC_VER >= 1000
#pragma once
#endif // _MSC_VER >= 1000

class CMouserView : public CView
{
protected: // create from serialization only
    CMouserView();
    DECLARE_DYNCREATE(CMouserView)
    CPoint CaretPosition;
    boolean CaretCreated;
    int x, y;
```

```
// Attributes
public:
    CMouserDoc* GetDocument();

// Operations
public:

// Overrides
    // ClassWizard generated virtual function overrides
    //{{AFX_VIRTUAL(CMouserView)
    public:
    virtual void OnDraw(CDC* pDC);   // overridden to draw this view
    virtual BOOL PreCreateWindow(CREATESTRUCT& cs);
    protected:
    virtual BOOL OnPreparePrinting(CPrintInfo* pInfo);
    virtual void OnBeginPrinting(CDC* pDC, CPrintInfo* pInfo);
    virtual void OnEndPrinting(CDC* pDC, CPrintInfo* pInfo);
    //}}AFX_VIRTUAL

// Implementation
public:
    virtual ~CMouserView();
#ifdef _DEBUG
    virtual void AssertValid() const;
    virtual void Dump(CDumpContext& dc) const;
#endif

protected:

// Generated message map functions
protected:
    //{{AFX_MSG(CMouserView)
    afx_msg void OnChar(UINT nChar, UINT nRepCnt, UINT nFlags);
    afx_msg void OnLButtonDown(UINT nFlags, CPoint point);
    //}}AFX_MSG
    DECLARE_MESSAGE_MAP()
};

#ifndef _DEBUG  // debug version in mouserView.cpp
inline CMouserDoc* CMouserView::GetDocument()
   { return (CMouserDoc*)m_pDocument; }
#endif

/////////////////////////////////////////////////////////////////////////

//{{AFX_INSERT_LOCATION}}
// Microsoft Developer Studio will insert additional declarations immediately
// before the previous line.
```

Skill 4

```
#endif //
!defined(AFX_MOUSERVIEW_H__AF4DCFE1_9222_11D0_8860_444553540000__INCLUDED_)



// mouserView.cpp : implementation of the CMouserView class
//

#include "stdafx.h"
#include "mouser.h"

#include "mouserDoc.h"
#include "mouserView.h"

#ifdef _DEBUG
#define new DEBUG_NEW
#undef THIS_FILE
static char THIS_FILE[] = __FILE__;
#endif

/////////////////////////////////////////////////////////////////////////
// CMouserView

IMPLEMENT_DYNCREATE(CMouserView, CView)

BEGIN_MESSAGE_MAP(CMouserView, CView)
    //{{AFX_MSG_MAP(CMouserView)
    ON_WM_CHAR()
    ON_WM_LBUTTONDOWN()
    ON_WM_KILLFOCUS()
    ON_WM_SETFOCUS()
    //}}AFX_MSG_MAP
    // Standard printing commands
    ON_COMMAND(ID_FILE_PRINT, CView::OnFilePrint)
    ON_COMMAND(ID_FILE_PRINT_DIRECT, CView::OnFilePrint)
    ON_COMMAND(ID_FILE_PRINT_PREVIEW, CView::OnFilePrintPreview)
END_MESSAGE_MAP()

/////////////////////////////////////////////////////////////////////////
// CMouserView construction/destruction

CMouserView::CMouserView()
{
    // TODO: add construction code here
    CaretCreated = false;
    x = y = 0;
}
```

```
CMouserView::~CMouserView()
{
}

BOOL CMouserView::PreCreateWindow(CREATESTRUCT& cs)
{
    // TODO: Modify the Window class or styles here by modifying
    //   the CREATESTRUCT cs

    return CView::PreCreateWindow(cs);
}

/////////////////////////////////////////////////////////////////////////
// CMouserView drawing

void CMouserView::OnDraw(CDC* pDC)
{
    CMouserDoc* pDoc = GetDocument();
    ASSERT_VALID(pDoc);

        if(!CaretCreated){
        TEXTMETRIC textmetric;

        pDC->GetTextMetrics(&textmetric);

        CreateSolidCaret(textmetric.tmAveCharWidth/8, textmetric.tmHeight);
        CaretPosition.x = CaretPosition.y = 0;

        SetCaretPos(CaretPosition);
        ShowCaret();
        CaretCreated = true;
    }

    pDC->TextOut(x, y, pDoc->StringData);

    CSize size = pDC->GetTextExtent(pDoc->StringData);

    HideCaret();

    CaretPosition.x = x + size.cx;
    CaretPosition.y = y;
    SetCaretPos(CaretPosition);

    ShowCaret();

    // TODO: add draw code for native data here
}
```

```
/////////////////////////////////////////////////////////////////////////
// CMouserView printing

BOOL CMouserView::OnPreparePrinting(CPrintInfo* pInfo)
{
    // default preparation
    return DoPreparePrinting(pInfo);
}

void CMouserView::OnBeginPrinting(CDC* /*pDC*/, CPrintInfo* /*pInfo*/)
{
    // TODO: add extra initialization before printing
}

void CMouserView::OnEndPrinting(CDC* /*pDC*/, CPrintInfo* /*pInfo*/)
{
    // TODO: add cleanup after printing
}

/////////////////////////////////////////////////////////////////////////
// CMouserView diagnostics

#ifdef _DEBUG
void CMouserView::AssertValid() const
{
    CView::AssertValid();
}

void CMouserView::Dump(CDumpContext& dc) const
{
    CView::Dump(dc);
}

CMouserDoc* CMouserView::GetDocument() // non-debug version is inline
{
    ASSERT(m_pDocument->IsKindOf(RUNTIME_CLASS(CMouserDoc)));
    return (CMouserDoc*)m_pDocument;
}
#endif //_DEBUG

/////////////////////////////////////////////////////////////////////////
// CMouserView message handlers

void CMouserView::OnChar(UINT nChar, UINT nRepCnt, UINT nFlags)
{
    // TODO: Add your message handler code here and/or call default
    CMouserDoc* pDoc = GetDocument();
    ASSERT_VALID(pDoc);
```

```
      pDoc->StringData += nChar;
      Invalidate();

      CView::OnChar(nChar, nRepCnt, nFlags);
}

void CMouserView::OnLButtonDown(UINT nFlags, CPoint point)
{
      // TODO: Add your message handler code here and/or call default
      x = point.x;
      y = point.y;

      CMouserDoc* pDoc = GetDocument();
      ASSERT_VALID(pDoc);
      pDoc->StringData.Empty();

      Invalidate();

      CView::OnLButtonDown(nFlags, point);
}

void CMouserView::OnKillFocus(CWnd* pNewWnd)
{
      CView::OnKillFocus(pNewWnd);
      HideCaret();

      // TODO: Add your message handler code here

}

void CMouserView::OnSetFocus(CWnd* pOldWnd)
{
      CView::OnSetFocus(pOldWnd);
      ShowCaret();

      // TODO: Add your message handler code here

}
```

That completes our mouse exercises for right now. In this skill, we've seen how to support a caret in our programs, then we've put that to use, allowing the user to click anywhere in our window and type text there. We've seen how to use the mouse down and other mouse events. In the next skill, we'll continue our Visual C++ exploration as we turn to a very popular topic—menus.

Are You Experienced?

Now You Can...

- ☑ Use the ClassWizard tool to connect mouse messages to event-handler methods
- ☑ Create, show, and hide carets in a window
- ☑ Understand how working with many mouse events works
- ☑ Use Textmetrics to determine characteristics of the current font

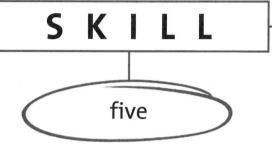

S K I L L

five

Creating Menus, Toolbar Buttons, Status Bar Prompts, and More

- ❑ Creating menus and menu items
- ❑ Using menu editor
- ❑ Creating submenus
- ❑ Tool tips
- ❑ Status bar prompts
- ❑ Adding Toolbar buttons
- ❑ Accelerator keys
- ❑ Shortcut keys

In this skill, we are going to start working with menus in Visual C++. Everyone's familiar with menus, the pop-down windows that display a set of options, or menu items, that the user can select from. They provide a convenient way to present the user with a list of options and then hide the list away again until it's needed (instead of working like a toolbar, displaying a number of buttons, one for each option, which will stay in view even when not needed and clutter up your program's appearance).

In this chapter we'll see how to place menu items into menus, and how to create whole new menus as well. We'll also see all the menu tricks of the trade: graying out or checking menu items; using shortcut keys, accelerator keys, and status bar prompts; even how to create and use submenus (menus that pop up when you rest the mouse on a menu item). We'll also see how to place a new button in the toolbar.

With all this on our agenda for this skill, let's start at once with our first menu.

Our First Menu Example

Our beginning menu example will be a pretty simple one so that we can learn the basics of menu-handling. In particular, we will add a new menu item to a program's File menu, and this menu item will be "Print Welcome":

```
 -------------------------------------------------
|Untitled - menus                                 |
|File Edit View Help                              |
| |New ----------                                 |
| |Open           |----------------------------------|
| |Save As        |                                  |
| |-------------- |                                  |
| |Print          |                                  |
| |Print Preview  |                                  |
-->     | |Print Welcome  |                                  |
| |Print Setup... |                                  |
| |-------------- |                                  |
| |Recent File    |                                  |
| |-------------- |                                  |
| |Exit           |                                  |
|  --------------                                  |
|                                                 |
|                                                 |
 -------------------------------------------------
```

When the user selects this new menu item, we'll display the text "Welcome to menus!" in the client area of our window:

```
-----------------------------------------------------
|Untitled - menus                                   |
|File Edit View Help                                |
|[ ]  [ ]  [ ]  [ ]                                 |
|---------------------------------------------------|
|Welcome to menus!                                  |
|                                                   |
|                                                   |
|                                                   |
|                                                   |
|                                                   |
|                                                   |
|                                                   |
|                                                   |
|                                                   |
-----------------------------------------------------
```

This program, menus, will give us our start in menu handling. Create this program now using AppWizard, making it an SDI program.

To begin our menu work, we'll use the Visual C++ menu editor to add our new menu item to the program's file menu.

Using the Menu Editor

The Visual C++ menu editor is one of the most useful of Visual C++ tools, and it lets us design menus easily. To open the menu editor, click the Resources tab in the Visual C++ viewer window (the window on the extreme left in Visual C++), because a menu is considered a *resource* in a Windows program (the specification of Windows resources are held in the project's .rc file). This opens the menus program's resources folder.

Next, find the folder marked Menus and open it, as shown in Figure 5.1. Then double-click the entry in that folder, IDR_MAINFRAME, opening the menu editor, as also shown in Figure 5.1 (in the document window at right).

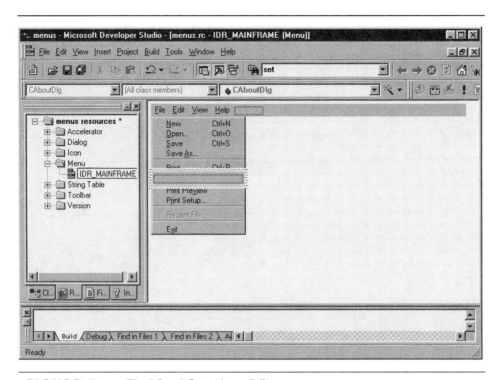

FIGURE 5.1: The Visual C++ Menu Editor

 NOTE   Note that the menu's resource ID is IDR_MAINFRAME (a resource ID is a numeric value given to a resource to identify it). As this name indicates, the menu system is part of our mainframe window object.

Adding a New Menu Item

Now we're ready to add our new menu item, Print Welcome. To do that, click the File menu in the menu editor, opening that menu, as shown in Figure 5.1. This new menu item will go between the existing Print and Print Preview menu items, so click the Print Preview menu item and press the Ins key to insert a new, blank menu item, as also shown in Figure 5.1 (the new menu item is surrounded by a multi-dotted box).

Double-click this new menu item now, opening the Menu Item Properties box, as shown in Figure 5.2. Place the caption Print Welcome in the Caption box of that dialog box, and close the box. This automatically gives the ID ID_FILE_PRINTWELCOME to our new menu item (the "FILE" part of the ID name is there because our new menu item is an item in the File menu).

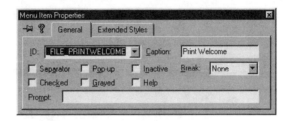

FIGURE 5.2: The Menu Item Properties box

We've designed our new menu item, so close the menu editor. The next step is to connect that menu item to our code so we can handle the case when the user clicks that item.

Connecting Menu Items to Code

We'll use ClassWizard to connect our new menu item to an event-handler that will be called when the user clicks the item. Open ClassWizard now, as shown in Figure 5.3.

You'll find that our new menu item's ID, ID_FILE_PRINTWELCOME, is listed in the Object IDs box in ClassWizard. We'll connect an event-handling method to that new menu item now. Click that item's entry in ClassWizard, then click the item's Command entry in the Messages box (the Command entry corresponds to the case in which the menu item is clicked). This makes ClassWizard suggest a name for the event-handler of OnFilePrintwelcome()—click OK to accept that name. When you do, this new method appears in the ClassWizard Member functions box, as also shown in Figure 5.3.

Double-click the OnFilePrintwelcome() entry in the ClassWizard Member functions box now, opening that new method:

```
void CMenusView::OnFilePrintwelcome()
{
    // TODO: Add your command handler code here

}
```

Skill 5

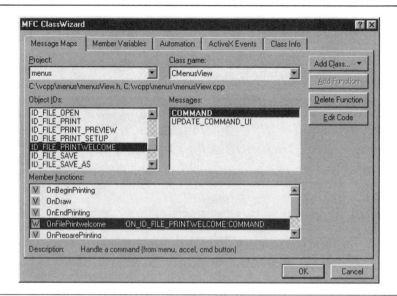

FIGURE 5.3: Connecting a menu item to Visual C++ code in ClassWizard

This is the method that will be called when the user clicks the new Print Welcome menu item, and we'll place the code here that will respond to that click. In particular, we want to print out the string "Welcome to menus!" when the user clicks our new menu item, so we set aside storage for that string in the document:

```
// menusDoc.h : interface of the CMenusDoc class
        .
        .
        .
// Implementation
public:
    virtual ~CMenusDoc();
    CString StringData;
        .
        .
        .
```

We also initialize that object to the empty string in the document's constructor:

```
CMenusDoc::CMenusDoc()

{
```

```
→      StringData = "";
}
```

Now, in the view object, we get a pointer, pDoc, to the document in OnFilePrintwelcome():

```
void CMenusView::OnFilePrintwelcome()
{
→      CMenusDoc* pDoc = GetDocument();
→      ASSERT_VALID(pDoc);
          .
          .
          .
}
```

All that remains is to place the string "Welcome to menus!" in the StringData object and display that string. We do that by invalidating the view so the code we place in OnDraw() will display the string for us:

```
void CMenusView::OnFilePrintwelcome()
{
       CMenusDoc* pDoc = GetDocument();
       ASSERT_VALID(pDoc);

→      pDoc->StringData = "Welcome to menus!";
→      Invalidate();
}
```

Finally, we add the code to OnDraw() to display the text in the StringData object:

```
void CMenusView::OnDraw(CDC* pDC)
{
       CMenusDoc* pDoc = GetDocument();
       ASSERT_VALID(pDoc);

→      pDC->TextOut(0, 0, pDoc->StringData);
}
```

That finishes the code; run this program now, as shown in Figure 5.4.

As you can see in that figure, our new menu item appears in the File menu. Click that item now, and the "Welcome to menus!" message appears in the program's client area, as shown in Figure 5.5. Our new program is a success—now we're working with menus!

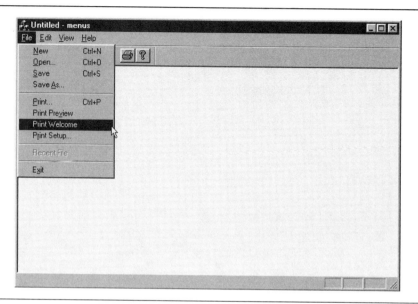

FIGURE 5.4: Our new menu item appears in the File menu.

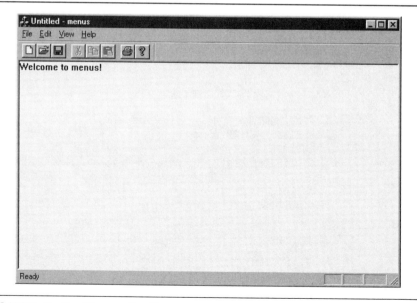

FIGURE 5.5: We use the file menu.

The code for this program appears in menusView.h/menusView.cpp.

menusView.h and *menusView.cpp*

```
// menusView.h : interface of the CMenusView class
//
/////////////////////////////////////////////////////////////////////

#if !defined(AFX_MENUSVIEW_H__F9003AAD_925D_11D0_8860_444553540000__INCLUDED_)
#define AFX_MENUSVIEW_H__F9003AAD_925D_11D0_8860_444553540000__INCLUDED_

#if _MSC_VER >= 1000
#pragma once
#endif // _MSC_VER >= 1000

class CMenusView : public CView
{
protected: // create from serialization only
    CMenusView();
    DECLARE_DYNCREATE(CMenusView)

// Attributes
public:
    CMenusDoc* GetDocument();

// Operations
public:

// Overrides
    // ClassWizard generated virtual function overrides
    //{{AFX_VIRTUAL(CMenusView)
    public:
    virtual void OnDraw(CDC* pDC);  // overridden to draw this view
    virtual BOOL PreCreateWindow(CREATESTRUCT& cs);
    protected:
    virtual BOOL OnPreparePrinting(CPrintInfo* pInfo);
    virtual void OnBeginPrinting(CDC* pDC, CPrintInfo* pInfo);
    virtual void OnEndPrinting(CDC* pDC, CPrintInfo* pInfo);
    //}}AFX_VIRTUAL

// Implementation
public:
    virtual ~CMenusView();
#ifdef _DEBUG
    virtual void AssertValid() const;
    virtual void Dump(CDumpContext& dc) const;
#endif
```

```
protected:

// Generated message map functions
protected:
    //{{AFX_MSG(CMenusView)
    afx_msg void OnFilePrintwelcome();
    //}}AFX_MSG
    DECLARE_MESSAGE_MAP()
};

#ifndef _DEBUG  // debug version in menusView.cpp
inline CMenusDoc* CMenusView::GetDocument()
   { return (CMenusDoc*)m_pDocument; }
#endif

/////////////////////////////////////////////////////////////////////////////

//{{AFX_INSERT_LOCATION}}
// Microsoft Developer Studio will insert additional declarations immediately
// before the previous line.

#endif // !defined(AFX_MENUSVIEW_H__F9003AAD_925D_11D0_8860_444553540000__
➡INCLUDED_)



// menusView.cpp : implementation of the CMenusView class
//

#include "stdafx.h"
#include "menus.h"

#include "menusDoc.h"
#include "menusView.h"

#ifdef _DEBUG
#define new DEBUG_NEW
#undef THIS_FILE
static char THIS_FILE[] = __FILE__;
#endif

/////////////////////////////////////////////////////////////////////////////
// CMenusView

IMPLEMENT_DYNCREATE(CMenusView, CView)

BEGIN_MESSAGE_MAP(CMenusView, CView)
```

```
        //{{AFX_MSG_MAP(CMenusView)
        ON_COMMAND(ID_FILE_PRINTWELCOME, OnFilePrintwelcome)
        //}}AFX_MSG_MAP
        // Standard printing commands
        ON_COMMAND(ID_FILE_PRINT, CView::OnFilePrint)
        ON_COMMAND(ID_FILE_PRINT_DIRECT, CView::OnFilePrint)
        ON_COMMAND(ID_FILE_PRINT_PREVIEW, CView::OnFilePrintPreview)
END_MESSAGE_MAP()


/////////////////////////////////////////////////////////////////////////////
// CMenusView construction/destruction

CMenusView::CMenusView()
{
        // TODO: add construction code here

}

CMenusView::~CMenusView()
{
}

BOOL CMenusView::PreCreateWindow(CREATESTRUCT& cs)
{
        // TODO: Modify the Window class or styles here by modifying
        //  the CREATESTRUCT cs

        return CView::PreCreateWindow(cs);
}


/////////////////////////////////////////////////////////////////////////////
// CMenusView drawing

void CMenusView::OnDraw(CDC* pDC)
{
        CMenusDoc* pDoc = GetDocument();
        ASSERT_VALID(pDoc);

        pDC->TextOut(0, 0, pDoc->StringData);
        // TODO: add draw code for native data here
}


/////////////////////////////////////////////////////////////////////////////
// CMenusView printing

BOOL CMenusView::OnPreparePrinting(CPrintInfo* pInfo)
{
        // default preparation
```

```
        return DoPreparePrinting(pInfo);
}

void CMenusView::OnBeginPrinting(CDC* /*pDC*/, CPrintInfo* /*pInfo*/)
{
        // TODO: add extra initialization before printing
}

void CMenusView::OnEndPrinting(CDC* /*pDC*/, CPrintInfo* /*pInfo*/)
{
        // TODO: add cleanup after printing
}

///////////////////////////////////////////////////////////////////////////
// CMenusView diagnostics

#ifdef _DEBUG
void CMenusView::AssertValid() const
{
        CView::AssertValid();
}

void CMenusView::Dump(CDumpContext& dc) const
{
        CView::Dump(dc);
}

CMenusDoc* CMenusView::GetDocument() // non-debug version is inline
{
        ASSERT(m_pDocument->IsKindOf(RUNTIME_CLASS(CMenusDoc)));
        return (CMenusDoc*)m_pDocument;
}
#endif //_DEBUG

///////////////////////////////////////////////////////////////////////////
// CMenusView message handlers

void CMenusView::OnFilePrintwelcome()
{
        CMenusDoc* pDoc = GetDocument();
        ASSERT_VALID(pDoc);

        pDoc->StringData = "Welcome to menus!";
        Invalidate();
        // TODO: Add your command handler code here

}
```

Our first program, menus, gives us the basics of menu handling. But there are still many unanswered questions: How do we add a whole new menu? How do we implement shortcut keys? How do we create submenus? We'll look into those questions and more now.

Creating the Fullmenu Example

Now that we've gotten the basics down, we'll go wild with menus in this next example. We'll see how to create whole new menus, make menu items inactive by "graying" them out (that is, making them appear in gray so there is no response when the user selects them), and check menu items (placing a check in front of their names in the menu). We'll also add submenus, shortcut keys (keys you can press to select a menu item when that menu is open), status bar prompts (the status bar appears at the bottom of our program's main window), toolbar buttons, and tool tips (a tool tip is a small yellow window that displays a prompt when you place the mouse cursor over a control like a button). Finally, we'll see how to create accelerator keys, which are control keys you can press to select a menu item even when the menu is not open.

In our new example program, fullmenus, we'll add a new menu to our program, naming that menu Demo. This new menu will have a grayed out menu item, a checked menu item, and an item that will display a submenu:

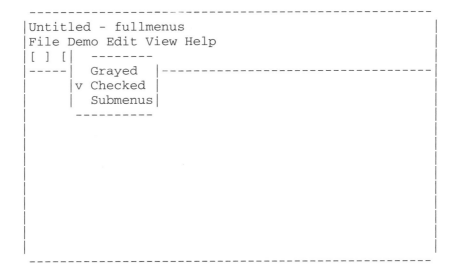

```
---------------------------------------------------------------
|Untitled - fullmenus                                          |
|File Demo Edit View Help                                      |
|[ ] [|  --------                                              |
|-----|  Grayed  |------------------------------------------|
|     |v Checked |                                            |
|     |  Submenus|                                            |
|      ----------                                             |
|                                                             |
|                                                             |
|                                                             |
|                                                             |
|                                                             |
|                                                             |
|                                                             |
---------------------------------------------------------------
```

When the user selects the submenu item, a new submenu will pop open, giving the user a new menu to select from:

```
 -----------------------------------------------------
|Untitled - fullmenus                                 |
|File Demo Edit View Help                             |
|[ ] [|   --------                                    |
|-----|  Grayed   |----------------------------------|
|     |v Checked  |--------------------              |
|     | Submenus |Sub item 1         |              |
|      --------- |Sub Item 2    Ctrl+F5 |           |
|                 --------------------               |
|                                                     |
|                                                     |
|                                                     |
|                                                     |
|                                                     |
|                                                     |
|                                                     |
|                                                     |
 -----------------------------------------------------
```

In addition, we'll use accelerator keys, tool tips, status bar prompts, and more. There's a great deal going on here, so let's start with this new example, fullmenus.

Create that program now, making it an SDI AppWizard program. Open the new program's menu resource, IDR_MAINFRAME, in the menu editor, as shown in Figure 5.6.

Our first task is to add the new Demo menu. That menu will go between the File and Edit menus, so just highlight (by clicking) the Edit menu in the menu editor and press the Ins key. This adds a new menu to our menu bar; double-click the new menu and give it the name Demo in the Menu Item Properties box that opens (even though this is a new menu, Visual C++ still uses the menu item properties box, because there is no menu properties box). This adds our new Demo menu, as shown in Figure 5.6.

Next, we will add the new menu items we want in the Demo menu. The menu editor has placed one blank item in the Demo menu already—click that item and give it the name Grayed, as shown in Figure 5.7. The menu editor gives it the ID ID_DEMO_GRAYED automatically.

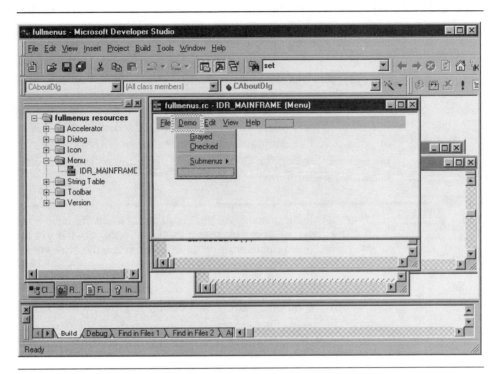

FIGURE 5.6: Creating our new program's menu system

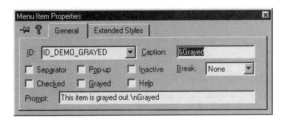

FIGURE 5.7: Adding the Grayed menu item

This will be the item we gray out, to make it inactive. In the same way, add two more menu items, Checked and Submenus. Just give these new menu items the names Checked and Submenus, and the menu editor will give them new IDs automatically.

You may also notice the small underlines under the letter D in Demo, G in Grayed, and so on in Figure 5.6. These are *shortcut* keys, and we'll see what they are all about next.

Adding Shortcut Keys

The D in our Demo menu is underlined, which means that when the user presses Alt+D, the Demo menu opens. In this way, the user can use the keyboard to reach our menu. In the Demo menu, the Submenu item's shortcut key is S. If the user presses Alt+S when the Demo menu is open, the submenu item will be activated, showing its submenus.

 **WARNING** Whether selecting menus for the menu bar or menu items in a menu, make sure that the shortcut keys you select are unique; otherwise the program will not know which item the user refers to when they use the shortcut key.

Adding shortcut keys is very easy—we just place an ampersand, &, in front of the letter in the menu's name or menu item's name that we want to make into the shortcut. For example, to make the G in Grayed the shortcut key, we set that item's caption to &Grayed, as shown in Figure 5.8.

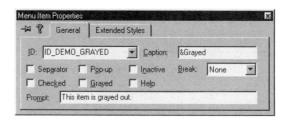

FIGURE 5.8: Adding a shortcut key to the Grayed menu item

In a similar way, we set the other item's shortcut keys, making them active. Now the shortcut keys are ready to be used.

You might notice the text "This item is grayed out." in the Prompt box of the Menu Items properties box in Figure 5.8. This is a status bar prompt, and you'll learn about them next.

Adding Status Bar Prompts

When the user highlights a menu item, we can explain more about that item in the status bar—the bar at the bottom of our program's window. To do that, we simply place the text we want to appear in the status bar in the Prompt box of the Menu Item Properties box, as shown in Figure 5.8.

In Figure 5.8, we create the prompt "This item is grayed out." in the status bar when the user highlights the Grayed menu item. It's as simple as that—now this text will appear in the status bar when the user lets the mouse rest on this menu item.

Let's move on now to add submenus to our new Demo menu.

Adding Submenus to Our Demo Menu

To add submenus to the Submenus item, just double-click that item now in the menu editor to open the Menu Item Properties box, as shown in Figure 5.9. Click the Pop-up item in that box now, as also shown in Figure 5.9.

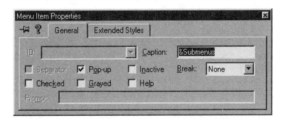

FIGURE 5.9: Adding a shortcut key to the Grayed menu item

This adds a new submenu with one blank item to the Submenu menu item. When you click that item in the menu editor, the new submenu opens, as shown in Figure 5.10.

We can add two new items to that submenu now: Sub Item 1 and Sub Item 2, as shown in Figure 5.10. We add these items in the usual way, by double-clicking a blank menu item and filling in the new item's name in the Menu Item Properties box. And that's all it takes to set up our submenus. We'll add code to them shortly.

You might also notice the text Ctrl+F5 in the Sub Item 1's caption, as shown in Figure 5.10. This is an *accelerator* key.

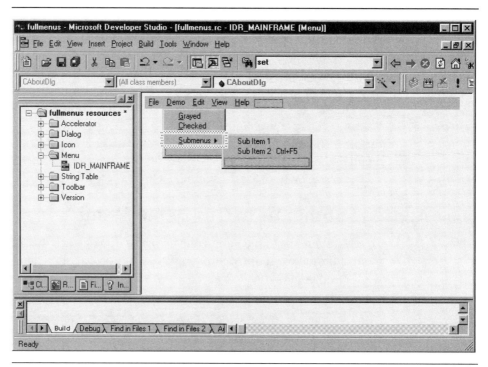

FIGURE 5.10: Our new submenus

Adding Accelerator Keys

An accelerator key is a control key that the user can press at any time (even when the menu is not open), and doing so is the same as clicking the menu item. In this case, pressing Ctrl+F5 is the same as clicking the Sub item 2 menu item.

To add an accelerator key to a menu item, we go to the viewer window and open the Accelerator folder. Double-click the IDR_MAINFRAME entry in the Accelerator folder now, opening the accelerator editor, as shown in Figure 5.11.

Double-click the last blank entry in the accelerator editor, opening the Accel Properties box, as shown in Figure 5.12. Select the ID for the Sub Item 2, ID_DEMO_SUBMENUS_SUBITEM2.

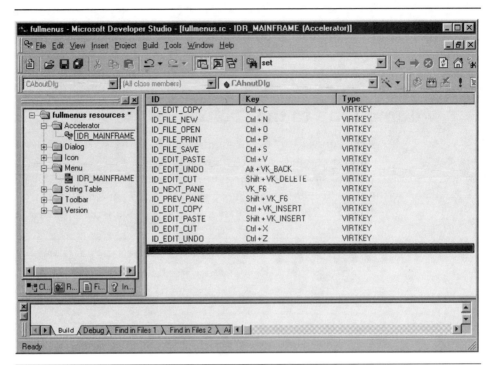

FIGURE 5.11: Adding an accelerator key

To connect Ctrl+F5 to this ID, we click the Ctrl box in the Modifiers box, as shown in Figure 5.12. In addition, select VK_F5 in the Key combo box, as also shown in Figure 5.12 (VK stands for virtual key). Now close the Accel Properties box. This adds Ctrl+F5 as an accelerator key to the Sub Item 2 menu item for us.

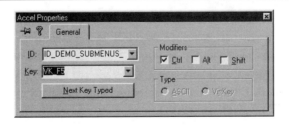

FIGURE 5.12: Connecting an accelerator key

To indicate that we have a new accelerator key for Sub Item 2, change that item's caption to "Sub Item 2\tCtrl+F5" in the menu editor. The "\t" is the code for a tab character, and this new caption will have the text "Ctrl+F5" at right, showing that this is the accelerator key for that menu item. Now we've set up our new accelerator key. Our next step will be to add a new button to the toolbar.

Adding Tools to the Toolbar

We can connect any of our menu items to buttons in the toolbar. For example, let's connect Sub Item 1 to a new button.

We will start by designing the new button for our toolbar. Do that by opening the Toolbar folder in the viewer window now, and clicking the IDR_MAINFRAME entry there. This opens the toolbar editor, as shown in Figure 5.13.

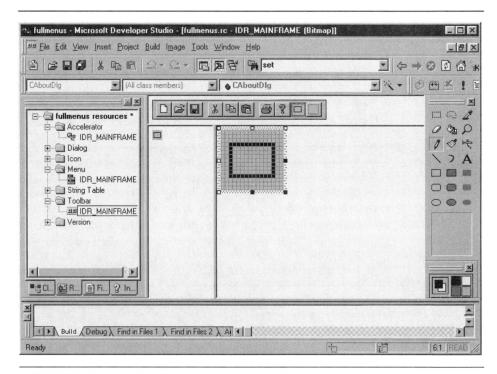

F I G U R E   5 . 1 3 :   Creating a new toolbar button

We'll create a simple button here, showing just a box. We use the drawing tool in the toolbar editor's toolbox—the small pencil in the toolbox on the right side of

Figure 5.13. Click the blank new button at left in the toolbar and use this drawing tool to draw a small box in the new button, as shown in Figure 5.13.

Next, double-click the new button in the toolbar, opening the Toolbar Button Properties box, as shown in Figure 5.14. Select ID_DEMO_SUBMENUS_SUBITEM1 to connect that menu item to the toolbar button.

In addition, give this button the prompt "Sub menu 1\nSub menu 1" in the prompt box. Doing so means that "Sub menu 1" will appear in the status bar when the user places the mouse cursor over the new button in the toolbar. In addition, the text following the "\n" will appear as a tool tip for the button. In this case, that means our tool tip will be "Sub menu 1".

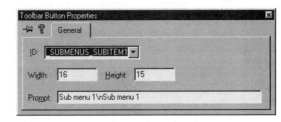

FIGURE 5.14: Connecting a toolbar button to a menu ID

We've come far in our new menu system already, but there's still more menu power to come. Our next step will be to make our grayed menu item grayed out, which is to say inactive.

Graying Out Menu Items

Our next step will be graying out a menu item. Open ClassWizard and find the ID_DEMO_GRAYED item in the Object IDs box, as shown in Figure 5.15. Now connect an event-handler to this ID—but click the UPDATE_COMMAND_UI item (UI stands for User Interface) in the Messages box, not the COMMAND item, as shown in Figure 5.15.

This creates the new method OnUpdateDemoGrayed():

```
void CFullmenusView::OnUpdateDemoGrayed(CCmdUI* pCmdUI)
{
    // TODO: Add your command update UI handler code here
}
```

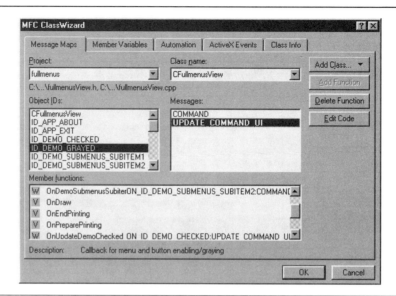

FIGURE 5.15: Using ClassWizard to connect an update method

This method is called when the program is about to display our new menu item, and we can make the menu item gray. In this method, we are passed a parameter, pCmdUI, that is a pointer to CCmdUI object—the methods of this class appear in Table 5.1.

TABLE 5.1 The CCmdUI Class Methods

Method	Does This
ContinueRouting	Tells the command-routing mechanism to continue routing the current message down the chain of handlers.
Enable	Enables or disables the user-interface item for this command.
SetCheck	Sets the check state of the user-interface item for this command.
SetRadio	Like the SetCheck member function, but operates on radio groups.
SetText	Sets the text for the user-interface item for this command.

In this method, we want to gray out the menu item, so we call the CCmdUI object's Enable() method, passing that method a value of false to make the item grayed out:

```
void CFullmenusView::OnUpdateDemoGrayed(CCmdUI* pCmdUI)
{
→    pCmdUI->Enable(false);
}
```

In this way, you can gray out menu items, making them inaccessible to the user. Just place code in that item's update event-handler, which is how the program checks to see how it should display a menu item before that item is actually shown on the screen.

Similarly, we can also place a check mark in front of our "Checked" menu item, which we'll do next.

Checking Menu Items

The next step will be to connect a method named OnUpdateDemoChecked()to the UPDATE_COMMAND_UI message of the Checked menu item:

```
void CFullmenusView::OnUpdateDemoChecked(CCmdUI* pCmdUI)
{
    // TODO: Add your command update UI handler code here

}
```

To check the Checked menu item, we first enable it with Enable(), and then call the CCMdUI object's SetCheck() method with an argument of 1 (an argument of 0 removes a check mark):

```
void CFullmenusView::OnUpdateDemoChecked(CCmdUI* pCmdUI)
{
→    pCmdUI->Enable(true);
→    pCmdUI->SetCheck(1);

}
```

That's it, now the Checked menu item will appear with a check mark in front of it. Our program is almost complete—all we will do now is add code to the submenu items to display a text string when the user clicks them.

Adding Code to the Submenu Items

Adding code to submenus is just as easy as adding code to normal menu items. To add code to Sub Item 1, just find ID_SUBMENUS_SUBITEM1 in ClassWizard and add an event-handler to it:

```
void CFullmenusView::OnDemoSubmenusSubitem1()
{

}
```

Here, we'll just place a new string, StringData, in the document, and place the text "Sub menu item 1 clicked." in the view when the user clicks this menu item:

```
void CFullmenusView::OnDemoSubmenusSubitem1()

{
    CFullmenusDoc* pDoc = GetDocument();
    ASSERT_VALID(pDoc);

    pDoc->StringData = "Sub menu item 1 clicked.";
    Invalidate();
}
```

We do the same for Sub Item 2, displaying the string "Sub menu item 2 clicked.":

```
void CFullmenusView::OnDemoSubmenusSubitem2()
{
    CFullmenusDoc* pDoc = GetDocument();
    ASSERT_VALID(pDoc);

    pDoc->StringData = "Sub menu item 2 clicked.";
    Invalidate();

}
```

Now our program is complete, and can be run as shown in Figure 5.16.

You can see our menu items in the new Demo menu now: the first item grayed out, the second item with a check, and the third item with its two submenu items. You can also see our accelerator and shortcut keys in Figure 5.16.

In addition, you can see our new button in the toolbar, as shown in Figure 5.17. When the user lets the mouse cursor rest on the new button, our program displays a tool tip, as also shown in Figure 5.17. When the user clicks the new button, it's the same as clicking Sub Item 1.

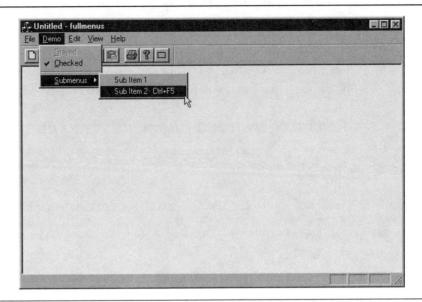

FIGURE 5.16: Our fullmenus program shows its new Demo menu.

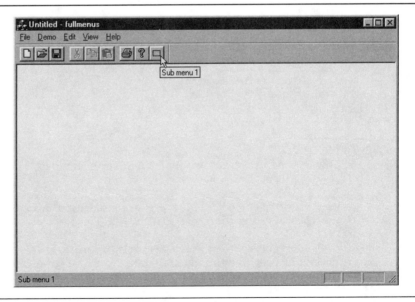

FIGURE 5.17: Our fullmenus program shows its new toolbar button.

Our fullmenus program works just as we planned it, and it's shown us a great deal about working with menus in Visual C++: from tool tips to toolbars, from check marks to graying out menu items, from shortcut keys to accelerators.

The code for this program appears in `fullmenusView.h/FullmenusView.cpp`. In addition, we include the pertinent portion of the resource file, `fullmenus.rc` below, because that is where the definition of our new menu is placed.

fullmenusView.h and *fullmenusView.cpp*

```
// fullmenusView.h : interface of the CFullmenusView class
//
/////////////////////////////////////////////////////////////////////////

#if !defined(AFX_FULLMENUSVIEW_H__F9003AC1_925D_11D0_8860_444553540000__
➥INCLUDED_)
#define AFX_FULLMENUSVIEW_H__F9003AC1_925D_11D0_8860_444553540000__INCLUDED_

#if _MSC_VER >= 1000
#pragma once
#endif // _MSC_VER >= 1000

class CFullmenusView : public CView
{
protected: // create from serialization only
    CFullmenusView();
    DECLARE_DYNCREATE(CFullmenusView)

// Attributes
public:
    CFullmenusDoc* GetDocument();

// Operations
public:

// Overrides
    // ClassWizard generated virtual function overrides
    //{{AFX_VIRTUAL(CFullmenusView)
    public:
    virtual void OnDraw(CDC* pDC);  // overridden to draw this view
    virtual BOOL PreCreateWindow(CREATESTRUCT& cs);
    protected:
    virtual BOOL OnPreparePrinting(CPrintInfo* pInfo);
    virtual void OnBeginPrinting(CDC* pDC, CPrintInfo* pInfo);
    virtual void OnEndPrinting(CDC* pDC, CPrintInfo* pInfo);
    //}}AFX_VIRTUAL
```

```
// Implementation
public:
     virtual ~CFullmenusView();
#ifdef _DEBUG
     virtual void AssertValid() const;
     virtual void Dump(CDumpContext& dc) const;
#endif

protected:

// Generated message map functions
protected:
     //{{AFX_MSG(CFullmenusView)
     afx_msg void OnUpdateDemoGrayed(CCmdUI* pCmdUI);
     afx_msg void OnUpdateDemoChecked(CCmdUI* pCmdUI);
     afx_msg void OnDemoSubmenusSubitem1();
     afx_msg void OnDemoSubmenusSubitem2();
     //}}AFX_MSG
     DECLARE_MESSAGE_MAP()
};

#ifndef _DEBUG  // debug version in fullmenusView.cpp
inline CFullmenusDoc* CFullmenusView::GetDocument()
   { return (CFullmenusDoc*)m_pDocument; }
#endif

/////////////////////////////////////////////////////////////////////////

//{{AFX_INSERT_LOCATION}}
// Microsoft Developer Studio will insert additional declarations immediately
// before the previous line.

#endif // !defined(AFX_FULLMENUSVIEW_H__F9003AC1_925D_11D0_8860_444553540000__
➡INCLUDED_)


// fullmenusView.cpp : implementation of the CFullmenusView class
//

#include "stdafx.h"
#include "fullmenus.h"

#include "fullmenusDoc.h"
#include "fullmenusView.h"

#ifdef _DEBUG
#define new DEBUG_NEW
#undef THIS_FILE
```

Skill 5

```
static char THIS_FILE[] = __FILE__;
#endif

/////////////////////////////////////////////////////////////////////////////
// CFullmenusView

IMPLEMENT_DYNCREATE(CFullmenusView, CView)

BEGIN_MESSAGE_MAP(CFullmenusView, CView)
    //{{AFX_MSG_MAP(CFullmenusView)
    ON_UPDATE_COMMAND_UI(ID_DEMO_GRAYED, OnUpdateDemoGrayed)
    ON_UPDATE_COMMAND_UI(ID_DEMO_CHECKED, OnUpdateDemoChecked)
    ON_COMMAND(ID_DEMO_SUBMENUS_SUBITEM1, OnDemoSubmenusSubitem1)
    ON_COMMAND(ID_DEMO_SUBMENUS_SUBITEM2, OnDemoSubmenusSubitem2)
    //}}AFX_MSG_MAP
    // Standard printing commands
    ON_COMMAND(ID_FILE_PRINT, CView::OnFilePrint)
    ON_COMMAND(ID_FILE_PRINT_DIRECT, CView::OnFilePrint)
    ON_COMMAND(ID_FILE_PRINT_PREVIEW, CView::OnFilePrintPreview)
END_MESSAGE_MAP()

/////////////////////////////////////////////////////////////////////////////
// CFullmenusView construction/destruction

CFullmenusView::CFullmenusView()
{
    // TODO: add construction code here

}

CFullmenusView::~CFullmenusView()
{
}

BOOL CFullmenusView::PreCreateWindow(CREATESTRUCT& cs)
{
    // TODO: Modify the Window class or styles here by modifying
    //   the CREATESTRUCT cs

    return CView::PreCreateWindow(cs);
}

/////////////////////////////////////////////////////////////////////////////
// CFullmenusView drawing

void CFullmenusView::OnDraw(CDC* pDC)
{
    CFullmenusDoc* pDoc = GetDocument();
    ASSERT_VALID(pDoc);
```

```
        pDC->TextOut(0, 0, pDoc->StringData);
        // TODO: add draw code for native data here
}

/////////////////////////////////////////////////////////////////////////
// CFullmenusView printing

BOOL CFullmenusView::OnPreparePrinting(CPrintInfo* pInfo)
{
    // default preparation
    return DoPreparePrinting(pInfo);
}

void CFullmenusView::OnBeginPrinting(CDC* /*pDC*/, CPrintInfo* /*pInfo*/)
{
    // TODO: add extra initialization before printing
}

void CFullmenusView::OnEndPrinting(CDC* /*pDC*/, CPrintInfo* /*pInfo*/)
{
    // TODO: add cleanup after printing
}

/////////////////////////////////////////////////////////////////////////
// CFullmenusView diagnostics

#ifdef _DEBUG
void CFullmenusView::AssertValid() const
{
    CView::AssertValid();
}

void CFullmenusView::Dump(CDumpContext& dc) const
{
    CView::Dump(dc);
}

CFullmenusDoc* CFullmenusView::GetDocument() // non-debug version is inline
{
    ASSERT(m_pDocument->IsKindOf(RUNTIME_CLASS(CFullmenusDoc)));
    return (CFullmenusDoc*)m_pDocument;
}
#endif //_DEBUG

/////////////////////////////////////////////////////////////////////////
// CFullmenusView message handlers

void CFullmenusView::OnUpdateDemoGrayed(CCmdUI* pCmdUI)
{
```

```
        // TODO: Add your command update UI handler code here
        pCmdUI->Enable(false);
}

void CFullmenusView::OnUpdateDemoChecked(CCmdUI* pCmdUI)
{
        // TODO: Add your command update UI handler code here
        pCmdUI->Enable(true);
        pCmdUI->SetCheck(1);

}

void CFullmenusView::OnDemoSubmenusSubitem1()
{
        // TODO: Add your command handler code here
        CFullmenusDoc* pDoc = GetDocument();
        ASSERT_VALID(pDoc);

        pDoc->StringData = "Sub menu item 1 clicked.";
        Invalidate();
}

void CFullmenusView::OnDemoSubmenusSubitem2()
{
        // TODO: Add your command handler code here
        CFullmenusDoc* pDoc = GetDocument();
        ASSERT_VALID(pDoc);

        pDoc->StringData = "Sub menu item 2 clicked.";
        Invalidate();

}
```

Section of *fullmenu.rc*

```
/////////////////////////////////////////////////////////////////////////////
//
// Toolbar
//

IDR_MAINFRAME TOOLBAR DISCARDABLE  16, 15
BEGIN
    BUTTON          ID_FILE_NEW
    BUTTON          ID_FILE_OPEN
    BUTTON          ID_FILE_SAVE
    SEPARATOR
    BUTTON          ID_EDIT_CUT
```

```
        BUTTON       ID_EDIT_COPY
        BUTTON       ID_EDIT_PASTE
        SEPARATOR
        BUTTON       ID_FILE_PRINT
        BUTTON       ID_APP_ABOUT
        BUTTON       ID_DEMO_SUBMENUS_SUBITEM1
END


/////////////////////////////////////////////////////////////////////////
//
// Menu
//

IDR_MAINFRAME MENU PRELOAD DISCARDABLE
BEGIN
    POPUP "&File"
    BEGIN
        MENUITEM "&New\tCtrl+N",              ID_FILE_NEW
        MENUITEM "&Open...\tCtrl+O",          ID_FILE_OPEN
        MENUITEM "&Save\tCtrl+S",             ID_FILE_SAVE
        MENUITEM "Save &As...",               ID_FILE_SAVE_AS
        MENUITEM SEPARATOR
        MENUITEM "&Print...\tCtrl+P",         ID_FILE_PRINT
        MENUITEM "Print Pre&view",            ID_FILE_PRINT_PREVIEW
        MENUITEM "P&rint Setup...",           ID_FILE_PRINT_SETUP
        MENUITEM SEPARATOR
        MENUITEM "Recent File",               ID_FILE_MRU_FILE1, GRAYED
        MENUITEM SEPARATOR
        MENUITEM "E&xit",                     ID_APP_EXIT
    END
    POPUP "&Demo"
    BEGIN
        MENUITEM "&Grayed",                   ID_DEMO_GRAYED
        MENUITEM "&Checked",                  ID_DEMO_CHECKED
        MENUITEM SEPARATOR
        POPUP "&Submenus"
        BEGIN
            MENUITEM "Sub Item 1",               ID_DEMO_SUBMENUS_SUBITEM1

            MENUITEM "Sub Item 2\tCtrl+F5",      ID_DEMO_SUBMENUS_SUBITEM2

        END
    END
    POPUP "&Edit"
    BEGIN
        MENUITEM "&Undo\tCtrl+Z",             ID_EDIT_UNDO
        MENUITEM SEPARATOR
```

Skill 5

```
        MENUITEM "Cu&t\tCtrl+X",                ID_EDIT_CUT
        MENUITEM "&Copy\tCtrl+C",               ID_EDIT_COPY
        MENUITEM "&Paste\tCtrl+V",              ID_EDIT_PASTE
    END
    POPUP "&View"
    BEGIN
        MENUITEM "&Toolbar",                    ID_VIEW_TOOLBAR
        MENUITEM "&Status Bar",                 ID_VIEW_STATUS_BAR
    END
    POPUP "&Help"
    BEGIN
        MENUITEM "&About fullmenus...",         ID_APP_ABOUT
    END
END


/////////////////////////////////////////////////////////////////////////////
//
// Accelerator
//

IDR_MAINFRAME ACCELERATORS PRELOAD MOVEABLE PURE
BEGIN
    "C",            ID_EDIT_COPY,               VIRTKEY, CONTROL, NOINVERT
    "N",            ID_FILE_NEW,                VIRTKEY, CONTROL, NOINVERT
    "O",            ID_FILE_OPEN,               VIRTKEY, CONTROL, NOINVERT
    "P",            ID_FILE_PRINT,              VIRTKEY, CONTROL, NOINVERT
    "S",            ID_FILE_SAVE,               VIRTKEY, CONTROL, NOINVERT
    "V",            ID_EDIT_PASTE,              VIRTKEY, CONTROL, NOINVERT
    VK_BACK,        ID_EDIT_UNDO,               VIRTKEY, ALT, NOINVERT
    VK_DELETE,      ID_EDIT_CUT,                VIRTKEY, SHIFT, NOINVERT
    VK_F5,          ID_DEMO_SUBMENUS_SUBITEM2, VIRTKEY, CONTROL, NOINVERT
    VK_F6,          ID_NEXT_PANE,               VIRTKEY, NOINVERT
    VK_F6,          ID_PREV_PANE,               VIRTKEY, SHIFT, NOINVERT
    VK_INSERT,      ID_EDIT_COPY,               VIRTKEY, CONTROL, NOINVERT
    VK_INSERT,      ID_EDIT_PASTE,              VIRTKEY, SHIFT, NOINVERT
    "X",            ID_EDIT_CUT,                VIRTKEY, CONTROL, NOINVERT
    "Z",            ID_EDIT_UNDO,               VIRTKEY, CONTROL, NOINVERT
END
```

This completes our menu skill. We've seen a great deal in this skill: from the basics of menus to adding submenus to menus, from toolbar buttons to tool tips, from shortcut keys to accelerator keys, and more. That's a significant amount of menu power. In the next skill, we'll start working with another very popular Visual C++ resource: dialog boxes.

Are You Experienced?

Now You Can...

- ☑ Create new menus and menu items
- ☑ Use the ClassWizard tool to connect menu items to event-handler methods
- ☑ Create new buttons in the toolbar
- ☑ Add tool tips to a toolbar button
- ☑ Create shortcut keys and accelerator keys
- ☑ Add prompts to the status bar
- ☑ Check and Gray out menu items

Skill 5

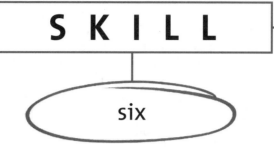

Dialog Boxes: Using Buttons and Text Boxes

❑ Creating dialog boxes

❑ Using buttons

❑ Using text boxes

❑ Retrieving data from a text box

❑ Basing an application's window on a dialog box

❑ Dialog member variables

❑ Dialog member objects

In this chapter, we will see how to create and use our own dialog boxes in Visual C++. Everyone knows what dialog boxes are—those windows with lots of buttons and list boxes and other items that you use to pass some information to a program. The strong advantage dialog boxes have over other windows in Visual C++ is that it's far easier to place controls (buttons, text boxes, check boxes and so on are called *controls*) in a dialog box than in other windows. In fact, Visual C++ has a special tool, the dialog editor, especially for use in creating dialog boxes.

We'll see how to create a dialog box, and how to add controls to that dialog box. And we'll see how to connect the controls to our code, and how to refer to the various *properties* of such controls as well, such as the text in a text box. When the user dismisses the dialog box from the screen, we'll see how to read the information that they placed in that dialog box (getting information from users is usually the point of dialog boxes).

We'll also cover a very powerful Visual C++ topic in this chapter—how to use a dialog box as our main window. That is, instead of a main window, view, and document objects, we'll just base our main window on a dialog box. This is very useful in Visual C++, because it's so easy to place and work with controls in a dialog box. If you have a program in which you want to present the user with a number of controls, using a dialog box as your main window is a very useful option.

Let's start at once by creating our first working dialog box example.

Creating Our First Dialog Box

Our first dialog box example, named dialogs, will show us all the aspects of working with dialog boxes. We will set up a menu item in our File menu, Show Dialog... (note the ellipsis—"..."—after "Show Dialog," indicating that selecting this menu item opens a dialog box; this is standard Windows usage), as shown in the following graphic.

```
------------------------------------------------------------
|Untitled - dialogs                                        |
|File Edit View Help                                       |
| |New ----------                                          |
| |Open              |-------------------------------------|
| |Save As           |                                     |
| |-------------     |                                     |
--> | |Show Dialog...|                                     |
| |-------------     |                                     |
| |Print             |                                     |
| |Print Preview     |                                     |
| |Print Welcome     |                                     |
| |Print Setup...    |                                     |
| |-------------     |                                     |
| |Recent File       |                                     |
| |-------------     |                                     |
| |Exit              |                                     |
|  -------------                                           |
|                                                          |
------------------------------------------------------------
```

When the user clicks this menu item, we place a dialog box on the screen with an OK button, a Cancel button, a button labeled Click Me, and a text box. Text boxes are those controls that can take and display text this way:

```
------------------------------------------------------------
|Dialog                                                    |
|----------------------------------------------------------|
|                                                          |
|                                        ----------        |
|                                       |   OK     |       |
|                                        ----------        |
|                                                          |
|                                        ----------        |
|                                       | Cancel   |       |
|                                        ----------        |
|                                                          |
|      -----------     --------------------              |
|     | Click Me  |   |                    |             |
|      -----------     --------------------              |
|                                                          |
|                                                          |
------------------------------------------------------------
```

When the user clicks the Click Me button, we can display some text in the text box: "Welcome to dialog boxes.":

```
---------------------------------------------------------
|Dialog                                                 |
|-------------------------------------------------------|
|                                                       |
|                                       -----------     |
|                                      |    OK     |    |
|                                       -----------     |
|                                                       |
|                                       -----------     |
|                                      |   Cancel  |    |
|                                       -----------     |
|                                                       |
|      -----------      -------------------------       |
|     | Click Me  |    | Welcome to dialog boxes. |     |
|      -----------      -------------------------       |
|                                                       |
|                                                       |
|                                                       |
---------------------------------------------------------
```

When the user clicks the OK button, the dialog box will be dismissed from the screen. However, the whole point of dialog boxes is usually to pass information back to the program, so in this case we'll pass the text from the text box back to the main program, which will display that text in its client area:

```
---------------------------------------------------------
|Untitled - dialogs                                     |
|File Edit View Help                                    |
|-------------------------------------------------------|
|Welcome to dialog boxes.                               |
|                                                       |
|                                                       |
|                                                       |
|                                                       |
|                                                       |
|                                                       |
|                                                       |
|                                                       |
|                                                       |
|                                                       |
---------------------------------------------------------
```

Let's start this new dialog box example now. Create a new SDI program named dialogs, and add a new menu item using the menu editor to the File menu: "Show Dialog...". Using ClassWizard, add an event-handling method to this new menu item, `OnFileShowdialog()`:

```
void CDialogsView::OnFileShowdialog()
{
    // TODO: Add your command handler code here
}
```

When the user clicks this menu item, we want to place our new dialog box on the screen. But how do we do that? It turns out that we have to create a new dialog box class, and then we can declare an object of that class in `OnFileShowdialog()`. To pop the dialog box on the screen, we will use its `DoModal()` method—placing a dialog box on the screen as a modal dialog box means that the user has to dismiss it before continuing on with the program. Let's see how to create our new dialog box class now.

Creating a Dialog Box

To create a new dialog box, select the Resource item in the Visual C++ Insert menu now. This opens the Insert Resource box, as shown in Figure 6.1. Select the Dialog entry and click the New button.

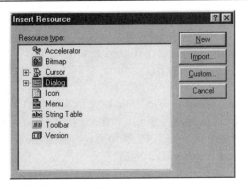

FIGURE 6.1: Creating a new dialog box

Clicking the New button opens the dialog box editor, as shown in Figure 6.2.

Skill 6

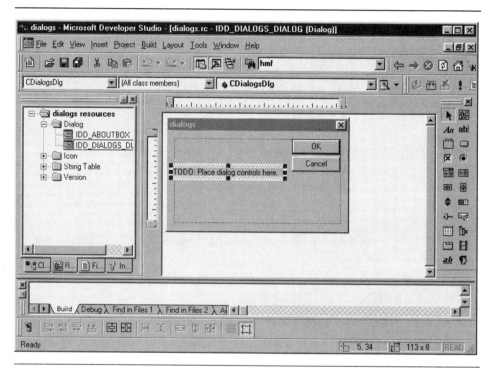

FIGURE 6.2: The dialog box editor

You can already see our new dialog box in the dialog box editor. Like menus, dialog boxes are considered resources in Windows programs. The resource ID given to our new dialog box is IDD_DIALOG1, as you can see in Figure 6.2. You can also see two buttons in the dialog box already: OK and Cancel. These are the two usual buttons in a dialog box—OK accepts the actions the user has made, and Cancel rejects them. If the user clicks the OK button, the DoModal() method returns the value IDOK, and if the user clicks the Cancel button, the DoModal() method returns IDCANCEL.

In addition, you see a label in the dialog box: "TODO: Place dialog controls here." Get rid of that prompt now by clicking that label (giving it a fuzzy border as shown in Figure 6.2) and pressing the Del key. This removes the label.

At right in Figure 6.2, you see the dialog editor's toolbox, and that's how we'll add the controls—a button and a text box—that we will use in this dialog box example.

NOTE   One Windows convention is to always have a Cancel button in a dialog box, in case the user has popped your dialog box on the screen by mistake.

Adding Controls to a Dialog Box

To add a control to the dialog box, you just drag a new control from the toolbox onto the dialog box under design. In our case, we will drag a button and a text box onto the dialog box, as shown in Figure 6.3. To do that, simply press the mouse button when the cursor is over the tool you want in the toolbox (the button tool is the third tool down on the right, and the text box tool is the second tool down on the right) and drag that tool to the dialog box.

TIP   If you want to find out what control a tool in the toolbox represents, let the mouse cursor rest over that tool for a moment, and a tool tip will tell you the name of the control that tool stands for.

The result appears in Figure 6.3. Click the text box now, which gives it a fuzzy outline with small boxes named *sizing handles*. Using the mouse, you can grasp a sizing handle and stretch controls as you like. In Figure 6.3, we are extending the text box horizontally (note the mouse cursor has changed to a right-left arrow to stretch the control).

So far, we have a text box and a button with the caption Button1. We want to give the button the caption Click Me, so let's do that now.

Labeling Controls

To give a control a new caption, you just select it by clicking it with the mouse, and typing the new caption. For our button, this opens the Push Button Properties box, as shown in Figure 6.4.

Skill 6

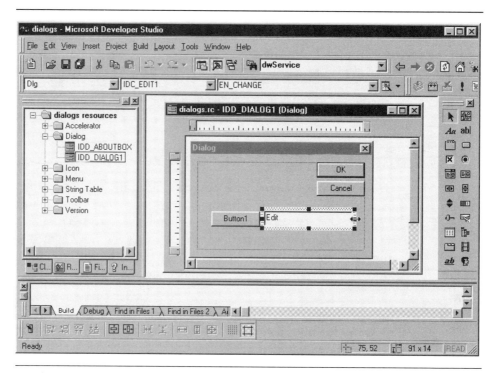

FIGURE 6.3 : Creating a new dialog box class

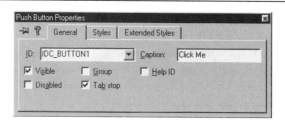

FIGURE 6.4 : Labeling our button

We give the button the caption Click Me. Note also the control ID the dialog editor has given our button: IDC_BUTTON1. In the same way, our text box has the control ID IDC_EDIT1 (text boxes are also called edit controls). The new version of our dialog box appears in Figure 6.5.

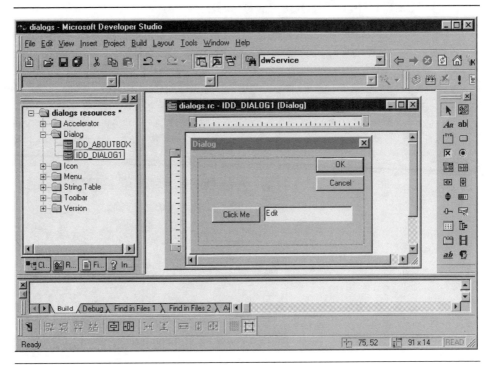

FIGURE 6.5: We've designed our dialog box.

This is the dialog box we'll use in our program. But how do we actually use that dialog box? Presently, our dialog box is just a resource as set up in the file dialogs.rc, and its specification looks like this:

```
IDD_DIALOG1 DIALOG DISCARDABLE  0, 0, 186, 95
STYLE DS_MODALFRAME | WS_POPUP | WS_CAPTION | WS_SYSMENU
CAPTION "Dialog"
FONT 8, "MS Sans Serif"
BEGIN
    DEFPUSHBUTTON    "OK",IDOK,129,7,50,14
    PUSHBUTTON       "Cancel",IDCANCEL,129,24,50,14
    EDITTEXT         IDC_EDIT1,75,52,91,14,ES_AUTOHSCROLL
    PUSHBUTTON       "Button1",IDC_BUTTON1,21,53,50,14
END
```

We'll need an object of some sort corresponding to this dialog box so that we can use dialog box methods like DoModal(). That's the usual way you add a dialog box to your program—design it and then connect it to a new class. We will create that new class now.

Creating a Dialog Box Class

You create a new dialog box class with ClassWizard, as you might guess from that tool's name. Start ClassWizard and click the Add Class button, then click the New item in the pop-up menu that appears. This opens the New Class box, as shown in Figure 6.6. Type the name **Dlg** for the new class in the Name box now. Next, select CDialog as the new dialog box's base class in the Base class box, as shown in Figure 6.6. CDialog is the MFC base class for dialog boxes, and its methods appear in Table 6.1. Click the OK button in the New Class box now.

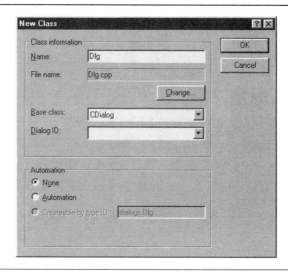

FIGURE 6.6: Creating a new dialog box class

TABLE 6.1 The CDialog Class Methods

Method	Does This
Cdialog	Constructs a CDialog object.
Create	Initializes the CDialog object.
CreateIndirect	Creates a modeless dialog box from a dialog-box template in memory.
DoModal	Calls a modal dialog box and returns when done.
EndDialog	Closes a modal dialog box.
GetDefID	Gets the ID of the default pushbutton control.

TABLE 6.1 CONTINUED: The CDialog Class Methods

Method	Does This
GotoDlgCtrl	Moves the focus to a specified dialog-box control in the dialog box.
InitModalIndirect	Creates a modal dialog box from a dialog-box template in memory; parameters are stored until the function DoModal is called.
MapDialogRect	Converts the dialog-box units to screen units.
NextDlgCtrl	Moves the focus to the next dialog-box control.
OnCancel	Override to perform the Cancel button or ESC key action.
OnInitDialog	Override to augment dialog-box initialization.
OnOK	Override to perform the OK button action in a modal dialog box.
OnSetFont	Override to specify the font that a dialog-box control is to use when it displays text.
PrevDlgCtrl	Moves the focus to the previous dialog-box control.
SetDefID	Changes the default pushbutton control for a dialog box to an indicated pushbutton.
SetHelpID	Sets a context-sensitive help ID.

Clicking OK opens ClassWizard again, as shown in Figure 6.7. Make sure our new class, Dlg, is selected in the Class name box. In Figure 6.7, you see the controls in our dialog box listed: IDC_BUTTON1, IDC_EDIT1, IDOK (the OK button) and IDCANCEL (the Cancel button).

Now we can connect Visual C++ code to our button.

Connecting Methods to Dialog Box Controls

When the user clicks the Click Me button, we want to display the text "Welcome to dialog boxes." in the text box. To do that, we'll first need some way of determining when the user clicks that button. We can connect an event-handling method to that button now, using ClassWizard.

To connect an event-handler to the button, select IDC_BUTTON1 now in ClassWizard and double-click the BN_CLICKED entry in the Messages box. This is a special message that buttons send (the BN prefix stands for button) when they are clicked; the other button message is BN_DOUBLECLICKED, sent when a button is double-clicked. When you double-click the BN_CLICKED entry, ClassWizard suggests the name OnButton1() for the new event-handler. Click OK to create the new event-handler OnButton1(), as shown in Figure 6.8.

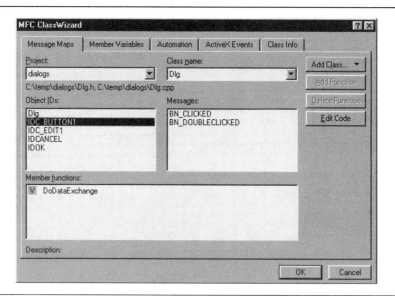

F I G U R E   6 . 7 :   ClassWizard displays our dialog box controls.

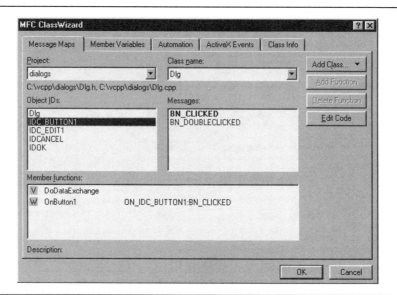

F I G U R E   6 . 8 :   ClassWizard creates a new event-handler.

We open that new event-handler now:

```
void Dlg::OnButton1()
{
    // TODO: Add your control notification handler code here
}
```

This is the method that the program will call when the user clicks the Click Me button in the dialog box.

We've made quite a bit of progress so far—we've designed our new dialog box by placing the controls we want in it, customized those controls, connected the dialog box to a new dialog box class, and connected a method to button clicks. However, we still need some way of reaching the text box, because when the user clicks the button, we should place our message in the text box. But how do we refer to the text box? Right now, the text box is only a specification in our dialogs.rc file:

```
IDD_DIALOG1 DIALOG DISCARDABLE  0, 0, 186, 95
STYLE DS_MODALFRAME | WS_POPUP | WS_CAPTION | WS_SYSMENU
CAPTION "Dialog"
FONT 8, "MS Sans Serif"
BEGIN
     DEFPUSHBUTTON    "OK",IDOK,129,7,50,14
     PUSHBUTTON       "Cancel",IDCANCEL,129,24,50,14
  →  EDITTEXT         IDC_EDIT1,75,52,91,14,ES_AUTOHSCROLL
     PUSHBUTTON       "Button1",IDC_BUTTON1,21,53,50,14
END
```

We need to be able to refer to the text box in a way that will let us insert our message into that text. Visual C++ allows us to connect member variables to a control in a dialog box, and we'll make use of that capability here. For example, we can name the text in the text box m_text, and when the user clicks the Click Me button, all we have to do is to set that text to "Welcome to dialog boxes." this way:

```
m_text = "Welcome to dialog boxes.";
```

As you can see, this is a powerful technique, so let's see how it works.

Connecting Variables to Dialog Box Controls

We use ClassWizard to connect a member variable to a control in a dialog box. Start ClassWizard now, and click the Member Variables tab, as shown in Figure 6.9. Make sure our dialog box class, Dlg, is selected in the Class name box. Now select the text box control, IDC_EDIT1, as shown in Figure 6.9, and click the Add Variable button.

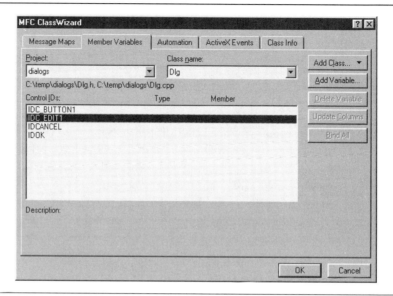

FIGURE 6.9: ClassWizard lets us create member variables.

This opens the Add Member Variable box, as shown in Figure 6.10. Here we will be able to give a name to the text in the text box. Give the new member variable the name m_text in the Member variable name box, as shown in Figure 6.10, and make sure Value shows in the Category box and CString in the Variable type box. This connects a CString variable named m_text to the text in the text box.

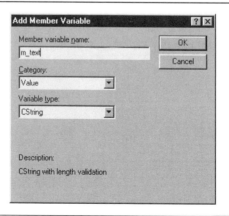

FIGURE 6.10: ClassWizard creates a member variable.

TIP   Besides member variables, you can also give a name to the whole control itself, not just to a *property* of that control. (A property is a "value" of the control, such as the text in a text box.) We'll see how that works in the next example.

Now click the OK button in the Add Member Variable box to close it, bringing ClassWizard back up, as shown in Figure 6.11. You can see our new member variable, m_text, in that figure.

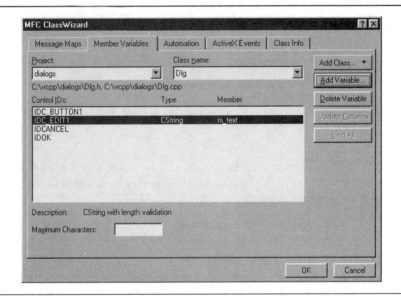

FIGURE 6.11: ClassWizard lists a member variable.

Now that we've set up our new member variable to refer to the text in the text box, we can place text in that text box this way in OnButton1() (which is the method called when the user clicks the Click Me button):

```
void Dlg::OnButton1()
{
    m_text = "Welcome to dialog boxes.";
          .
          .
          .
}
```

This doesn't quite do what we wanted, though, which was place the text in the text box. Simply assigning the m_text variable to our new text doesn't make that text appear in the text box. That variable is connected to the IDC_EDIT1 control in a special method the ClassWizard has added to our Dlg dialog box class:

```
void Dlg::DoDataExchange(CDataExchange* pDX)
{
    CDialog::DoDataExchange(pDX);
    //{{AFX_DATA_MAP(Dlg)
    DDX_Text(pDX, IDC_EDIT1, m_text);
    //}}AFX_DATA_MAP
}
```

We still have to do a little bit of work to make sure the text box is updated with the new data, and we do that by calling the UpdateData() method:

```
void Dlg::OnButton1()
{
    m_text = "Welcome to dialog boxes.";
    UpdateData(false);
}
```

Calling this method with a value of false updates the text box from the value in m_text. Calling this method with a value of true updates m_text from the text in the text box:

➜UpdateData(false) means: IDC_EDIT1   m_text
➜UpdateData(true) means: m_text   IDC_EDIT1

WARNING   One of the hardest things to remember about using member variables in a dialog box is to use UpdateData() to get or set the actual value in the control. If your program doesn't seem to do anything when you change a member variable's value in your code, check to make sure you've used UpdateData().

We've moved the message into the text box, but what if the user edits the text in the text box before clicking the OK button? We want to display the text from the text box in our client window, so we'll need to reload m_text with the text from the text box before closing the text box. Let's do that now.

Overriding the OK Button

You can add code to the OK button just like any other button. Using ClassWizard, connect a method named OnOK() to the OK button, whose ID is IDOK:

```
void Dlg::OnOK()
{
    // TODO: Add extra validation here
    CDialog::OnOK();
}
```

Notice the call to the CDialog class OnOK() method. Calling this method closes the dialog box and returns the value IDOK. We want to make sure the m_text variable holds the text from the text box, so we just call UpdateData() with a value of true here:

```
void Dlg::OnOK()
{
➜       UpdateData(true);
        CDialog::OnOK();
}
```

Now even if the user edits the text in the text box, we'll be able to display exactly the same text that was in the text box when they clicked the OK button.

Our Dlg class, the dialog box class, is complete, so we're ready to display that dialog box on the screen. Let's look into that now.

Displaying a Dialog Box

We want to display our new dialog box on the screen when the user clicks the "Show Dialog..." item in our program's File menu, and we've connected that to the view class's method OnFileShowdialog():

```
void CDialogsView::OnFileShowdialog()
{
    // TODO: Add your command handler code here
}
```

We will create a new object of our dialog box's class, Dlg, here, and display it with that object's DoModal() method. Before we do that, however, we have to let our view class know about the Dlg class. This might seem surprising—isn't the

Dlg class part of the same project as the view class? Yes, it is, but the support for the Dlg class is in a separate file, Dlg.cpp.

To let the view class know about the members of the Dlg class, we have to include the Dlg class's header file, Dlg.h, in the view class:

```
// dialogsView.cpp : implementation of the CDialogsView class
//

#include "stdafx.h"
#include "dialogs.h"

#include "dialogsDoc.h"
#include "dialogsView.h"
➜#include "Dlg.h"
          .
          .
          .
```

Finally, we are able to make use of the Dlg class in our view class. We first create a new object of that class named dlg:

```
void CDialogsView::OnFileShowdialog()
    {
➜       Dlg dlg;
          .
          .
          .

    }
```

Next, we display the dialog box on the screen. We do that with the DoModal() method. This method returns an integer value, which we store as the integer result:

```
void CDialogsView::OnFileShowdialog()
    {
        Dlg dlg;
➜       int result = dlg.DoModal();
          .
          .
          .

    }
```

At this point, the dialog box appears on the screen. The user can then click the Click Me button if they want to, placing our message in the text variable m_text. If they click the OK button, we can display the text from the text box, m_text, in our program's client area. First, we check to make sure the user did indeed click the OK button:

```
void CDialogsView::OnFileShowdialog()
{
    Dlg dlg;
    int result = dlg.DoModal();

→   if(result == IDOK){
        .
        .
        .

→   }
}
```

If the user did click OK, we want to get the string from the text box, m_text. We'll store that string in our document, so we get a pointer to the document now:

```
void CDialogsView::OnFileShowdialog()
{
    Dlg dlg;
    int result = dlg.DoModal();

    if(result == IDOK){
→       CDialogsDoc* pDoc = GetDocument();
→       ASSERT_VALID(pDoc);
        .
        .
        .

    }
}
```

We can set up a new CString object named StringData in the document (initializing it in the constructor):

```
// dialogsDoc.h : interface of the CDialogsDoc class
        .
        .
        .
class CDialogsDoc : public CDocument
{
protected: // create from serialization only
    CDialogsDoc();
```

Skill 6

```
        DECLARE_DYNCREATE(CDialogsDoc)

    // Attributes
    public:
→       CString StringData;
                   .
                   .
                   .
```

And we place the text in the dialog box's `m_text` variable in the `StringData` object:

```
    void CDialogsView::OnFileShowdialog()
    {
    Dlg dlg;
        int result = dlg.DoModal();

        if(result == IDOK){
            CDialogsDoc* pDoc = GetDocument();
            ASSERT_VALID(pDoc);

→           pDoc->StringData = dlg.m_text;
                   .
                   .
                   .

        }
    }
```

Getting data from a dialog box is as simple as that. Even though the dialog box is closed, its object still exists, and the data in that object is still intact.

Now we've retrieved the `m_text` string from the dialog box. The next task is to display that text, and we'll do that in the `OnDraw()` method, so we force a call to that method now with `Invalidate()`:

```
    void CDialogsView::OnFileShowdialog()
    {
        Dlg dlg;
        int result = dlg.DoModal();

        if(result == IDOK){
            CDialogsDoc* pDoc = GetDocument();
            ASSERT_VALID(pDoc);

            pDoc->StringData = dlg.m_text;
→           Invalidate();
        }
    }
```

And in the view's OnDraw() method, we draw the text from the dialog box:

```
void CDialogsView::OnDraw(CDC* pDC)
{
    CDialogsDoc* pDoc = GetDocument();
    ASSERT_VALID(pDoc);

    pDC->TextOut(0, 0, pDoc->StringData);

}
```

Now the program is complete. Run it as shown in Figure 6.12. Click the Show Dialog... item in the File menu to open the dialog box.

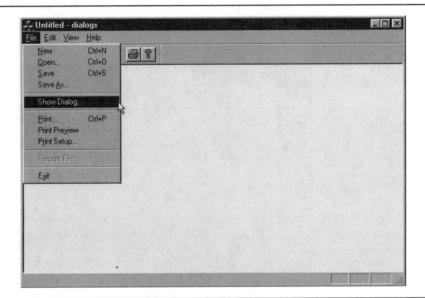

FIGURE 6.12: Our dialogs program

The dialog box opens as shown in Figure 6.13. Click the Click Me button now to make our message, "Welcome to dialog boxes." appear in the text box, as shown in Figure 6.13.

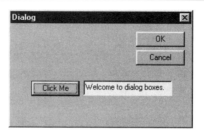

FIGURE 6.13: Our new dialog box

Next, close the dialog box. When you do, we read the text from the text box and display it in our main window's client area, as shown in Figure 6.14.

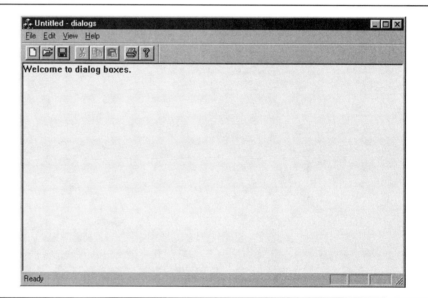

FIGURE 6.14: We retrieve data from a dialog box.

Our dialogs program works just as we want it to—we're supporting a dialog box and reading data from that dialog box when the user closes it. Now we're able to use dialog boxes in Visual C++.

The code for this program appears in `dialogsView.h`/`dialogsView.cpp`.

dialogsView.h and *dialogsView.cpp*

```cpp
// dialogsView.h : interface of the CDialogsView class
//
/////////////////////////////////////////////////////////////////////

#if !defined(AFX_DIALOGSVIEW_H__B5C0A5ED_9307_11D0_8860_444553540000__INCLUDED_)
#define AFX_DIALOGSVIEW_H__B5C0A5ED_9307_11D0_8860_444553540000__INCLUDED_

#if _MSC_VER >= 1000
#pragma once
#endif // _MSC_VER >= 1000

class CDialogsView : public CView
{
protected: // create from serialization only
    CDialogsView();
    DECLARE_DYNCREATE(CDialogsView)

// Attributes
public:
    CDialogsDoc* GetDocument();

// Operations
public:

// Overrides
    // ClassWizard generated virtual function overrides
    //{{AFX_VIRTUAL(CDialogsView)
    public:
    virtual void OnDraw(CDC* pDC);  // overridden to draw this view
    virtual BOOL PreCreateWindow(CREATESTRUCT& cs);
    protected:
    virtual BOOL OnPreparePrinting(CPrintInfo* pInfo);
    virtual void OnBeginPrinting(CDC* pDC, CPrintInfo* pInfo);
    virtual void OnEndPrinting(CDC* pDC, CPrintInfo* pInfo);
    //}}AFX_VIRTUAL

// Implementation
public:
    virtual ~CDialogsView();
#ifdef _DEBUG
    virtual void AssertValid() const;
    virtual void Dump(CDumpContext& dc) const;
#endif

protected:
```

```
// Generated message map functions
protected:
    //{{AFX_MSG(CDialogsView)
    afx_msg void OnFileShowdialog();
    //}}AFX_MSG
    DECLARE_MESSAGE_MAP()
};

#ifndef _DEBUG  // debug version in dialogsView.cpp
inline CDialogsDoc* CDialogsView::GetDocument()
   { return (CDialogsDoc*)m_pDocument; }
#endif

/////////////////////////////////////////////////////////////////////////////

//{{AFX_INSERT_LOCATION}}
// Microsoft Developer Studio will insert additional declarations immediately
// before the previous line.

#endif // !defined(AFX_DIALOGSVIEW_H__B5C0A5ED_9307_11D0_8860_444553540000__
➥INCLUDED_)


// dialogsView.cpp : implementation of the CDialogsView class
//

#include "stdafx.h"
#include "dialogs.h"

#include "dialogsDoc.h"
#include "dialogsView.h"
#include "Dlg.h"

#ifdef _DEBUG
#define new DEBUG_NEW
#undef THIS_FILE
static char THIS_FILE[] = __FILE__;
#endif

/////////////////////////////////////////////////////////////////////////////
// CDialogsView

IMPLEMENT_DYNCREATE(CDialogsView, CView)

BEGIN_MESSAGE_MAP(CDialogsView, CView)
    //{{AFX_MSG_MAP(CDialogsView)
    ON_COMMAND(ID_FILE_SHOWDIALOG, OnFileShowdialog)
    //}}AFX_MSG_MAP
    // Standard printing commands
```

```
        ON_COMMAND(ID_FILE_PRINT, CView::OnFilePrint)
        ON_COMMAND(ID_FILE_PRINT_DIRECT, CView::OnFilePrint)
        ON_COMMAND(ID_FILE_PRINT_PREVIEW, CView::OnFilePrintPreview)
END_MESSAGE_MAP()

/////////////////////////////////////////////////////////////////////////////
// CDialogsView construction/destruction

CDialogsView::CDialogsView()
{
        // TODO: add construction code here

}

CDialogsView::~CDialogsView()
{
}

BOOL CDialogsView::PreCreateWindow(CREATESTRUCT& cs)
{
        // TODO: Modify the Window class or styles here by modifying
        //   the CREATESTRUCT cs

        return CView::PreCreateWindow(cs);
}

/////////////////////////////////////////////////////////////////////////////
// CDialogsView drawing

void CDialogsView::OnDraw(CDC* pDC)
{
        CDialogsDoc* pDoc = GetDocument();
        ASSERT_VALID(pDoc);

        pDC->TextOut(0, 0, pDoc->StringData);

        // TODO: add draw code for native data here
}

/////////////////////////////////////////////////////////////////////////////
// CDialogsView printing

BOOL CDialogsView::OnPreparePrinting(CPrintInfo* pInfo)
{
        // default preparation
        return DoPreparePrinting(pInfo);
}

void CDialogsView::OnBeginPrinting(CDC* /*pDC*/, CPrintInfo* /*pInfo*/)
```

Skill 6

```
{
    // TODO: add extra initialization before printing
}

void CDialogsView::OnEndPrinting(CDC* /*pDC*/, CPrintInfo* /*pInfo*/)
{
    // TODO: add cleanup after printing
}

///////////////////////////////////////////////////////////////////////
// CDialogsView diagnostics

#ifdef _DEBUG
void CDialogsView::AssertValid() const
{
    CView::AssertValid();
}

void CDialogsView::Dump(CDumpContext& dc) const
{
    CView::Dump(dc);
}

CDialogsDoc* CDialogsView::GetDocument() // non-debug version is inline
{
    ASSERT(m_pDocument->IsKindOf(RUNTIME_CLASS(CDialogsDoc)));
    return (CDialogsDoc*)m_pDocument;
}
#endif //_DEBUG

///////////////////////////////////////////////////////////////////////
// CDialogsView message handlers

void CDialogsView::OnFileShowdialog()
{
    // TODO: Add your command handler code here
    Dlg dlg;
    int result = dlg.DoModal();

    if(result == IDOK){
        CDialogsDoc* pDoc = GetDocument();
        ASSERT_VALID(pDoc);
        pDoc->StringData = dlg.m_text;
        Invalidate();
    }
}
```

Dlg.h and Dlg.cpp

```
#if !defined(AFX_DLG_H__B5C0A5F5_9307_11D0_8860_444553540000__INCLUDED_)
#define AFX_DLG_H__B5C0A5F5_9307_11D0_8860_444553540000__INCLUDED_

#if _MSC_VER >= 1000
#pragma once
#endif // _MSC_VER >= 1000
// Dlg.h : header file
//


/////////////////////////////////////////////////////////////////////////
// Dlg dialog

class Dlg : public CDialog
{
// Construction
public:
    Dlg(CWnd* pParent = NULL);    // standard constructor

// Dialog Data
    //{{AFX_DATA(Dlg)
    enum { IDD = IDD_DIALOG1 };
    CString     m_text;
    //}}AFX_DATA


// Overrides
    // ClassWizard generated virtual function overrides
    //{{AFX_VIRTUAL(Dlg)
    protected:
    virtual void DoDataExchange(CDataExchange* pDX);    // DDX/DDV support
    //}}AFX_VIRTUAL

// Implementation
protected:

    // Generated message map functions
    //{{AFX_MSG(Dlg)
    afx_msg void OnButton1();
    //}}AFX_MSG
    DECLARE_MESSAGE_MAP()
};

//{{AFX_INSERT_LOCATION}}
// Microsoft Developer Studio will insert additional declarations immediately
// before the previous line.
```

```
#endif // !defined(AFX_DLG_H__B5C0A5F5_9307_11D0_8860_444553540000__INCLUDED_)


// Dlg.cpp : implementation file
//

#include "stdafx.h"
#include "dialogs.h"
#include "Dlg.h"

#ifdef _DEBUG
#define new DEBUG_NEW
#undef THIS_FILE
static char THIS_FILE[] = __FILE__;
#endif

/////////////////////////////////////////////////////////////////////////////
// Dlg dialog


Dlg::Dlg(CWnd* pParent /*=NULL*/)
    : CDialog(Dlg::IDD, pParent)
{
    //{{AFX_DATA_INIT(Dlg)
    m_text = _T("");
    //}}AFX_DATA_INIT
}


void Dlg::DoDataExchange(CDataExchange* pDX)
{
    CDialog::DoDataExchange(pDX);
    //{{AFX_DATA_MAP(Dlg)
    DDX_Text(pDX, IDC_EDIT1, m_text);
    //}}AFX_DATA_MAP
}


BEGIN_MESSAGE_MAP(Dlg, CDialog)
    //{{AFX_MSG_MAP(Dlg)
    ON_BN_CLICKED(IDC_BUTTON1, OnButton1)
    //}}AFX_MSG_MAP
END_MESSAGE_MAP()

/////////////////////////////////////////////////////////////////////////////
// Dlg message handlers

void Dlg::OnButton1()
{
```

```
        // TODO: Add your control notification handler code here
        m_text = "Welcome to dialog boxes.";
        UpdateData(false);
}

void Dlg::OnOK()
{
        // TODO: Add extra validation here
        UpdateData(true);
        CDialog::OnOK();
}
```

We've gotten a strong introduction to dialog boxes at this point. We've seen how to create a dialog box, put controls into it, connect those controls to code, display the dialog box, and retrieve data from it.

For our next example, we'll see that it's even possible to use a dialog box as our program's main window.

Using a Dialog Box as a Main Window

Sometimes a program has many controls that you want to present to the user in your main window; for example, you might be creating a calculator program full of buttons. Visual C++ provides an easy way of doing this—you can use a dialog box as your main window. For this example, we'll use a dialog box as our main window with a Click Me button and a text box:

```
 ---------------------------------------------------
|buttons                                            |
| ------------------------------------------------- |
|                                                   |
|                                    ----------      |
|                                   |    OK    |  |  |
|           -----------              ----------      |
|          | Click Me  |                            |
|           -----------                             |
|                                    ----------      |
|                                   |  Cancel  |  |  |
|                                    ----------      |
|                                                   |
|      ---------------------                        |
|     |                     |                       |
|      ---------------------                        |
|                                                   |
|                                                   |
 ---------------------------------------------------
```

When the user clicks the Click Me button, we can display the text "Dialog box window!" in the text box:

```
---------------------------------------------------------
|buttons                                                |
|-------------------------------------------------------|
|                                                       |
|                                        -----------    |
|              -----------              |     OK      | |
|             |  Click Me  |             -----------    |
|              -----------                              |
|                                        -----------    |
|                                       |   Cancel    | |
|                                        -----------    |
|                                                       |
|              --------------------                     |
|             |Dialog box window!       |                |
|              --------------------                     |
|                                                       |
|                                                       |
|                                                       |
---------------------------------------------------------
```

TIP   Although we will retain the OK and Cancel buttons in this example, you can remove these buttons just like any other buttons in a dialog box. Just select them in the dialog editor and press Del.

Now let's start this new program, named buttons. This time in AppWizard's Step 1, however, click the option marked "Dialog based", as shown in Figure 6.15, to base our new program on the CDialog class. Now click Finish to create the new program.

Next, click the Resources tab, open the Dialog folder, and click the entry for our program's main window, IDD_BUTTONS_DIALOG. This opens the dialog editor, as shown in Figure 6.16.

Add a new button with the caption Click Me and a new text box to the dialog box, as also shown in Figure 6.16, then open ClassWizard to connect the Click Me button to our code.

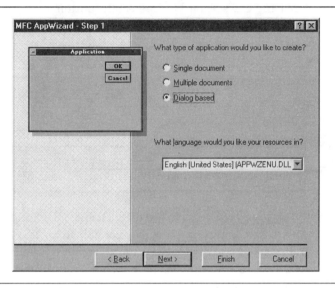

FIGURE 6.15: Creating a dialog-based program

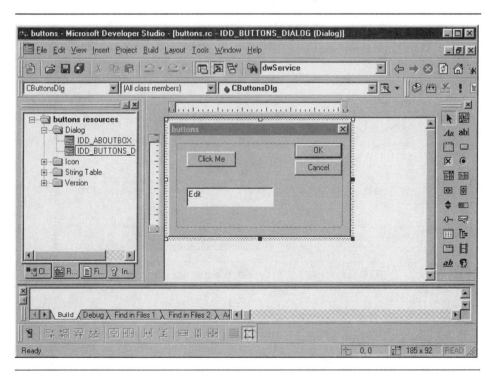

FIGURE 6.16: Designing a dialog-based program

We use ClassWizard to connect the button to an event-handler, `OnButton1()`, as we did in the previous example. Double-click `IDC_BUTTON1` in the Object IDs box, and double-click `BN_CLICKED` in the Messages box. This creates `OnButton1()`:

```
void CButtonsDlg::OnButton1()
{

}
```

NOTE   We did not have to create a new class for our dialog box in this example, because AppWizard has already done so when it created our program.

Here, we want to place the text "Dialog box window!" in the text box. We could do that by connecting a member variable to the text in the text box, such as `m_text` in the last example. However, there is a more general way of working with controls—we can give a name to the whole control, and work with the whole control at once, not just one property inside the control. Let's look into this now.

Open ClassWizard and click the Member Variables tab. Next, select IDC_EDIT1 in the Control IDs box. Then click the Add Variable button, opening the Add Member Variable box, as shown in Figure 6.17.

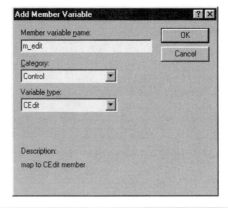

FIGURE 6.17: Creating a member object

We will give a name to the text box: `m_edit`. To do that, enter **m_edit** in the Member Name Variable box, make sure "Control" is showing in the Category combo box and CEdit is showing in the Variable type box, then click OK. This creates a new member variable, m_edit, as shown in Figure 6.18.

Now we have a new name for the text box in our dialog box, so we can make use of that text box directly, and thus use all the methods built into the new m_edit object. The CEdit class methods appear in Table 6.2.

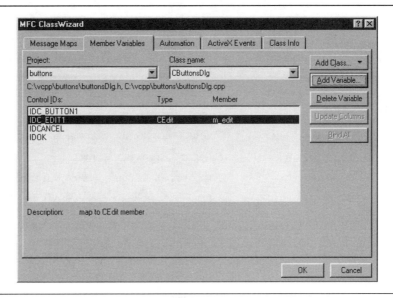

FIGURE 6.18: Our new m_edit **variable is created.**

TABLE 6.2: The CEdit **Class Methods**

Method	Does This
CanUndo	Indicates whether an edit-control operation can be undone.
CEdit	Constructs a CEdit control.
CharFromPos	Retrieves the line and character indices for the character closest to a specified position.
Clear	Deletes the current selection in the edit control.
Copy	Copies the current selection in the edit control to the Clipboard.
Create	Creates the Windows edit control and attaches it to the CEdit object.

T A B L E   6 . 2   C O N T I N U E D : The CEdit Class Methods

Method	Does This
Cut	Deletes the current selection in the edit control and copies that text to the Clipboard.
EmptyUndoBuffer	Resets the undo flag of an edit control.
FmtLines	Sets the inclusion of soft line-break characters on or off.
GetFirstVisibleLine	Determines the topmost visible line in an edit control.
GetHandle	Retrieves a handle to the memory currently allocated for a multiple-line edit control.
GetLimitText	Gets the maximum amount of text this CEdit can contain.
GetLine	Gets a line of text from an edit control.
GetLineCount	Gets the number of lines in a multiple-line edit control.
GetMargins	Gets the left and right margins.
GetModify	Indicates whether the contents of an edit control have been modified.
GetPasswordChar	Retrieves the password character displayed in an edit control when the user enters text.
GetRect	Gets the formatting rectangle.
GetSel	Gets the starting and ending character positions of the current selection.
LimitText	Limits the length of the text that the user may enter into an edit control.
LineFromChar	Retrieves the line number of the line that contains the specified character index.
LineIndex	Retrieves the character index of a line within a multiple-line edit control.
LineLength	Retrieves the length of a line in an edit control.
LineScroll	Scrolls the text of a multiple-line edit control.
Paste	Inserts the data from the Clipboard into the edit control.
PosFromChar	Gets the coordinates of the upper-left corner of a specified character index.
ReplaceSel	Replaces the current selection in an edit control with the specified text.
SetHandle	Sets the handle to the local memory that will be used by a multiple-line edit control.
SetLimitText	Sets the maximum amount of text this CEdit can contain.
SetMargins	Sets the left and right margins for this CEdit.

TABLE 6.2 CONTINUED: The CEdit Class Methods

Method	Does This
SetModify	Sets or clears the modification flag.
SetPasswordChar	Sets or removes a password character displayed in an edit control.
SetReadOnly	Sets the read-only state of an edit control.
SetRect	Sets the formatting rectangle of a multiple-line edit control and updates the control.
SetRectNP	Sets the formatting rectangle of a multiple-line edit control; does not redraw the window.
SetSel	Selects a range of characters in an edit control.
SetTabStops	Sets the tab stops in a multiple-line edit control.
Undo	Reverses the last edit-control operation.

For example, the CEdit text box class is based on the CWindow class, and CWindow contains a method called SetWindowText() to set the window's text, so we can set the text in the text box to "Dialog box window!" this way:

```
void CButtonsDlg::OnButton1()
{
    m_edit.SetWindowText(CString("Dialog box window!"));

}
```

That's all there is to it—run the program now, as shown in Figure 6.19, and click the Click Me button. This displays our message in the text box, as also shown in Figure 6.19.

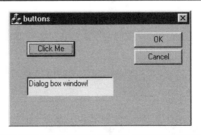

FIGURE 6.19: Our buttons program uses a dialog box as its main window.

Now we're able to use a dialog box as our program's main window. This is especially important because, using the dialog editor, we can add and customize controls in a dialog box very easily. The code for this program appears in buttonsDlg.h/buttonsDlg.cpp.

buttonsDlg.h and *buttonsDlg.cpp*

```
// buttonsDlg.h : header file
//

#if !defined(AFX_BUTTONSDIG_H__C89D1407_9190_11D0_8860_444553540000__INCLUDED_)
#define AFX_BUTTONSDLG_H__C89D1407_9190_11D0_8860_444553540000__INCLUDED_

#if _MSC_VER >= 1000
#pragma once
#endif // _MSC_VER >= 1000

/////////////////////////////////////////////////////////////////////////////
// CButtonsDlg dialog

class CButtonsDlg : public CDialog
{
// Construction
public:
    CButtonsDlg(CWnd* pParent = NULL);       // standard constructor

// Dialog Data
    //{{AFX_DATA(CButtonsDlg)
    enum { IDD = IDD_BUTTONS_DIALOG };
    CEdit      m_edit;
    //}}AFX_DATA

    // ClassWizard generated virtual function overrides
    //{{AFX_VIRTUAL(CButtonsDlg)
    protected:
    virtual void DoDataExchange(CDataExchange* pDX);      // DDX/DDV support
    //}}AFX_VIRTUAL

// Implementation
protected:
    HICON m_hIcon;

    // Generated message map functions
    //{{AFX_MSG(CButtonsDlg)
    virtual BOOL OnInitDialog();
    afx_msg void OnSysCommand(UINT nID, LPARAM lParam);
    afx_msg void OnPaint();
    afx_msg HCURSOR OnQueryDragIcon();
```

```
        virtual void OnOK();
        afx_msg void OnButton1();
    //}}AFX_MSG
    DECLARE_MESSAGE_MAP()
};

//{{AFX_INSERT_LOCATION}}
// Microsoft Developer Studio will insert additional declarations immediately
// before the previous line.

#endif //
!defined(AFX_BUTTONSDLG_H__C89D1407_9190_11D0_8860_444553540000__INCLUDED_)


// buttonsDlg.cpp : implementation file
//

#include "stdafx.h"
#include "buttons.h"
#include "buttonsDlg.h"

#ifdef _DEBUG
#define new DEBUG_NEW
#undef THIS_FILE
static char THIS_FILE[] = __FILE__;
#endif

/////////////////////////////////////////////////////////////////////////////
// CAboutDlg dialog used for App About

class CAboutDlg : public CDialog
{
public:
    CAboutDlg();

// Dialog Data
    //{{AFX_DATA(CAboutDlg)
    enum { IDD = IDD_ABOUTBOX };
    //}}AFX_DATA


    // ClassWizard generated virtual function overrides
    //{{AFX_VIRTUAL(CAboutDlg)
    protected:
    virtual void DoDataExchange(CDataExchange* pDX);    // DDX/DDV support
    //}}AFX_VIRTUAL

// Implementation
protected:
    //{{AFX_MSG(CAboutDlg)
```

Skill 6

```
     //}}AFX_MSG
     DECLARE_MESSAGE_MAP()
};

CAboutDlg::CAboutDlg() : CDialog(CAboutDlg::IDD)
{
     //{{AFX_DATA_INIT(CAboutDlg)
     //}}AFX_DATA_INIT
}

void CAboutDlg::DoDataExchange(CDataExchange* pDX)
{
     CDialog::DoDataExchange(pDX);
     //{{AFX_DATA_MAP(CAboutDlg)
     //}}AFX_DATA_MAP
}

BEGIN_MESSAGE_MAP(CAboutDlg, CDialog)
     //{{AFX_MSG_MAP(CAboutDlg)
          // No message handlers
     //}}AFX_MSG_MAP
END_MESSAGE_MAP()

///////////////////////////////////////////////////////////////////////
// CButtonsDlg dialog

CButtonsDlg::CButtonsDlg(CWnd* pParent /*=NULL*/)
     : CDialog(CButtonsDlg::IDD, pParent)
{
     //{{AFX_DATA_INIT(CButtonsDlg)
          // NOTE: the ClassWizard will add member initialization here
     //}}AFX_DATA_INIT
     // Note that LoadIcon does not require a subsequent DestroyIcon in Win32
     m_hIcon = AfxGetApp()->LoadIcon(IDR_MAINFRAME);
}

void CButtonsDlg::DoDataExchange(CDataExchange* pDX)
{
     CDialog::DoDataExchange(pDX);
     //{{AFX_DATA_MAP(CButtonsDlg)
     DDX_Control(pDX, IDC_EDIT1, m_edit);
     //}}AFX_DATA_MAP
}

BEGIN_MESSAGE_MAP(CButtonsDlg, CDialog)
     //{{AFX_MSG_MAP(CButtonsDlg)
     ON_WM_SYSCOMMAND()
     ON_WM_PAINT()
     ON_WM_QUERYDRAGICON()
```

```
        ON_BN_CLICKED(IDC_BUTTON1, OnButton1)
        //}}AFX_MSG_MAP
END_MESSAGE_MAP()

/////////////////////////////////////////////////////////////////////////////
// CButtonsDlg message handlers

BOOL CButtonsDlg::OnInitDialog()
{
        CDialog::OnInitDialog();

        // Add "About..." menu item to system menu.

        // IDM_ABOUTBOX must be in the system command range.
        ASSERT((IDM_ABOUTBOX & 0xFFF0) == IDM_ABOUTBOX);
        ASSERT(IDM_ABOUTBOX < 0xF000);

        CMenu* pSysMenu = GetSystemMenu(FALSE);
        if (pSysMenu != NULL)
        {
            CString strAboutMenu;
            strAboutMenu.LoadString(IDS_ABOUTBOX);
            if (!strAboutMenu.IsEmpty())
            {
                pSysMenu->AppendMenu(MF_SEPARATOR);
                pSysMenu->AppendMenu(MF_STRING, IDM_ABOUTBOX, strAboutMenu);
            }
        }

        // Set the icon for this dialog.  The framework does this automatically
        //  when the application's main window is not a dialog
        SetIcon(m_hIcon, TRUE);                  // Set big icon
        SetIcon(m_hIcon, FALSE);          // Set small icon

        // TODO: Add extra initialization here

        return TRUE;  // return TRUE  unless you set the focus to a control
}

void CButtonsDlg::OnSysCommand(UINT nID, LPARAM lParam)
{
        if ((nID & 0xFFF0) == IDM_ABOUTBOX)
        {
            CAboutDlg dlgAbout;
            dlgAbout.DoModal();
        }
        else
        {
            CDialog::OnSysCommand(nID, lParam);
        }
```

Skill 6

```
}

// If you add a minimize button to your dialog, you will need the code below
//  to draw the icon.  For MFC applications using the document/view model,
//  this is automatically done for you by the framework.

void CButtonsDlg::OnPaint()
{
    if (IsIconic())
    {
        CPaintDC dc(this); // device context for painting

        SendMessage(WM_ICONERASEBKGND, (WPARAM) dc.GetSafeHdc(), 0);

        // Center icon in client rectangle
        int cxIcon = GetSystemMetrics(SM_CXICON);
        int cyIcon = GetSystemMetrics(SM_CYICON);
        CRect rect;
        GetClientRect(&rect);
        int x = (rect.Width() - cxIcon + 1) / 2;
        int y = (rect.Height() - cyIcon + 1) / 2;

        // Draw the icon
        dc.DrawIcon(x, y, m_hIcon);
    }
    else
    {
        CDialog::OnPaint();
    }
}

// The system calls this to obtain the cursor to display while the user drags
//  the minimized window.
HCURSOR CButtonsDlg::OnQueryDragIcon()
{
    return (HCURSOR) m_hIcon;
}

void CButtonsDlg::OnOK()
{
    CDialog::OnOK();
}

void CButtonsDlg::OnButton1()
{
    m_edit.SetWindowText(CString("Dialog box window!"));

}
```

That completes our chapter on dialog boxes. You've gained a lot of expertise here, and seen how to create a dialog box and put buttons and text boxes in it, connect the button to an event-handler, and reach the text in the text box from code. You've also learned how to use the dialog editor, create member variables from control properties and from the controls themselves, display a dialog box, retrieve data from a dialog box when the user closes it, check which button the user clicked, and how to use a dialog box as our program's main window. In the next chapter, we'll continue on with two new controls that are also usually associated with dialog boxes: check boxes and radio buttons.

Are You Experienced?

Now You Can...

- ☑ Create a dialog box
- ☑ Display a dialog box from code
- ☑ Retrieve data from a dialog box
- ☑ Connect a dialog box's controls to code
- ☑ Use a dialog box as a program's main window
- ☑ Determine which button the user clicked in a dialog box
- ☑ Create member variables from a dialog box's controls and control properties

Skill 6

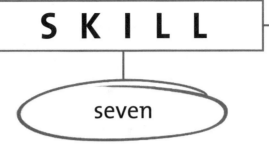

SKILL

seven

Creating Check Boxes and Radio Buttons

- ❑ Creating and using check boxes
- ❑ Creating and using radio buttons
- ❑ Connecting check boxes and radio buttons to code
- ❑ Grouping check boxes and radio buttons together
- ❑ Using check boxes and radio buttons together
- ❑ Creating button member variables
- ❑ Exploring button styles

In this skill, we will explore two new controls: check boxes and radio buttons. In Visual C++, these controls are really buttons with a different button style than the buttons we've used already (the simple buttons we've used up to now are called *pushbuttons*, and they revert to their unpressed state when you release the mouse).

You have seen check boxes in Windows, they are those little boxes that are either empty inside or display a small check mark. When you click a check box, it changes its *state* to either checked or unchecked. You use check boxes to let the user select one or more options from a number of options, such as the contents of a sandwich (e.g., tomato, lettuce, ham, turkey and so on).

Radio buttons, on the other hand, only let the user select one option, such as the current day of the week (for example, Monday, Tuesday, Wednesday, and so on). Radio buttons (also called option buttons) are small circular buttons that display a black dot in the middle when clicked, and are empty otherwise. Like check boxes, clicking a radio button causes it to change the state to checked or unchecked. Unlike check boxes, however, radio buttons are coordinated into groups, and function together.

Only one radio button in a group of radio buttons can be checked at a time. When one radio button is clicked, it displays its dot in the middle, and all the other radio buttons are cleared, so only the clicked radio button displays a dot. There are two ways to group radio buttons together in Visual C++; either with a group box control or by placing them in the same window (that is, all the radio buttons in the same window function together if there is no group box). We'll see how both methods work in this skill.

Finally, we'll see how to use both radio buttons and check boxes in the same program. In that program, we'll create a small program for a flower shop, allowing the user to select from various flower arrangements (which they select by clicking radio buttons so they can only select one arrangement at a time) and letting them see what flowers are in each arrangement (by clicking various check boxes appropriately—note that several check boxes may be clicked at the same time).

With all this going on, then, let's start at once with our first check box program.

Working with Check Boxes

We'll base our check box program on a dialog box, using that dialog box as our main window and displaying three check boxes, as illustrated in the following graphic.

```
 --------------------------------------------------------
| checks                                                 |
|--------------------------------------------------------|
|      -                           ------------          |
|     | |  Check 1              |     OK      |          |
|      -                           ------------          |
|                                                        |
|      -                           ------------          |
|     | |  Check 2              |   Cancel    |          |
|      -                           ------------          |
|                                                        |
|      -                                                 |
|     | |  Check 3                                       |
|      -                                                 |
|                                                        |
|      -------------------------------------------       |
|     |                                           |      |
|      -------------------------------------------       |
|                                                        |
 --------------------------------------------------------
```

We use a dialog box as our main window so we can then use the dialog editor to create and position our check boxes in that window. When the user clicks one of our three check boxes, we indicate which check box they've clicked in a text box:

```
 --------------------------------------------------------
| checks                                                 |
|--------------------------------------------------------|
|      -                           ------------          |
|     | |  Check 1              |     OK      |          |
|      -                           ------------          |
|                                                        |
|      -                           ------------          |
|     |v|  Check 2              |   Cancel    |          |
|      -                           ------------          |
|                                                        |
|      -                                                 |
|     | |  Check 3                                       |
|      -                                                 |
|                                                        |
|      -------------------------------------------       |
|     |Check 2 clicked                            |      |
|      -------------------------------------------       |
|                                                        |
 --------------------------------------------------------
```

Skill 7

Create this program now, naming it checks, and making it a dialog-based program in AppWizard. After you have created the program, open the dialog box for our main window, ID = IDD_CHECKS_DIALOG, in the dialog editor, as shown in Figure 7.1.

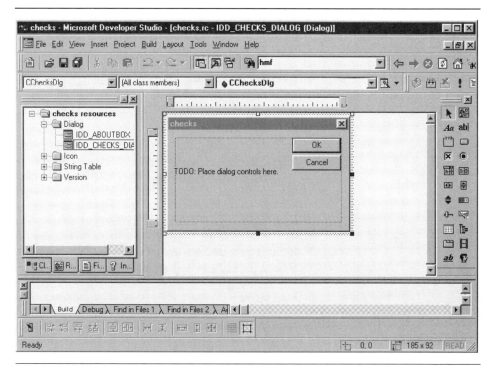

FIGURE 7.1: Designing our checks program

Start by deleting the "TODO: Place dialog controls here" label (just select that label and press Del). Now we will add the controls we'll need for our checks program—three check boxes and a text box.

Adding Check Boxes to a Program

Adding the three check boxes and the text box to our dialog window is not hard. Just drag those controls over to the dialog box from the dialog editor's toolbox (the check box tool is the fourth tool down on the left), and stretch the text box as shown in Figure 7.2. The dialog editor gives them the captions Check1, Check2, and so on.

TIP

To set a check box's caption yourself in the dialog editor, just right click the check box, click the Properties item in the pop-up menu that appears, and type in the new caption.

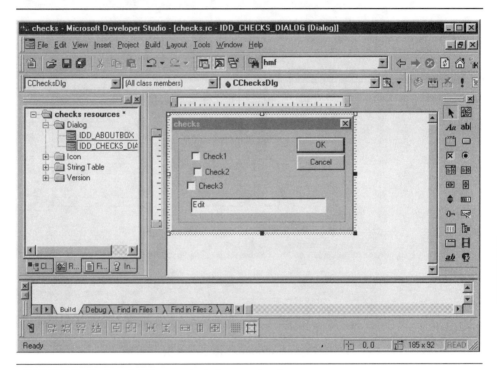

FIGURE 7.2: Adding controls to our checks program

As you can see, the check boxes aren't exactly neatly lined up in our first attempt. Arranging controls exactly (that is, to the screen pixel) is always a problem when you're designing a dialog box with a number of controls in it, but the dialog editor can help here.

Aligning Controls in the Dialog Editor

To align these new check boxes, hold down the Ctrl key and click each one, giving all three a fuzzy outline, as shown in Figure 7.3. Make sure you click the top check box last, giving it solid sizing handles, and the other two check boxes hollow sizing handles, as also shown in Figure 7.3. Giving the top check box solid sizing handles makes it the reference control, and the other controls will be aligned with respect to it.

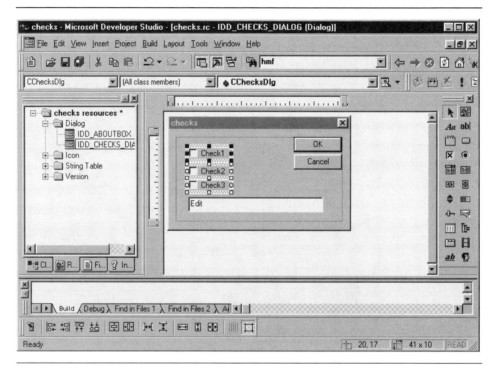

FIGURE 7.3: Aligning the check boxes

To align the controls horizontally, select the Align menu item in the Layout menu now. This opens a submenu—select Left in that submenu to align the check box controls to the left edge of the reference check box.

We've aligned our controls horizontally now. We can also make the vertical spacing between them even. To do that, select the Space Evenly item in the Layout menu, opening a new submenu. Select the Down item in the new submenu, aligning the controls now as shown in Figure 7.4.

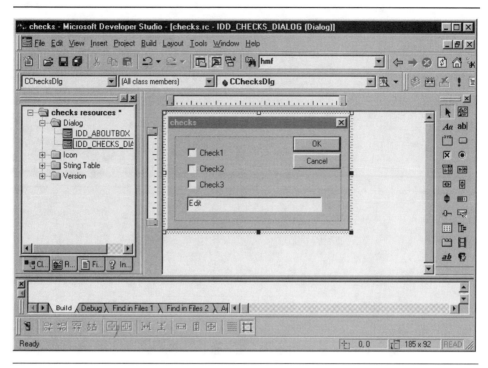

FIGURE 7.4: Our checks program in finished form

We've arranged the controls we want in our program. The next step is connecting them to our code.

Connecting Check Boxes to Code

We connect event-handling methods to the check boxes with ClassWizard. Open ClassWizard now as shown in Figure 7.5, and find the three check boxes, IDC_ CHECK1, IDC_CHECK2, and IDC_CHECK3. Add event-handlers to these controls by clicking those ID values one by one, and double-clicking the BN_CLICKED message in the Messages box.

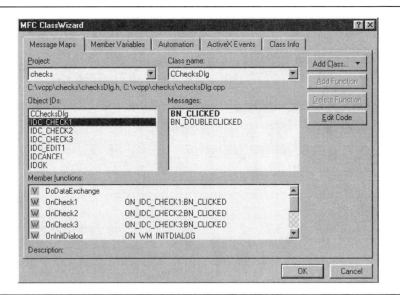

FIGURE 7.5: Connecting our check boxes to code

This creates the event-handlers OnCheck1(), OnCheck2, and OnCheck3().
ClassWizard can be used to connect a member variable to the text in the text box,
which we will name m_text.

```
Now open OnCheck1():
void CChecksDlg::OnCheck1()
{
    // TODO: Add your control notification handler code here
}
```

This is the method that is called when the user clicks the first check box.
Clicking the check box automatically changes its state from checked to unchecked
or from unchecked to checked. You can determine the current state of the check
box at any time by connecting a member variable to the check box control and
using the GetCheck() method. Like radio buttons, check boxes are derived from
the CButton class, so you can use the CButton methods with check boxes. The
methods of the CButton class appear in Table 7.1.

TIP   Besides using GetCheck() to determine a check box's state, you can use
SetCheck() to set its state.

T A B L E   7 . 1 : The CButton Class Methods

Method	Does This
Cbutton	Constructs a CButton object.
Create	Creates a button control and attaches it to the Cbutton object.
DrawItem	Override this method to draw an owner-drawn button.
GetBitmap	Gets the handle of the bitmap set with SetBitmap.
GetButtonStyle	Gets the button control style.
GetCheck	Gets the check state of a button control.
GetCursor	Gets the handle of the cursor image set with SetCursor.
GetIcon	Gets the handle of the icon set with SetIcon.
GetState	Gets the check state, highlight state, and focus state of a button.
SetBitmap	Specifies a bitmap to be displayed on the button.
SetButtonStyle	Changes the style of a button.
SetCheck	Sets the check state of a button.
SetCursor	Sets the cursor image to be displayed on the button.
SetIcon	Specifies the icon to be displayed on the button.
SetState	Sets the highlight state of a button.

What really distinguishes the various types of buttons from each other is their button *style*. The possible styles of buttons appear in Table 7.2.

T A B L E   7 . 2 : The CButton Class Styles

Button Style	Description
BS_3STATE	Same style as a check box, but the box can be dimmed as well as checked.
BS_AUTO3STATE	Same style as a three-state check box, but the box changes state when the user selects it.
BS_AUTOCHECKBOX	Identical to a check box, but a check mark appears in the check box when the user selects the box.
BS_AUTORADIOBUTTON	Identical to a radio button, but when the user selects it, automatically highlights itself and de-selects any other radio button.

Skill 7

TABLE 7.2 CONTINUED: The CButton Class Styles

Button Style	Description
BS_CHECKBOX	Creates a small square button that has text displayed to its right.
BS_DEFPUSHBUTTON	Creates a button that has a heavy black border.
BS_GROUPBOX	Creates a rectangle in which other buttons can be grouped.
BS_LEFTTEXT	Makes text appear on the left side of the button.
BS_OWNERDRAW	Creates an owner-drawn button.
BS_PUSHBUTTON	Creates a pushbutton that posts a WM_COMMAND message to the owner window when the user selects the button.
BS_RADIOBUTTON	Creates a small circular button that has text displayed to its right.

When the user clicks check box 1, we will simply display the string "Check 1 clicked" this way in the text box:

```
    void CChecksDlg::OnCheck1()
    {
→       m_text = "Check 1 clicked";
→       UpdateData(false);
    }
```

And we display a similar string for check box 2 and check box 3:

```
    void CChecksDlg::OnCheck2()
    {
        m_text = "Check 2 clicked";
        UpdateData(false);
    }

    void CChecksDlg::OnCheck3()
    {
        m_text = "Check 3 clicked";
        UpdateData(false);

    }
```

That is all we need; run the program now, as shown in Figure 7.6. As you can see there, we report which check box was clicked when the user clicks one. Now we're able to use check boxes!

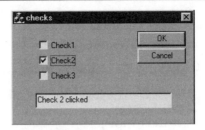

FIGURE 7.6: Our checks program at work

The code for this program appears in checksDlg.h/checksDlg.cpp.

checksDlg.h and *checksDlg.cpp*

```
// checksDlg.h : header file
//

#if !defined(AFX_CHECKSDLG_H__B5C0A5FC_9307_11D0_8860_444553540000__INCLUDED_)
#define AFX_CHECKSDLG_H__B5C0A5FC_9307_11D0_8860_444553540000__INCLUDED_

#if _MSC_VER >= 1000
#pragma once
#endif // _MSC_VER >= 1000


/////////////////////////////////////////////////////////////////////////
// CChecksDlg dialog

class CChecksDlg : public CDialog
{
// Construction
public:
    CChecksDlg(CWnd* pParent = NULL);      // standard constructor

// Dialog Data
    //{{AFX_DATA(CChecksDlg)
    enum { IDD = IDD_CHECKS_DIALOG };
    CString     m_text;
    //}}AFX_DATA

    // ClassWizard generated virtual function overrides
    //{{AFX_VIRTUAL(CChecksDlg)
    protected:
```

```
        virtual void DoDataExchange(CDataExchange* pDX);       // DDX/DDV support
        //}}AFX_VIRTUAL

// Implementation
protected:
        HICON m_hIcon;

        // Generated message map functions
        //{{AFX_MSG(CChecksDlg)
        virtual BOOL OnInitDialog();
        afx_msg void OnSysCommand(UINT nID, LPARAM lParam);
        afx_msg void OnPaint();
        afx_msg HCURSOR OnQueryDragIcon();
        afx_msg void OnCheck1();
        afx_msg void OnCheck2();
        afx_msg void OnCheck3();
        //}}AFX_MSG
        DECLARE_MESSAGE_MAP()
};

//{{AFX_INSERT_LOCATION}}
// Microsoft Developer Studio will insert additional declarations immediately
// before the previous line.

#endif // !defined(AFX_CHECKSDLG_H__B5C0A5FC_9307_11D0_8860_444553540000__
➥INCLUDED_)




// checksDlg.cpp : implementation file
//

#include "stdafx.h"
#include "checks.h"
#include "checksDlg.h"

#ifdef _DEBUG
#define new DEBUG_NEW
#undef THIS_FILE
static char THIS_FILE[] = __FILE__;
#endif

/////////////////////////////////////////////////////////////////////////////
// CAboutDlg dialog used for App About

class CAboutDlg : public CDialog
{
```

```
public:
    CAboutDlg();

// Dialog Data
    //{{AFX_DATA(CAboutDlg)
    enum { IDD = IDD_ABOUTBOX };
    //}}AFX_DATA

    // ClassWizard generated virtual function overrides
    //{{AFX_VIRTUAL(CAboutDlg)
    protected:
    virtual void DoDataExchange(CDataExchange* pDX);      // DDX/DDV support
    //}}AFX_VIRTUAL

// Implementation
protected:
    //{{AFX_MSG(CAboutDlg)
    //}}AFX_MSG
    DECLARE_MESSAGE_MAP()
};

CAboutDlg::CAboutDlg() : CDialog(CAboutDlg::IDD)
{
    //{{AFX_DATA_INIT(CAboutDlg)
    //}}AFX_DATA_INIT
}

void CAboutDlg::DoDataExchange(CDataExchange* pDX)
{
    CDialog::DoDataExchange(pDX);
    //{{AFX_DATA_MAP(CAboutDlg)
    //}}AFX_DATA_MAP
}

BEGIN_MESSAGE_MAP(CAboutDlg, CDialog)
    //{{AFX_MSG_MAP(CAboutDlg)
        // No message handlers
    //}}AFX_MSG_MAP
END_MESSAGE_MAP()

/////////////////////////////////////////////////////////////////////////////
// CChecksDlg dialog

CChecksDlg::CChecksDlg(CWnd* pParent /*=NULL*/)
    : CDialog(CChecksDlg::IDD, pParent)
{
    //{{AFX_DATA_INIT(CChecksDlg)
    m_text = _T("");
```

Skill 7

```
    //}}AFX_DATA_INIT
    // Note that LoadIcon does not require a subsequent DestroyIcon in Win32
    m_hIcon = AfxGetApp()->LoadIcon(IDR_MAINFRAME);
}

void CChecksDlg::DoDataExchange(CDataExchange* pDX)
{
    CDialog::DoDataExchange(pDX);
    //{{AFX_DATA_MAP(CChecksDlg)
    DDX_Text(pDX, IDC_EDIT1, m_text);
    //}}AFX_DATA_MAP
}

BEGIN_MESSAGE_MAP(CChecksDlg, CDialog)
    //{{AFX_MSG_MAP(CChecksDlg)
    ON_WM_SYSCOMMAND()
    ON_WM_PAINT()
    ON_WM_QUERYDRAGICON()
    ON_BN_CLICKED(IDC_CHECK1, OnCheck1)
    ON_BN_CLICKED(IDC_CHECK2, OnCheck2)
    ON_BN_CLICKED(IDC_CHECK3, OnCheck3)
    //}}AFX_MSG_MAP
END_MESSAGE_MAP()

/////////////////////////////////////////////////////////////////////////////
// CChecksDlg message handlers

BOOL CChecksDlg::OnInitDialog()
{
    CDialog::OnInitDialog();

    // Add "About..." menu item to system menu.

    // IDM_ABOUTBOX must be in the system command range.
    ASSERT((IDM_ABOUTBOX & 0xFFF0) == IDM_ABOUTBOX);
    ASSERT(IDM_ABOUTBOX < 0xF000);

    CMenu* pSysMenu = GetSystemMenu(FALSE);
    if (pSysMenu != NULL)
    {
        CString strAboutMenu;
        strAboutMenu.LoadString(IDS_ABOUTBOX);
        if (!strAboutMenu.IsEmpty())
        {
            pSysMenu->AppendMenu(MF_SEPARATOR);
            pSysMenu->AppendMenu(MF_STRING, IDM_ABOUTBOX, strAboutMenu);
        }
    }
```

```
        // Set the icon for this dialog.  The framework does this automatically
        //  when the application's main window is not a dialog
        SetIcon(m_hIcon, TRUE);                  // Set big icon
        SetIcon(m_hIcon, FALSE);              // Set small icon

        // TODO: Add extra initialization here

        return TRUE;   // return TRUE  unless you set the focus to a control
}

void CChecksDlg::OnSysCommand(UINT nID, LPARAM lParam)
{
        if ((nID & 0xFFF0) == IDM_ABOUTBOX)
        {
                CAboutDlg dlgAbout;
                dlgAbout.DoModal();
        }
        else
        {
                CDialog::OnSysCommand(nID, lParam);
        }
}

// If you add a minimize button to your dialog, you will need the code below
//  to draw the icon.  For MFC applications using the document/view model,
//  this is automatically done for you by the framework.

void CChecksDlg::OnPaint()
{
        if (IsIconic())
        {
                CPaintDC dc(this); // device context for painting

                SendMessage(WM_ICONERASEBKGND, (WPARAM) dc.GetSafeHdc(), 0);

                // Center icon in client rectangle
                int cxIcon = GetSystemMetrics(SM_CXICON);
                int cyIcon = GetSystemMetrics(SM_CYICON);
                CRect rect;
                GetClientRect(&rect);
                int x = (rect.Width() - cxIcon + 1) / 2;
                int y = (rect.Height() - cyIcon + 1) / 2;

                // Draw the icon
                dc.DrawIcon(x, y, m_hIcon);
        }
        else
        {
```

Skill 7

```
            CDialog::OnPaint();
        }
}

// The system calls this to obtain the cursor to display while the user drags
//   the minimized window.
HCURSOR CChecksDlg::OnQueryDragIcon()
{
        return (HCURSOR) m_hIcon;
}

void CChecksDlg::OnCheck1()
{
        // TODO: Add your control notification handler code here
        m_text = "Check 1 clicked";
        UpdateData(false);
}

void CChecksDlg::OnCheck2()
{
        // TODO: Add your control notification handler code here
        m_text = "Check 2 clicked";
        UpdateData(false);
}

void CChecksDlg::OnCheck3()
{
        // TODO: Add your control notification handler code here
        m_text = "Check 3 clicked";
        UpdateData(false);

}
```

The user can, in fact, click several check boxes in the checks program, and there can be as many as three checked check boxes showing at once. That's not appropriate for all programs—sometimes, you only want to let the user select one option, not multiple options. And that's what radio buttons are all about.

Working with Radio Buttons

In our radio button example, named radios, we'll have three radio buttons arranged vertically, as illustrated in the following graphic.

```
-----------------------------------------------------------
|radios                                                    |
|---------------------------------------------------------|
|                                        -----------       |
|    ( )  Radio 1                       |     OK     |      |
|                                        -----------       |
|                                                          |
|                                        -----------       |
|    ( )  Radio 2                       |   Cancel   |      |
|                                        -----------       |
|                                                          |
|                                                          |
|    ( )  Radio 3                                          |
|                                                          |
|       --------------------------------------------       |
|    |                                               |  |
|       --------------------------------------------       |
|                                                          |
-----------------------------------------------------------
```

When the user clicks one of the radio buttons, we'll indicate which button was clicked with a message in a text box:

```
-----------------------------------------------------------
|radios                                                    |
|---------------------------------------------------------|
|                                        -----------       |
|    ( )  Radio 1                       |     OK     |      |
|                                        -----------       |
|                                                          |
|                                        -----------       |
|    (*)  Radio 2                       |   Cancel   |      |
|                                        -----------       |
|                                                          |
|                                                          |
|    ( )  Radio 3                                          |
|                                                          |
|       --------------------------------------------       |
|    |Radio 2 clicked                                |  |
|       --------------------------------------------       |
|                                                          |
-----------------------------------------------------------
```

Besides using a different type of control, this example is different from the previous example because only one radio button at a time can appear clicked in this instance. In the checks example, any of the check boxes could appear checked independent of the others, but in the radios example, all buttons are coordinated.

Create this new, dialog-based example now using AppWizard, naming it radios. Open the dialog box for our main window, ID = IDD_RADIOS_DIALOG, as shown in Figure 7.7.

We place a text box in the main window, as shown in Figure 7.7, and we also add three radio buttons, Radio1, Radio2, and Radio3 to the main window, as shown in Figure 7.7 (the radio button tool is the fourth tool down on the right; as with check boxes, the dialog editor gives the radio buttons these captions, but you can change them as you like).

In addition, align the three radio buttons vertically and horizontally as we did for the check boxes in the checks program. Now open ClassWizard and find the three radio buttons: IDC_RADIO1, IDC_RADIO2, and IDC_RADIO3, and connect the event-handlers to each of these new controls, OnRadio1(), OnRadio2(), and OnRadio3(). Finally, connect a new member variable, m_text, to the text in the text box.

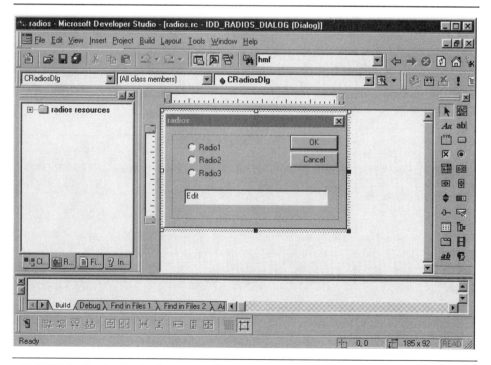

FIGURE 7.7: Designing our radios program

Connecting Radio Buttons to Code

Now open OnRadio1():

```
void CRadiosDlg::OnRadio1()
{
        // TODO: Add your control notification handler code here
}
```

This is the event-handler that is called when the user clicks radio button 1. Here, we just report the user's action in the text box with the message "Radio 1 clicked." this way:

```
void CRadiosDlg::OnRadio1()
{
→       m_text = "Radio 1 clicked.";
→       UpdateData(false);
}
```

Coordinating Radio Buttons

Note that we make no other provisions here for de-selecting the other radio buttons when the user clicks this radio button. That's because the three radio buttons *already* function as a group automatically—they are all in the same window, so they are already coordinated. When the user clicks one of our radio buttons, the program de-selects the other automatically, because they all share the same window. If we used group boxes, as we will in the next example, we could break down our radio button groupings still further, as only one radio button in a group box will appear checked at any one time.

At this point, we can add code for the second and third radio buttons as well:

```
void CRadiosDlg::OnRadio2()
{
    m_text = "Radio 2 clicked.";
    UpdateData(false);

}

void CRadiosDlg::OnRadio3()
{
    m_text = "Radio 3 clicked.";
    UpdateData(false);

}
```

Now the radios program is ready to go. Run it, as shown in Figure 7.8, and click a button. The program reports which button you clicked, as shown in Figure 7.8.

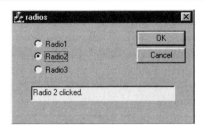

FIGURE 7.8: Our radios program at work

You can click other radio buttons as well, but no matter how many you click, only the most recently clicked radio button stays clicked, displaying the dot in its center. Now we're using radio buttons in Visual C++!

 TIP   To get or set the state of a radio button in code, you can use the `GetState()` and `SetState()` methods.

The code for this program appears in `radiosDlg.h/radiosDlg.cpp`.

radiosDlg.h and *radiosDlg.cpp*

```
// radiosDlg.h : header file
//

#if !defined(AFX_RADIOSDLG_H__ED674067_9309_11D0_8860_444553540000__INCLUDED_)
#define AFX_RADIOSDLG_H__ED674067_9309_11D0_8860_444553540000__INCLUDED_

#if _MSC_VER >= 1000
#pragma once
#endif // _MSC_VER >= 1000


/////////////////////////////////////////////////////////////////////////////
// CRadiosDlg dialog

class CRadiosDlg : public CDialog
{
// Construction
public:
    CRadiosDlg(CWnd* pParent = NULL);     // standard constructor

// Dialog Data
    //{{AFX_DATA(CRadiosDlg)
    enum { IDD = IDD_RADIOS_DIALOG };
```

```
        CString      m_text;
        //}}AFX_DATA

        // ClassWizard generated virtual function overrides
        //{{AFX_VIRTUAL(CRadiosDlg)
        protected:
        virtual void DoDataExchange(CDataExchange* pDX);        // DDX/DDV support
        //}}AFX_VIRTUAL

// Implementation
protected:
        HICON m_hIcon;

        // Generated message map functions
        //{{AFX_MSG(CRadiosDlg)
        virtual BOOL OnInitDialog();
        afx_msg void OnSysCommand(UINT nID, LPARAM lParam);
        afx_msg void OnPaint();
        afx_msg HCURSOR OnQueryDragIcon();
        afx_msg void OnRadio1();
        afx_msg void OnRadio2();
        afx_msg void OnRadio3();
        //}}AFX_MSG
        DECLARE_MESSAGE_MAP()
};

//{{AFX_INSERT_LOCATION}}
// Microsoft Developer Studio will insert additional declarations immediately
// before the previous line.

#endif // !defined(AFX_RADIOSDLG_H__ED674067_9309_11D0_8860_444553540000__
➡INCLUDED_)




// radiosDlg.cpp : implementation file
//

#include "stdafx.h"
#include "radios.h"
#include "radiosDlg.h"

#ifdef _DEBUG
#define new DEBUG_NEW
#undef THIS_FILE
static char THIS_FILE[] = __FILE__;
#endif

/////////////////////////////////////////////////////////////////////////////
// CAboutDlg dialog used for App About
```

```
class CAboutDlg : public CDialog
{
public:
    CAboutDlg();

// Dialog Data
    //{{AFX_DATA(CAboutDlg)
    enum { IDD = IDD_ABOUTBOX };
    //}}AFX_DATA

    // ClassWizard generated virtual function overrides
    //{{AFX_VIRIUAL(CAboutDlg)
    protected:
    virtual void DoDataExchange(CDataExchange* pDX);    // DDX/DDV support
    //}}AFX_VIRTUAL

// Implementation
protected:
    //{{AFX_MSG(CAboutDlg)
    //}}AFX_MSG
    DECLARE_MESSAGE_MAP()
};

CAboutDlg::CAboutDlg() : CDialog(CAboutDlg::IDD)
{
    //{{AFX_DATA_INIT(CAboutDlg)
    //}}AFX_DATA_INIT
}

void CAboutDlg::DoDataExchange(CDataExchange* pDX)
{
    CDialog::DoDataExchange(pDX);
    //{{AFX_DATA_MAP(CAboutDlg)
    //}}AFX_DATA_MAP
}

BEGIN_MESSAGE_MAP(CAboutDlg, CDialog)
    //{{AFX_MSG_MAP(CAboutDlg)
        // No message handlers
    //}}AFX_MSG_MAP
END_MESSAGE_MAP()

/////////////////////////////////////////////////////////////////////////
// CRadiosDlg dialog

CRadiosDlg::CRadiosDlg(CWnd* pParent /*=NULL*/)
    : CDialog(CRadiosDlg::IDD, pParent)
{
    //{{AFX_DATA_INIT(CRadiosDlg)
```

```
        m_text = _T("");
        //}}AFX_DATA_INIT
        // Note that LoadIcon does not require a subsequent DestroyIcon in Win32
        m_hIcon = AfxGetApp()->LoadIcon(IDR_MAINFRAME);
}

void CRadiosDlg::DoDataExchange(CDataExchange* pDX)
{
        CDialog::DoDataExchange(pDX);
        //{{AFX_DATA_MAP(CRadiosDlg)
        DDX_Text(pDX, IDC_EDIT1, m_text);
        //}}AFX_DATA_MAP
}

BEGIN_MESSAGE_MAP(CRadiosDlg, CDialog)
        //{{AFX_MSG_MAP(CRadiosDlg)
        ON_WM_SYSCOMMAND()
        ON_WM_PAINT()
        ON_WM_QUERYDRAGICON()
        ON_BN_CLICKED(IDC_RADIO1, OnRadio1)
        ON_BN_CLICKED(IDC_RADIO2, OnRadio2)
        ON_BN_CLICKED(IDC_RADIO3, OnRadio3)
        //}}AFX_MSG_MAP
END_MESSAGE_MAP()

/////////////////////////////////////////////////////////////////////////////
// CRadiosDlg message handlers

BOOL CRadiosDlg::OnInitDialog()
{
        CDialog::OnInitDialog();

        // Add "About..." menu item to system menu.

        // IDM_ABOUTBOX must be in the system command range.
        ASSERT((IDM_ABOUTBOX & 0xFFF0) == IDM_ABOUTBOX);
        ASSERT(IDM_ABOUTBOX < 0xF000);

        CMenu* pSysMenu = GetSystemMenu(FALSE);
        if (pSysMenu != NULL)
        {
                CString strAboutMenu;
                strAboutMenu.LoadString(IDS_ABOUTBOX);
                if (!strAboutMenu.IsEmpty())
                {
                        pSysMenu->AppendMenu(MF_SEPARATOR);
                        pSysMenu->AppendMenu(MF_STRING, IDM_ABOUTBOX, strAboutMenu);
                }
        }
```

```
        // Set the icon for this dialog.  The framework does this automatically
        //  when the application's main window is not a dialog
        SetIcon(m_hIcon, TRUE);                 // Set big icon
        SetIcon(m_hIcon, FALSE);            // Set small icon

        // TODO: Add extra initialization here

        return TRUE;  // return TRUE  unless you set the focus to a control
}

void CRadiosDlg::OnSysCommand(UINT nID, LPARAM lParam)
{
        if ((nID & 0xFFF0) == IDM_ABOUTBOX)
        {
                CAboutDlg dlgAbout;
                dlgAbout.DoModal();
        }
        else
        {
                CDialog::OnSysCommand(nID, lParam);
        }
}

// If you add a minimize button to your dialog, you will need the code below
//  to draw the icon.  For MFC applications using the document/view model,
//  this is automatically done for you by the framework.

void CRadiosDlg::OnPaint()
{
        if (IsIconic())
        {
                CPaintDC dc(this); // device context for painting

                SendMessage(WM_ICONERASEBKGND, (WPARAM) dc.GetSafeHdc(), 0);

                // Center icon in client rectangle
                int cxIcon = GetSystemMetrics(SM_CXICON);
                int cyIcon = GetSystemMetrics(SM_CYICON);
                CRect rect;
                GetClientRect(&rect);
                int x = (rect.Width() - cxIcon + 1) / 2;
                int y = (rect.Height() - cyIcon + 1) / 2;

                // Draw the icon
                dc.DrawIcon(x, y, m_hIcon);
        }
        else
        {
                CDialog::OnPaint();
```

```
        }
}

// The system calls this to obtain the cursor to display while the user drags
//   the minimized window.
HCURSOR CRadiosDlg::OnQueryDragIcon()
{
        return (HCURSOR) m_hIcon;
}

void CRadiosDlg::OnRadio1()
{
        // TODO: Add your control notification handler code here
        m_text = "Radio 1 clicked.";
        UpdateData(false);
}

void CRadiosDlg::OnRadio2()
{
        // TODO: Add your control notification handler code here
        m_text = "Radio 2 clicked.";
        UpdateData(false);

}

void CRadiosDlg::OnRadio3()
{
        // TODO: Add your control notification handler code here
        m_text = "Radio 3 clicked.";
        UpdateData(false);

}
```

At this point, then, we've seen how to use both check boxes and radio buttons, but we haven't seen them working together yet. Because of their unique capabilities—check boxes display options and radio buttons display exclusive (i.e., "select one only") options, these controls often work well together, and we'll see an example of that next.

Putting Check Boxes and Radio Buttons Together

In this next example, we can imagine that we've been commissioned to write a program for a flower shop, listing the various arrangements they have for sale and the flowers in each of them.

```
 ----------------------------------------------------------
|seller                                                    |
|----------------------------------------------------------|
|                                                          |
|   --Arrangement-    ----Flowers-----                     |
|  |              |  | |                |                  |
|  |              |  | | -              |   ------------    |
|  |  ( ) Type 1  |  | | | Roses        |  |    OK      |  |
|  |              |  | | -              |   ------------    |
|  |              |  | | -              |   ------------    |
|  |  ( ) Type 2  |  | | | Lilies       |  |   Cancel   |  |
|  |              |  | | -              |   ------------    |
|  |              |  | | -              |                   |
|  |  ( ) Type 3  |  | | | Carnations   |   ------------    |
|  |              |  | | -              |  |            |  |
|  |              |  | | -              |   ------------    |
|  |  ( ) Type 4  |  | | | Petunias     |                   |
|  |              |  | | -              |                   |
|   --------------    --------------                       |
|                                                          |
 ----------------------------------------------------------
```

When the user clicks a radio button corresponding to a particular arrangement, the program is supposed to check the various check boxes corresponding to the flowers in that arrangement, and indicate the arrangement's price in a text box:

```
 ----------------------------------------------------------
|seller                                                    |
|----------------------------------------------------------|
|                                                          |
|   --Arrangement-    ----Flowers-----                     |
|  |              |  | |                |                  |
|  |              |  | | -              |   ------------    |
|  |  (*) Type 1  |  | |v| Roses        |  |    OK      |  |
|  |              |  | | -              |   ------------    |
|  |              |  | | -              |   ------------    |
|  |  ( ) Type 2  |  | |v| Lilies       |  |   Cancel   |  |
|  |              |  | | -              |   ------------    |
|  |              |  | | -              |                   |
|  |  ( ) Type 3  |  | |v| Carnations   |   ------------    |
|  |              |  | | -              |  |Price: $4.95 |  |
|  |              |  | | -              |   ------------    |
|  |  ( ) Type 4  |  | |v| Petunias     |                   |
|  |              |  | | -              |                   |
|   --------------    --------------                       |
|                                                          |
 ----------------------------------------------------------
```

When the user clicks another radio button, the program should indicate the flowers in the new arrangement type, and give that arrangement's price:

```
 ----------------------------------------------------------
|seller                                                    |
| -------------------------------------------------------- |
|                                                          |
|   --Arrangement-    ----Flowers-----                     |
|  |              |  | -              |    ------------     |
|  |  ( )  Type 1 |  ||v|  Roses      |   |     OK     |    |
|  |              |  | -              |    ------------     |
|  |              |  | -              |    ------------     |
|  |  (*)  Type 2 |  || |  Lilies     |   |   Cancel   |    |
|  |              |  | -              |    ------------     |
|  |              |  | -              |    ------------     |
|  |  ( )  Type 3 |  ||v|  Carnations |   ------------      |
|  |              |  | -              |  |Price: $3.95 |     |
|  |              |  | -              |   ------------       |
|  |  ( )  Type 4 |  || |  Petunias   |                     |
|  |              |  | -              |                     |
|   --------------    ---------------                       |
|                                                          |
 ----------------------------------------------------------
```

In this way, we combine the exclusive nature of radio buttons with the nonexclusive nature of check boxes. Let's create this program now.

We'll call this program "seller". Create it now using AppWizard, making it a dialog-based application, and open the dialog for our main window now, IDD_SELLER_DIALOG in the dialog editor, as shown in Figure 7.9.

After deleting the TODO label, we will add two group boxes.

Using Group Boxes

Group boxes arrange controls both visually, and functionally. In particular, the radio buttons in the same group box function in concert, so you can arrange various independent groups of radio buttons in your program. To add two group boxes to our seller program, simply drag them from the dialog editor's toolbox (the group box tool is the third tool down on the left), as shown in Figure 7.10.

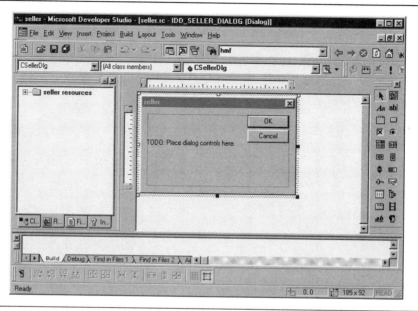

FIGURE 7.9:   Designing our seller program

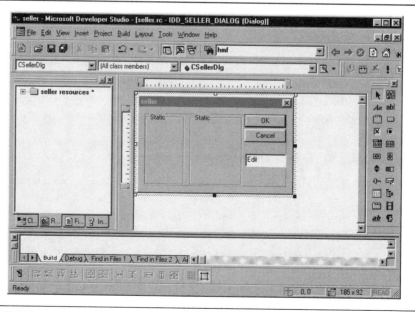

FIGURE 7.10:   Adding group boxes to our seller program

The dialog editor gives these new group boxes the caption "Static", but we can change that. To give a group box a new caption, just right click the group box in the dialog editor, select Properties in the pop-up menu, and type in the new caption in the Properties box that opens. In this case, we'll give the left group box the caption Arrangement, and the right group box the caption Flowers, as shown in Figure 7.11.

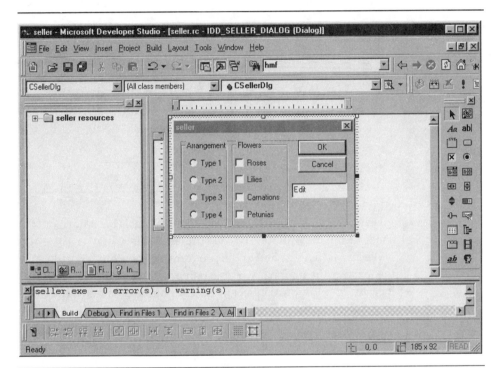

FIGURE 7.11: Customizing the group boxes in our seller program

We want the user to be able to select a flower arrangement using radio buttons, and indicate which flowers are in each arrangement with check boxes, so we add four option buttons to the Arrangement group and four check boxes to the Flowers group, as shown in Figure 7.11, giving each of these controls the appropriate captions.

```
-------------------------------------------------------------------
|seller                                                            |
|-----------------------------------------------------------------|
|                                                                  |
|   --Arrangement-     ----Flowers-----                            |
|  |              |   | |          -      |                        |
|  |              |   | |   _      |     ------------              |
|  |  ( )  Type 1 |   | | | Roses  |    |     OK     |             |
|  |              |   | |   _      |     ------------              |
|  |              |   | |   _      |     ------------              |
|  |  ( )  Type 2 |   | | | Lilies |    |   Cancel   |             |
|  |              |   | |   _      |     ------------              |
|  |              |   | |   _      |                               |
|  |  ( )  Type 3 |   | | | Carnations |  ------------             |
|  |              |   | |   _      |    |            |             |
|  |              |   | |   _      |     ------------              |
|  |  ( )  Type 4 |   | | | Petunias|                              |
|  |              |   | |   _      |                               |
|   --------------     ----------------                            |
|                                                                  |
-------------------------------------------------------------------
```

Using the dialog editor, arrange these controls both horizontally and vertically, as we did in the previous two examples in this skill.

We also add a text box to the program, as shown in Figure 7.11. Give the text in the text box the member variable name m_text with ClassWizard so we may reach it easily. In addition, connect the event-handlers OnRadio1() to OnRadio4() to the four radio buttons using ClassWizard and open OnRadio1():

```
void CSellerDlg::OnRadio1()
{
    // TODO: Add your control notification handler code here
}
```

At this point, we want to place checks in the check boxes; let's say clicking the first radio button causes all check boxes to appear checked. But how do we reach the check boxes?

Adding Member Variables to Check Box Controls

We can add member variables for the check boxes using ClassWizard, and then refer to the check boxes using those variables. As discussed earlier, you can add two different categories of member variables: those that represent properties of a

control, and those that represent the control itself. In this case, we want the first
kind, those member variables that represent the control's properties.

Start ClassWizard now, and select the Member Variables tab. Now click the
first check box, IDC_CHECK1, and click the Add Variable button. This opens the
Add Member Variable box, as shown in Figure 7.12.

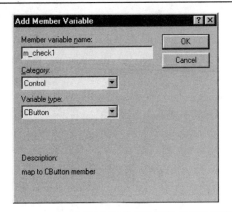

FIGURE 7.12: Adding a check box member variable

Give this new variable the name m_check1, and make sure you select the
Control option in the Category combo box. Then click OK and do the same for the
other three check boxes, giving them the variables m_check2 to m_check4. At this
point, all of our check boxes have member variables, as indicated in ClassWizard
in Figure 7.13.

All that's left is to set the state of the various check boxes in the radio button's
click event-handlers. We do that like this in OnRadio1():

```
void CSellerDlg::OnRadio1()
{
    m_check1 = true;              <
    m_check2 = true;              <
    m_check3 = true;              <
    m_check4 = true;              <
            .
            .
            .
}
```

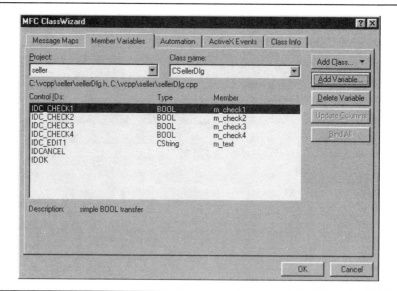

FIGURE 7.13: All our check boxes have member variables.

Then we place the price of the arrangement in the text box and call
`UpdateData()`:

```
void CSellerDlg::OnRadio1()
{
    m_check1 = true;
    m_check2 = true;
    m_check3 = true;
    m_check4 = true;
    m_text = "Price: $4.95";
    UpdateData(false);
}
```

We can do the same for the other three radio buttons as well, setting up other
flower arrangements:

```
void CSellerDlg::OnRadio2()
{
    m_check1 = true;
    m_check2 = false;
    m_check3 = true;
    m_check4 = false;
    m_text = "Price: $3.95";
```

```
        UpdateData(false);
}

void CSellerDlg::OnRadio3()
{
        m_check1 = false;
        m_check2 = true;
        m_check3 = false;
        m_check4 = true;
        m_text = "Price: $2.95";
        UpdateData(false);
}

void CSellerDlg::OnRadio4()
{
        m_check1 = false;
        m_check2 = false;
        m_check3 = false;
        m_check4 = false;
        m_text = "Price: $0.00";
        UpdateData(false);
}
```

Our seller program is ready to run now. We've set up our two group boxes, filled them with radio buttons and check boxes, and connected those controls in our code. All that remains is to run the program, so run it now, as shown in Figure 7.14.

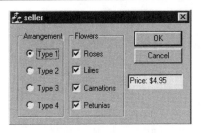

FIGURE 7.14: Our seller program lets the user see what flower arrangements are for sale.

When the user clicks a radio button, we indicate what flowers are in that arrangement, as shown in Figure 7.14 (note the check boxes, which indicate the flower types in the arrangement). When the user clicks another radio button for another flower arrangement, we display the flower types in that arrangement as well, as shown in Figure 7.15. Our seller program is a success—now we're using both check boxes and radio buttons at the same time.

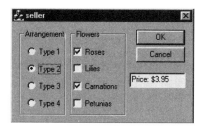

FIGURE 7.15: Selecting a different flower arrangement in seller

The code for this program appears in `sellerDlg.h/sellerDlg.cpp`.

sellerDlg.h and sellerDlg.cpp

```
// sellerDlg.h : header file
//

#if !defined(AFX_SELLERDLG_H__1FA88027_9477_11D0_8860_444553540000__INCLUDED_)
#define AFX_SELLERDLG_H__1FA88027_9477_11D0_8860_444553540000__INCLUDED_

#if _MSC_VER >= 1000
#pragma once
#endif // _MSC_VER >= 1000


/////////////////////////////////////////////////////////////////////////////
// CSellerDlg dialog

class CSellerDlg : public CDialog
{
// Construction
public:
        CSellerDlg(CWnd* pParent = NULL);    // standard constructor

// Dialog Data
        //{{AFX_DATA(CSellerDlg)
        enum { IDD = IDD_SELLER_DIALOG };
        BOOL    m_check1;
        BOOL    m_check2;
        BOOL    m_check3;
        BOOL    m_check4;
        CString m_text;
        //}}AFX_DATA
```

```
        // ClassWizard generated virtual function overrides
        //{{AFX_VIRTUAL(CSellerDlg)
        protected:
        virtual void DoDataExchange(CDataExchange* pDX);      // DDX/DDV support
        //}}AFX_VIRTUAL

// Implementation
protected:
        HICON m_hIcon;

        // Generated message map functions
        //{{AFX_MSG(CSellerDlg)
        virtual BOOL OnInitDialog();
        afx_msg void OnSysCommand(UINT nID, LPARAM lParam);
        afx_msg void OnPaint();
        afx_msg HCURSOR OnQueryDragIcon();
        afx_msg void OnRadio1();
        afx_msg void OnRadio2();
        afx_msg void OnRadio3();
        afx_msg void OnRadio4();
        //}}AFX_MSG
        DECLARE_MESSAGE_MAP()
};

//{{AFX_INSERT_LOCATION}}
// Microsoft Developer Studio will insert additional declarations
immediately before the previous line.

#endif //
!defined(AFX_SELLERDLG_H__1FA88027_9477_11D0_8860_444553540000__INCLUDED_)

// sellerDlg.cpp : implementation file
//

#include "stdafx.h"
#include "seller.h"
#include "sellerDlg.h"

#ifdef _DEBUG
#define new DEBUG_NEW
#undef THIS_FILE
static char THIS_FILE[] = __FILE__;
#endif

/////////////////////////////////////////////////////////////////////////////
// CAboutDlg dialog used for App About

class CAboutDlg : public CDialog
{
public:
```

```
        CAboutDlg();

// Dialog Data
    //{{AFX_DATA(CAboutDlg)
    enum { IDD = IDD_ABOUTBOX };
    //}}AFX_DATA

    // ClassWizard generated virtual function overrides
    //{{AFX_VIRTUAL(CAboutDlg)
    protected:
    virtual void DoDataExchange(CDataExchange* pDX);     // DDX/DDV support
    //}}AFX_VIRTUAL

// Implementation
protected:
    //{{AFX_MSG(CAboutDlg)
    //}}AFX_MSG
    DECLARE_MESSAGE_MAP()
};

CAboutDlg::CAboutDlg() : CDialog(CAboutDlg::IDD)
{
    //{{AFX_DATA_INIT(CAboutDlg)
    //}}AFX_DATA_INIT
}

void CAboutDlg::DoDataExchange(CDataExchange* pDX)
{
    CDialog::DoDataExchange(pDX);
    //{{AFX_DATA_MAP(CAboutDlg)
    //}}AFX_DATA_MAP
}

BEGIN_MESSAGE_MAP(CAboutDlg, CDialog)
    //{{AFX_MSG_MAP(CAboutDlg)
        // No message handlers
    //}}AFX_MSG_MAP
END_MESSAGE_MAP()

//////////////////////////////////////////////////////////////////////
// CSellerDlg dialog

CSellerDlg::CSellerDlg(CWnd* pParent /*=NULL*/)
    : CDialog(CSellerDlg::IDD, pParent)
{
    //{{AFX_DATA_INIT(CSellerDlg)
    m_check1 = FALSE;
    m_check2 = FALSE;
```

```
    m_check3 = FALSE;
    m_check4 = FALSE;
    m_text = _T("");
    //}}AFX_DATA_INIT
    // Note that LoadIcon does not require a subsequent DestroyIcon in Win32
    m_hIcon = AfxGetApp()->LoadIcon(IDR_MAINFRAME);
}

void CSellerDlg::DoDataExchange(CDataExchange* pDX)
{
    CDialog::DoDataExchange(pDX);
    //{{AFX_DATA_MAP(CSellerDlg)
    DDX_Check(pDX, IDC_CHECK1, m_check1);
    DDX_Check(pDX, IDC_CHECK2, m_check2);
    DDX_Check(pDX, IDC_CHECK3, m_check3);
    DDX_Check(pDX, IDC_CHECK4, m_check4);
    DDX_Text(pDX, IDC_EDIT1, m_text);
    //}}AFX_DATA_MAP
}

BEGIN_MESSAGE_MAP(CSellerDlg, CDialog)
    //{{AFX_MSG_MAP(CSellerDlg)
    ON_WM_SYSCOMMAND()
    ON_WM_PAINT()
    ON_WM_QUERYDRAGICON()
    ON_BN_CLICKED(IDC_RADIO1, OnRadio1)
    ON_BN_CLICKED(IDC_RADIO2, OnRadio2)
    ON_BN_CLICKED(IDC_RADIO3, OnRadio3)
    ON_BN_CLICKED(IDC_RADIO4, OnRadio4)
    //}}AFX_MSG_MAP
END_MESSAGE_MAP()

/////////////////////////////////////////////////////////////////////////
// CSellerDlg message handlers

BOOL CSellerDlg::OnInitDialog()
{
    CDialog::OnInitDialog();

    // Add "About..." menu item to system menu.

    // IDM_ABOUTBOX must be in the system command range.
    ASSERT((IDM_ABOUTBOX & 0xFFF0) == IDM_ABOUTBOX);
    ASSERT(IDM_ABOUTBOX < 0xF000);

    CMenu* pSysMenu = GetSystemMenu(FALSE);
    if (pSysMenu != NULL)
    {
```

Skill 7

```
            CString strAboutMenu;
            strAboutMenu.LoadString(IDS_ABOUTBOX);
            if (!strAboutMenu.IsEmpty())
            {
                pSysMenu->AppendMenu(MF_SEPARATOR);
                pSysMenu->AppendMenu(MF_STRING, IDM_ABOUTBOX, strAboutMenu);
            }
      }

      // Set the icon for this dialog.  The framework does this automatically
      //  when the application's main window is not a dialog
      SetIcon(m_hIcon, TRUE);                  // Set big icon
      SetIcon(m_hIcon, FALSE);                 // Set small icon

      // TODO: Add extra initialization here

      return TRUE;   // return TRUE  unless you set the focus to a control
}

void CSellerDlg::OnSysCommand(UINT nID, LPARAM lParam)
{
      if ((nID & 0xFFF0) == IDM_ABOUTBOX)
      {
            CAboutDlg dlgAbout;
            dlgAbout.DoModal();
      }
      else
      {
            CDialog::OnSysCommand(nID, lParam);
      }
}

// If you add a minimize button to your dialog, you will need the code below
//  to draw the icon.  For MFC applications using the document/view model,
//  this is automatically done for you by the framework.

void CSellerDlg::OnPaint()
{
      if (IsIconic())
      {
            CPaintDC dc(this); // device context for painting

            SendMessage(WM_ICONERASEBKGND, (WPARAM) dc.GetSafeHdc(), 0);

            // Center icon in client rectangle
            int cxIcon = GetSystemMetrics(SM_CXICON);
            int cyIcon = GetSystemMetrics(SM_CYICON);
            CRect rect;
```

```
        GetClientRect(&rect);
        int x = (rect.Width() - cxIcon + 1) / 2;
        int y = (rect.Height() - cyIcon + 1) / 2;

        // Draw the icon
        dc.DrawIcon(x, y, m_hIcon);
    }
    else
    {
        CDialog::OnPaint();
    }
}

// The system calls this to obtain the cursor to display while the user drags
//  the minimized window.
HCURSOR CSellerDlg::OnQueryDragIcon()
{
    return (HCURSOR) m_hIcon;
}

void CSellerDlg::OnRadio1()
{
    // TODO: Add your control notification handler code here
    m_check1 = true;
    m_check2 = true;
    m_check3 = true;
    m_check4 = true;
    m_text = "Price: $4.95";
    UpdateData(false);
}

void CSellerDlg::OnRadio2()
{
    m_check1 = true;
    m_check2 = false;
    m_check3 = true;
    m_check4 = false;
    m_text = "Price: $3.95";
    UpdateData(false);
}

void CSellerDlg::OnRadio3()
{
    m_check1 = false;
    m_check2 = true;
    m_check3 = false;
    m_check4 = true;
    m_text = "Price: $2.95";
```

Skill 7

```
        UpdateData(false);
}

void CSellerDlg::OnRadio4()
{
    m_check1 = false;
    m_check2 = false;
    m_check3 = false;
    m_check4 = false;
    m_text = "Price: $0.00";
    UpdateData(false);
}
```

That completes our skill on check boxes and radio buttons. We've seen quite a lot in this skill, including how to create and use check boxes and radio buttons, how to use them together, and how to set and get a button's state. We've also covered how to arrange controls in a dialog box and how to add and use group boxes in a dialog box. In the next skill, we'll see even more new controls: list boxes, combo boxes, and sliders.

Are You Experienced?

Now You Can...

- ☑ **Create a check box**
- ☑ **Create a radio button**
- ☑ **Align controls in a dialog box**
- ☑ **Get or set a radio button or check box's state**
- ☑ **Give button controls a member variable**
- ☑ **Use group boxes to arrange your controls**
- ☑ **Work with check boxes and radio buttons in the same program**

List Boxes, Combo Boxes, and Sliders

- ❏ **Creating List boxes**

- ❏ **Creating Combo boxes**

- ❏ **Creating Sliders**

- ❏ **Adding items to list boxes and combo boxes**

- ❏ **Handling item selections and double-clicks**

In this skill, we are going to examine three new controls: list boxes, combo boxes, and sliders. These are all popular controls that any Visual C++ programmer should be familiar with, and we'll get a guided tour of these controls, and how to use them, in this skill.

You've seen list boxes before—these controls present the user with a list of items displayed in a box. The user can click an item to highlight it, and double-click that item to select it. In our list box example, we'll see how to add a dozen new items to a list box, and how to find out which item the user selects.

Combo boxes are a combination of a text box, drop-down list box, and a button the user can press to open the list box. In this skill, we'll see how to place items in a combo box and report which item the user selects.

Sliders are relatively new controls and are popular among programmers. They present the user with a small sliding box, called a *thumb*, that the user moves along a "groove," like the controls on a stereo. We'll see how to set up and use a slider control, reporting the new slider position as the user moves the slider. We have three new controls to explore, and we'll start with list boxes.

Handling List Boxes

In our first example, we'll see how to fill a list box with a dozen items, and the list box will present these items as a list to the user. Since we'll add a dozen items to the list box, the list box won't be able to display all the items at once, so it will display a scroll-bar control on the right:

```
 --------------------------------------------------------------
|lists                                                         |
|-------------------------------------------------------------|
| Double-click an item:                                        |
|  ---------                               ----------          |
| |Item 01 |^|                            |   OK     |         |
| |Item 02 |-|                             ----------          |
| |Item 03 | |                                                 |
| |Item 04 | |                             ----------          |
| |Item 05 | |                            | Cancel   |         |
| |Item 06 | |                             ----------          |
| |Item 07 |-|           You chose:                            |
| |Item 08 |V|            ------------                          |
|  ---------            |            |                         |
|                        ------------                          |
|                                                              |
|                                                              |
 --------------------------------------------------------------
```

When the user double-clicks a list box item, we will display which item they've selected in a text box:

```
 -----------------------------------------------------
|lists                                                |
|-----------------------------------------------------|
| Double-click an item:                               |
|  ---------                         ---------         |
| |Item 01  |^|                     |   OK    |        |
| |Item 02  |-|                      ---------         |
| |Item 03  | |                                        |
| |Item 04  | |                      ---------         |
| |Item 05  | |                     | Cancel  |        |
| |Item 06  | |                      ---------         |
| |Item 07  |-|      You chose:                        |
| |Item 08  |V|       -------------                    |
|  ---------         |Item 02      |                   |
|                     -------------                    |
|                                                     |
|                                                     |
 -----------------------------------------------------
```

Let's start this example now. This example, as well as the others in this skill, will be dialog-based, because it's easier to add controls to dialog boxes and to connect them to code using ClassWizard. Call this example "lists," and create it now with AppWizard, making this a dialog-based application.

 TIP   You can also display controls in a standard (non-dialog) window, although you can't use the dialog editor to create and position them. For example, to add a list box, you would declare a new object of the list box class, CListBox, and call its Create() method. You have to specify the style of list box you want, and be sure to include the WS_VISIBLE style to make your list box visible. Note, however, that you can't also use ClassWizard with your new list box, so to connect messages from your list box to your program, you'll have to do what ClassWizard usually does for you—edit message maps, set resource IDs, and so on.

Now we'll add the controls we'll need to this program. Double-click the main window's dialog resource ID, IDD_LISTS_DIALOG, in the Visual C++ viewer window to open that dialog in the dialog editor, as shown in Figure 8.1.

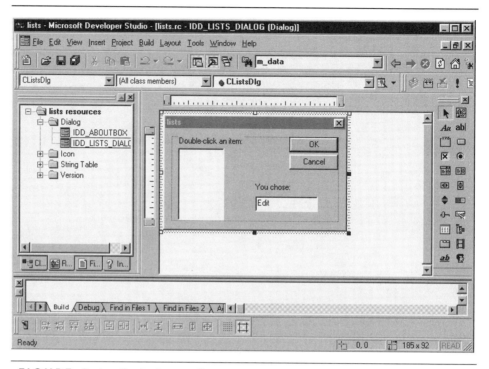

FIGURE 8.1: Designing our lists program

We'll need a list box to start—that control's tool is the fifth one down on the right in the dialog editor's toolbox, so drag a new list box to the dialog window and size it as shown in Figure 8.1.

Next, add the text box shown in Figure 8.1, and two *labels*.

Using Labels to Display Text

A label control is used simply to display text. These controls are handy, because, as their name implies, you can use them to label other controls, giving the user a prompt. The label control is the second control down on the left in the dialog editor's tool box. Drag a new label to the top of the list box and then simply type the text: **Double-click an item:**; when you do, that text appears in the label, as shown in Figure 8.1.

Add another label on top of the text box in which we will indicate the user's selection, and give that label the text, **You chose:**, as also shown in Figure 8.1.

We have designed our lists program's appearance. The next step is to place the items we want to display to the user in the list box.

Giving Our List Box a Member Object

To add a dozen items to our list box, we have to be able to refer to that list box from our code, which means giving it a name. We do that in ClassWizard, by connecting this new list box, which the dialog editor has given the ID IDC_LIST1, to a new object of the list box class, CListBox.

Start ClassWizard now and select the Member Variables tab. Select the IDC_LIST1 item in the Control IDs box, and click the Add Variable button. This opens the Add Member Variable box, as shown in Figure 8.2.

In this case, we will connect the member variable m_list to the list box IDC_LIST1. Type the name **m_list** in the Member variable name box, as shown in Figure 8.2 (ClassWizard has already placed "m_" in that box for us), and make sure you select "Control" in the Category box, so that we add a member variable for the whole control, not just its value (which, for a list box, corresponds to the currently selected item). ClassWizard will give the new member variable the type CListBox, as shown in Figure 8.2. Now click the OK button to close the Add Member Variable box.

Skill 8

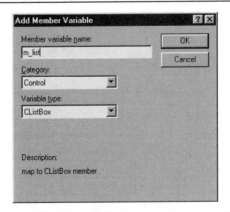

FIGURE 8.2: The Member Variable Box

This adds the member variable m_list, of class CListBox, to our program; now we have a way to refer to our list box in code: as m_list. This means we're ready to initialize the data in that list box. The methods of the CListBox class appear in Table 8.1.

T A B L E 8 . 1 : The CListBox Class Methods

Method	Does This
AddString	Adds a string to a list box.
CharToItem	Override to provide custom WM_CHAR handling.
CListBox	Constructs a CListBox object.
CompareItem	Called to determine position of a new item in a sorted owner-draw list box.
Create	Creates the list box and attaches it to the CListBox object.
DeleteItem	Called when the user deletes an item from an owner-draw list box.
DeleteString	Deletes a string from a list box.
Dir	Adds filenames from the current directory to a list box.
DrawItem	Called when a visual aspect of an owner-draw list box changes.
FindString	Searches for a string in a list box.
FindStringExact	Finds the first list-box string that matches an indicated string.
GetAnchorIndex	Gets the zero-based index of the current anchor item in a list box.
GetCaretIndex	Gets the index of the item that has the focus rectangle in a multiple-selection list box.
GetCount	Returns the number of strings in a list box.
GetCurSel	Returns the zero-based index of the currently selected string.
GetHorizontalExtent	Returns the width in pixels that a list box can be scrolled horizontally.
GetItemData	Returns the 32-bit value associated with the list-box item.
GetItemDataPtr	Returns a pointer to a list-box item.
GetItemHeight	Determines the height of items in a list box.
GetItemRect	Returns the bounding rectangle of the list-box item as it is currently displayed.
GetLocale	Gets the locale identifier for a list box.
GetSel	Returns the selection state of a list-box item.

TABLE 8.1 CONTINUED: The CListBox Class Methods

Method	Does This
GetSelCount	Returns the number of strings currently selected in a multiple-selection list box.
GetSelItems	Returns the indices of the strings currently selected in a list box.
GetText	Copies a list-box item into a buffer.
GetTextLen	Returns the length in bytes of a list-box item.
GetTopIndex	Returns the index of the first visible string in a list box.
InitStorage	Preallocates blocks of memory for list box items and strings.
InsertString	Inserts a string at a specific location in a list box.
ItemFromPoint	Returns the index of the list-box item nearest a point.
MeasureItem	Called when an owner-drawn list box is created to determine listbox dimensions.
ResetContent	Clears all the entries from a list box.
SelectString	Searches for and selects a string in a single-selection list box.
SelItemRange	Selects or deselects a range of strings in a multiple-selection list box.
SetAnchorIndex	Sets the anchor in a multiple-selection list box to begin an extended selection.
SetCaretIndex	Sets the focus rectangle to the item at an indicated index in a multiple-selection list box.
SetColumnWidth	Sets the column width of a multicolumn list box.
SetCurSel	Selects a list-box string.
SetHorizontalExtent	Sets the width in pixels that a list box can be scrolled horizontally.
SetItemData	Sets the 32-bit value associated with the list-box item.
SetItemDataPtr	Sets a pointer to the list-box item.
SetItemHeight	Sets the height of items in a list box.
SetLocale	Sets the locale identifier for a list box.
SetSel	Selects or deselects a list-box item in a multiple-selection list box.
SetTabStops	Sets the tab-stop positions in a list box.
SetTopIndex	Sets the zero-based index of the first visible string in a list box.
VKeyToItem	Override to provide WM_KEYDOWN handling for list boxes.

Skill 8

Initializing the Data in a List Box

To initialize data in a dialog box, we add code to the OnInitDialog()method, so find that method now in the program's code (it's a long method, and we've omitted almost all of its code here for brevity):

```
BOOL CListsDlg::OnInitDialog()
{
    CDialog::OnInitDialog();
        .
        .
        .

}
```

NOTE   We add code to the OnInitDialog() method in a dialog box instead of a constructor, because by the time we reach OnInitDialog(), the controls and the dialog window itself are set up for us to use.

Here's where we'll place the items we want to display in the list box in that control so when the dialog box appears on the screen, the list box will already hold our items. We'll add 12 items to the list box, naming them item 01, item 02, and so on. To do that, we use m_list's AddString() method:

```
BOOL CListsDlg::OnInitDialog()
{
    CDialog::OnInitDialog();

→       m_list.AddString("Item 01");
→       m_list.AddString("Item 02");
→       m_list.AddString("Item 03");
→       m_list.AddString("Item 04");
→       m_list.AddString("Item 05");
→       m_list.AddString("Item 06");
→       m_list.AddString("Item 07");
→       m_list.AddString("Item 08");
→       m_list.AddString("Item 09");
→       m_list.AddString("Item 10");
→       m_list.AddString("Item 11");
→       m_list.AddString("Item 12");

        // Add "About..." menu item to system menu.
        .
        .
        .

}
```

You may wonder why we used "Item 01" rather than just "Item 1". We did that here because we want the items to appear in order, 1 to 12, and by default, list boxes sort the items you place in them alphabetically. That is, if we gave item 2 the name "Item 2", item 12—beginning with a 1—would come before it in our list.

TIP If you do not want a list box to sort the items you place in it, right click the list box in the dialog editor, select Properties in the pop-up menu, click Styles in the Properties box that opens, and de-select the Sort check box.

TIP The items in a list are numbered automatically when you place them in the list, and you refer to them by an *index* value. This index value is 0 for the first item in the list box, 1 for the next, and so on. When we ask the list box in code which item the user has selected, it passes back that item's index.

TIP Besides simply giving each item in a list box its own string to appear in the list box, you can also associate other data with each item, using the SetItemData() method. For example, you might want to associate the name of a path and file with each item in a list box, and to retrieve such an item's data, you would use the GetItemData()method.

Now our list box is initialized, and when we run the program, all our items will appear in the list box. But when the user double-clicks an item in the list box, how will you know which one they've selected? Let's work on that now.

Handling List Box Double-Clicks

When the user double-clicks our list box, we want to be able to display the selection they've made in our text box, so connect a member variable to the text in the text box now, named m_text. This is the variable we'll fill with the string the user has double-clicked in the list box.

The next step is determining when the user double-clicks the list box, and we'll do that with ClassWizard's help. Open ClassWizard now, as shown in Figure 8.3. Select the list box, IDC_LIST1, and double-click the LBN_DBLCLICK message in the Messages box now (LBN_DBLCLICK is the message that the list box sends to our program when the user double-clicks it. LBN stands for list box notification, and the possible LBN messages are: LBN_DBLCLICK, LBN_ERRSPACE, LBN_KILLFOCUS, LBN_SELCANCEL, LBN_SELCHANGE, and LBN_SETFOCUS). ClassWizard then suggests the name OnDblclkList1() for this new event-handler. Accept that name by clicking OK.

ClassWizard now creates the new method, OnDblclkList1():

```
void CListsDlg::OnDblclkList1()
{
     // TODO: Add your control notification handler code here
}
```

This is the new method that the program will call when the user double-clicks an item in the list box. But which item did the user double-click?

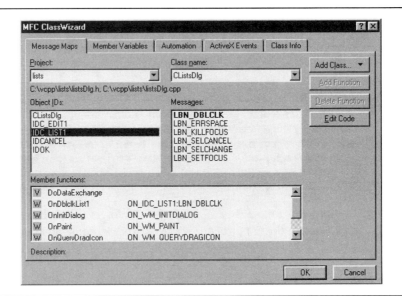

FIGURE 8.3: Using ClassWizard to catch list box's double-click events

Determining Which Item Is Selected in a List Box

We will use the CListBox method GetCurSel() to get the list box's current selection. This returns the index of the item the user double-clicked. How do we get the actual name of that item as we've placed it into the list box (e.g., "Item 02")?

We do that with the `CListBox` method `GetText()`, which fills a string object that you pass to it with the item's text:

```
void CListsDlg::OnDblclkList1()
{
➔     m_list.GetText(m_list.GetCurSel(), m_text);
                .
                .
                .
}
```

This places the item's text into `m_text`. We call `UpdateData()` to update `m_text` on the screen and we're done:

```
void CListsDlg::OnDblclkList1()
{
      m_list.GetText(m_list.GetCurSel(), m_text);
➔     UpdateData(false);
}
```

Run the program now, as shown in Figure 8.4, and double-click an item. When you do, the program reports which item you've chosen in the text box, as also shown in Figure 8.4. Now we're making use of list boxes in our programs, and we've added a good deal of power to our Visual C++ arsenal.

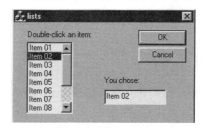

FIGURE 8.4: Our lists program lets the user select items in a list box.

The code for this program appears in `listsDlg.h`/`listsDlg.cpp`.

listsDlg.h and listsDlg.cpp

```
// listsDlg.h : header file
//

#if !defined(AFX_LISTSDLG_H__ED674075_9309_11D0_8860_444553540000__INCLUDED_)
```

```
#define AFX_LISTSDLG_H__ED674075_9309_11D0_8860_444553540000__INCLUDED_

#if _MSC_VER >= 1000
#pragma once
#endif // _MSC_VER >= 1000

/////////////////////////////////////////////////////////////////////////
// CListsDlg dialog

class CListsDlg : public CDialog
{
// Construction
public:
    CListsDlg(CWnd* pParent = NULL);      // standard constructor

// Dialog Data
    //{{AFX_DATA(CListsDlg)
    enum { IDD = IDD_LISTS_DIALOG };
    CListBox    m_list;
    CString     m_text;
    //}}AFX_DATA

    // ClassWizard generated virtual function overrides
    //{{AFX_VIRTUAL(CListsDlg)
    protected:
    virtual void DoDataExchange(CDataExchange* pDX);     // DDX/DDV support
    //}}AFX_VIRTUAL

// Implementation
protected:
    HICON m_hIcon;

    // Generated message map functions
    //{{AFX_MSG(CListsDlg)
    virtual BOOL OnInitDialog();
    afx_msg void OnSysCommand(UINT nID, LPARAM lParam);
    afx_msg void OnPaint();
    afx_msg HCURSOR OnQueryDragIcon();
    afx_msg void OnDblclkList1();
    //}}AFX_MSG
    DECLARE_MESSAGE_MAP()
};

//{{AFX_INSERT_LOCATION}}
// Microsoft Developer Studio will insert additional declarations immediately
// before the previous line.
```

```
#endif // !defined(AFX_LISTSDLG_H__ED674075_9309_11D0_8860_444553540000__
➡INCLUDED_)
```

```
// listsDlg.cpp : implementation file
//

#include "stdafx.h"
#include "lists.h"
#include "listsDlg.h"

#ifdef _DEBUG
#define new DEBUG_NEW
#undef THIS_FILE
static char THIS_FILE[] = __FILE__;
#endif

/////////////////////////////////////////////////////////////////////////
// CAboutDlg dialog used for App About

class CAboutDlg : public CDialog
{
public:
    CAboutDlg();

// Dialog Data
    //{{AFX_DATA(CAboutDlg)
    enum { IDD = IDD_ABOUTBOX };
    //}}AFX_DATA

    // ClassWizard generated virtual function overrides
    //{{AFX_VIRTUAL(CAboutDlg)
    protected:
    virtual void DoDataExchange(CDataExchange* pDX);    // DDX/DDV support
    //}}AFX_VIRTUAL

// Implementation
protected:
    //{{AFX_MSG(CAboutDlg)
    //}}AFX_MSG
    DECLARE_MESSAGE_MAP()
};

CAboutDlg::CAboutDlg() : CDialog(CAboutDlg::IDD)
{
```

```
        //{{AFX_DATA_INIT(CAboutDlg)
        //}}AFX_DATA_INIT
    }

    void CAboutDlg::DoDataExchange(CDataExchange* pDX)
    {
        CDialog::DoDataExchange(pDX);
        //{{AFX_DATA_MAP(CAboutDlg)
        //}}AFX_DATA_MAP
    }

    BEGIN_MESSAGE_MAP(CAboutDlg, CDialog)
        //{{AFX_MSG_MAP(CAboutDlg)
            // No message handlers
        //}}AFX_MSG_MAP
    END_MESSAGE_MAP()

    /////////////////////////////////////////////////////////////////////////
    // CListsDlg dialog

    CListsDlg::CListsDlg(CWnd* pParent /*=NULL*/)
        : CDialog(CListsDlg::IDD, pParent)
    {
        //{{AFX_DATA_INIT(CListsDlg)
        m_text = _T("");
        //}}AFX_DATA_INIT
        // Note that LoadIcon does not require a subsequent DestroyIcon in Win32
        m_hIcon = AfxGetApp()->LoadIcon(IDR_MAINFRAME);
    }

    void CListsDlg::DoDataExchange(CDataExchange* pDX)
    {
        CDialog::DoDataExchange(pDX);
        //{{AFX_DATA_MAP(CListsDlg)
        DDX_Control(pDX, IDC_LIST1, m_list);
        DDX_Text(pDX, IDC_EDIT1, m_text);
        //}}AFX_DATA_MAP
    }

    BEGIN_MESSAGE_MAP(CListsDlg, CDialog)
        //{{AFX_MSG_MAP(CListsDlg)
        ON_WM_SYSCOMMAND()
        ON_WM_PAINT()
        ON_WM_QUERYDRAGICON()
        ON_LBN_DBLCLK(IDC_LIST1, OnDblclkList1)
        //}}AFX_MSG_MAP
    END_MESSAGE_MAP()
```

```
//////////////////////////////////////////////////////////////////////
// CListsDlg message handlers

BOOL CListsDlg::OnInitDialog()
{
    CDialog::OnInitDialog();

    m_list.AddString("Item 01");
    m_list.AddString("Item 02");
    m_list.AddString("Item 03");
    m_list.AddString("Item 04");
    m_list.AddString("Item 05");
    m_list.AddString("Item 06");
    m_list.AddString("Item 07");
    m_list.AddString("Item 08");
    m_list.AddString("Item 09");
    m_list.AddString("Item 10");
    m_list.AddString("Item 11");
    m_list.AddString("Item 12");

    // Add "About..." menu item to system menu.

    // IDM_ABOUTBOX must be in the system command range.
    ASSERT((IDM_ABOUTBOX & 0xFFF0) == IDM_ABOUTBOX);
    ASSERT(IDM_ABOUTBOX < 0xF000);

    CMenu* pSysMenu = GetSystemMenu(FALSE);
    if (pSysMenu != NULL)
    {
        CString strAboutMenu;
        strAboutMenu.LoadString(IDS_ABOUTBOX);
        if (!strAboutMenu.IsEmpty())
        {
            pSysMenu->AppendMenu(MF_SEPARATOR);
            pSysMenu->AppendMenu(MF_STRING, IDM_ABOUTBOX, strAboutMenu);
        }
    }

    // Set the icon for this dialog.  The framework does this automatically
    //  when the application's main window is not a dialog
    SetIcon(m_hIcon, TRUE);                    // Set big icon
    SetIcon(m_hIcon, FALSE);           // Set small icon

    // TODO: Add extra initialization here

    return TRUE;  // return TRUE  unless you set the focus to a control
}
```

```
void CListsDlg::OnSysCommand(UINT nID, LPARAM lParam)
{
    if ((nID & 0xFFF0) == IDM_ABOUTBOX)
    {
        CAboutDlg dlgAbout;
        dlgAbout.DoModal();
    }
    else
    {
        CDialog::OnSysCommand(nID, lParam);
    }
}

// If you add a minimize button to your dialog, you will need the code below
//   to draw the icon.  For MFC applications using the document/view model,
//   this is automatically done for you by the framework.

void CListsDlg::OnPaint()
{
    if (IsIconic())
    {
        CPaintDC dc(this); // device context for painting

        SendMessage(WM_ICONERASEBKGND, (WPARAM) dc.GetSafeHdc(), 0);

        // Center icon in client rectangle
        int cxIcon = GetSystemMetrics(SM_CXICON);
        int cyIcon = GetSystemMetrics(SM_CYICON);
        CRect rect;
        GetClientRect(&rect);
        int x = (rect.Width() - cxIcon + 1) / 2;
        int y = (rect.Height() - cyIcon + 1) / 2;

        // Draw the icon
        dc.DrawIcon(x, y, m_hIcon);
    }
    else
    {
        CDialog::OnPaint();
    }
}

// The system calls this to obtain the cursor to display while the user drags
//   the minimized window.
HCURSOR CListsDlg::OnQueryDragIcon()
```

```
{
    return (HCURSOR) m_hIcon;
}

void CListsDlg::OnDblclkList1()
{
    // TODO: Add your control notification handler code here
    m_list.GetText(m_list.GetCurSel(), m_text);
    UpdateData(false);
}
```

We've explored list boxes and seen how they work—now it's time to move on to a new control: combo boxes.

Working with Combo Boxes

We will get a guided tour of combo boxes next. In this example, we'll include a combo box and a text box in which to display the user's selections:

```
------------------------------------------------------
|lists                                               |
|----------------------------------------------------|
|                                                    |
|  Choose an item:                                   |
|  ---------                          ---------       |
| |Item 01 |V|                       |   OK    |      |
|  ---------                          ---------       |
|                                                    |
|                                     ---------       |
|                                    | Cancel  |      |
|                                     ---------       |
|                                                    |
|  You chose:                                        |
|  -------------                                     |
| |           |                                      |
|  -------------                                     |
|                                                    |
------------------------------------------------------
```

When the user clicks the downward arrow in the combo box, a list of items will appear.

```
---------------------------------------------------------------
|lists                                                        |
|------------------------------------------------------------|
|                                                             |
| Choose an item:                                             |
|    ----------                                               |
|   |Item 01  |V|                       ----------            |
|   |-------- |-|                      |   OK    |   |         |
|   |Item 03  |^|                       ----------            |
|   |Item 04  |-|                                             |
|   |Item 05  | |                       ----------            |
|   |Item 06  | |                      | Cancel  |   |        |
|   |Item 07  |-|e:                     ----------            |
|   |Item 08  |V|-----                                        |
|    ----------         |                                     |
|      --------------                                         |
|                                                             |
---------------------------------------------------------------
```

When the user selects one of these items, we'll indicate which one they chose in the text box:

```
---------------------------------------------------------------
|lists                                                        |
|------------------------------------------------------------|
|                                                             |
| Choose an item:                                             |
|    ----------                                               |
|   |Item 02  |V|                       ----------            |
|    ----------                        |   OK    |   |        |
|                                       ----------            |
|                                                             |
|                                       ----------            |
|                                      | Cancel  |   |        |
| You chose:                            ----------            |
|    --------------                                           |
|   |Item 02      |                                           |
|    --------------                                           |
|                                                             |
---------------------------------------------------------------
```

Let's start this program; call it combos and make it a dialog-based AppWizard program. Now we're ready to place our data in the combo box.

Initializing a Combo Box

We'll initialize our combo box in `OnInitDialog()`:

```
BOOL CCombosDlg::OnInitDialog()
{
     CDialog::OnInitDialog();
          .
          .
          .
}
```

Here we can initialize our combo box, just as we initialized our list box in the previous example. Use ClassWizard to connect a member variable to the combo box control, and name this variable m_combo, making it a variable of class CComboBox. The CComboBox methods appear in Table 8.2.

T A B L E 8 . 2 : The ComboBox Class Methods

Method	Does This
AddString	Adds a string to the end of the list in the list box of a combo box.
CComboBox	Constructs a CComboBox object.
Clear	Deletes the current selection in the text box.
CompareItem	Called to determine the position of a new list item in a sorted owner-drawn combo box.
Copy	Copies the current selection onto the Clipboard.
Create	Creates the combo box and attaches it to the CComboBox object.
Cut	Deletes the current selection.
DeleteItem	Called when a list item is deleted from an owner-drawn combo box.
DeleteString	Deletes a string from the list box of a combo box.
Dir	Adds a list of filenames to the list box of a combo box.
DrawItem	Called when a visual aspect of an owner-drawn combo box changes.
FindString	Finds the first string that contains the indicated prefix in the list box of a combo box.
FindStringExact	Finds the first list-box string that matches the indicated string.
GetCount	Retrieves the number of items in the list box of a combo box.
GetCurSel	Retrieves the index of the currently selected item, if any, in the list box of a combo box.

Skill 8

T A B L E   8 . 2   C O N T I N U E D :   The ComboBox Class Methods

Method	Does This
GetDroppedControlRect	Retrieves the screen coordinates of the visible list box of a drop-down combo box.
GetDroppedState	Determines whether the list box of a drop-down combo box is visible.
GetDroppedWidth	Retrieves the minimum allowable width for the drop-down list-box portion of a combo box.
GetEditSel	Gets the starting and ending character positions of the current selection in the text box.
GetExtendedUI	Determines whether a combo box has the default user interface or the extended user interface.
GetHorizontalExtent	Returns the width that the list-box portion of the combo box can be scrolled horizontally.
GetItemData	Retrieves the application-supplied 32-bit value associated with the indicated combo-box item.
GetItemDataPtr	Retrieves a pointer to the application-supplied 32-bit value associated with the indicated combo-box item.
GetItemHeight	Retrieves the height of list items in a combo box.
GetLBText	Gets a string from the list box of a combo box.
GetLBTextLen	Gets the length of a string in the list box.
GetLocale	Retrieves the locale identifier for a combo box.
GetTopIndex	Returns the index of the first visible item in the list-box portion of the combo box.
InitStorage	Preallocates blocks of memory for items and strings in the list-box portion of the combo box.
InsertString	Inserts a string into the list box of a combo box.
LimitText	Limits the length of the text that the user can enter into the text box of a combo box.
MeasureItem	Called to determine combo box dimensions when an owner-drawn combo box is created.
Paste	Inserts the data from the Clipboard into the text box.
ResetContent	Removes all items from the list box and text box of a combo box.
SelectString	Searches for a string in the list box of a combo box.
SetCurSel	Selects a string in the list box of a combo box.

TABLE 8.2 CONTINUED: The ComboBox Class Methods

Method	Does This
SetDroppedWidth	Sets the minimum allowable width for the drop-down list-box portion of a combo box.
SetEditSel	Selects characters in the text box of a combo box.
SetExtendedUI	Selects either the default user interface or the extended user interface.
SetHorizontalExtent	Sets the width in pixels that the list-box portion of the combo box can be scrolled horizontally.
SetItemData	Sets the 32-bit value associated with the indicated item in a combo box.
SetItemDataPtr	Sets the 32-bit value associated with the indicated item in a combo box to the indicated pointer.
SetItemHeight	Sets the height of list items in a combo box or the height of the text box portion of a combo box.
SetLocale	Sets the locale identifier for a combo box.
SetTopIndex	Tells the list-box portion of the combo box to display an item at the top.
ShowDropDown	Shows or hides the list box.

TIP

You can also connect a member variable to the value of a combo box. The value property for a combo box holds the text in the combo's text box.

Just as we did in the previous example, we'll use the AddString() method to add the strings we want ("Item 01" to "Item 12") to the combo box:

```
BOOL CCombosDlg::OnInitDialog()
{
     CDialog::OnInitDialog();

➜    m_combo.AddString("Item 01");
➜    m_combo.AddString("Item 02");
➜    m_combo.AddString("Item 03");
➜    m_combo.AddString("Item 04");
➜    m_combo.AddString("Item 05");
➜    m_combo.AddString("Item 06");
```

Skill 8

```
➜        m_combo.AddString("Item 07");
➜        m_combo.AddString("Item 08");
➜        m_combo.AddString("Item 09");
➜        m_combo.AddString("Item 10");
➜        m_combo.AddString("Item 11");
➜        m_combo.AddString("Item 12");

         // Add "About..." menu item to system menu.
                   .
                   .
                   .
    }
```

In addition, we select the first item in the combo box's list ("Item 01") so that that item's text will appear in the combo box's text box when the dialog window first appears (otherwise the text box would be blank):

```
    BOOL CCombosDlg::OnInitDialog()
    {
        CDialog::OnInitDialog();

        m_combo.AddString("Item 01");
        m_combo.AddString("Item 02");
        m_combo.AddString("Item 03");
        m_combo.AddString("Item 04");
        m_combo.AddString("Item 05");
        m_combo.AddString("Item 06");
        m_combo.AddString("Item 07");
        m_combo.AddString("Item 08");
        m_combo.AddString("Item 09");
        m_combo.AddString("Item 10");
        m_combo.AddString("Item 11");
        m_combo.AddString("Item 12");
➜       m_combo.SetCurSel(0);

        // Add "About..." menu item to system menu.
                   .
                   .
                   .
    }
```

Now we're ready to handle the selections the user makes.

Determining Which Selection the User Made

We want to be able to report which item in the drop-down list box the user selects. When the user selects an item from that list box, the combo box will send our program a CBN_SELCHANGE message (CBN stands for combo box notification—the CBN messages are: CBN_CLOSEUP, CBN_DBLCLICK, CBN_DROPDOWN, CBN_EDITCHANGE, CBN_EDITUPDATE, CBN_ERRSPACE, CBN_KILLFOCUS, CBN_SELCHANGE, CBN_SELEND–CANCEL, CBN_SELENDOK, and CBN_SETFOCUS). Using ClassWizard, connect an event-handling method to that message now.

TIP   If you're ever in doubt about what messages a control can send to your program, just take a look at that control in ClassWizard, clicking the Message Maps tab. All the possible messages from this control will be listed in the Messages box.

ClassWizard will suggest the name OnSelchangeCombo1() for the new method. Accept that name and open the new method now:

```
void CCombosDlg::OnSelchangeCombo1()
{
    // TODO: Add your control notification handler code here
}
```

When this method is called, the user has made a new selection, and we want to report that selection in the text box, using the text box's m_text variable. We do that just as we did with our list box, using the GetCurSel() method and then calling UpdateData() to update the text in the text box:

```
void CCombosDlg::OnSelchangeCombo1()
{
    m_combo.GetLBText(m_combo.GetCurSel(), m_text);
    UpdateData(false);

}
```

TIP   To catch changes made to the text in the text box of a combo box, use ClassWizard to handle CBN_EDITCHANGE messages in your program.

Run the program now, as you see in Figure 8.5. When you select a new item, the program indicates which item you chose by displaying its text in the text box, as also shown in Figure 8.5. That's it—our combos program lets the user make selections in a combo box, just as we designed it to. Our example is a success.

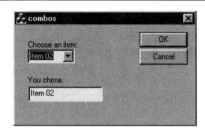

FIGURE 8.5: Our combos program lets the user select items in a combo box.

The code for this program appears in combosDlg.h/combosDlg/cpp.

combosDlg.h and *combosDlg.cpp*

```
// combosDlg.h : header file
//

#if !defined(AFX_COMBOSDLG_H__ED674083_9309_11D0_8860_444553540000__INCLUDED_)
#define AFX_COMBOSDLG_H__ED674083_9309_11D0_8860_444553540000__INCLUDED_

#if _MSC_VER >= 1000
#pragma once
#endif // _MSC_VER >= 1000


/////////////////////////////////////////////////////////////////////////////
// CCombosDlg dialog

class CCombosDlg : public CDialog
{
// Construction
public:
    CCombosDlg(CWnd* pParent = NULL);    // standard constructor

// Dialog Data
    //{{AFX_DATA(CCombosDlg)
    enum { IDD = IDD_COMBOS_DIALOG };
    CComboBox      m_combo;
    CString        m_text;
```

```
        CString      m_combotext;
        //}}AFX_DATA

        // ClassWizard generated virtual function overrides
        //{{AFX_VIRTUAL(CCombosDlg)
        protected:
        virtual void DoDataExchange(CDataExchange* pDX);      // DDX/DDV support
        //}}AFX_VIRTUAL

// Implementation
protected:
        HICON m_hIcon;

        // Generated message map functions
        //{{AFX_MSG(CCombosDlg)
        virtual BOOL OnInitDialog();
        afx_msg void OnSysCommand(UINT nID, LPARAM lParam);
        afx_msg void OnPaint();
        afx_msg HCURSOR OnQueryDragIcon();
        afx_msg void OnSelchangeCombo1();
        //}}AFX_MSG
        DECLARE_MESSAGE_MAP()
};

//{{AFX_INSERT_LOCATION}}
// Microsoft Developer Studio will insert additional declarations immediately
// before the previous line.

#endif // !defined(AFX_COMBOSDLG_H__ED674083_9309_11D0_8860_444553540000__
➥INCLUDED_)
```

```
// CAboutDlg dialog used for App About

class CAboutDlg : public CDialog
{
public:
    CAboutDlg();

// Dialog Data
    //{{AFX_DATA(CAboutDlg)
    enum { IDD = IDD_ABOUTBOX };
    //}}AFX_DATA

    // ClassWizard generated virtual function overrides
    //{{AFX_VIRTUAL(CAboutDlg)
    protected:
    virtual void DoDataExchange(CDataExchange* pDX);    // DDX/DDV support
    //}}AFX_VIRTUAL

// Implementation
protected:
    //{{AFX_MSG(CAboutDlg)
    //}}AFX_MSG
    DECLARE_MESSAGE_MAP()
};

CAboutDlg::CAboutDlg() : CDialog(CAboutDlg::IDD)
{
    //{{AFX_DATA_INIT(CAboutDlg)
    //}}AFX_DATA_INIT
}

void CAboutDlg::DoDataExchange(CDataExchange* pDX)
{
    CDialog::DoDataExchange(pDX);
    //{{AFX_DATA_MAP(CAboutDlg)
    //}}AFX_DATA_MAP
}

BEGIN_MESSAGE_MAP(CAboutDlg, CDialog)
    //{{AFX_MSG_MAP(CAboutDlg)
        // No message handlers
    //}}AFX_MSG_MAP
END_MESSAGE_MAP()

/////////////////////////////////////////////////////////////////////////////
// CCombosDlg dialog

CCombosDlg::CCombosDlg(CWnd* pParent /*=NULL*/)
```

```
        : CDialog(CCombosDlg::IDD, pParent)
{
    //{{AFX_DATA_INIT(CCombosDlg)
    m_text = _T("");
    //}}AFX_DATA_INIT
    // Note that LoadIcon does not require a subsequent DestroyIcon in Win32
    m_hIcon = AfxGetApp()->LoadIcon(IDR_MAINFRAME);
}

void CCombosDlg::DoDataExchange(CDataExchange* pDX)
{
    CDialog::DoDataExchange(pDX);
    //{{AFX_DATA_MAP(CCombosDlg)
    DDX_Control(pDX, IDC_COMBO1, m_combo);
    DDX_Text(pDX, IDC_EDIT1, m_text);
    //}}AFX_DATA_MAP
}

BEGIN_MESSAGE_MAP(CCombosDlg, CDialog)
    //{{AFX_MSG_MAP(CCombosDlg)
    ON_WM_SYSCOMMAND()
    ON_WM_PAINT()
    ON_WM_QUERYDRAGICON()
    ON_CBN_SELCHANGE(IDC_COMBO1, OnSelchangeCombo1)
    //}}AFX_MSG_MAP
END_MESSAGE_MAP()

/////////////////////////////////////////////////////////////////////////////
// CCombosDlg message handlers

BOOL CCombosDlg::OnInitDialog()
{
    CDialog::OnInitDialog();

    m_combo.AddString("Item 01");
    m_combo.AddString("Item 02");
    m_combo.AddString("Item 03");
    m_combo.AddString("Item 04");
    m_combo.AddString("Item 05");
    m_combo.AddString("Item 06");
    m_combo.AddString("Item 07");
    m_combo.AddString("Item 08");
    m_combo.AddString("Item 09");
    m_combo.AddString("Item 10");
    m_combo.AddString("Item 11");
    m_combo.AddString("Item 12");
    m_combo.SetCurSel(0);
```

Skill 8

```
    // Add "About..." menu item to system menu.

    // IDM_ABOUTBOX must be in the system command range.
    ASSERT((IDM_ABOUTBOX & 0xFFF0) == IDM_ABOUTBOX);
    ASSERT(IDM_ABOUTBOX < 0xF000);

    CMenu* pSysMenu = GetSystemMenu(FALSE);
    if (pSysMenu != NULL)
    {
        CString strAboutMenu;
        strAboutMenu.LoadString(IDS_ABOUTBOX);
        if (!strAboutMenu.IsEmpty())
        {
            pSysMenu->AppendMenu(MF_SEPARATOR);
            pSysMenu->AppendMenu(MF_STRING, IDM_ABOUTBOX, strAboutMenu);
        }
    }

    // Set the icon for this dialog.  The framework does this automatically
    //  when the application's main window is not a dialog
    SetIcon(m_hIcon, TRUE);              // Set big icon
    SetIcon(m_hIcon, FALSE);            // Set small icon

    // TODO: Add extra initialization here

    return TRUE;  // return TRUE  unless you set the focus to a control
}

void CCombosDlg::OnSysCommand(UINT nID, LPARAM lParam)
{
    if ((nID & 0xFFF0) == IDM_ABOUTBOX)
    {
        CAboutDlg dlgAbout;
        dlgAbout.DoModal();
    }
    else
    {
        CDialog::OnSysCommand(nID, lParam);
    }
}

// If you add a minimize button to your dialog, you will need the code below
//  to draw the icon.  For MFC applications using the document/view model,
//  this is automatically done for you by the framework.

void CCombosDlg::OnPaint()
{
```

```
    if (IsIconic())
    {
        CPaintDC dc(this); // device context for painting

        SendMessage(WM_ICONERASEBKGND, (WPARAM) dc.GetSafeHdc(), 0);

        // Center icon in client rectangle
        int cxIcon = GetSystemMetrics(SM_CXICON);
        int cyIcon = GetSystemMetrics(SM_CYICON);
        CRect rect;
        GetClientRect(&rect);
        int x = (rect.Width() - cxIcon + 1) / 2;
        int y = (rect.Height() - cyIcon + 1) / 2;

        // Draw the icon
        dc.DrawIcon(x, y, m_hIcon);
    }
    else
    {
        CDialog::OnPaint();
    }
}

// The system calls this to obtain the cursor to display while the user drags
//  the minimized window.
HCURSOR CCombosDlg::OnQueryDragIcon()
{
    return (HCURSOR) m_hIcon;
}

void CCombosDlg::OnSelchangeCombo1()
{
    // TODO: Add your control notification handler code here
    m_combo.GetLBText(m_combo.GetCurSel(), m_text);
    UpdateData(false);

}
```

So far, we've gotten an introduction to both list boxes and combo boxes. We started this skill off with those two controls because they work in a similar way—a combo box includes a list box, and you use AddString() to place items in both controls, and so on. However, the next control we look at, the slider control, is completely different.

Adding Scroll Power with Sliders

In this example, we'll show how to use slider controls. These controls are useful when you want to get a number from the user, such as when you want to set a color value (which values range from 0 to 255, as we'll see in the next skill). Sliders present the user with a small scrollable box (the thumb) that moves along a groove:

```
----------------------------------------------------
|sliders                                           |
|------------------------------------------------- |
|                                                  |
| Move the slider:                                 |
|                                                  |
| []-------------                                  |
|                                                  |
| Slider's position (1-100):                       |
|   ----------                                     |
| |1          |                                    |
|   ----------                                     |
|                                                  |
----------------------------------------------------
```

When the user moves the slider's thumb with the mouse, we can report the thumb's new position on a scale of 1 to 100 (1 = extreme left, 100 = extreme right):

```
----------------------------------------------------
|sliders                                           |
|------------------------------------------------- |
|                                                  |
| Move the slider:                                 |
|                                                  |
| -------[]-------                                 |
|                                                  |
| Slider's position (1-100):                       |
|   ----------                                     |
| |50         |                                    |
|   ----------                                     |
|                                                  |
----------------------------------------------------
```

Let's put this into practice now.

We start by creating a dialog-based AppWizard program named sliders. Next, we add the controls we want to the slider, as shown in Figure 8.6, including a text box, two labels, and a new slider control (the slider tool is the eighth down on the left in the dialog editor's toolbox). The slider's ID value is IDC_SLIDER1.

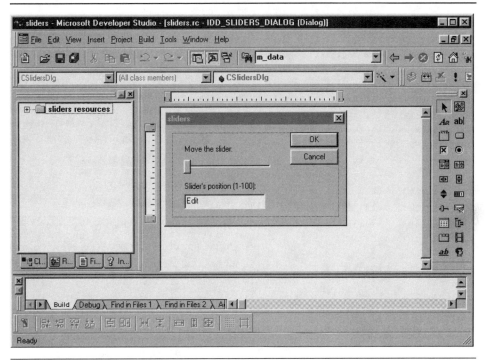

FIGURE 8.6: We design our sliders program.

Now we're ready to use ClassWizard to add a new member variable of class CSlider to our program. Do that now, basing the new member variable on theCSlider class. That class's methods appear in Table 8.3.

TABLE 8.3: The CSlider Class Methods

Method	Does This
ClearSel	Clears the current selection.
ClearTics	Removes the current tick marks.
Create	Creates a slider and attaches it to a CSliderCtrl object.
CSliderCtrl	Constructs a CSliderCtrl object.
GetChannelRect	Gets the size of the slider's channel.

TABLE 8.3 CONTINUED: The CSlider Class Methods

Method	Does This
GetLineSize	Gets the line size of a slider.
GetNumTics	Gets the number of tick marks in a slider.
GetPageSize	Gets the page size of a slider.
GetPos	Gets the current position of the slider.
GetRange	Gets the minimum and maximum positions for a slider.
GetRangeMax	Gets the maximum position for a slider.
GetRangeMin	Gets the minimum position for a slider.
Gets election	Gets the range of the current selection.
GetThumbRect	Gets the size of the slider's thumb.
GetTic	Gets the position of the specified tick mark.
GetTicArray	Gets the array of tick mark positions for a slider.
GetTicPos	Gets the position of the specified tick mark, in client coordinates.
SetLineSize	Sets the line size of a slider.
SetPageSize	Sets the page size of a slider.
SetPos	Sets the current position of the slider.
SetRange	Sets the minimum and maximum positions for a slider.
SetRangeMax	Sets the maximum position for a slider.
SetRangeMin	Sets the minimum position for a slider.
SetSelection	Sets the range of the current selection.
SetTic	Sets the position of the specified tick mark.
SetTicFreq	Sets the frequency of tick marks per slider increment.
VerifyPos	Verifies that the position of a slider is between the minimum and maximum values.

Now we're ready to initialize our new slider.

Initializing a Slider Control

When you create a new slider control, you should set its *range*. The range represents the allowable values the slider can take, from the extreme left position of the thumb to the extreme right position. In our example, we'll let the slider return values from 1 to 100 using the `CSlider SetRangeMin()` and `SetRangeMax()` methods (The second parameter in the call to these methods indicates whether or not we want the slider redrawn after we set its range. Here we indicate that we do not want it redrawn by passing a value of `false`.):

```
BOOL CSlidersDlg::OnInitDialog()
{
     CDialog::OnInitDialog();

➜    m_slider.SetRangeMin(1, false);
➜    m_slider.SetRangeMax(100, false);

     // Add "About..." menu item to system menu.
          .
          .
          .
}
```

In addition, we can display the initial value of the slider (that initial value is 1) in the text box by attaching a member variable to the text in the text box and setting it to "1" this way:

```
BOOL CSlidersDlg::OnInitDialog()
{
     CDialog::OnInitDialog();

     m_slider.SetRangeMin(1, false);
     m_slider.SetRangeMax(100, false);
➜    m_text = "1";
➜    UpdateData(false);

     // Add "About..." menu item to system menu.
          .
          .
          .
}
```

Now our slider control is set up. But how do we know when the user slides the slider?

TIP You can make sliders either horizontal (the default) or vertical. Just select the correct orientation in a slider control's Properties box in the dialog editor (right-click the slider and select Properties in the pop-up menu that appears to display the Properties box).

Handling Slider Events

When the user moves the slider's thumb, it passes us a WM_HSCROLL message (WM_VSCROLL for vertical sliders). Using ClassWizard, connect WM_HSCROLL to the OnHScroll() method (for vertical sliders, you would use OnVScroll()):

```
void CSlidersDlg::OnHScroll(UINT nSBCode, UINT nPos, CScrollBar* pScrollBar)
{
    // TODO: Add your message handler code here and/or call default

}
```

In this method, we are passed a scroll bar code, the new position of the scrollable control, and a pointer to the scrollable control that sent the message. The scroll bar code is one of the Windows scroll messages that appear in Table 8.4.

T A B L E 8 . 4 : The Windows Scroll Messages

Scroll Message	Means This
SB_ENDSCROLL	Ends scroll.
SB_LEFT	Scrolls to far left.
SB_LINELEFT	Scrolls left.
SB_LINERIGHT	Scrolls right.
SB_PAGELEFT	Scrolls one page left.
SB_PAGERIGHT	Scrolls one page right.
SB_RIGHT	Scrolls to far right.
SB_THUMBPOSITION	Scrolls to absolute position.
SB_THUMBTRACK	Drags scroll box to specified position.

In this case, we'll intercept the SB_THUMBPOSITION message, sent to us when the user moves the slider's thumb (note that if you want to handle other scroll messages, such as when the user clicks the scroll bar itself instead of just the thumb, you can add them to our code here):

```
void CSlidersDlg::OnHScroll(UINT nSBCode, UINT nPos, CScrollBar* pScrollBar)
{
➔       if(nSBCode == SB_THUMBPOSITION){
```

```
                  .
                  .
                  .
→         }
→         else{
              CDialog::OnHScroll(nSBCode, nPos, pScrollBar);
→         }
      }
```

If the message we got was indeed SB_THUMBPOSITION, the user has moved the slider's thumb, and we want to indicate the new slider position.

We start the process of displaying the slider's new position by connecting a member variable to the text in the text box, m_text. We want to display the value of the nPos parameter in m_text—but how do we do that? The m_text object is a CString object and the nPos parameter is an integer; in the next section we'll look at how to display a numeric value in a text string.

Displaying Numbers in Text Boxes

We can use the CString class's Format() method here. This method takes a format string, just as you would use for the normal C string-handling functions (if you are not familiar with the C formatting codes, take a look at the Visual C++ documentation, searching for "Format specification fields"). That means that we can format our nPos parameter as a long integer and place it in our text box this way:

```
void CSlidersDlg::OnHScroll(UINT nSBCode, UINT nPos, CScrollBar* pScrollBar)
{
      if(nSBCode == SB_THUMBPOSITION){
→         m_text.Format("%ld", nPos);
→         UpdateData(false);
      }
      else{
          CDialog::OnHScroll(nSBCode, nPos, pScrollBar);
      }
}
```

Now run the program, as shown in Figure 8.7. As you can see in that figure, when you move the slider's thumb, the program reports the new location of the slider. The sliders program works as intended—you're now using sliders.

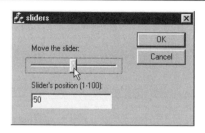

F I G U R E   8 . 7 :   The sliders program at work.

The code for this program appears in `slidersDlg.h/slidersDlg.cpp`.

 TIP   If you have more than one type of scroll bar in your program (sliders and standard scroll bars and so on) you should be aware that all these controls will call OnHScroll() for vertical scroll movements. To determine which control is calling OnHScroll(), you can compare the control passed to that method (that is, the control pointed to by pScrollbar) to the various scrollable controls in your program. Alternatively, you can determine the *type* of control that is calling OnHScroll() by using the Visual C++ RUNTIME_CLASS macro (a macro is just a name given to a prewritten set of instructions). This macro returns a pointer to a CRuntimeClass object, which indicates the object's class.

slidersDlg.h and *slidersDlg.cpp*

```
// slidersDlg.h : header file
//

#if !defined(AFX_SLIDERSDLG_H__ED674091_9309_11D0_8860_444553540000__INCLUDED_)
#define AFX_SLIDERSDLG_H__ED674091_9309_11D0_8860_444553540000__INCLUDED_

#if _MSC_VER >= 1000
#pragma once
#endif // _MSC_VER >= 1000

/////////////////////////////////////////////////////////////////////////////
// CSlidersDlg dialog

class CSlidersDlg : public CDialog
{
// Construction
```

```
public:
    CSlidersDlg(CWnd* pParent = NULL);      // standard constructor

// Dialog Data
    //{{AFX_DATA(CSlidersDlg)
    enum { IDD = IDD_SLIDERS_DIALOG };
    CEdit      m_textbox;
    CSliderCtrl     m_slider;
    CString     m_text;
    //}}AFX_DATA

    // ClassWizard generated virtual function overrides
    //{{AFX_VIRTUAL(CSlidersDlg)
    protected:
    virtual void DoDataExchange(CDataExchange* pDX);      // DDX/DDV support
    //}}AFX_VIRTUAL

// Implementation
protected:
    HICON m_hIcon;

    // Generated message map functions
    //{{AFX_MSG(CSlidersDlg)
    virtual BOOL OnInitDialog();
    afx_msg void OnSysCommand(UINT nID, LPARAM lParam);
    afx_msg void OnPaint();
    afx_msg HCURSOR OnQueryDragIcon();
    afx_msg void OnHScroll(UINT nSBCode, UINT nPos, CScrollBar* pScrollBar);
    //}}AFX_MSG
    DECLARE_MESSAGE_MAP()
};

//{{AFX_INSERT_LOCATION}}
// Microsoft Developer Studio will insert additional declarations immediately
// before the previous line.

#endif //
!defined(AFX_SLIDERSDLG_H__ED674091_9309_11D0_8860_444553540000__INCLUDED_)




// slidersDlg.cpp : implementation file
//

#include "stdafx.h"
#include "sliders.h"
#include "slidersDlg.h"
```

Skill 8

```
#ifdef _DEBUG
#define new DEBUG_NEW
#undef THIS_FILE
static char THIS_FILE[] = __FILE__;
#endif


/////////////////////////////////////////////////////////////////////////////
// CAboutDlg dialog used for App About

class CAboutDlg : public CDialog
{
public:
    CAboutDlg();

// Dialog Data
    //{{AFX_DATA(CAboutDlg)
    enum { IDD = IDD_ABOUTBOX };
    //}}AFX_DATA

    // ClassWizard generated virtual function overrides
    //{{AFX_VIRTUAL(CAboutDlg)
    protected:
    virtual void DoDataExchange(CDataExchange* pDX);    // DDX/DDV support
    //}}AFX_VIRTUAL

// Implementation
protected:
    //{{AFX_MSG(CAboutDlg)
    //}}AFX_MSG
    DECLARE_MESSAGE_MAP()
};

CAboutDlg::CAboutDlg() : CDialog(CAboutDlg::IDD)
{
    //{{AFX_DATA_INIT(CAboutDlg)
    //}}AFX_DATA_INIT
}

void CAboutDlg::DoDataExchange(CDataExchange* pDX)
{
    CDialog::DoDataExchange(pDX);
    //{{AFX_DATA_MAP(CAboutDlg)
    //}}AFX_DATA_MAP
}

BEGIN_MESSAGE_MAP(CAboutDlg, CDialog)
    //{{AFX_MSG_MAP(CAboutDlg)
        // No message handlers
```

```
        //}}AFX_MSG_MAP
END_MESSAGE_MAP()


///////////////////////////////////////////////////////////////////
// CSlidersDlg dialog

CSlidersDlg::CSlidersDlg(CWnd* pParent /*=NULL*/)
    : CDialog(CSlidersDlg::IDD, pParent)
{
    //{{AFX_DATA_INIT(CSlidersDlg)
    m_text = _T("");
    //}}AFX_DATA_INIT
    // Note that LoadIcon does not require a subsequent DestroyIcon in Win32
    m_hIcon = AfxGetApp()->LoadIcon(IDR_MAINFRAME);
}

void CSlidersDlg::DoDataExchange(CDataExchange* pDX)
{
    CDialog::DoDataExchange(pDX);
    //{{AFX_DATA_MAP(CSlidersDlg)
    DDX_Control(pDX, IDC_EDIT1, m_textbox);
    DDX_Control(pDX, IDC_SLIDER1, m_slider);
    DDX_Text(pDX, IDC_EDIT1, m_text);
    //}}AFX_DATA_MAP
}

BEGIN_MESSAGE_MAP(CSlidersDlg, CDialog)
    //{{AFX_MSG_MAP(CSlidersDlg)
    ON_WM_SYSCOMMAND()
    ON_WM_PAINT()
    ON_WM_QUERYDRAGICON()
    ON_WM_HSCROLL()
    //}}AFX_MSG_MAP
END_MESSAGE_MAP()


///////////////////////////////////////////////////////////////////
// CSlidersDlg message handlers

BOOL CSlidersDlg::OnInitDialog()
{
    CDialog::OnInitDialog();

    m_slider.SetRangeMin(1, false);
    m_slider.SetRangeMax(100, false);
    m_text = "1";
    UpdateData(false);

    // Add "About..." menu item to system menu.
```

```
    // IDM_ABOUTBOX must be in the system command range.
    ASSERT((IDM_ABOUTBOX & 0xFFF0) == IDM_ABOUTBOX);
    ASSERT(IDM_ABOUTBOX < 0xF000);

    CMenu* pSysMenu = GetSystemMenu(FALSE);
    if (pSysMenu != NULL)
    {
        CString strAboutMenu;
        strAboutMenu.LoadString(IDS_ABOUTBOX);
        if (!strAboutMenu.IsEmpty())
        {
            pSysMenu->AppendMenu(MF_SEPARATOR);
            pSysMenu->AppendMenu(MF_STRING, IDM_ABOUTBOX, strAboutMenu);
        }
    }

    // Set the icon for this dialog.  The framework does this automatically
    //  when the application's main window is not a dialog
    SetIcon(m_hIcon, TRUE);              // Set big icon
    SetIcon(m_hIcon, FALSE);             // Set small icon

    // TODO: Add extra initialization here

    return TRUE;  // return TRUE  unless you set the focus to a control
}

void CSlidersDlg::OnSysCommand(UINT nID, LPARAM lParam)
{
    if ((nID & 0xFFF0) == IDM_ABOUTBOX)
    {
        CAboutDlg dlgAbout;
        dlgAbout.DoModal();
    }
    else
    {
        CDialog::OnSysCommand(nID, lParam);
    }
}

// If you add a minimize button to your dialog, you will need the code below
//  to draw the icon.  For MFC applications using the document/view model,
//  this is automatically done for you by the framework.

void CSlidersDlg::OnPaint()
{
    if (IsIconic())
    {
        CPaintDC dc(this); // device context for painting
```

```
        SendMessage(WM_ICONERASEBKGND, (WPARAM) dc.GetSafeHdc(), 0);

        // Center icon in client rectangle
        int cxIcon = GetSystemMetrics(SM_CXICON);
        int cyIcon = GetSystemMetrics(SM_CYICON);
        CRect rect;
        GetClientRect(&rect);
        int x = (rect.Width() - cxIcon + 1) / 2;
        int y = (rect.Height() - cyIcon + 1) / 2;

        // Draw the icon
        dc.DrawIcon(x, y, m_hIcon);
    }
    else
    {
        CDialog::OnPaint();
    }
}

// The system calls this to obtain the cursor to display while the user drags
//  the minimized window.
HCURSOR CSlidersDlg::OnQueryDragIcon()
{
    return (HCURSOR) m_hIcon;
}

void CSlidersDlg::OnHScroll(UINT nSBCode, UINT nPos, CScrollBar* pScrollBar)
{
    // TODO: Add your message handler code here and/or call default
    if(nSBCode == SB_THUMBPOSITION){
        m_text.Format("%ld", nPos);
        UpdateData(false);
    }
    else{
        CDialog::OnHScroll(nSBCode, nPos, pScrollBar);
    }
}
```

That completes our skill on list boxes, combo boxes, and sliders. In this skill, we've seen how to handle all three of those controls, as well as how to connect them to code, and handle the various ways the user interacts with them. We've determined which item the user double-clicked in a list box, which item they chose in a combo box, and what location they've scrolled a slider to. We've added more skills to our already pretty extensive Visual C++ repertoire. And in the next skill, we're going to dig into something really powerful—creating graphics.

Are You Experienced?

Now You Can...

☑ Create and fill a list box with items

☑ Create a combo box, filling it with items

☑ Create a slider, initializing its range

☑ Determine which item the user chose in a list box

☑ Determine which item the user chose in a combo box

☑ Handle the case where the user scrolls a slider's thumb

☑ Read the new value of a slider after it's been scrolled

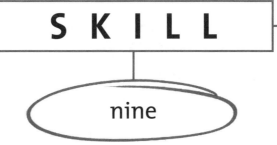

Graphics and a Complete Mouse-Driven Paint Program

- ❏ Creating a full mouse- and toolbar-driven paint program
- ❏ Drawing rectangles
- ❏ Drawing circles and ellipses
- ❏ Drawing lines
- ❏ Implementing easy screen refreshes
- ❏ Filling graphics figures in with color
- ❏ Letting the user "stretch" a graphics image on the screen
- ❏ Saving our graphics images to disk

In this skill we'll look at using Visual C++ for graphics, and you'll learn a lot about some very powerful techniques. We're going to create a whopper of a program: a fully functional, mouse-driven paint program named painter. This program will let us create new graphics images easily, drawing them with the mouse, and we will be able to save those images to disk. Even though this is a larger program (our first skill-long example!), it will be broken up into many bite-sized methods, easy to handle and understand. And we'll get a complete guided tour of graphics handling in Visual C++ as we build our painter program step-by-step in this skill.

When the user runs our painter program, we'll present them with a new menu—the Tools menu—that will let them select various drawing options, such as drawing lines, rectangles, and ellipses. Those tools will also appear in the program's toolbar, so the user can easily select the kind of graphics figure they want to draw.

After they've selected the kind of figure they want to draw, they can press the mouse button at any location in our program's client area, and stretch the new graphics figure as they want it, just as in professional paint programs (like the one that comes with Windows). As they drag the mouse, the new line or rectangle or ellipse appears to stretch on the screen, following the mouse's movements. When they release the mouse button, the figure is drawn, and it appears in the client area as the user has drawn it.

They can even select a "fill" tool and, by clicking in any hollow figure (such as an ellipse), fill that figure with color. We'll also see how to use the mouse to draw freehand figures.

After the painter program's window is minimized or uncovered (as when the user moves another window), we'll see an easy way of redrawing the graphics that the user has already created *without* having to remember all the steps they took to create those graphics. We'll do this by using Windows *metafiles* as a backup for our graphics. In this way, the user can minimize or cover our program without worrying that the graphics they've already created will be lost.

In fact, the user can even save the graphics they've created to disk. We'll see how to save our graphics in .wmf (Windows metafile) format, a format that many programs can read, including ours. That is, we'll also let the painter program read in the graphics files it's created, displaying the graphics images in them once again. In this way, the user can save and retrieve their graphics images to and from the disk.

We'll also see other little touches in this program, such as how to change the mouse cursor from the standard arrow to a cross so the user knows the program is ready to draw.

There's a lot coming up in this skill, so let's get started at once, designing our painter program.

Designing Our Painter Program

There are really two parts to the painter program, the part that interacts with the user, and the part that draws the actual graphics. In a larger program like this, it's good programming practice to break things up as much as possible (this helps confine any problems to a smaller section of the program, and also makes the program easier to work with conceptually by breaking it into bite-sized pieces). To keep things simple, then, we'll divide the program into two parts: the part that reads menu items, button clicks, and mouse events, and the part that actually draws.

This will make things easier because when the user clicks a menu item, or a button in the toolbar, or works with the mouse, we will simply set a boolean flag. The other part of the program—the part that draws—then only needs to look at those flags to know what to do. The drawing part doesn't need to watch menu items or button clicks at all, it just draws.

For example, when the user clicks the line-drawing menu item or toolbar button, we will set a flag, bLineFlag, to true. Then the user moves the mouse, and when they release the mouse button, the drawing part of the program can simply check which figure to draw by noticing that the bLineFlag flag is true, and so it draws a line. In this way, we've compartmentalized the program into a user interface and a drawing section. Let's set up the user interface now.

Creating a User-Friendly Interface for Painter

The painter program's user interface consists of the menu items, toolbar buttons, and mouse events that we will handle in the program. For example, let's say the user wanted to draw a line. They would first select the Line drawing tool in the Tools menu or the Line drawing button in the toolbar. Selecting this menu item or button makes a check mark appear in front of the menu item and leaves the Line drawing button in the toolbar in a pressed (selected) state, as shown in the following graphic.

Skill 9

```
 ------------------------------------------------------------
|Untitled - painter                                          |
| ---------------------------------------------------------- |
|File Edit View Help Tools                                   |
| ------------------|    -------------------------------     |
|[ ] [ ] [ ]  [ ] [ ]|  Draw freehand|] [ ] [ ] [ ]  |
| ------------------|v Line          | ------------- |
|                   |  Rectangle     |               |
|                   |  Ellipse       |               |
|                   |  Fill figure   |               |
|                    ---------------                       |
|                                                            |
|                                                            |
|                                                            |
|                                                            |
|                                                            |
|                                                            |
|                                                            |
|                                                            |
 ------------------------------------------------------------
```

They then click the mouse at the location where they want to start the line; we'll
call this the *Anchor* point:

```
 ------------------------------------------------------------
|Untitled - painter                                          |
| ---------------------------------------------------------- |
|File Edit View Help Tools                                   |
| ---------------------------------------------------------- |
|[ ] [ ] [ ]  [ ] [ ] [ ]   [ ] [ ] [ ] [ ] [ ] [ ]  |
| ---------------------------------------------------------- |
|                                                            |
|                                                            |
|                                                            |
|                x                                           |
|             Anchor point                                   |
|                                                            |
|                                                            |
|                                                            |
|                                                            |
|                                                            |
 ------------------------------------------------------------
```

Next, they drag the mouse to a new point, the *Draw To* point, and release the
mouse button. When they do, we draw the line, from Anchor to Draw To point,
as shown in the following graphic.

```
---------------------------------------------------------
|Untitled - painter                                     |
|-------------------------------------------------------|
|File Edit View Help Tools                              |
|-------------------------------------------------------|
|[ ] [ ] [ ]  [ ] [ ] [ ]   [ ] [ ] [ ] [ ] [ ] [ ]    |
|-------------------------------------------------------|
|                                                       |
|                                                       |
|                                                       |
|            x--------------------x                     |
|            Anchor point         Draw To point         |
|                                                       |
|                                                       |
|                                                       |
|                                                       |
|                                                       |
---------------------------------------------------------
```

While they drag the mouse, we keep drawing lines, so it appears that the user is stretching the line. When they release the line, it becomes permanent.

They can draw rectangles and other figures in the same way, using an Anchor point and a Draw To point:

```
---------------------------------------------------------
|Untitled - painter                                     |
|-------------------------------------------------------|
|File Edit View Help Tools                              |
|-------------------------------------------------------|
|[ ] [ ] [ ]  [ ] [ ] [ ]   [ ] [ ] [ ] [ ] [ ] [ ]    |
|-------------------------------------------------------|
|                                                       |
|              Anchor point                             |
|              x--------------------                    |
|              |                   |                    |
|              |                   |                    |
|              |                   |                    |
|              |                   |                    |
|              --------------------x                    |
|                                  Draw To point        |
|                                                       |
---------------------------------------------------------
```

The user interface's job is to set up Boolean flags to communicate to the drawing part of the program, and we'll look into working with those flags now.

Setting Painter Flags

Here is the sequence of events : the user selects a drawing tool, and we set the appropriate drawing tool flag so we know what kind of figure we are to draw: bDrawFlag (for freehand drawing), bLineFlag, bRectangleFlag, bEllipseFlag, or bFillFlag (the bFillFlag is set if the user wants to start filling figures with color).

Next, the user clicks to establish the Anchor point. We record the Anchor point when the mouse goes down.

The user then drags the mouse to the Draw To point and releases the mouse button. Because we already have the Anchor point, and the correct tool flag (such as bLineFlag) is set, we can simply draw the figure they want when the mouse button goes up.

Let's start now. Create the painter program using AppWizard, making it an SDI program. We'll begin by declaring all the flags we'll need, as well as the Anchor and Draw To points:

```
class CPainterView : public CView
{
         .
         .
         .
protected:
→        CPoint Anchor;
→        CPoint DrawTo;
→        CPoint OldPoint;
→        boolean bDrawFlag;
→        boolean bLineFlag;
→        boolean bRectangleFlag;
→        boolean bEllipseFlag;
→        boolean bFillFlag;
         .
         .
         .
}
class CPainterView : public CView
{
protected: // create from serialization only
         .
         .
         .
```

In addition, we set all those flags to false in the constructor. In fact, we'll want to clear all the flags by setting them to false each time the user clicks a new drawing tool (i.e., only one drawing tool can be active at once), so we set up a new method, MakeAllFlagsFalse(), declaring it our view class's header file, painterView.h:

```
class CPainterView : public CView
{
            .
            .
            .
protected:
        CPoint Anchor;
        CPoint DrawTo;
        CPoint OldPoint;
        boolean bDrawFlag;
        boolean bLineFlag;
        boolean bRectangleFlag;
        boolean bEllipseFlag;
        boolean bFillFlag;
➜       void MakeAllFlagsFalse();
            .
            .
            .
}
```

And we write that method like this, simply setting all flags as false:

```
void CPainterView::MakeAllFlagsFalse()
{
        bDrawFlag = false;
        bLineFlag = false;
        bRectangleFlag = false;
        bEllipseFlag = false;
        bFillFlag = false;
}
```

Next, we can call this new method in the view class's constructor to turn off all drawing tools when the program first starts:

```
CPainterView::CPainterView()
{
        // TODO: add construction code here
➜       MakeAllFlagsFalse();
}
```

We've set up our flags—the next step is to connect them to menu items.

Skill 9

Creating the Tools Menu and Toolbar Buttons

Open the menu editor now, as shown in Figure 9.1. We add a new menu named Tools to the menu bar, as shown in Figure 9.1, giving that menu five items: Draw freehand, Line, Rectangle, Ellipse, and Fill figure. The menu editor gives these new menu items IDs like ID_TOOLS_LINE for the Line menu item.

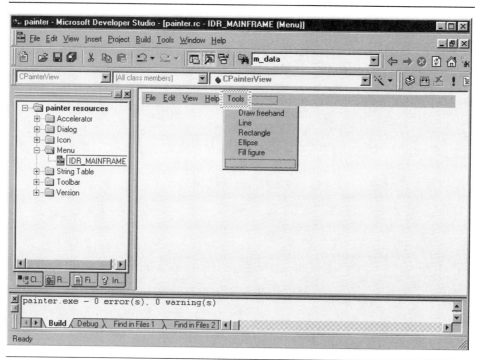

FIGURE 9.1: Designing our menu system

In addition, we open the program's toolbar, as shown in Figure 9.2. Add five new buttons to the end of the toolbar (every time you draw anything in a toolbar button, the toolbar editor adds a new, blank button at the end of the toolbar), and drag them off to their own group of buttons in the toolbar, as shown in Figure 9.2. Now we design these toolbar buttons. For example, we place a short line in the line-drawing button, a box in the rectangle button, and so on, keeping the buttons in order: draw freehand, line, rectangle, ellipse, and fill. The new buttons appear in Figure 9.2.

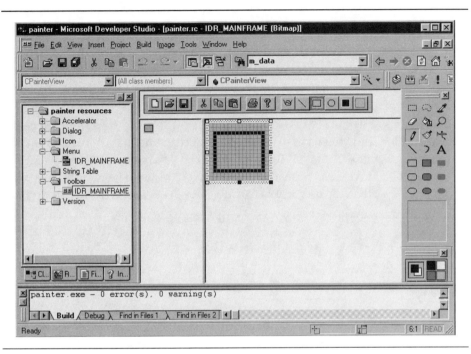

FIGURE 9.2: Designing our toolbar

Finally, connect these new buttons to the menu items they represent by double-clicking a button and finding the correct menu item ID in the ID box of the Properties dialog box that opens. For example, set the ID of the rectangle button to ID_TOOLS_RECTANGLE, as shown in Figure 9.3.

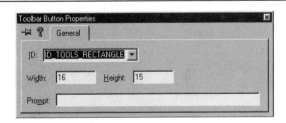

FIGURE 9.3: Assigning IDs to toolbar buttons

Now we've designed the user interface—both menu items and toolbar buttons. The next step is to connect these items to code.

Connecting the Flags to the Drawing Tools

Our next job is to set the appropriate flags when the user selects a drawing tool to use. Using ClassWizard, connect a method to each new menu item, such as OnToolsEllipse() to the Ellipse menu item, OnToolsDrawfreehand() to the Draw freehand item, and so on (accept the ClassWizard defaults for the names of these methods). Then we set all flags false in each menu item's event-handler and set the particular drawing tool the menu item represents to true. For example, when the user wants to draw lines, we set bLineFlag true and all other false:

```
void CPainterView::OnToolsDrawfreehand()
{
    MakeAllFlagsFalse();
    bDrawFlag = true;

}

void CPainterView::OnToolsEllipse()
{
    MakeAllFlagsFalse();
    bEllipseFlag = true;

}

void CPainterView::OnToolsFillfigure()
{
    MakeAllFlagsFalse();
    bFillFlag = true;

}

void CPainterView::OnToolsLine()
{
    MakeAllFlagsFalse();
    bLineFlag = true;

}

void CPainterView::OnToolsRectangle()
{
    MakeAllFlagsFalse();
    bRectangleFlag = true;

}
```

Our drawing tools are now active, insofar as they can set the flags like bLineFlag in our program (and those flags will communicate with the drawing part of the program). There is one more thing to do here, however, before finishing the user interface. We should report to the user which drawing tool is currently selected, and we do that with SetCheck().

Setting Check Marks in Menus

As you know, the program calls an update method for each menu item before it displays the menu, so we can set a check in front of the currently active drawing tool. Using ClassWizard, connect an update method to each menu item (by connecting that menu item's event-handler to the item's UPDATE_COMMAND_UI message). Now we can place (or remove) check marks in front of the various menu items simply by examining the flag associated with that menu item:

```
void CPainterView::OnUpdateToolsDrawfreehand(CCmdUI* pCmdUI)
{
    pCmdUI->SetCheck(bDrawFlag);
}

void CPainterView::OnUpdateToolsEllipse(CCmdUI* pCmdUI)
{
    pCmdUI->SetCheck(bEllipseFlag);

}

void CPainterView::OnUpdateToolsFillfigure(CCmdUI* pCmdUI)
{
    pCmdUI->SetCheck(bFillFlag);

}

void CPainterView::OnUpdateToolsLine(CCmdUI* pCmdUI)
{
    pCmdUI->SetCheck(bLineFlag);

}

void CPainterView::OnUpdateToolsRectangle(CCmdUI* pCmdUI)
{
    pCmdUI->SetCheck(bRectangleFlag);

}
```

Skill 9

Besides placing a check mark in front of the currently active drawing tool in the Tools menu, this also makes the corresponding drawing tool button in the toolbar appear pressed, so the user will know at all times which drawing tool is active.

Now we've handled the user interface, which really means setting the correct Boolean flags. When it comes time to draw, we just have to see which flag is active to know what kind of figure we're supposed to draw. The user interface is ready, and we're ready to move on to handling the mouse.

Handling Mouse Down Events

When the user moves the mouse to our program's client area, they are ready to draw. When they press the mouse button, they are establishing the Anchor point, so add an OnLButtonDown() method now using ClassWizard and add this code so that we can record the Anchor point:

```
void CPainterView::OnLButtonDown(UINT nFlags, CPoint point)
{
→       Anchor.x = point.x;
→       Anchor.y = point.y;

        CView::OnLButtonDown(nFlags, point);
}
```

That's it—now we've recorded the Anchor point, and we know what kind of figure the user wants to draw. The next step is to actually draw that figure.

Drawing Lines

When the user presses the mouse button, establishing the Anchor point, then moves to another location and releases the mouse button, establishing the Draw To point, our program should draw the graphics figure they want, stretching from Anchor to Draw To point.

Let's start by handling the case in which we're supposed to draw lines—that is, the bLineFlag flag is true. We draw lines when the mouse button goes up, so add the OnLButtonUp() method to our program now:

```
void CPainterView::OnLButtonUp(UINT nFlags, CPoint point)
{
        CView::OnLButtonUp(nFlags, point);

}
```

When the mouse goes up, the user is establishing the Draw To point, so we start by recording that point:

```
void CPainterView::OnLButtonUp(UINT nFlags, CPoint point)
{

    DrawTo.x = point.x;
    DrawTo.y = point.y;
        .
        .
        .

}
```

Now we're ready to draw lines.

In a typical program, we'd set up a few variables and then call `Invalidate()` so the actual screen drawing would be handled in the `OnDraw()` method. That's not good enough here, however. The user may have drawn a great many graphics figures before they drew the current line, and our program would have to remember everything they did and re-create it in the `OnDraw()` method each time they draw a new figure.

Instead, we are going to use *metafiles* to handle our screen refreshes in `OnDraw()`, and so it makes much more sense to simply draw the new graphics figures as the user releases the mouse button instead of calling `OnDraw()`. Drawing the figures as they are created will also show us how to get a device context for our view any time we need one, not just in `OnDraw()`, and we do that with the `CClientDC` class. This class is derived from the `CDC` class, so it already has all the drawing methods that the `CDC` class has. (These methods appear in Table 2.4.) And, unlike the `CDC` class, it has a constructor that is easy to use—you just pass that constructor a pointer to the current view object to construct a device context for that object:

```
void CPainterView::OnLButtonUp(UINT nFlags, CPoint point)
{

    DrawTo.x = point.x;
    DrawTo.y = point.y;

→   CClientDC* pDC = new CClientDC(this);
        .
        .
        .

}
```

The CClientDC class constructor needs a pointer to the current view object, and we pass it that pointer using the *this* keyword. The this keyword is a very handy pointer that all C++ objects have, and it points to the current object. In this way, we're able to indicate that we want the new device context attached to our current view.

Now we have our own device context, pDC, and we can draw in it, just as if we were in the OnDraw() method (and, because of the structure of our program, it's actually better to draw graphics from the current method rather than having the program call OnDraw()).

Next, we make sure we're supposed to be drawing lines by checking the bLineFlag flag:

```
void CPainterView::OnLButtonUp(UINT nFlags, CPoint point)
{

    DrawTo.x = point.x;
    DrawTo.y = point.y;

    CClientDC* pDC = new CClientDC(this);

→   if(bLineFlag){

→   }
        .
        .
        .
}
```

If bLineFlag is true, we're ready to draw a line. We do that by moving to the Anchor point first with the CClientDC method MoveTo(), and then drawing a line from that point to the Draw To point using the LineTo() method:

```
void CPainterView::OnLButtonUp(UINT nFlags, CPoint point)
{

    DrawTo.x = point.x;
    DrawTo.y = point.y;

    CClientDC* pDC = new CClientDC(this);

    if(bLineFlag){
→       pDC->MoveTo(Anchor.x, Anchor.y);
→       pDC->LineTo(DrawTo.x, DrawTo.y);
```

```
    }
            .
            .
            .
}
```

That's it: a line appears—in fact, as many lines as you want—in the device context's current drawing color (the default is black) on the screen, as shown in Figure 9.4. Now we're drawing lines with Visual C++!

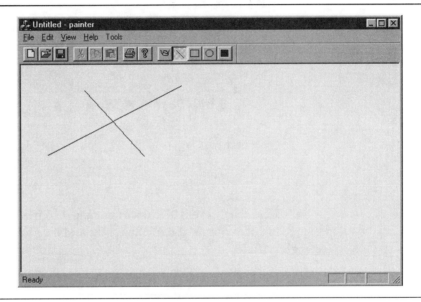

FIGURE 9.4: Drawing lines in painter

TIP   If you want to draw in a particular color, you have to create a new device context *pen* object with the CPen class and install it in a device context with the device context's SelectObject() method. We'll see more about selecting such objects soon.

Now let's turn to drawing rectangles.

Skill 9

Drawing Rectangles

Drawing rectangles is almost as easy as drawing lines. We just check to make sure that we are supposed to be drawing rectangles by looking at the bRectangleFlag flag:

```
void CPainterView::OnLButtonUp(UINT nFlags, CPoint point)
{

    DrawTo.x = point.x;
    DrawTo.y = point.y;

    CClientDC* pDC = new CClientDC(this);

    if(bLineFlag){
        pDC->MoveTo(Anchor.x, Anchor.y);
        pDC->LineTo(DrawTo.x, DrawTo.y);
    }

➜    if(bRectangleFlag){

➜    }
}
```

If so, we use the CClientDC class's Rectangle() method to draw the rectangle, passing it the two points, the Anchor point and the Draw To point, that define the rectangle:

```
void CPainterView::OnLButtonUp(UINT nFlags, CPoint point)
{

    DrawTo.x = point.x;
    DrawTo.y = point.y;

    CClientDC* pDC = new CClientDC(this);

    if(bLineFlag){
        pDC->MoveTo(Anchor.x, Anchor.y);
        pDC->LineTo(DrawTo.x, DrawTo.y);
    }

    if(bRectangleFlag){
➜        pDC->SelectStockObject(NULL_BRUSH);
➜        pDC->Rectangle(Anchor.x, Anchor.y, DrawTo.x, DrawTo.y);
    }
}
```

This isn't quite right, however, because this actually draws a rectangle that is filled in with the current background color. This is fine as long as you don't draw the rectangle over other figures, but if you do, a filled rectangle will erase everything that should appear inside it.

To avoid disturbing other graphics already on the screen (for example, the user may be using this rectangle to draw a border for other graphics figures), we install a *null brush* into our device context using the CCLientDC method SelectStockObject(). The interior of a filled figure is filled with a Windows "brush" and if we set that to the null brush, the interior of the rectangle is not disturbed:

```
void CPainterView::OnLButtonUp(UINT nFlags, CPoint point)
{

    DrawTo.x = point.x;
    DrawTo.y = point.y;

    CClientDC* pDC = new CClientDC(this);

    if(bLineFlag){
        pDC->MoveTo(Anchor.x, Anchor.y);
        pDC->LineTo(DrawTo.x, DrawTo.y);
    }

    if(bRectangleFlag){
        pDC->SelectStockObject(NULL_BRUSH);
        pDC->Rectangle(Anchor.x, Anchor.y, DrawTo.x, DrawTo.y);
    }
}
```

TIP   Besides the NULL_BRUSH, Windows also defines various other default brushes, such as the BLACK_BRUSH and the WHITE_BRUSH. You can also define your brush with the CBrush class.

That's how you draw in device contexts—using the current pen object to draw (you can set the pen object with SelectStockObject() to pens like the default BLACK_PEN or the WHITE_PEN, or create your own pen with the CPen class and install it with SelectObject()) and the current brush object to fill figures in (and you can use a stock brush like BLACK_BRUSH or create your own with the CBrush class).

At this point, the rectangle(s) that the user drew appears on the screen, as shown in Figure 9.5. Now we're able to draw rectangles!

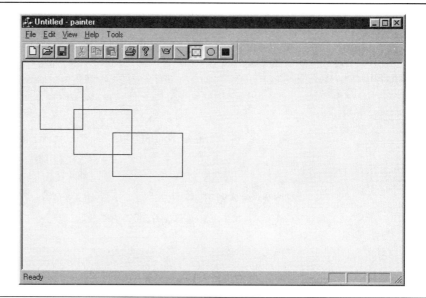

FIGURE 9.5: Drawing rectangles in painter

The next graphics figure we'll work with are ellipses.

Drawing Ellipses and Circles

Visual C++ considers circles simply ellipses with the same major and minor axes, so both circles and ellipses are drawn with the same method: `Ellipse()`. We can determine if we're supposed to be drawing ellipses with the `bEllipseFlag` flag, and if so, we place a null brush in the device context and display the ellipse this way:

```
void CPainterView::OnLButtonUp(UINT nFlags, CPoint point)
{

        DrawTo.x = point.x;
        DrawTo.y = point.y;
```

```
CClientDC* pDC = new CClientDC(this);

if(bLineFlag){
    pDC->MoveTo(Anchor.x, Anchor.y);
    pDC->LineTo(DrawTo.x, DrawTo.y);
}

if(bRectangleFlag){
    pDC->SelectStockObject(NULL_BRUSH);
    pDC->Rectangle(Anchor.x, Anchor.y, DrawTo.x, DrawTo.y);
}

if(bEllipseFlag){
    pDC->SelectStockObject(NULL_BRUSH);
    pDC->Ellipse(Anchor.x, Anchor.y, DrawTo.x, DrawTo.y);
}
}
```

It's as easy as that—now you can draw ellipses as shown in Figure 9.6.

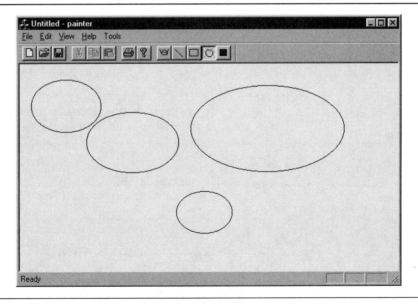

FIGURE 9.6: Drawing ellipses in painter

Next, we'll turn to filling graphics figures with color.

Filling Graphics Figures with Solid Color

So far, all of our figures have been hollow. However, we can change that with the
FloodFill() method. This handy method lets you indicate a point in a device
context and a bounding color. The FloodFill() method will then fill the figure
in (as bounded by the bounding color, which will be black for our figures) with
the current brush.

We will use a BLACK_BRUSH for the filling brush in the case, which means that
we can use FloodFill() to fill around the location at which the mouse went
down (the Anchor point) this way:

```
void CPainterView::OnLButtonUp(UINT nFlags, CPoint point)
{

    DrawTo.x = point.x;
    DrawTo.y = point.y;

    CClientDC* pDC = new CClientDC(this);

    if(bLineFlag){
        pDC->MoveTo(Anchor.x, Anchor.y);
        pDC->LineTo(DrawTo.x, DrawTo.y);
    }

    if(bRectangleFlag){
        pDC->SelectStockObject(NULL_BRUSH);
        pDC->Rectangle(Anchor.x, Anchor.y, DrawTo.x, DrawTo.y);
    }

    if(bEllipseFlag){
        pDC->SelectStockObject(NULL_BRUSH);
        pDC->Ellipse(Anchor.x, Anchor.y, DrawTo.x, DrawTo.y);
    }

    if(bFillFlag){
➜        pDC->SelectStockObject(BLACK_BRUSH);
➜        pDC->FloodFill(Anchor.x, Anchor.y, RGB(0, 0, 0));
    }

    delete pDC;

    CView::OnLButtonUp(nFlags, point);
}
```

This fills figures with black when the user clicks inside them with the mouse. Note how we indicated that we want black to be the bounding color to FloodFill()—we used the RGB macro. This macro returns a value of type COLORREF, which is how Windows refers to colors. There are three color values that you pass to the RGB macro to specify the amounts of red, green, and blue that you want in your color. Each color value can go from 0 to 255, and so we specify black this way: RGB(0, 0, 0). Bright red is RGB(255, 0, 0), bright green is RGB(0, 255, 0), bright blue is RGB(0, 0, 255), gray is RGB(128, 128, 128), and so on.

> **TIP**   As with pens, if you want to fill figures in a particular color, you can create a new brush with the CBrush class, and install that brush into the device context with SelectObject().

Run the painter program and, using the Fill tool, fill in a few figures as you like, as shown in Figure 9.7. Now we're filling in figures!

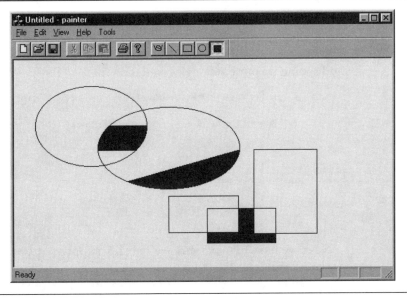

FIGURE 9.7: Filling figures in painter

Skill 9

We've drawn lines, rectangles, ellipses, and filled figures in. The next step is to draw freehand, and we'll look at that now.

Drawing Freehand with the Mouse

Drawing with the mouse is not very difficult—we will get a series of mouse locations as the mouse moves, and we'll just connect the dots by drawing lines between these locations.

 TIP   Because only a certain number of mouse movements are generated per second, we don't get a mouse move event for each pixel the mouse moves over, so coloring only one pixel each time we get a new mouse move message would only leave a scattered trail of dots on the screen, not a freehand drawing.

Drawing freehand works like this: when the mouse button goes down, we set the Anchor point. When the mouse moves to a new point, we draw a line from the Anchor point to the new point, and then we should make the new point the Anchor point in preparation for the next mouse move.

We begin by adding an event-handler for mouse movements, `OnMouseMove()`, and setting up our own device context:

```
void CPainterView::OnMouseMove(UINT nFlags, CPoint point)
{
➔      CClientDC* pDC = new CClientDC(this);
             .
             .
             .
➔      delete pDC;

       CView::OnMouseMove(nFlags, point);
}
```

Next, we have to make sure we're really supposed to be drawing freehand, and we check that with the `bDrawFlag`. In addition, we're only supposed to be drawing when the user is dragging the mouse—that is, moving the mouse with the left button pressed—so we check if the left button is pressed by comparing the `nFlags` parameter passed to us in `OnMouseMove()` with the Visual C++ constant `MK_LBUTTON`:

```
void CPainterView::OnMouseMove(UINT nFlags, CPoint point)
{
```

```
        CClientDC* pDC = new CClientDC(this);

→       if((nFlags && MK_LBUTTON) && bDrawFlag){
                    .
                    .
                    .
→       }

        delete pDC;

        CView::OnMouseMove(nFlags, point);
    }
```

> **TIP**
>
> Besides MK_LBUTTON, you can check if the right button is down with the MK_RBUTTON constant, the middle button with the MK_MBUTTON constant, the Ctrl key with the MK_CONTROL constant, and the shift key with the MK_SHIFT constant.

If we are supposed to be drawing freehand, we just draw a line from the Anchor point to the current point, then make the current point the Anchor point, getting ready for the next time we get a mouse move event:

```
void CPainterView::OnMouseMove(UINT nFlags, CPoint point)
{
        CClientDC* pDC = new CClientDC(this);

        if((nFlags && MK_LBUTTON) && bDrawFlag){
→           pDC->MoveTo(Anchor.x, Anchor.y);
→           pDC->LineTo(point.x, point.y);
→           Anchor.x = point.x;
→           Anchor.y = point.y;
        }

        delete pDC;

        CView::OnMouseMove(nFlags, point);
    }
```

Before drawing freehand, we make one more change to the program. We'll change the default cursor for our view from the standard mouse cursor to a cross, which is common in paint programs.

Skill 9

Changing the Mouse Cursor's Appearance

We can install a new cursor for our view when that view is created in the PreCreateWindow() method, which already looks like this in our view class:

```
BOOL CPainterView::PreCreateWindow(CREATESTRUCT& cs)
{
    // TODO: Modify the Window class or styles here by modifying
    //   the CREATESTRUCT cs

    return CView::PreCreateWindow(cs);
}
```

We have to change the window's creation structure, passed to us as cs, which we do by installing a new cross cursor, IDC_CROSS. Here we're modifying the actual window class to support a cross cursor instead of the standard arrow one:

```
BOOL CPainterView::PreCreateWindow(CREATESTRUCT& cs)
{
    // TODO: Modify the Window class or styles here by modifying
    //   the CREATESTRUCT cs
→   cs.lpszClass = AfxRegisterWndClass(CS_DBLCLKS, AfxGetApp()
  ->LoadStandardCursor(IDC_CROSS), (HBRUSH)(COLOR_WINDOW+1), AfxGetApp()
  ->LoadIcon(IDR_MAINFRAME));
    return CView::PreCreateWindow(cs);
}
```

Now we have a new cursor, which appears in Figure 9.8, that we're going to use to draw freehand with the mouse. We're able to let the user move the mouse directly to draw.

We've come far in this skill already, drawing various graphics figures as the user moves the mouse. But we also want to let the user see the figures they're creating as they move the mouse, and we can do that now.

Stretching Graphics Figures

In professional paint programs, the user can "stretch" graphics figures with the mouse—that is, they can shape graphics visually as they create them—and we can allow the user to do that here, too.

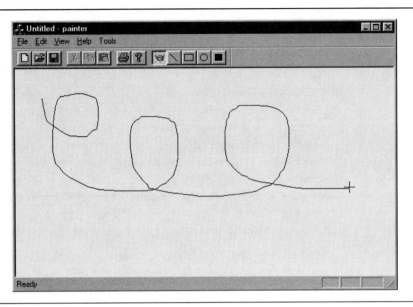

FIGURE 9.8: Drawing freehand in painter

We'll add our new code for making the graphics figures seem to stretch as the user moves the mouse in the OnMouseMove() event-handler. Let's work on stretching lines first.

First, we must determine if we are supposed to be stretching a line. In other words, if the Line drawing tool is selected, if the left mouse button is down, and if the mouse is moving, we use:

```
void CPainterView::OnMouseMove(UINT nFlags, CPoint point)
{
    CClientDC* pDC = new CClientDC(this);

    if((nFlags && MK_LBUTTON) && bDrawFlag){
        pDC->MoveTo(Anchor.x, Anchor.y);
        pDC->LineTo(point.x, point.y);
        Anchor.x = point.x;
        Anchor.y = point.y;
    }

➜    if((nFlags && MK_LBUTTON) && bLineFlag){
```

```
            .
            .
            .
      }
}
```

If we are supposed to be stretching a line from the Anchor point to the present point, we will take the following steps: first, erase the current line from the Anchor point to the mouse's previous location, then draw a new line from the Anchor point to the current mouse location.

To erase the old line from the Anchor point to the old mouse location, we have to store that location, which we do by adding a new CPoint object to our program, named OldPoint. This point will hold the previous mouse location when the code is called in OnMouseMove(). We first place a value in OldPoint when the mouse goes down to make sure that point always has a valid location in it:

```
    void CPainterView::OnLButtonDown(UINT nFlags, CPoint point)
    {
        Anchor.x = point.x;
        Anchor.y = point.y;
➜       OldPoint.x = Anchor.x;
➜       OldPoint.y = Anchor.y;

        CView::OnLButtonDown(nFlags, point);
    }
```

Now our task breaks up into these stages: erase the line from the Anchor point to OldPoint, draw a new line from the Anchor point to the current point, then copy the current point into OldPoint for the next mouse movement.

What Are Binary Raster Operations?

To erase the line from the Anchor point to OldPoint, we just set the device context's *binary raster mode* to R2_NOT and draw that line again. What does this mean? The binary raster mode indicates *how* what you draw will appear on the screen (the possible settings are shown in Table 9.1). Setting the binary raster mode to R2_NOT means that you *invert* the color on the screen each time you draw a new pixel. Because our lines are black and the background is white in our program, redrawing a line in this new mode will change the line to white, erasing it. In addition, if the stretched line passes over a black region on the screen, that portion of the line will appear white, so the user can still see it.

T A B L E   9 . 1 : The Windows Binary Raster Modes

R2 Mode	Means This
R2_BLACK	Pixel is always black.
R2_COPYPEN	Pixel is the pen color.
R2_MASKNOTPEN	Pixel = (NOT pen) AND screen pixel.
R2_MASKPEN	Pixel = pen AND screen pixel.
R2_MASKPENNOT	Pixel = (NOT screen pixel) AND pen.
R2_MERGENOTPEN	Pixel = (NOT pen) OR screen pixel.
R2_MERGEPEN	Pixel = pen OR screen pixel.
R2_MERGEPENNOT	Pixel = (NOT screen pixel) OR pen.
R2_NOP	Pixel remains unchanged.
R2_NOT	Pixel is the inverse of the screen color.
R2_NOTCOPYPEN	Pixel is the inverse of the pen color.
R2_NOTMASKPEN	Pixel = NOT(pen AND screen pixel).
R2_NOTMERGEPEN	Pixel = NOT(pen OR screen pixel).
R2_NOTXORPEN	Pixel = NOT(pen XOR screen pixel).
R2_WHITE	Pixel is always white.
R2_XORPEN	Pixel = pen XOR screen pixel).

Here, then is how we erase the previous line. Note that we save the old binary raster mode (an integer value) so that we can restore it later:

```
void CPainterView::OnMouseMove(UINT nFlags, CPoint point)
{
➜      int nOldMode;

       CClientDC* pDC = new CClientDC(this);

       if((nFlags && MK_LBUTTON) && bLineFlag){
➜            nOldMode = pDC->GetROP2();
➜            pDC->SetROP2(R2_NOT);
➜            pDC->MoveTo(Anchor.x, Anchor.y);
➜            pDC->LineTo(OldPoint.x, OldPoint.y);
                .
                .
                .
       }
}
```

Next we draw the new line, update OldPoint, and restore the binary raster mode in the device context:

```
void CPainterView::OnMouseMove(UINT nFlags, CPoint point)
{
    int nOldMode;

    CClientDC* pDC = new CClientDC(this);

    if((nFlags && MK_LBUTTON) && bLineFlag){
        nOldMode = pDC->GetROP2();
        pDC->SetROP2(R2_NOT);
        pDC->MoveTo(Anchor.x, Anchor.y);
        pDC->LineTo(OldPoint.x, OldPoint.y);
→       pDC->MoveTo(Anchor.x, Anchor.y);
→       pDC->LineTo(point.x, point.y);
→       OldPoint.x = point.x;
→       OldPoint.y = point.y;
→       pDC->SetROP2(nOldMode);
    }
}
```

Now when the user draws a line, they can stretch the line as they want it, as shown in Figure 9.9. Note that the stretched line appears in white when passing over a black object.

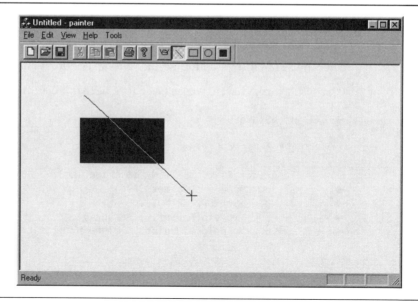

FIGURE 9.9: Stretching a line in painter

In the same way, we add code to stretch rectangles and ellipses as well:

```
void CPainterView::OnMouseMove(UINT nFlags, CPoint point)
{
     int nOldMode;

     CClientDC* pDC = new CClientDC(this);
                .
                .
                .
     if((nFlags && MK_LBUTTON) && bRectangleFlag){
          CClientDC dc(this);
          nOldMode = pDC->GetROP2();
          pDC->SetROP2(R2_NOT);
          pDC->SelectStockObject(NULL_BRUSH);
          pDC->Rectangle(OldPoint.x, OldPoint.y, Anchor.x, Anchor.y);
          pDC->Rectangle(Anchor.x, Anchor.y, point.x, point.y);
          OldPoint.x = point.x;
          OldPoint.y = point.y;
          pDC->SetROP2(nOldMode);
     }

     if((nFlags && MK_LBUTTON) && bEllipseFlag){
          CClientDC dc(this);
          nOldMode = pDC->GetROP2();
          pDC->SetROP2(R2_NOT);
          pDC->SelectStockObject(NULL_BRUSH);
          pDC->Ellipse(OldPoint.x, OldPoint.y, Anchor.x, Anchor.y);
          pDC->Ellipse(Anchor.x, Anchor.y, point.x, point.y);
          OldPoint.x = point.x;
          OldPoint.y = point.y;
          pDC->SetROP2(nOldMode);
     }

     delete pDC;

     CView::OnMouseMove(nFlags, point);
}
```

Skill 9

When the user presses the mouse and drags it to the Draw To point, they stretch a figure of the type they want to draw, so they can see how that figure will look when complete. This is a very powerful technique, and now it's part of our painter program.

There is still one step missing from our painter demo program—adding code to OnDraw(). The code in OnDraw() handles cases in which the program's display needs to be refreshed. In fact, placing code in OnDraw() can be a problem for programmers with complex programs, because the program is supposed to re-create its display in that method, no matter how complex that display might be.

In our case, for example, the user may have drawn all kinds of graphics in our window. Are we supposed to remember each mouse movement? The answer lies in the use of metafiles, as we'll see next.

Refreshing Painter's Display

A metafile is a memory object that supports a device context. When the user performs any device context action, we can mirror that action in a metafile. Then, when it comes time to re-create all the actions the user performed, as when it's time to refresh the screen, we can simply *play back* that metafile. That will repeat all the graphics calls for us, automatically re-creating our display. Let's look into this now—the CMetaFileDC class methods appear in Table 9.2.

T A B L E 9 . 2 : The CMetaFileDC Class Methods

Method	Does This
Close	Closes the device context, creates a metafile handle.
CloseEnhanced	Closes an enhanced-metafile device context, creates an enhanced-metafile handle.
CMetaFileDC	Constructs a CMetaFileDC object.
Create	Creates the Windows metafile device context, attaches it to the CmetaFileDC object.
CreateEnhanced	Creates a metafile device context for an enhanced-format metafile.

The screen refreshing takes place in OnDraw(). Currently, that method looks like this in our program:

```
void CPainterView::OnDraw(CDC* pDC)
{
    CPainterDoc* pDoc = GetDocument();
    ASSERT_VALID(pDoc);

    // TODO: add draw code for native data here
}
```

Let's add code to handle screen refreshes now. We'll create a device context for a metafile and then we'll be able to draw in that device context to back up all our graphics. When it's time to refresh the screen, we'll just play that metafile back.

We begin by adding a new pointer to the metafile device context that we'll use in our program, pMetaFileDC, in our program's document header:

```
// painterDoc.h : interface of the CPainterDoc class
        .
        .
        .
// Implementation
public:
    virtual ~CPainterDoc();
➜   CMetaFileDC* pMetaFileDC;
        .
        .
        .
}
```

Next, we allocate a new CMetaFileDC object and call its Create() method to create it in the document's constructor:

```
CPainterDoc::CPainterDoc()
{
➜   pMetaFileDC = new CMetaFileDC();
➜   pMetaFileDC->Create();

}
```

This is the metafile device context in which we'll mirror all the user's actions. But how do we mirror those actions in the metafile device context?

Mirroring Graphics Calls in a MetaFile

We must mirror everything the user does on-screen in the metafile. That means that each time we call a device context method for our view, we'll also make the same call in the metafile device context, like this where we draw lines and rectangles:

```
void CPainterView::OnLButtonUp(UINT nFlags, CPoint point)
{

    CPainterDoc* pDoc = GetDocument();
    ASSERT_VALID(pDoc);

    DrawTo.x = point.x;
    DrawTo.y = point.y;

    CClientDC* pDC = new CClientDC(this);
```

```
          if(bLineFlag){
              pDC->MoveTo(Anchor.x, Anchor.y);
              pDC->LineTo(DrawTo.x, DrawTo.y);
→             pDoc->pMetaFileDC->MoveTo(Anchor.x, Anchor.y);
→             pDoc->pMetaFileDC->LineTo(DrawTo.x, DrawTo.y);
          }

          if(bRectangleFlag){
              pDC->SelectStockObject(NULL_BRUSH);
              pDC->Rectangle(Anchor.x, Anchor.y, DrawTo.x, DrawTo.y);
→             pDoc->pMetaFileDC->SelectStockObject(NULL_BRUSH);
→             pDoc->pMetaFileDC->Rectangle(Anchor.x, Anchor.y, DrawTo.x,
   ➥DrawTo.y);
          }
                      .
                      .
                      .

     }
```

We place such mirror code throughout our program so that every step we make in the view's device context, we also make in the metafile device context. This stores all those actions in the metafile, where they are ready to be played back.

At this point, we have a complete backup of all of the user's drawing actions in the metafile device context. Now we can use that metafile to restore the screen graphics as needed.

Playing Back a Metafile

In OnDraw(), we are supposed to re-create the painter program's display, which now just means playing back the metafile. Playing back a metafile means that you have to close it, which gives you a handle to that metafile, and you use the handle to play the metafile back; that process looks like this in OnDraw():

```
void CPainterView::OnDraw(CDC* pDC)
{
     CPainterDoc* pDoc = GetDocument();
     ASSERT_VALID(pDoc);

→    HMETAFILE MetaFileHandle = pDoc->pMetaFileDC->Close();
→    pDC->PlayMetaFile(MetaFileHandle);
                 .
                 .
                 .

}
```

However, closing a metafile means that we can't write to it anymore. Does that mean that we've lost all the current graphics when we need to refresh the screen the next time? No, we can create a new metafile and play the old one (which we have a handle to) in the new metafile:

```
void CPainterView::OnDraw(CDC* pDC)
{
    CPainterDoc* pDoc = GetDocument();
    ASSERT_VALID(pDoc);

    HMETAFILE MetaFileHandle = pDoc->pMetaFileDC->Close();
    pDC->PlayMetaFile(MetaFileHandle);
→   CMetaFileDC* ReplacementMetaFile = new CMetaFileDC();
→   ReplacementMetaFile->Create();
→   ReplacementMetaFile->PlayMetaFile(MetaFileHandle);
            .
            .
            .

}
```

At this point we can install the new replacement metafile in our program as the backup metafile, and delete the old metafile this way:

```
void CPainterView::OnDraw(CDC* pDC)
{
    CPainterDoc* pDoc = GetDocument();
    ASSERT_VALID(pDoc);

    HMETAFILE MetaFileHandle = pDoc->pMetaFileDC->Close();
    pDC->PlayMetaFile(MetaFileHandle);
    CMetaFileDC* ReplacementMetaFile = new CMetaFileDC();
    ReplacementMetaFile->Create();
    ReplacementMetaFile->PlayMetaFile(MetaFileHandle);
→   DeleteMetaFile(MetaFileHandle);
→   delete pDoc->pMetaFileDC;
→   pDoc->pMetaFileDC = ReplacementMetaFile;
}
```

Now we've replayed the graphics in the client area as we were supposed to in OnDraw(), and created a new metafile for next time.

This solves an old Visual C++ problem: restoring a program's display in OnDraw(). Using metafiles, the solution was easy. Now we're able to refresh our graphics display whenever it's needed.

Skill 9

We can do more with metafiles; for example, now that we have our program's graphics stored in a metafile, we can store that metafile on disk.

Saving Graphics Files

To store a metafile on disk, we just use the CMetaFileDC CopyMetaFile() method. Let's put this in action. Using ClassWizard, connect member functions to the three File menu items, New, Save, and Open, in our program.

We'll add code to these menu items to create a new painter document, to save our graphics in a file named painter.wmf (.wmf is the usual extension for a Windows metafile on disk), and to read that file back in.

Open the new OnFileSave() method now:

```
void CPainterView::OnFileSave()
{
    // TODO: Add your command handler code here

}
```

Here, we will close the current metafile, creating a new metafile handle, and we'll pass this handle to CopyMetaFile(), giving that method the name of the file to save the metafile to:

```
    void CPainterView::OnFileSave()
    {
➜       CPainterDoc* pDoc = GetDocument();
➜       ASSERT_VALID(pDoc);

➜       HMETAFILE MetaFileHandle = pDoc->pMetaFileDC->Close();
```

```
→        CopyMetaFile(MetaFileHandle, "painter.wmf");
                     .
                     .
                     .
    }
```

This writes the metafile to disk. In addition, we create a replacement metafile, and play the old metafile in that new metafile:

```
    void CPainterView::OnFileSave()
    {
        CPainterDoc* pDoc = GetDocument();
        ASSERT_VALID(pDoc);

        HMETAFILE MetaFileHandle = pDoc->pMetaFileDC->Close();
        CopyMetaFile(MetaFileHandle, "painter.wmf");

→        CMetaFileDC* ReplacementMetaFile = new CMetaFileDC();
→        ReplacementMetaFile->Create();
→        ReplacementMetaFile->PlayMetaFile(MetaFileHandle);
                     .
                     .
                     .
    }
```

Now we install the new metafile and delete the old one:

```
    void CPainterView::OnFileSave()
    {
        CPainterDoc* pDoc = GetDocument();
        ASSERT_VALID(pDoc);

        HMETAFILE MetaFileHandle = pDoc->pMetaFileDC->Close();
        CopyMetaFile(MetaFileHandle, "painter.wmf");

→        CMetaFileDC* ReplacementMetaFile = new CMetaFileDC();
→        ReplacementMetaFile->Create();
→        ReplacementMetaFile->PlayMetaFile(MetaFileHandle);
→        DeleteMetaFile(MetaFileHandle);
→        delete pDoc->pMetaFileDC;
→        pDoc->pMetaFileDC = ReplacementMetaFile;
    }
```

Skill 9

In this way, we've stored the graphics from our painter program on disk in the file painter.wmf, and created a new copy of the metafile that we've installed in our program.

Now we've stored our graphics on disk in a file—but how do we read that file back in?

Opening Graphics Files

We will read the painter.wmf file back in using the OnFileOpen() method:

```
void CPainterView::OnFileOpen()
{
    // TODO: Add your command handler code here

}
```

In this case, we just use the GetMetaFile() method this way to read painter.wmf back in:

```
    void CPainterView::OnFileOpen()
    {
→       CPainterDoc* pDoc = GetDocument();
→       ASSERT_VALID(pDoc);

→       HMETAFILE MetaFileHandle = GetMetaFile("painter.wmf");
                .
                .
                .
    }
```

This creates a new metafile handle, and we want to use that to create a new metafile in our program. To do that, we create a new CMetaFileDC object, play the metafile we read from disk into this new metafile, then install the new metafile in our program after deleting the old metafile:

```
    void CPainterView::OnFileOpen()
    {
        CPainterDoc* pDoc = GetDocument();
        ASSERT_VALID(pDoc);

        HMETAFILE MetaFileHandle = GetMetaFile("painter.wmf");

→       CMetaFileDC* ReplacementMetaFile = new CMetaFileDC();
→       ReplacementMetaFile->Create();
```

```
→      ReplacementMetaFile->PlayMetaFile(MetaFileHandle);
→      DeleteMetaFile(MetaFileHandle);
→      delete pDoc->pMetaFileDC;
→      pDoc->pMetaFileDC = ReplacementMetaFile;

→      Invalidate();
   }
```

Note also that at the end of this method, we call `Invalidate()` so the new metafile is displayed in the program's view.

Now we're able to store our graphics images on disk and read them back in. There's only one more task to complete here—letting the user create a new document with the New menu item.

Creating a New Document

Currently, the `OnFileNew()` method looks like this:

```
void CPainterView::OnFileNew()
{
       // TODO: Add your command handler code here

}
```

If the user clicks the New item in the File menu, they want to create a new document. We will do that by creating a new empty metafile, installing that metafile in our program, and calling `Invalidate()` so the empty metafile is played. The `Invalidate()` method first clears the view, so the result of playing our blank metafile will be a blank screen, associated with a blank metafile, and the user is free to start drawing again.

First, we create the new metafile:

```
   void CPainterView::OnFileNew()
   {
→      CPainterDoc* pDoc = GetDocument();
→      ASSERT_VALID(pDoc);

→      CMetaFileDC* ReplacementMetaFile = new CMetaFileDC();
→      ReplacementMetaFile->Create();
          .
          .
          .
   }
```

Skill 9

Then we delete the old metafile, put the new, empty one in its place, and call Invalidate() to blank the screen:

```
void CPainterView::OnFileNew()
{
    CPainterDoc* pDoc = GetDocument();
    ASSERT_VALID(pDoc);

    CMetaFileDC* ReplacementMetaFile = new CMetaFileDC();
    ReplacementMetaFile->Create();
➡   delete pDoc->pMetaFileDC;
➡   pDoc->pMetaFileDC = ReplacementMetaFile;

➡   Invalidate();
}
```

And that finishes our graphics file handling for the moment!

The Painter Program Is Complete

The painter program is complete—we've allowed the user to draw rectangles, lines, circles, ellipses, fill figures with color, draw freehand, use the tools we put in the toolbar, stretch graphics figures, save those figures to disk, restore them, and create a new document. Quite a lot for one skill!

The code for this program appears in painterView.h/painterView.cpp.

painterView.h and *painterView.cpp*

```
// painterView.h : interface of the CPainterView class
//
////////////////////////////////////////////////////////////////////////////

#if !defined(AFX_PAINTERVIEW_H__A4A35E0D_94AC_11D0_8860_444553540000__INCLUDED_)
#define AFX_PAINTERVIEW_H__A4A35E0D_94AC_11D0_8860_444553540000__INCLUDED_

#if _MSC_VER >= 1000
#pragma once
#endif // _MSC_VER >= 1000

class CPainterView : public CView
{
protected: // create from serialization only
    CPainterView();
    DECLARE_DYNCREATE(CPainterView)

// Attributes
```

```
public:
     CPainterDoc* GetDocument();

// Operations
public:

// Overrides
     // ClassWizard generated virtual function overrides
     //{{AFX_VIRTUAL(CPainterView)
     public:
     virtual void OnDraw(CDC* pDC);   // overridden to draw this view
     virtual BOOL PreCreateWindow(CREATESTRUCT& cs);
     protected:
     virtual BOOL OnPreparePrinting(CPrintInfo* pInfo);
     virtual void OnBeginPrinting(CDC* pDC, CPrintInfo* pInfo);
     virtual void OnEndPrinting(CDC* pDC, CPrintInfo* pInfo);
     //}}AFX_VIRTUAL

// Implementation
public:
     virtual ~CPainterView();
#ifdef _DEBUG
     virtual void AssertValid() const;
     virtual void Dump(CDumpContext& dc) const;
#endif

protected:
     CPoint Anchor;
     CPoint DrawTo;
     CPoint OldPoint;
     boolean bDrawFlag;
     boolean bLineFlag;
     boolean bRectangleFlag;
     boolean bEllipseFlag;
     boolean bFillFlag;
     void MakeAllFlagsFalse();

// Generated message map functions
protected:
     //{{AFX_MSG(CPainterView)
     afx_msg void OnLButtonDown(UINT nFlags, CPoint point);
     afx_msg void OnLButtonUp(UINT nFlags, CPoint point);
     afx_msg void OnMouseMove(UINT nFlags, CPoint point);
     afx_msg void OnToolsDrawfreehand();
     afx_msg void OnToolsEllipse();
     afx_msg void OnToolsFillfigure();
     afx_msg void OnToolsLine();
     afx_msg void OnToolsRectangle();
```

```
        afx_msg void OnUpdateToolsDrawfreehand(CCmdUI* pCmdUI);
        afx_msg void OnUpdateToolsEllipse(CCmdUI* pCmdUI);
        afx_msg void OnUpdateToolsFillfigure(CCmdUI* pCmdUI);
        afx_msg void OnUpdateToolsLine(CCmdUI* pCmdUI);
        afx_msg void OnUpdateToolsRectangle(CCmdUI* pCmdUI);
        //}}AFX_MSG
        DECLARE_MESSAGE_MAP()
};

#ifndef _DEBUG   // debug version in painterView.cpp
inline CPainterDoc* CPainterView::GetDocument()
    { return (CPainterDoc*)m_pDocument; }
#endif

/////////////////////////////////////////////////////////////////////////

//{{AFX_INSERT_LOCATION}}
// Microsoft Developer Studio will insert additional declarations immediately
// before the previous line.

#endif // !defined(AFX_PAINTERVIEW_H__A4A35E0D_94AC_11D0_8860_444553540000__
➥INCLUDED_)




// painterView.cpp : implementation of the CPainterView class
//

#include "stdafx.h"
#include "painter.h"

#include "painterDoc.h"
#include "painterView.h"

#ifdef _DEBUG
#define new DEBUG_NEW
#undef THIS_FILE
static char THIS_FILE[] = __FILE__;
#endif

/////////////////////////////////////////////////////////////////////////
// CPainterView

IMPLEMENT_DYNCREATE(CPainterView, CView)

BEGIN_MESSAGE_MAP(CPainterView, CView)
    //{{AFX_MSG_MAP(CPainterView)
    ON_WM_LBUTTONDOWN()
    ON_WM_LBUTTONUP()
```

```
        ON_WM_MOUSEMOVE()
        ON_COMMAND(ID_TOOLS_DRAWFREEHAND, OnToolsDrawfreehand)
        ON_COMMAND(ID_TOOLS_ELLIPSE, OnToolsEllipse)
        ON_COMMAND(ID_TOOLS_FILLFIGURE, OnToolsFillfigure)
        ON_COMMAND(ID_TOOLS_LINE, OnToolsLine)
        ON_COMMAND(ID_TOOLS_RECTANGLE, OnToolsRectangle)
        ON_UPDATE_COMMAND_UI(ID_TOOLS_DRAWFREEHAND, OnUpdateToolsDrawfreehand)
        ON_UPDATE_COMMAND_UI(ID_TOOLS_ELLIPSE, OnUpdateToolsEllipse)
        ON_UPDATE_COMMAND_UI(ID_TOOLS_FILLFIGURE, OnUpdateToolsFillfigure)
        ON_UPDATE_COMMAND_UI(ID_TOOLS_LINE, OnUpdateToolsLine)
        ON_UPDATE_COMMAND_UI(ID_TOOLS_RECTANGLE, OnUpdateToolsRectangle)
        ON_COMMAND(ID_FILE_SAVE, OnFileSave)
        ON_COMMAND(ID_FILE_OPEN, OnFileOpen)
        ON_COMMAND(ID_FILE_NEW, OnFileNew)
        //}}AFX_MSG_MAP
        // Standard printing commands
        ON_COMMAND(ID_FILE_PRINT, CView::OnFilePrint)
        ON_COMMAND(ID_FILE_PRINT_DIRECT, CView::OnFilePrint)
        ON_COMMAND(ID_FILE_PRINT_PREVIEW, CView::OnFilePrintPreview)
END_MESSAGE_MAP()

/////////////////////////////////////////////////////////////////////////////
// CPainterView construction/destruction

CPainterView::CPainterView()
{
        // TODO: add construction code here
        MakeAllFlagsFalse();
}


CPainterView::~CPainterView()
{
}


BOOL CPainterView::PreCreateWindow(CREATESTRUCT& cs)
{
        // TODO: Modify the Window class or styles here by modifying
        //   the CREATESTRUCT cs
        cs.lpszClass = AfxRegisterWndClass(CS_DBLCLKS, AfxGetApp()
➥->LoadStandardCursor(IDC_CROSS), (HBRUSH)(COLOR_WINDOW+1), AfxGetApp()
➥->LoadIcon(IDR_MAINFRAME));
        return CView::PreCreateWindow(cs);
}


/////////////////////////////////////////////////////////////////////////////
// CPainterView drawing

void CPainterView::OnDraw(CDC* pDC)
{
```

Skill 9

```
    CPainterDoc* pDoc = GetDocument();
    ASSERT_VALID(pDoc);

    HMETAFILE MetaFileHandle = pDoc->pMetaFileDC->Close();
    pDC->PlayMetaFile(MetaFileHandle);
    CMetaFileDC* ReplacementMetaFile = new CMetaFileDC();
    ReplacementMetaFile->Create();
    ReplacementMetaFile->PlayMetaFile(MetaFileHandle);
    DeleteMetaFile(MetaFileHandle);
    delete pDoc->pMetaFileDC;
    pDoc->pMetaFileDC = ReplacementMetaFile;

    // TODO: add draw code for native data here
}

/////////////////////////////////////////////////////////////////////////////
// CPainterView printing

BOOL CPainterView::OnPreparePrinting(CPrintInfo* pInfo)
{
    // default preparation
    return DoPreparePrinting(pInfo);
}

void CPainterView::OnBeginPrinting(CDC* /*pDC*/, CPrintInfo* /*pInfo*/)
{
    // TODO: add extra initialization before printing
}

void CPainterView::OnEndPrinting(CDC* /*pDC*/, CPrintInfo* /*pInfo*/)
{
    // TODO: add cleanup after printing
}

/////////////////////////////////////////////////////////////////////////////
// CPainterView diagnostics

#ifdef _DEBUG
void CPainterView::AssertValid() const
{
    CView::AssertValid();
}

void CPainterView::Dump(CDumpContext& dc) const
{
    CView::Dump(dc);
}

CPainterDoc* CPainterView::GetDocument() // non-debug version is inline
```

```
{
    ASSERT(m_pDocument->IsKindOf(RUNTIME_CLASS(CPainterDoc)));
    return (CPainterDoc*)m_pDocument;
}
#endif //_DEBUG

/////////////////////////////////////////////////////////////////////////
// CPainterView message handlers

void CPainterView::OnLButtonDown(UINT nFlags, CPoint point)
{
    Anchor.x = point.x;
    Anchor.y = point.y;
    OldPoint.x = Anchor.x;
    OldPoint.y = Anchor.y;

    CView::OnLButtonDown(nFlags, point);
}

void CPainterView::OnLButtonUp(UINT nFlags, CPoint point)
{

    CPainterDoc* pDoc = GetDocument();
    ASSERT_VALID(pDoc);

    DrawTo.x = point.x;
    DrawTo.y = point.y;

    CClientDC* pDC = new CClientDC(this);

    if(bLineFlag){
        pDC->MoveTo(Anchor.x, Anchor.y);
        pDC->LineTo(DrawTo.x, DrawTo.y);
        pDoc->pMetaFileDC->MoveTo(Anchor.x, Anchor.y);
        pDoc->pMetaFileDC->LineTo(DrawTo.x, DrawTo.y);
    }

    if(bRectangleFlag){
        pDC->SelectStockObject(NULL_BRUSH);
        pDC->Rectangle(Anchor.x, Anchor.y, DrawTo.x, DrawTo.y);
        pDoc->pMetaFileDC->SelectStockObject(NULL_BRUSH);
        pDoc->pMetaFileDC->Rectangle(Anchor.x, Anchor.y, DrawTo.x, DrawTo.y);
    }

    if(bEllipseFlag){
        pDC->SelectStockObject(NULL_BRUSH);
        pDC->Ellipse(Anchor.x, Anchor.y, DrawTo.x, DrawTo.y);
        pDoc->pMetaFileDC->SelectStockObject(NULL_BRUSH);
        pDoc->pMetaFileDC->Ellipse(Anchor.x, Anchor.y, DrawTo.x, DrawTo.y);
```

Skill 9

```
        }

        if(bFillFlag){
            pDC->SelectStockObject(BLACK_BRUSH);
            pDC->FloodFill(Anchor.x, Anchor.y, RGB(0, 0, 0));
            pDoc->pMetaFileDC->SelectStockObject(BLACK_BRUSH);
            pDoc->pMetaFileDC->FloodFill(Anchor.x, Anchor.y, RGB(0, 0, 0));
        }

        delete pDC;

        CView::OnLButtonUp(nFlags, point);
}

void CPainterView::OnMouseMove(UINT nFlags, CPoint point)
{
        CPainterDoc* pDoc = GetDocument();
        ASSERT_VALID(pDoc);

        int nOldMode;

        CClientDC* pDC = new CClientDC(this);

        if((nFlags && MK_LBUTTON) && bDrawFlag){
            pDC->MoveTo(Anchor.x, Anchor.y);
            pDC->LineTo(point.x, point.y);
            pDoc->pMetaFileDC->MoveTo(Anchor.x, Anchor.y);
            pDoc->pMetaFileDC->LineTo(point.x, point.y);
            Anchor.x = point.x;
            Anchor.y = point.y;
        }

        if((nFlags && MK_LBUTTON) && bLineFlag){
            nOldMode = pDC->GetROP2();
            pDC->SetROP2(R2_NOT);
            pDC->MoveTo(Anchor.x, Anchor.y);
            pDC->LineTo(OldPoint.x, OldPoint.y);
            pDC->MoveTo(Anchor.x, Anchor.y);
            pDC->LineTo(point.x, point.y);
            OldPoint.x = point.x;
            OldPoint.y = point.y;
            pDC->SetROP2(nOldMode);
        }

        if((nFlags && MK_LBUTTON) && bRectangleFlag){
            CClientDC dc(this);
            nOldMode = pDC->GetROP2();
            pDC->SetROP2(R2_NOT);
```

```
                pDC->SelectStockObject(NULL_BRUSH);
                pDC->Rectangle(OldPoint.x, OldPoint.y, Anchor.x, Anchor.y);
                pDC->Rectangle(Anchor.x, Anchor.y, point.x, point.y);
                OldPoint.x = point.x;
                OldPoint.y = point.y;
                pDC->SetROP2(nOldMode);
        }

    if((nFlags && MK_LBUTTON) && bEllipseFlag){
                CClientDC dc(this);
                nOldMode = pDC->GetROP2();
                pDC->SetROP2(R2_NOT);
                pDC->SelectStockObject(NULL_BRUSH);
                pDC->Ellipse(OldPoint.x, OldPoint.y, Anchor.x, Anchor.y);
                pDC->Ellipse(Anchor.x, Anchor.y, point.x, point.y);
                OldPoint.x = point.x;
                OldPoint.y = point.y;
                pDC->SetROP2(nOldMode);
        }

        delete pDC;

        CView::OnMouseMove(nFlags, point);
}

void CPainterView::MakeAllFlagsFalse()
{
        bDrawFlag = false;
        bLineFlag = false;
        bRectangleFlag = false;
        bEllipseFlag = false;
        bFillFlag = false;
}


void CPainterView::OnToolsDrawfreehand()
{
        MakeAllFlagsFalse();
        bDrawFlag = true;


}

void CPainterView::OnToolsEllipse()
{
        MakeAllFlagsFalse();
        bEllipseFlag = true;


}
```

Skill 9

```
void CPainterView::OnToolsFillfigure()
{
    MakeAllFlagsFalse();
    bFillFlag = true;

}

void CPainterView::OnToolsLine()
{
    MakeAllFlagsFalse();
    bLineFlag = true;

}

void CPainterView::OnToolsRectangle()
{
    MakeAllFlagsFalse();
    bRectangleFlag = true;

}

void CPainterView::OnUpdateToolsDrawfreehand(CCmdUI* pCmdUI)
{
    pCmdUI->SetCheck(bDrawFlag);
}

void CPainterView::OnUpdateToolsEllipse(CCmdUI* pCmdUI)
{
    pCmdUI->SetCheck(bEllipseFlag);

}

void CPainterView::OnUpdateToolsFillfigure(CCmdUI* pCmdUI)
{
    pCmdUI->SetCheck(bFillFlag);

}

void CPainterView::OnUpdateToolsLine(CCmdUI* pCmdUI)
{
    pCmdUI->SetCheck(bLineFlag);

}

void CPainterView::OnUpdateToolsRectangle(CCmdUI* pCmdUI)
{
    pCmdUI->SetCheck(bRectangleFlag);
```

```
    }

    void CPainterView::OnFileSave()
    {
        // TODO: Add your command handler code here
        CPainterDoc* pDoc = GetDocument();
        ASSERT_VALID(pDoc);

        HMETAFILE MetaFileHandle = pDoc->pMetaFileDC->Close();
        CopyMetaFile(MetaFileHandle, "painter.wmf");

        CMetaFileDC* ReplacementMetaFile = new CMetaFileDC();
        ReplacementMetaFile->Create();
        ReplacementMetaFile->PlayMetaFile(MetaFileHandle);
        DeleteMetaFile(MetaFileHandle);
        delete pDoc->pMetaFileDC;
        pDoc->pMetaFileDC = ReplacementMetaFile;

    }

    void CPainterView::OnFileOpen()
    {
        // TODO: Add your command handler code here
        CPainterDoc* pDoc = GetDocument();
        ASSERT_VALID(pDoc);

        HMETAFILE MetaFileHandle = GetMetaFile("painter.wmf");

        CMetaFileDC* ReplacementMetaFile = new CMetaFileDC();
        ReplacementMetaFile->Create();
        ReplacementMetaFile->PlayMetaFile(MetaFileHandle);
        DeleteMetaFile(MetaFileHandle);
        delete pDoc->pMetaFileDC;
        pDoc->pMetaFileDC = ReplacementMetaFile;

        Invalidate();
    }

    void CPainterView::OnFileNew()
    {
        // TODO: Add your command handler code here
        CPainterDoc* pDoc = GetDocument();
        ASSERT_VALID(pDoc);

        CMetaFileDC* ReplacementMetaFile = new CMetaFileDC();
        ReplacementMetaFile->Create();
        delete pDoc->pMetaFileDC;
```

Skill 9

```
pDoc->pMetaFileDC = ReplacementMetaFile;

Invalidate();
}
```

We've seen a great deal about graphics and metafiles in this skill. In the next skill, we're going to turn to another powerful aspect of Visual C++—file handling.

Are You Experienced?

Now You Can...

- ☑ Draw lines, rectangles, circles, and ellipses from code
- ☑ "Stretch" graphics figures and use various binary raster drawing modes
- ☑ Fill graphics figures with color
- ☑ Let the user draw freehand with the mouse
- ☑ Use metafiles to save and restore your program's display
- ☑ Save and retrieve graphics in a file on disk

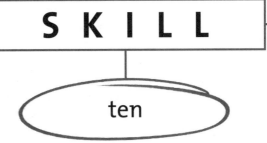

S K I L L

ten

Getting the Most Out of
File Handling

❑ **Writing data to disk and reading it back in**

❑ **How Visual C++ serialization works**

❑ **Serializing common Visual C++ objects**

❑ **Serializing your own custom objects**

❑ **Standard file handling with the CFile class**

This is our skill on Visual C++ file handling, and we'll see that Visual C++ has already added considerable file support, both in our programs' menus and behind the scenes.

As we've discussed, our non-dialog AppWizard programs already have a File menu built in, with menu items such as Save As and Open and New, and we'll see how to put those menu items to work in this skill. Doing so means using the built-in file-handling capabilities of those programs, which is a technique called *serializing* data. When we set up our programs to serialize our data in the document's `Serialize()` method, the user can use the File menu's file-handling menu items like Open and Save and the rest. We'll see how to do that in this skill, showing how to serialize—that is, write to or read from disk—both the built-in classes of Visual C++, like `CString`, and custom classes that we build ourselves.

You don't always have a document object to do serializing for you, however. For example, dialog-based programs don't use Visual C++ documents; in such cases, you use the MFC `CFile` class instead. This class offers us the support we'll need in document-less programs to work with files, both writing data out to disk and reading it back in.

What Is Visual C++ Serializing All About?

Serializing is the process of writing or reading an object of some type to a "persistent storage medium," which means a disk. The document handles our data in normal Visual C++ programs, and this is the skill where we specialize in looking at handling the document object. In particular, when we place code in the document's `Serialize()` function to serialize our data to and from disk, we will automatically support our program's file-handling items in its File menu.

We'll put an example together now, since it's always better to learn about a new concept at work rather than talk about it in the abstract. This new example is called writer, and it will write a string of text that the user types in to disk, and read it back in again on demand.

Creating the Writer Program

Using AppWizard, create the writer program now as an SDI program. We'll add the code to let writer accept and display keystrokes first. As we have done before,

we will store the characters the user types in a CString object named
StringData, which we place in the document:

```
// writerDoc.h : interface of the CWriterDoc class

            .
            .
            .
class CWriterDoc : public CDocument
{
protected: // create from serialization only
    CWriterDoc();
    DECLARE_DYNCREATE(CWriterDoc)

// Attributes
public:
    CString StringData;
            .
            .
            .
```

We also initialize that object to the empty string in the document's constructor:

```
CWriterDoc::CWriterDoc()
{
    StringData = "";
}
```

Using ClassWizard, we connect the WM_CHAR message to the method OnChar(),
and we add the code we need to store the character the user has just typed in the
StringData object:

```
void CWriterView::OnChar(UINT nChar, UINT nRepCnt, UINT nFlags)
{
    CWriterDoc* pDoc = GetDocument();
    ASSERT_VALID(pDoc);

    pDoc->StringData += nChar;
    Invalidate();

    CView::OnChar(nChar, nRepCnt, nFlags);
}
```

Note that we also invalidate the view when the user types a new character. To
display the new string of text in OnDraw(), we add this line:

```
void CWriterView::OnDraw(CDC* pDC)
{
    CWriterDoc* pDoc = GetDocument();
```

```
        ASSERT_VALID(pDoc);

→       pDC->TextOut(0, 0, pDoc->StringData);

}
```

Now the program can read and display characters that the user types, and it stores those characters in the StringData object. The next step is letting the user store and retrieve our program's data—that is, the StringData object—to and from disk.

Serializing the StringData Object

You'll find that the document class already has a Serialize() method built right in, and that method looks like this now (from writerDoc.cpp):

```
void CWriterDoc::Serialize(CArchive& ar)
{
    if (ar.IsStoring())
    {
        // TODO: add storing code here
    }
    else
    {
        // TODO: add loading code here
    }
}
```

This is where we'll serialize StringData. We are passed a reference named ar to a CArchive object in Serialize() (a reference holds an item's address, but you treat it in code as you would the item itself), and we can use ar just as we used cout and cin in Skill 1. That is, we first check ar's IsStoring() method to see if we are writing data to disk, in which case we serialize StringData this way:

```
void CWriterDoc::Serialize(CArchive& ar)
{
    if (ar.IsStoring())
    {
→       ar << StringData;
    }
    else
    {
        // TODO: add loading code here
    }
}
```

If, on the other hand, we are loading the StringData object back in from disk, we use this line of code:

```
void CWriterDoc::Serialize(CArchive& ar)
{
    if (ar.IsStoring())
    {
        ar << StringData;
    }
    else
    {
➔       ar >> StringData;
    }
}
```

That's it for serializing the StringData string. There is one more touch we'll add here before running the program—when the user adds more data to the StringData object, we can let the document know that the data it is to store has been modified. This means that if the user quits before saving the new data to disk, the program will pop up a dialog box of the kind Windows users are very familiar with: "Save changes to document1?".

We indicate to the document that its data has changed by calling the document method SetModifiedFlag() in OnChar():

```
void CWriterView::OnChar(UINT nChar, UINT nRepCnt, UINT nFlags)
{
    CWriterDoc* pDoc = GetDocument();
    ASSERT_VALID(pDoc);

    pDoc->StringData += nChar;
    Invalidate();
➔   pDoc->SetModifiedFlag();

    CView::OnChar(nChar, nRepCnt, nFlags);
}
```

TIP   The document's modified flag is reset when the user saves the document to disk.

Skill 10

Now we're ready to run the program, as shown in Figure 10.1. In that example, we've typed some text into the writer program, and we're ready to save it to disk.

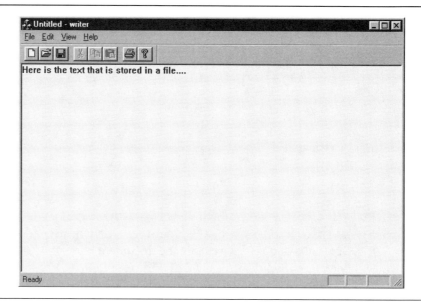

FIGURE 10.1: Typing characters in writer

When the user selects the File menu's Save As item, the Save As dialog box appears, as shown in Figure 10.2. We save the program's data in a file named `text.dat`.

FIGURE 10.2: The Save As dialog box

The user can now read the file back in by selecting the Open item in the File menu, which makes the Open dialog box appear, as in Figure 10.3. Here we select `text.dat` and read that file back in.

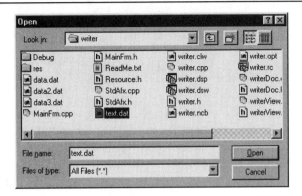

FIGURE 10.3: The Open dialog box

This opens the file and displays its contents, as shown in Figure 10.4 (when a file is read in and the document changed, the view is invalidated so it refreshes itself automatically and displays the new document). Note that the title bar now reads "text.dat - writer" instead of "Untitled - writer" as it did before. In this way, the program indicates what the current document is.

There are one or two things to add to this program. First, we should add some code to clear the text in `StringData` when the user selects the New item in the File menu to create a new document. We do that in the document's `OnNewDocument()` method, which looks like this now (note the call to `UpdateAllViews()`; as we'll see in the next skill, this call causes the view of views in this program to refresh themselves with the document's new data):

```
BOOL CWriterDoc::OnNewDocument()
{
    if (!CDocument::OnNewDocument())
        return FALSE;

    // TODO: add reinitialization code here
    // (SDI documents will reuse this document)
    UpdateAllViews(NULL);

    return TRUE;
}
```

Skill 10

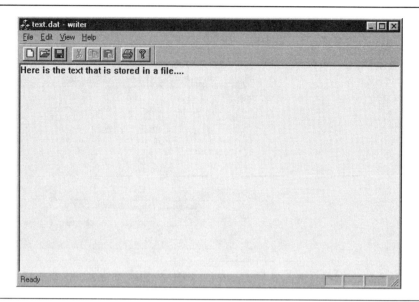

FIGURE 10.4: Reading text back in

This is how we add the code to empty the `StringData` object when the user creates a new document:

```
BOOL CWriterDoc::OnNewDocument()
{
    if (!CDocument::OnNewDocument())
        return FALSE;

    // TODO: add reinitialization code here
    // (SDI documents will reuse this document)
➜   StringData = "";
    UpdateAllViews(NULL);

    return TRUE;
}
```

Now we've made the File menu's New item active.

We should also note that if we had a number of objects to serialize (and they might be of different classes), we simply load them back into the program in the same order that we stored them to start with:

```
void CWriterDoc::Serialize(CArchive& ar)
{
```

```
            if (ar.IsStoring())
            {
→                ar << Data1;
→                ar << Data2;
            }
            else
            {
→                ar >> Data1;
→                ar >> Data2;
            }
        }
```

In this way, we're able to serialize a number of objects, not just one. The code for the writer program appears in writerView.h/writerView.cpp.

writerView.h and *writerView.cpp*

```cpp
// writerView.h : interface of the CWriterView class
//
/////////////////////////////////////////////////////////////////////////////

#if !defined(AFX_WRITERVIEW_H__6AE5A14D_9584_11D0_8860_444553540000__INCLUDED_)
#define AFX_WRITERVIEW_H__6AE5A14D_9584_11D0_8860_444553540000__INCLUDED_

#if _MSC_VER >= 1000
#pragma once
#endif // _MSC_VER >= 1000

class CWriterView : public CView
{
protected: // create from serialization only
    CWriterView();
    DECLARE_DYNCREATE(CWriterView)

// Attributes
public:
    CWriterDoc* GetDocument();

// Operations
public:

// Overrides
    // ClassWizard generated virtual function overrides
    //{{AFX_VIRTUAL(CWriterView)
    public:
    virtual void OnDraw(CDC* pDC);  // overridden to draw this view
    virtual BOOL PreCreateWindow(CREATESTRUCT& cs);
```

Skill 10

```
    protected:
    virtual BOOL OnPreparePrinting(CPrintInfo* pInfo);
    virtual void OnBeginPrinting(CDC* pDC, CPrintInfo* pInfo);
    virtual void OnEndPrinting(CDC* pDC, CPrintInfo* pInfo);
    //}}AFX_VIRTUAL

// Implementation
public:
    virtual ~CWriterView();
#ifdef _DEBUG
    virtual void AssertValid() const;
    virtual void Dump(CDumpContext& dc) const;
#endif

protected:

// Generated message map functions
protected:
    //{{AFX_MSG(CWriterView)
    afx_msg void OnChar(UINT nChar, UINT nRepCnt, UINT nFlags);
    //}}AFX_MSG
    DECLARE_MESSAGE_MAP()
};

#ifndef _DEBUG  // debug version in writerView.cpp
inline CWriterDoc* CWriterView::GetDocument()
   { return (CWriterDoc*)m_pDocument; }
#endif

/////////////////////////////////////////////////////////////////////////////

//{{AFX_INSERT_LOCATION}}
// Microsoft Developer Studio will insert additional declarations immediately
// before the previous line.

#endif //!defined(AFX_WRITERVIEW_H__6AE5A14D_9584_11D0_8860_444553540000__
➥INCLUDED_)


// writerView.cpp : implementation of the CWriterView class
//

#include "stdafx.h"
#include "writer.h"

#include "writerDoc.h"
#include "writerView.h"
```

```
#ifdef _DEBUG
#define new DEBUG_NEW
#undef THIS_FILE
static char THIS_FILE[] = __FILE__;
#endif

//////////////////////////////////////////////////////////////////////
// CWriterView

IMPLEMENT_DYNCREATE(CWriterView, CView)

BEGIN_MESSAGE_MAP(CWriterView, CView)
    //{{AFX_MSG_MAP(CWriterView)
    ON_WM_CHAR()
    //}}AFX_MSG_MAP
    // Standard printing commands
    ON_COMMAND(ID_FILE_PRINT, CView::OnFilePrint)
    ON_COMMAND(ID_FILE_PRINT_DIRECT, CView::OnFilePrint)
    ON_COMMAND(ID_FILE_PRINT_PREVIEW, CView::OnFilePrintPreview)
END_MESSAGE_MAP()

//////////////////////////////////////////////////////////////////////
// CWriterView construction/destruction

CWriterView::CWriterView()
{
    // TODO: add construction code here

}

CWriterView::~CWriterView()
{
}

BOOL CWriterView::PreCreateWindow(CREATESTRUCT& cs)
{
    // TODO: Modify the Window class or styles here by modifying
    //   the CREATESTRUCT cs

    return CView::PreCreateWindow(cs);
}

//////////////////////////////////////////////////////////////////////
// CWriterView drawing

void CWriterView::OnDraw(CDC* pDC)
{
    CWriterDoc* pDoc = GetDocument();
```

```
        ASSERT_VALID(pDoc);

        pDC->TextOut(0, 0, pDoc->StringData);

        // TODO: add draw code for native data here
}

/////////////////////////////////////////////////////////////////////////////
// CWriterView printing

BOOL CWriterView::OnPreparePrinting(CPrintInfo* pInfo)
{
        // default preparation
        return DoPreparePrinting(pInfo);
}

void CWriterView::OnBeginPrinting(CDC* /*pDC*/, CPrintInfo* /*pInfo*/)
{
        // TODO: add extra initialization before printing
}

void CWriterView::OnEndPrinting(CDC* /*pDC*/, CPrintInfo* /*pInfo*/)
{
        // TODO: add cleanup after printing
}

/////////////////////////////////////////////////////////////////////////////
// CWriterView diagnostics

#ifdef _DEBUG
void CWriterView::AssertValid() const
{
        CView::AssertValid();
}

void CWriterView::Dump(CDumpContext& dc) const
{
        CView::Dump(dc);
}

CWriterDoc* CWriterView::GetDocument() // non-debug version is inline
{
        ASSERT(m_pDocument->IsKindOf(RUNTIME_CLASS(CWriterDoc)));
        return (CWriterDoc*)m_pDocument;
}
#endif //_DEBUG

/////////////////////////////////////////////////////////////////////////////
```

```
// CWriterView message handlers

void CWriterView::OnChar(UINT nChar, UINT nRepCnt, UINT nFlags)
{
    // TODO: Add your message handler code here and/or call default
    CWriterDoc* pDoc = GetDocument();
    ASSERT_VALID(pDoc);

    pDoc->StringData += nChar;
    Invalidate();
    pDoc->SetModifiedFlag();

    CView::OnChar(nChar, nRepCnt, nFlags);
}
```

What we've done so far works well if you want to serialize objects of the classes that come with Visual C++. But what if you have your own classes? We'll see how to serialize your own custom objects next.

Serializing Your Own Objects

Let's say that we've set up our own new class, CData, and that we want to serialize objects of this class. In this class, we store a string of text, named data, this way:

```
    class CData {
    private:
➜       CString data;
            .
            .
            .
    }
```

We also provide a constructor to initialize that string to the empty string, as well as three methods to work with that string: AddText() to add more text to the end of the string, DrawText() to draw the text in a device context, and ClearText() to clear the string (note that we can define the method's bodies in the class declaration; this is called an *inline* definition):

```
    class CData {
    private:
        CString data;
    public:
➜       CData(){data = CString("");}
➜       void AddText(CString text){data += text;}
```

Skill 10

```
➜        void DrawText(CDC* pDC){pDC->TextOut(0, 0, data);}
➜        void ClearText(){data = "";}
    };
```

Now that we've got our new class, we can put it to work and serialize it. Create a new SDI program now named serializer. Next, using the New item in the Visual C++ File menu and clicking the Files tab in the New dialog box, add a new file to the project: CData.h, and place the above code in that file.

In addition, we include that new file in the document's header (so the document will know about our new CData class) and create a new object of the CData class named DataObject:

```
// serializerDoc.h : interface of the CSerializerDoc class
//
/////////////////////////////////////////////////////////////////////////////
➜#include "CData.h"
            .
            .
            .

// Attributes
public:
➜      CData DataObject;
            .
            .
            .

}
```

Now we're free to use our new DataObject. In this example, we'll record the characters the user types, much like we did in the last example. We do that by adding code to the view's OnChar() method, which adds the newly typed character to the internal data in DataObject using the AddText() method:

```
void CSerializerView::OnChar(UINT nChar, UINT nRepCnt, UINT nFlags)
{
    CSerializerDoc* pDoc = GetDocument();
    ASSERT_VALID(pDoc);

➜        pDoc->DataObject.AddText(CString(nChar));
    Invalidate();
    CView::OnChar(nChar, nRepCnt, nFlags);
}
```

Similarly, we can draw the text in the DataObject object using the DrawText() method like this in the view's OnDraw() method:

```
void CSerializerView::OnDraw(CDC* pDC)
{
    CSerializerDoc* pDoc = GetDocument();
```

```
        ASSERT_VALID(pDoc);

➜       pDoc->DataObject.DrawText(pDC);
    }
```

So far, this example works just like the last one, displaying the text that the user types. However, when it comes to serialization, there's a problem. We can't just use code like this to serialize DataObject:

```
void CWriterDoc::Serialize(CArchive& ar)
{
    if (ar.IsStoring())
    {
        ar << DataObject;         //Does not work
    }
    else
    {
        ar >> DataObject;         //Does not work
    }
}
```

The reason we can't serialize DataObject this way is that we haven't defined how serialization works for the CData class yet, and if we try to use the above code, Visual C++ will tell us that we can't use the << and >> operators with DataObject. Instead, we have to set up the serialization process ourselves, adding code to the CData class so it can be serialized.

Adding Serialization to a Class

To make a class *serializable*, we first must make sure that it's derived from the MFC CObject class (this class is the basis of all MFC classes):

```
➜class CData : public CObject {
 private:
     CString data;
 public:
     CData(){data = CString("");}
     void AddText(CString text){data += text;}
     void DrawText(CDC* pDC){pDC->TextOut(0, 0, data);}
     void ClearText(){data = "";}
};
```

Next, we must include the DECLARE_SERIAL macro in our class definition. This Visual C++ macro adds the declarations of the methods it will use for serialization:

```
class CData : public CObject {
 private:
```

```
        CString data;
→       DECLARE_SERIAL(CData);
    public:
        CData(){data = CString("");}
        void AddText(CString text){data += text;}
        void DrawText(CDC* pDC){pDC->TextOut(0, 0, data);}
        void ClearText(){data = "";}
    };
```

Finally, we must override CObject's Serialize() method:

```
    class CData : public CObject {
    private:
        CString data;
        DECLARE_SERIAL(CData);
    public:
        CData(){data = CString("");}
        void AddText(CString text){data += text;}
        void DrawText(CDC* pDC){pDC->TextOut(0, 0, data);}
        void ClearText(){data = "";}
→       void Serialize(CArchive& archive);
    };
```

To write a new version of Serialize(), we add a new file to the project: CData.cpp. Create that file now and define Serialize() in it this way:

```
    #include "stdafx.h"
    #include "serializerDoc.h"

    void CData::Serialize(CArchive& archive)
    {

    }
```

First, we call the base class's Serialize() method (the base class is CObject):

```
    #include "stdafx.h"

    #include "serializerDoc.h"

    void CData::Serialize(CArchive& archive)
    {
→       CObject::Serialize(archive);
            .
            .
            .
    }
```

Next, we serialize our internal CString data member using the << and >> operators:

```
#include "stdafx.h"
#include "serializerDoc.h"

void CData::Serialize(CArchive& archive)
{
    CObject::Serialize(archive);
→   if(archive.IsStoring()){
→       archive << data;
→   }
→   else{
→       archive >> data;
→   }
}
```

Finally, we use the IMPLEMENT_SERIAL macro, which adds the additional methods that Visual C++ will use for serialization:

```
#include "stdafx.h"
#include "serializerDoc.h"

void CData::Serialize(CArchive& archive)
{
    CObject::Serialize(archive);
    if(archive.IsStoring()){
        archive << data;
    }
    else{
        archive >> data;
    }
}

→IMPLEMENT_SERIAL(CData, CObject, 0)
```

And that's it — we've made our CData class serializable.

To serialize our DataObject object, we just call its Serialize() method in the document's Serialize() method, like this:

```
void CSerializerDoc::Serialize(CArchive& ar)
{
→   DataObject.Serialize(ar);
}
```

That's all it takes—now we're able to send our new object out to disk and to read it back in again, as shown in Figure 10.5. At this point, we're able to serialize our own customized objects.

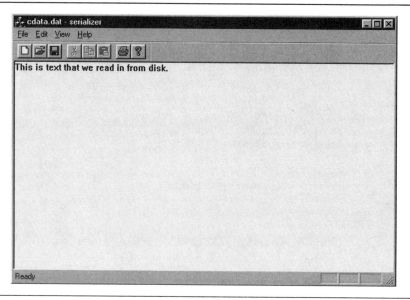

FIGURE 10.5: Serializing our custom object

The code for this program appears in CData.h/CData.cpp, serializerDoc.h/
serializerDoc.cpp, and seralizerView.h/serializerView.cpp.

CData.h and CData.cpp

```
class CData : public CObject {
private:
    CString data;
    DECLARE_SERIAL(CData);
public:
    CData(){data = CString("");}
    void AddText(CString text){data += text;}
    void DrawText(CDC* pDC){pDC->TextOut(0, 0, data);}
    void ClearText(){data = "";}
    void Serialize(CArchive& archive);
};



#include "stdafx.h"
#include "serializerDoc.h"

void CData::Serialize(CArchive& archive)
```

```
        {
            CObject::Serialize(archive);
            if(archive.IsStoring()){
                archive << data;
            }
            else{
                archive >> data;
            }
        }

        IMPLEMENT_SERIAL(CData, CObject, 0)
```

serializerDoc.h and serializerDoc.cpp

```
// serializerDoc.h : interface of the CSerializerDoc class
//
/////////////////////////////////////////////////////////////////////
#include "CData.h"

#if !defined(AFX_SERIALIZERDOC_H__FC0F69AD_9582_11D0_8860_444553540000__
➡INCLUDED_)
#define AFX_SERIALIZERDOC_H__FC0F69AD_9582_11D0_8860_444553540000__INCLUDED_

#if _MSC_VER >= 1000
#pragma once
#endif // _MSC_VER >= 1000

class CSerializerDoc : public CDocument
{
protected: // create from serialization only
    CSerializerDoc();
    DECLARE_DYNCREATE(CSerializerDoc)

// Attributes
public:
    CData DataObject;

// Operations
public:

// Overrides
    // ClassWizard generated virtual function overrides
    //{{AFX_VIRTUAL(CSerializerDoc)
    public:
    virtual BOOL OnNewDocument();
    virtual void Serialize(CArchive& ar);
    //}}AFX_VIRTUAL
```

```
// Implementation
public:
    virtual ~CSerializerDoc();
#ifdef _DEBUG
    virtual void AssertValid() const;
    virtual void Dump(CDumpContext& dc) const;
#endif

protected:

// Generated message map functions
protected:
    //{{AFX_MSG(CSerializerDoc)
        // NOTE - the ClassWizard will add and remove member functions here.
        //    DO NOT EDIT what you see in these blocks of generated code !
    //}}AFX_MSG
    DECLARE_MESSAGE_MAP()
};

/////////////////////////////////////////////////////////////////////////////

//{{AFX_INSERT_LOCATION}}
// Microsoft Developer Studio will insert additional declarations immediately
// before the previous line.

#endif // !defined(AFX_SERIALIZERDOC_H__FC0F69AD_9582_11D0_8860_444553540000__
➥INCLUDED_)




// serializerDoc.cpp : implementation of the CSerializerDoc class
//

#include "stdafx.h"
#include "serializer.h"

#include "serializerDoc.h"

#ifdef _DEBUG
#define new DEBUG_NEW
#undef THIS_FILE
static char THIS_FILE[] = __FILE__;
#endif

/////////////////////////////////////////////////////////////////////////////
// CSerializerDoc
```

```
IMPLEMENT_DYNCREATE(CSerializerDoc, CDocument)

BEGIN_MESSAGE_MAP(CSerializerDoc, CDocument)
    //{{AFX_MSG_MAP(CSerializerDoc)
        // NOTE - the ClassWizard will add and remove mapping macros here.
        //      DO NOT EDIT what you see in these blocks of generated code!
    //}}AFX_MSG_MAP
END_MESSAGE_MAP()

/////////////////////////////////////////////////////////////////////////////
// CSerializerDoc construction/destruction

CSerializerDoc::CSerializerDoc()
{
    // TODO: add one-time construction code here
}

CSerializerDoc::~CSerializerDoc()
{
}

BOOL CSerializerDoc::OnNewDocument()
{
    if (!CDocument::OnNewDocument())
        return FALSE;

    DataObject.ClearText();
    UpdateAllViews(NULL);

    // TODO: add reinitialization code here
    // (SDI documents will reuse this document)

    return TRUE;
}




/////////////////////////////////////////////////////////////////////////////
// CSerializerDoc serialization

void CSerializerDoc::Serialize(CArchive& ar)
{
    DataObject.Serialize(ar);
}

/////////////////////////////////////////////////////////////////////////////
// CSerializerDoc diagnostics
```

Skill 10

```
#ifdef _DEBUG
void CSerializerDoc::AssertValid() const
{
     CDocument::AssertValid();
}

void CSerializerDoc::Dump(CDumpContext& dc) const
{
     CDocument::Dump(dc);
}
#endif //_DEBUG


/////////////////////////////////////////////////////////////////////////////
// CSerializerDoc commands
```

serializerView.h and serializerView.cpp

```
// serializerView.h : interface of the CSerializerView class
//
/////////////////////////////////////////////////////////////////////////////

#if !defined(AFX_SERIALIZERVIEW_H__FC0F69AF_9582_11D0_8860_444553540000__
➥INCLUDED_)
#define AFX_SERIALIZERVIEW_H__FC0F69AF_9582_11D0_8860_444553540000__INCLUDED_

#if _MSC_VER >= 1000
#pragma once
#endif // _MSC_VER >= 1000

class CSerializerView : public CView
{
protected: // create from serialization only
     CSerializerView();
     DECLARE_DYNCREATE(CSerializerView)

// Attributes
public:
     CSerializerDoc* GetDocument();

// Operations
public:

// Overrides
     // ClassWizard generated virtual function overrides
     //{{AFX_VIRTUAL(CSerializerView)
     public:
     virtual void OnDraw(CDC* pDC);  // overridden to draw this view
     virtual BOOL PreCreateWindow(CREATESTRUCT& cs);
```

```
    protected:
        virtual BOOL OnPreparePrinting(CPrintInfo* pInfo);
        virtual void OnBeginPrinting(CDC* pDC, CPrintInfo* pInfo);
        virtual void OnEndPrinting(CDC* pDC, CPrintInfo* pInfo);
        //}}AFX_VIRTUAL

// Implementation
public:
        virtual ~CSerializerView();
#ifdef _DEBUG
        virtual void AssertValid() const;
        virtual void Dump(CDumpContext& dc) const;
#endif

protected:

// Generated message map functions
protected:
        //{{AFX_MSG(CSerializerView)
        afx_msg void OnChar(UINT nChar, UINT nRepCnt, UINT nFlags);
        //}}AFX_MSG
        DECLARE_MESSAGE_MAP()
};

#ifndef _DEBUG  // debug version in serializerView.cpp
inline CSerializerDoc* CSerializerView::GetDocument()
    { return (CSerializerDoc*)m_pDocument; }
#endif

/////////////////////////////////////////////////////////////////////////////

//{{AFX_INSERT_LOCATION}}
// Microsoft Developer Studio will insert additional declarations immediately
// before the previous line.

#endif // !defined(AFX_SERIALIZERVIEW_H__FC0F69AF_9582_11D0_8860_444553540000__
➥INCLUDED_)
```

```
// serializerView.cpp : implementation of the CSerializerView class
//

#include "stdafx.h"
#include "serializer.h"

#include "serializerDoc.h"
#include "serializerView.h"
```

```
#ifdef _DEBUG
#define new DEBUG_NEW
#undef THIS_FILE
static char THIS_FILE[] = __FILE__;
#endif

/////////////////////////////////////////////////////////////////////////////
// CSerializerView

IMPLEMENT_DYNCREATE(CSerializerView, CView)

BEGIN_MESSAGE_MAP(CSerializerView, CView)
    //{{AFX_MSG_MAP(CSerializerView)
    ON_WM_CHAR()
    //}}AFX_MSG_MAP
    // Standard printing commands
    ON_COMMAND(ID_FILE_PRINT, CView::OnFilePrint)
    ON_COMMAND(ID_FILE_PRINT_DIRECT, CView::OnFilePrint)
    ON_COMMAND(ID_FILE_PRINT_PREVIEW, CView::OnFilePrintPreview)
END_MESSAGE_MAP()

/////////////////////////////////////////////////////////////////////////////
// CSerializerView construction/destruction

CSerializerView::CSerializerView()
{
    // TODO: add construction code here

}

CSerializerView::~CSerializerView()
{
}

BOOL CSerializerView::PreCreateWindow(CREATESTRUCT& cs)
{
    // TODO: Modify the Window class or styles here by modifying
    //   the CREATESTRUCT cs

    return CView::PreCreateWindow(cs);
}

/////////////////////////////////////////////////////////////////////////////
// CSerializerView drawing

void CSerializerView::OnDraw(CDC* pDC)
{
    CSerializerDoc* pDoc = GetDocument();
```

```
        ASSERT_VALID(pDoc);

        pDoc->DataObject.DrawText(pDC);
        // TODO: add draw code for native data here
}

/////////////////////////////////////////////////////////////////////////
// CSerializerView printing

BOOL CSerializerView::OnPreparePrinting(CPrintInfo* pInfo)
{
        // default preparation
        return DoPreparePrinting(pInfo);
}

void CSerializerView::OnBeginPrinting(CDC* /*pDC*/, CPrintInfo* /*pInfo*/)
{
        // TODO: add extra initialization before printing
}

void CSerializerView::OnEndPrinting(CDC* /*pDC*/, CPrintInfo* /*pInfo*/)
{
        // TODO: add cleanup after printing
}

/////////////////////////////////////////////////////////////////////////
// CSerializerView diagnostics

#ifdef _DEBUG
void CSerializerView::AssertValid() const
{
        CView::AssertValid();
}

void CSerializerView::Dump(CDumpContext& dc) const
{
        CView::Dump(dc);
}

CSerializerDoc* CSerializerView::GetDocument() // non-debug version is inline
{
        ASSERT(m_pDocument->IsKindOf(RUNTIME_CLASS(CSerializerDoc)));
        return (CSerializerDoc*)m_pDocument;
}
#endif //_DEBUG

/////////////////////////////////////////////////////////////////////////
// CSerializerView message handlers
```

```
void CSerializerView::OnChar(UINT nChar, UINT nRepCnt, UINT nFlags)
{
    // TODO: Add your message handler code here and/or call default
    CSerializerDoc* pDoc = GetDocument();
    ASSERT_VALID(pDoc);

    pDoc->DataObject.AddText(CString(nChar));
    Invalidate();
    CView::OnChar(nChar, nRepCnt, nFlags);
}
```

The techniques we've developed work well if your program has a document so that you can serialize your data. However, not all programs use documents—a dialog-based program doesn't have a document, for example. Let's look into how to work with files in such programs now.

Just Plain Everyday File Handling

In this new program, we'll get an introduction to standard file handling in Visual C++. In this case, we'll just take a string that reads "Welcome to file handling.", and display it in a text box in a dialog-based program:

```
-----------------------------------------------------------------
| filer                                                         |
|---------------------------------------------------------------|
|                                                               |
|    ---------------------------        ----------              |
|    | Welcome to file handling. |      |    OK    |            |
|    ---------------------------        ----------              |
|                                                               |
|    ---------------------------        ----------              |
|    |  Write and read the file |       |  Cancel  |            |
|    ---------------------------        ----------              |
|                                                               |
|    ---------------------------                                |
|    |                         |                                |
|    ---------------------------                                |
|                                                               |
-----------------------------------------------------------------
```

When the user clicks a button labeled Write and read the file, we will write that string out to a file named `data.dat`, then read it back in and display the string we read in a second text box:

```
----------------------------------------------------------------
|filer                                                          |
|--------------------------------------------------------------|
|                                                               |
|    --------------------------------      ---------           |
|    | Welcome to file handling.  |       |   OK    |          |
|    --------------------------------      ---------           |
|                                                               |
|    --------------------------------      ---------           |
|    |  Write and read the file   |       | Cancel  |          |
|    --------------------------------      ---------           |
|                                                               |
|    --------------------------------                          |
|    | Welcome to file handling.  |                           |
|    --------------------------------                          |
|                                                               |
----------------------------------------------------------------
```

This new program will be named filer. Create it now with AppWizard, making this program a dialog-based program.

Dividing a File into Records

To show how file handling works in a little more depth, we will store our string "Welcome to file handling." as four separate character strings, each 20 characters long, in an array of strings named `OutString[]`:

```
OutString[0]    ←    "Welcome               "
OutString[1]    ←    "to                    "
OutString[2]    ←    "file                  "
OutString[3]    ←    "handling              "
```

We will treat each such string as a *record*, or data item, and write each record out to the file separately. In general, you can place whatever kind of data you want in a record, and treat your file as a huge storage area for such records, any one of which may be individually accessed at any time (see the following graphic).

Skill 10

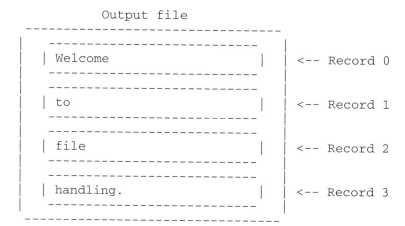

You don't have to break a file up into records at all if you don't want to—you can place whatever you want in a file—but by organizing our data into records, we make it easier to access, and we'll see how to use the *file pointer* to move around in a file. The file pointer holds our current location in a file. (This technique is called *random access* because you can access whatever record you want.)

When it's time to read each record back in, we'll read it and store it in a 20-character array named InString[]:

```
// filerDlg.h : header file
            .
            .
            .
protected:
     HICON m_hIcon;
→    char OutString[4][20];
→    char InString[20];
            .
            .
            .
}
```

Now we've set aside space for our data. Our plan of action is to write out each of the four character arrays, our records, to the data.dat file. Then, when we read them back in, we can see how to use the file pointer, positioning ourselves at the beginning of each of those records in data.dat to read them back in. The file pointer holds our present location in a file we're reading or writing. In fact, we broke our data up into records expressly so we could see how to use the file pointer.

The next step in our filer program is to initialize the character arrays we've just set up, so let's do that next.

Initializing Filer's Data

Now we will place the strings we'll use in the four character arrays. We'll use the standard C `strcpy()` function to fill each character array in `OnInitDialog()`:

```
BOOL CFilerDlg::OnInitDialog()
{
→       CDialog::OnInitDialog();
→       strcpy(OutString[0], "Welcome ");
→       strcpy(OutString[1], "to ");
→       strcpy(OutString[2], "file ");
→       strcpy(OutString[3], "handling. ");
             .
             .
             .
}
```

Next, add the controls we'll need to the main dialog window: two text boxes and a button, as shown in Figure 10.6.

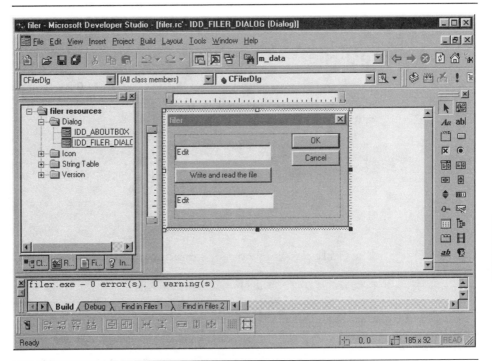

FIGURE 10.6: Laying out the filer program's controls

In addition, we connect the member variable m_text1 to the text in the top text box, and m_text2 to the text in the bottom text box. We can place the string we're going to send out to disk in the top text box with this code in OnInitDialog():

```
BOOL CFilerDlg::OnInitDialog()
{
    CDialog::OnInitDialog();
    strcpy(OutString[0], "Welcome ");
    strcpy(OutString[1], "to ");
    strcpy(OutString[2], "file ");
    strcpy(OutString[3], "handling. ");

    m_text1 = CString(OutString[0]) + CString(OutString[1]) +
    CString(OutString[2]) + CString(OutString[3]);
    UpdateData(false);
         .
         .
         .
}
```

Now we're all set to write our file when the user clicks the "Write and read the file" button. Let's turn to the process of writing the file out to disk next.

Writing a File

To write our four character arrays, OutString[0] to OutString[3] to disk, we use the CFile class and create an object of that class named OutFile in the button event-handler OnButton1():

```
void CFilerDlg::OnButton1()
{
    CFile OutFile("data.dat", CFile::modeCreate | CFile::modeWrite);
         .
         .
         .
}
```

The CFile class methods appear in Table 10.1.

TABLE 10.1: The CFile Class Methods

Method	Does This
Abort	Closes a file ignoring all warnings and errors.
CFile	Constructs a CFile object from a path or file handle.
Close	Closes a file and deletes the object.

TABLE 10.1 CONTINUED: The `CFile` Class Methods

Method	Does This
Flush	Flushes any data yet to be written.
GetFileName	Gets the filename of the selected file.
GetFilePath	Gets the full file path of the selected file.
GetFileTitle	Gets the title of the selected file.
GetLength	Gets the length of the file.
GetPosition	Gets the current file pointer.
GetStatus	Gets the status of the specified file (static, virtual function).
GetStatus	Gets the status of this open file.
LockRange	Locks a range of bytes in a file.
Open	Safely opens a file with an error-testing option.
Read	Reads data from a file at the current file position.
ReadHuge	Can read more than 64K of data from a file at the current file position. Outdated in 32-bit programming.
Remove	Deletes the specified file.
Rename	Renames the specified file.
Seek	Places the current file pointer.
SeekToBegin	Places the current file pointer at the beginning of the file.
SeekToEnd	Places the current file pointer at the end of the file.
SetFilePath	Sets the full file path of the selected file.
SetLength	Changes the length of the file.
SetStatus	Sets the status of the specified file.
UnlockRange	Unlocks a range of bytes in a file.
Write	Writes data in a file to the current file position.
WriteHuge	Can write more than 64K of data in a file to the current file position. Outdated in 32-bit programming.

This first line of code creates and opens a new file, data.dat, for us to write to. Note the constants we pass to the CFile constructor: CFile::modeCreate | CFile::modeWrite. The CFile:: prefix indicates that these constants are member constants of the CFile class, and, like all the CFile constructor constants, we can set several options at once by combining them with the Visual C++ | operator. Passing these constants indicates to CFile that we want to create and write to the new file. The possible constants we can pass to CFile's constructor appear in Table 10.2.

TABLE 10.2: The CFile File Open Modes

Mode Constant	Means This
CFile::modeCreate	Creates a new file.
CFile::modeNoInherit	Prevents the file from being inherited by child processes.
CFile::modeNoTruncate	Combine this value with modeCreate—if the file you are creating already exists, it is not truncated to zero length.
CFile::modeRead	Opens the file for reading only.
CFile::modeReadWrite	Opens the file for reading and writing.
CFile::modeWrite	Opens the file for writing only.
CFile::shareCompat	Maps to CFile::shareExclusive when used in CFile::Open.
CFile::shareDenyNone	Opens the file without denying other processes read or write access to the file.
CFile::shareDenyRead	Opens the file and denies other processes read access to the file.
CFile::shareDenyWrite	Opens the file and denies other processes write access to the file.
CFile::shareExclusive	Opens the file with exclusive mode, denying other processes both read and write access to the file.
CFile::typeBinary	Sets binary mode.
CFile::typeText	Sets text mode with special processing for carriage return–line-feed pairs.

Now the file is open and ready to write to. To actually write our four character strings to the file, we simply loop over all four strings, writing them to the file with the CFile Write() method:

```
void CFilerDlg::OnButton1()
{
    CFile OutFile("data.dat", CFile::modeCreate | CFile::modeWrite);
→   for(int loop_index = 0; loop_index < 4; loop_index++){
→       OutFile.Write(OutString[loop_index], 20);
→   }
→   OutFile.Close();
```

```
              .
              .
              .
    }
```

In this way, we can consider each string a separate record in the file, and organizing your data into such records provides an easy way to access them in a file. Note that at the end of the above code, we call CFile's Close() method to close the file.

That completes the writing process—we've created and filled our data.dat file, which now exists on the disk. The next step is to read that file back in.

Reading a File

To read the character strings in data.dat back in, we'll use the CFile Read() method. We start by opening the file and creating a new CFile object, InFile, which is set up to read the file:

```
void CFilerDlg::OnButton1()
{
    CFile OutFile("data.dat", CFile::modeCreate | CFile::modeWrite);
    for(int loop_index = 0; loop_index < 4; loop_index++){
        OutFile.Write(OutString[loop_index], 20);
    }
    OutFile.Close();

→   CFile InFile("data.dat", CFile::modeRead);
              .
              .
              .
}
```

Now we loop over the four character strings in our file. We've given each string a length of 20 characters, so we can use the CFile Seek() method to position the file pointer at the beginning of each successive string:

```
void CFilerDlg::OnButton1()
{
    CFile OutFile("data.dat", CFile::modeCreate | CFile::modeWrite);
    for(int loop_index = 0; loop_index < 4; loop_index++){
        OutFile.Write(OutString[loop_index], 20);
    }
    OutFile.Close();

    CFile InFile("data.dat", CFile::modeRead);
```

Skill 10

```
      for(loop_index = 0; loop_index < 4; loop_index++){
➜          InFile.Seek(20 * loop_index, CFile::begin);
                .
                .
                .
      }
  }
```

Moving the File Pointer

The Seek() method positions the file pointer in a file, which is where we'll write the next section of data we want to write or read the next section of data we want to read. That is, the CFile Write() and Read() methods perform their actions at the location of the file pointer. Using Seek(), you can position the file pointer where you want it.

Note the CFile::begin constant in the call to Seek():

```
      InFile.Seek(20 * loop_index, CFile::begin);
```

This means that we want to place the file pointer to a new location using the beginning of the file as our origin. The other possible origins for the file pointer are: CFile::begin, CFile::current (meaning the current location in the file), and CFile::end.

Now that we've placed the file pointer where we want it, we can read the 20 characters into the character array we've put aside for that purpose, InString, using the Read() method. This methods returns the number of characters actually read, and we store that value in the integer NumberCharacters:

```
void CFilerDlg::OnButton1()
{
    CFile OutFile("data.dat", CFile::modeCreate | CFile::modeWrite);
    for(int loop_index = 0; loop_index < 4; loop_index++){
        OutFile.Write(OutString[loop_index], 20);
    }
    OutFile.Close();

    CFile InFile("data.dat", CFile::modeRead);
    for(loop_index = 0; loop_index < 4; loop_index++){
        InFile.Seek(20 * loop_index, CFile::begin);
➜       int NumberCharacters = InFile.Read(InString, 20);
                .
                .
                .
    }
}
```

And now we've read in our data, record by record.

Note that we're using the Seek() method in this example to show how you can break a file up into separate records, which is very useful if a file like data.dat contains a million or more records. But in this short example, if you just wanted to read in all our data at once from data.dat, you could read in all 80 characters with one call to Read(), just by asking for 80 characters instead of 20.

> **TIP**   If you are unsure of a file's length, you can ask Read() for more data than is in the file, and Read() will return the number of bytes it actually read, which will be the actual length of the file on disk. Alternatively, you could read the file in sections, and when the number of bytes Read() actually read is less than the number you asked for, you've reached the end of the file.

The record we just read in is in the character array InString[]. We add that record to the text in the second text box in our program, and then close the file data.dat, and we're done:

```
void CFilerDlg::OnButton1()
{
    CFile OutFile("data.dat", CFile::modeCreate | CFile::modeWrite);
    for(int loop_index = 0; loop_index < 4; loop_index++){
        OutFile.Write(OutString[loop_index], 20);
    }
    OutFile.Close();

    CFile InFile("data.dat", CFile::modeRead);
    for(loop_index = 0; loop_index < 4; loop_index++){
        InFile.Seek(20 * loop_index, CFile::begin);
        int NumberCharacters = InFile.Read(InString, 20);
        m_text2 += CString(InString);
    }
    UpdateData(false);
    InFile.Close();
}
```

Now the program is ready to go. Run it, as shown in Figure 10.7. The text we are going to save as four records appears in the top text box in that figure.

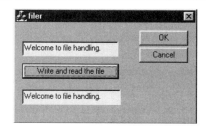

FIGURE 10.7: Our filer program writes and reads a file.

Click the "Write and read file" button now. When you do, the text is written to disk in `data.dat`, read back in again, and the program displays that text in the bottom text box, as shown in Figure 10.7.

Our program is a success; this example has given us a good introduction to the capabilities of CFile. The code for this program appears in `filerDlg.h`/`filerDlg.cpp`.

filerDlg.h and *filerDlg.cpp*

```
// filerDlg.h : header file
//

#if !defined(AFX_FILERDLG_H__D5ED9167_960A_11D0_8860_444553540000__INCLUDED_)
#define AFX_FILERDLG_H__D5ED9167_960A_11D0_8860_444553540000__INCLUDED_

#if _MSC_VER >= 1000
#pragma once
#endif // _MSC_VER >= 1000

/////////////////////////////////////////////////////////////////////////////
// CFilerDlg dialog

class CFilerDlg : public CDialog
{
// Construction
public:
    CFilerDlg(CWnd* pParent = NULL);    // standard constructor

// Dialog Data
    //{{AFX_DATA(CFilerDlg)
    enum { IDD = IDD_FILER_DIALOG };
    CString     m_text1;
```

```
        CString     m_text2;
        //}}AFX_DATA

        // ClassWizard generated virtual function overrides
        //{{AFX_VIRTUAL(CFilerDlg)
        protected:
        virtual void DoDataExchange(CDataExchange* pDX);        // DDX/DDV support
        //}}AFX_VIRTUAL

// Implementation
protected:
        HICON m_hIcon;
        char OutString[4][20];
        char InString[20];

        // Generated message map functions
        //{{AFX_MSG(CFilerDlg)
        virtual BOOL OnInitDialog();
        afx_msg void OnSysCommand(UINT nID, LPARAM lParam);
        afx_msg void OnPaint();
        afx_msg HCURSOR OnQueryDragIcon();
        afx_msg void OnButton1();
        //}}AFX_MSG
        DECLARE_MESSAGE_MAP()
};

//{{AFX_INSERT_LOCATION}}
// Microsoft Developer Studio will insert additional declarations immediately
// before the previous line.

#endif //!defined(AFX_FILERDLG_H__D5ED9167_960A_11D0_8860_444553540000__
➡INCLUDED_)


// filerDlg.cpp : implementation file
//

#include "stdafx.h"
#include "filer.h"
#include "filerDlg.h"

#ifdef _DEBUG
#define new DEBUG_NEW
#undef THIS_FILE
static char THIS_FILE[] = __FILE__;
#endif

////////////////////////////////////////////////////////////////////////
```

```
// CAboutDlg dialog used for App About

class CAboutDlg : public CDialog
{
public:
    CAboutDlg();

// Dialog Data
    //{{AFX_DATA(CAboutDlg)
    enum { IDD = IDD_ABOUTBOX };
    //}}AFX_DATA

    // ClassWizard generated virtual function overrides
    //{{AFX_VIRTUAL(CAboutDlg)
    protected:
    virtual void DoDataExchange(CDataExchange* pDX);    // DDX/DDV support
    //}}AFX_VIRTUAL

// Implementation
protected:
    //{{AFX_MSG(CAboutDlg)
    //}}AFX_MSG
    DECLARE_MESSAGE_MAP()
};

CAboutDlg::CAboutDlg() : CDialog(CAboutDlg::IDD)
{
    //{{AFX_DATA_INIT(CAboutDlg)
    //}}AFX_DATA_INIT
}

void CAboutDlg::DoDataExchange(CDataExchange* pDX)
{
    CDialog::DoDataExchange(pDX);
    //{{AFX_DATA_MAP(CAboutDlg)
    //}}AFX_DATA_MAP
}

BEGIN_MESSAGE_MAP(CAboutDlg, CDialog)
    //{{AFX_MSG_MAP(CAboutDlg)
        // No message handlers
    //}}AFX_MSG_MAP
END_MESSAGE_MAP()

/////////////////////////////////////////////////////////////////////////////
// CFilerDlg dialog

CFilerDlg::CFilerDlg(CWnd* pParent /*=NULL*/)
```

```
                 : CDialog(CFilerDlg::IDD, pParent)
{
    //{{AFX_DATA_INIT(CFilerDlg)
    m_text1 = _T("");
    m_text2 = _T("");
    //}}AFX_DATA_INIT
    // Note that LoadIcon does not require a subsequent DestroyIcon in Win32
    m_hIcon = AfxGetApp()->LoadIcon(IDR_MAINFRAME);
}

void CFilerDlg::DoDataExchange(CDataExchange* pDX)
{
    CDialog::DoDataExchange(pDX);
    //{{AFX_DATA_MAP(CFilerDlg)
    DDX_Text(pDX, IDC_EDIT1, m_text1);
    DDX_Text(pDX, IDC_EDIT2, m_text2);
    //}}AFX_DATA_MAP
}

BEGIN_MESSAGE_MAP(CFilerDlg, CDialog)
    //{{AFX_MSG_MAP(CFilerDlg)
    ON_WM_SYSCOMMAND()
    ON_WM_PAINT()
    ON_WM_QUERYDRAGICON()
    ON_BN_CLICKED(IDC_BUTTON1, OnButton1)
    //}}AFX_MSG_MAP
END_MESSAGE_MAP()

/////////////////////////////////////////////////////////////////////////////
// CFilerDlg message handlers

BOOL CFilerDlg::OnInitDialog()
{
    CDialog::OnInitDialog();

    strcpy(OutString[0], "Welcome ");
    strcpy(OutString[1], "to ");
    strcpy(OutString[2], "file ");
    strcpy(OutString[3], "handling. ");

    m_text1 = CString(OutString[0]) + CString(OutString[1]) +
➥CString(OutString[2]) + CString(OutString[3]);
    UpdateData(false);

    // Add "About..." menu item to system menu.

    // IDM_ABOUTBOX must be in the system command range.
    ASSERT((IDM_ABOUTBOX & 0xFFF0) == IDM_ABOUTBOX);
```

```
        ASSERT(IDM_ABOUTBOX < 0xF000);

        CMenu* pSysMenu = GetSystemMenu(FALSE);
        if (pSysMenu != NULL)
        {
            CString strAboutMenu;
            strAboutMenu.LoadString(IDS_ABOUTBOX);
            if (!strAboutMenu.IsEmpty())
            {
                pSysMenu->AppendMenu(MF_SEPARATOR);
                pSysMenu->AppendMenu(MF_STRING, IDM_ABOUTBOX, strAboutMenu);
            }
        }

        // Set the icon for this dialog.  The framework does this automatically
        //  when the application's main window is not a dialog
        SetIcon(m_hIcon, TRUE);              // Set big icon
        SetIcon(m_hIcon, FALSE);             // Set small icon

        // TODO: Add extra initialization here

        return TRUE;  // return TRUE  unless you set the focus to a control
}

void CFilerDlg::OnSysCommand(UINT nID, LPARAM lParam)
{
    if ((nID & 0xFFF0) == IDM_ABOUTBOX)
    {
        CAboutDlg dlgAbout;
        dlgAbout.DoModal();
    }
    else
    {
        CDialog::OnSysCommand(nID, lParam);
    }
}

// If you add a minimize button to your dialog, you will need the code below
//  to draw the icon.  For MFC applications using the document/view model,
//  this is automatically done for you by the framework.

void CFilerDlg::OnPaint()
{
    if (IsIconic())
    {
        CPaintDC dc(this); // device context for painting

        SendMessage(WM_ICONERASEBKGND, (WPARAM) dc.GetSafeHdc(), 0);
```

```
            // Center icon in client rectangle
            int cxIcon = GetSystemMetrics(SM_CXICON);
            int cyIcon = GetSystemMetrics(SM_CYICON);
            CRect rect;
            GetClientRect(&rect);
            int x = (rect.Width() - cxIcon + 1) / 2;
            int y = (rect.Height() - cyIcon + 1) / 2;

            // Draw the icon
            dc.DrawIcon(x, y, m_hIcon);
        }
        else
        {
            CDialog::OnPaint();
        }
    }

// The system calls this to obtain the cursor to display while the user drags
//   the minimized window.
HCURSOR CFilerDlg::OnQueryDragIcon()
{
    return (HCURSOR) m_hIcon;
}


void CFilerDlg::OnButton1()
{
    CFile OutFile("data.dat", CFile::modeCreate | CFile::modeWrite);
    for(int loop_index = 0; loop_index < 4; loop_index++){
        OutFile.Write(OutString[loop_index], 20);
    }
    OutFile.Close();

    CFile InFile("data.dat", CFile::modeRead);
    for(loop_index = 0; loop_index < 4; loop_index++){
        InFile.Seek(20 * loop_index, CFile::begin);
        int NumberCharacters = InFile.Read(InString, 20);
        m_text2 += CString(InString);
    }
    UpdateData(false);
    InFile.Close();
}
```

We've covered a lot of file-handling material in this skill, from serializing standard MFC objects to making your own objects serializable, from writing data to disk using CFile to reading it back in again, from letting Visual C++ handle all the details of how the data in your files is organized to organizing that data into records yourself.

In the next skill, we're going to go on to more ways of handling and presenting your data to the user as we turn to working with multiple views and multiple documents.

Are You Experienced?

Now You Can...

☑ Serialize (write out to and read from disk) MFC objects

☑ Customize your classes so they can be serialized

☑ Support the File menu items in a Visual C++ program

☑ Use CFile to write and read a file

☑ Position the file pointer in a file

☑ Organize your file into records

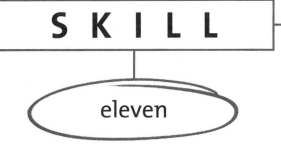

S K I L L

eleven

Using Multiple Documents and Multiple Views

- ❏ Handling more than one document in the same program
- ❏ Coordinating a number of views into the same document
- ❏ Using a document's Modified flag
- ❏ Scrolling a view
- ❏ Using text boxes as whole windows

In this skill, we'll start working with a very strong aspect of Visual C++, the ability to work with multiple documents and multiple views into those documents. Using this capability, we'll be able to open a number of documents—such as, `timetable.txt` and `phonenumbers.txt`—at the same time in a program, and work on them as we have designed our programs to do.

This is the first time we'll be working with multiple documents in the same program. So far, our programs have been purposely constructed to use only one document to keep things simple as we looked at other aspects of Visual C++ programming, but now the time has come to support multiple documents in the same program. As we'll see, these documents will appear as separate windows in our main window; this setup is called the Multiple Document Interface, MDI.

We'll see that a Visual C++ program can automatically create a new document object and view object from our customized document and view classes each time we select the New menu item in the File menu. Because each document gets its own document object, we'll be able to keep the data of each document separate from all the other documents automatically.

We'll also see how to support multiple views into each document. A view presents the data in a document, and when that document is too big to present on the screen at one time, the view presents just a portion of that document. It's possible to have several views open at once in the same document—each view can then show a different portion of the main document. With multiple views, the user can move around in the same document, working on different sections simultaneously. Each of these views will get its own window.

Because the user will now be able to work with multiple views in the same document, there is a new concern: what if the user makes a change in one view—will that change be echoed in the data displayed by the second view in the same document? As the AppWizard designs programs for us, the answer is no, so the user could actually view the same part of a document in two different view windows, make changes in one view and not see those changes appear in the other view of the same data. We'll see how to fix that in this skill.

In addition, since we're dealing with potentially large documents in this skill, we'll see how to make views scrollable, that is, support scroll bars on the side of the view window. Using these scroll bars, the user can scroll the data in our document smoothly.

In fact, we'll also see how to cover a whole view window with a text box so that all the standard editing functions, Cut, Copy, Paste, and so on, are already built in, as well as built-in scroll bars.

We've got a lot planned for this skill, so let's start at once with our first multiple document, multiple view program.

Our First Multiple Document Multiple View Example

In our first Multiple Document Interface (MDI), example, we'll present the user with a main window that can hold windows itself. Each window in the main window corresponds to a document, and each document corresponds to a document object in our program (as we'll see, Visual C++ handles the details of connecting the document objects to new documents as they are created).

Each document object also gets its own view object, so we can set up our user interface just as we did in previous skills. For example, we might let the user type text that the program will store in a document object and we can display from a view object. Note that the program calls this new document Multiv1 (it takes the name of the document from the name of our program, multiview):

```
--------------------------------------------------------
|multiview - Multiv2                                   |
|------------------------------------------------------|
|File Edit View Window Help                            |
|------------------------------------------------------|
|  --------------------------------                    |
| |Multiv1                        |                    |
| |-------------------------------|                    |
| |This is a test!                |                    |
| |                               |                    |
| |                               |                    |
| |                               |                    |
| |                               |                    |
| |                               |                    |
| |                               |                    |
| |                               |                    |
|  --------------------------------                    |
|                                                      |
|                                                      |
|                                                      |
|                                                      |
 --------------------------------------------------------
```

Skill 11

TIP You can change the default name given to documents by clicking the Advanced button in Step 4 of AppWizard, typing the default name you want for documents in the Doc Type Name box.

When the user selects the New menu item in the File menu, the program opens a new document window, `Multiv2`, and the user can type in that new document (the text in the new document will be entirely separate from the text in the first document):

```
-----------------------------------------------------
|multiview - Multiv2                                 |
|---------------------------------------------------|
|File Edit View Window Help                          |
|---------------------------------------------------|
|   ---------------------------                      |
| |Multiv1                    |                      |
| |-------------------------- |                      |
| |This is a test!            |                      |
| |   ---------------------------                    |
| |  |Multiv2                    |                    |
| |  |-------------------------- |                    |
| |  |This is also a test!       |                    |
| |  |                           |                    |
| |  |                           |                    |
| |  |                           |                    |
| |  |                           |                    |
| ---|                          |                    |
|    |                          |                    |
|    |                          |                    |
|     ---------------------------                    |
|                                                    |
|                                                    |
|                                                    |
-----------------------------------------------------
```

Now the user can save each document to disk, giving them whatever names they like, and load them in independently (assuming we add the correct code to the document's `Serialize()` method). In this way, we are able to support multiple documents.

We can also support multiple views into each document. For example, while editing `Multiv2`, the user can select the New Window menu item in the Window menu, opening a new view into `Multiv2`. This changes the text the title bar of `Multiv2`'s first view from "Multiv2" to "Multiv2:1" and the text in the new view's title bar to "Multiv2:2". This lets the user keep the various views into the same document straight:

```
-----------------------------------------------------------
|multiview - Multiv2                                      |
|-------------------------------------------------------- |
|File Edit View Window Help                               |
|-------------------------------------------------------- |
|  ---------------------------                            |
| |Multiv1                    |                           |
| |-------------------------- |                           |
| |This is a test!            |                           |
| |    ---------------------------                        |
| |   |Multiv2:1                 |                         |
| |   |------------------------- |                         |
| |   |This is also a test!      |                         |
| |   |                          |                         |
| |   |     ---------------------------                    |
| |   |    |Multiv2:2                 |                     |
| |   |    |------------------------- |                     |
| |   |    |This is also a test!      |                     |
| |---|    |                          |                     |
| |   |    |                          |                     |
| |   |    |                          |                     |
| |   ------|                         |                     |
| |        |                          |                     |
| |        |                          |                     |
| |        |                          |                     |
| |        ---------------------------                     |
|                                                         |
-----------------------------------------------------------
```

We'll see how to support scroll bars in a view in the next example, so the user can scroll to different parts of the same document in two different views. However, when they make changes to a document in one view, we must be sure that those changes are echoed in the data that the other view into the same document is displaying.

Let's get started at once. This time, when you create the multiview program in AppWizard, leave the Multiple documents option selected in AppWizard's Step 1, as shown in Figure 11.1. This makes multiview an MDI, not SDI, program.

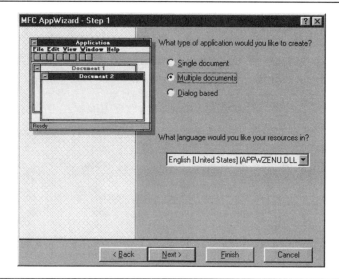

FIGURE 11.1: Making a program an MDI program

What's Different in an MDI Program?

Many of the programming details remain the same for us in an MDI program, because the program will automatically create a new document object for each new object, and a new view object to go along with that document object. This means that for pure data storage and display, we can simply assume there is only one document and one view in our program—Visual C++ will handle the rest.

How does it handle the details automatically? If we had made multiview an SDI program, we would have found this code in `multiview.cpp`, the program's application file:

```
BOOL CMultiviewApp::InitInstance()
{
    AfxEnableControlContainer();
        .
        .
        .
    CSingleDocTemplate* pDocTemplate;
```

```
pDocTemplate = new CSingleDocTemplate(
    IDR_MAINFRAME,
    RUNTIME_CLASS(CMultiviewDoc),
    RUNTIME_CLASS(CMainFrame),        // main SDI frame window
    RUNTIME_CLASS(CMultiviewView));
AddDocTemplate(pDocTemplate);
    .
    .
    .
}
```

Note that here the document *template*, used to create new documents, is of the MFC CSingleDocTemplate type, and that the program places the view, document, and main window classes into that template. Because we've made multiview an MDI program, however, multiview.cpp actually contains this code:

```
BOOL CMultiviewApp::InitInstance()
{
    AfxEnableControlContainer();
        .

        .
    CMultiDocTemplate* pDocTemplate;
    pDocTemplate = new CMultiDocTemplate(
        IDR_MULTIVTYPE,
        RUNTIME_CLASS(CMultiviewDoc),
        RUNTIME_CLASS(CChildFrame), // custom MDI child frame
        RUNTIME_CLASS(CMultiviewView));
    AddDocTemplate(pDocTemplate);
        .
        .
        .
}
```

Here, we're using the CMultiDocTemplate template for our MDI program, which is how the program handles multiple documents, and we connect our view and document classes to this document template, as well as to the CChildFrame class, which supports MDI *child windows*, the type of windows that appear inside the main window.

Two Window Types, Two Menu Types

Using two different window types raises an interesting issue in MDI programming—when the user is working in a document, we will want certain menus available for them to use: File, Edit, and so on. But when the user closes all windows, we don't want the Edit menu to appear any more, because there is nothing to edit, and other menus and menu items we may have added might not be appropriate either if no document is open.

Visual C++ allows us to handle this situation by defining two menu resources for our program: IDR_MAINFRAME, which is the menu system that will appear if there are no documents open, and IDR_MULTIVTYPE, which is the menu system that appears if one or more documents are open (you can think of it this way: when a document is open, its menu system takes over the program's main menu system). By default, IDR_MAINFRAME only includes the File, View, and Help menus, while IDR_MULTIVTYPE includes File, Edit, View, Window, and Help.

TIP   When the program starts, it opens a new, empty document automatically. Only if the user intentionally closes all documents does the IDR_MAINFRAME menu system take over.

Now that we've gotten a behind-the-scenes look into our program, let's start adding some code. We'll do that by letting multiview read characters from the keyboard.

Reading Keystrokes in Multiview

We'll add character-reading capabilities to multiview just as we did in previous programs in this book, emphasizing how working with multiple documents and views is very much like working with single documents and views—the program will handle most of the details for us.

We begin by setting up storage for our character data, a CString object named StringData:

```
// multiviewDoc.h : interface of the CMultiviewDoc class
        .
        .
        .
// Attributes
public:
➜       CString StringData;
        .
        .
        .
```

We also initialize that string to the empty string in the document's constructor:

```
CMultiviewDoc::CMultiviewDoc()
{
```

```
→      StringData = "";
   }
```

That's all we have to do to store our data, even though we're working with multiple documents and multiple views now. The program will create a new document object (using the document template) for each new document, so as far as data storage goes, we can write our program as though this is the only document the program supports.

When it's time to store our document on disk, we only need to store this document's version of the `StringData` object in the `Serialize()` method:

```
   void CMultiviewDoc::Serialize(CArchive& ar)
   {
       if (ar.IsStoring())
       {
→          ar << StringData;
       }
       else
       {
→          ar >> StringData;
       }
   }
```

Similarly, the program will create a new view object for each new document, so we can display our data in the view's `OnDraw()` method as we have before:

```
   void CMultiviewView::OnDraw(CDC* pDC)
   {
       CMultiviewDoc* pDoc = GetDocument();
       ASSERT_VALID(pDoc);

→      pDC->TextOut(0, 0, pDoc->StringData);
   }
```

We can also collect the characters the user types, placing them in the `StringData` string as we've done before in previous programs:

```
   void CMultiviewView::OnChar(UINT nChar, UINT nRepCnt, UINT nFlags)
   {
→      CMultiviewDoc* pDoc = GetDocument();
→      ASSERT_VALID(pDoc);

→      pDoc->StringData += nChar;
→      Invalidate();

       CView::OnChar(nChar, nRepCnt, nFlags);
   }
```

However, there is one new consideration. We perform a view-specific action here: we invalidate the view in order to refresh the view now that we've read a new character from the keyboard. Since we've refreshed one view, we should assume that there may be others, and perform the same action—redrawing the view—in the others. We do that by calling the document object's UpdateAllViews() method (the document object keeps a list of all the views into its data):

```
void CMultiviewView::OnChar(UINT nChar, UINT nRepCnt, UINT nFlags)
{
    CMultiviewDoc* pDoc = GetDocument();
    ASSERT_VALID(pDoc);

    pDoc->StringData += nChar;
    Invalidate();

➡        pDoc->UpdateAllViews(this, 0L, NULL);

    CView::OnChar(nChar, nRepCnt, nFlags);
}
```

This calls the OnUpdate() method of each view into this document, and the default action of OnUpdate() is the same as Invalidate()—it forces a redraw of the view. In this way, using UpdateAllViews(), we're able to refresh all the views into this document now that the user has typed a new character.

Note the parameters we pass to UpdateAllViews(): a keyword named this, a long integer whose value is 0, and a NULL pointer. What do those parameters do?

The first parameter in the UpdateAllViews() method is a pointer to the view that is calling that method (this is so the document will not call the present view's OnUpdate() method, because it assumes the present view already knows about the change to the document). We make this parameter a this pointer, which is simply a pointer to the current object.

The next two parameters let us pass *hints* (that's the Visual C++ name for them) to the other views about what part of the data needs to be updated.

Using View Hints

Although we do not use view update hints here (since we pass a parameter whose value is 0 and a NULL pointer), you can pass some kind of numeric code and a pointer to some object to the other views when you make a change to the document's data. Usually, you pass a pointer to the object in the document's data that's been changed. This means that the other views can update their displays in a "smart" way, updating only the data that needs to be updated and not having to redraw the entire view.

TIP   You don't have to use view hints in your programs, of course, but the thing to remember is that when you perform a view-specific data-displaying action (such as invalidating the view to reflect modifications to the document's data) in one view, you should at least call UpdateAllViews() to make sure all the other views are updated and redrawn as well.

The Document Modified Flag

Besides calling UpdateAllViews(), we also set the document's modified flag in our OnChar() method:

```
void CMultiviewView::OnChar(UINT nChar, UINT nRepCnt, UINT nFlags)
{
    CMultiviewDoc* pDoc = GetDocument();
    ASSERT_VALID(pDoc);

    pDoc->StringData += nChar;
    Invalidate();

    pDoc->UpdateAllViews(this, OL, NULL);
    pDoc->SetModifiedFlag();

    CView::OnChar(nChar, nRepCnt, nFlags);
}
```

We first saw SetModifiedFlag() in the last skill; setting the document's modified flag with SetModifiedFlag() means that if the user tries to close the current document without saving it, the program will ask if they want to save it before the data in it is lost.

Our multiview program is complete; run it now, as shown in Figure 11.1. As you can see in that figure, you can create multiple documents in this program. You can also create multiple views in each document, as shown in Figure 11.2. The user can save and open these documents as well. All in all, multiview is a powerful program, giving us a lot of insight into MDI programming.

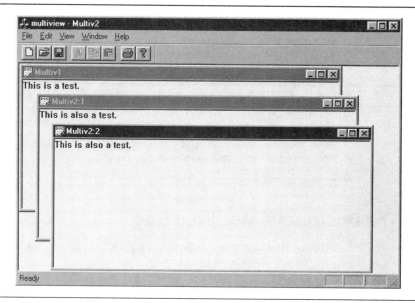

FIGURE 11.2: Our first multiview, multi-document program

The code for this program appears in multiviewView.h/multiviewView.cpp.

multiviewView.h and *multiviewView.cpp*

```
// multiviewView.h : interface of the CMultiviewView class
//
////////////////////////////////////////////////////////////////////////////

#if !defined(AFX_MULTIVIEWVIEW_H__12808D11_94CF_11D0_8860_444553540000__
➥INCLUDED_)
#define AFX_MULTIVIEWVIEW_H__12808D11_94CF_11D0_8860_444553540000__INCLUDED_

#if _MSC_VER >= 1000
#pragma once
#endif // _MSC_VER >= 1000

class CMultiviewView : public CView
{
protected: // create from serialization only
    CMultiviewView();
    DECLARE_DYNCREATE(CMultiviewView)
```

```
// Attributes
public:
    CMultiviewDoc* GetDocument();

// Operations
public:

// Overrides
    // ClassWizard generated virtual function overrides
    //{{AFX_VIRTUAL(CMultiviewView)
    public:
    virtual void OnDraw(CDC* pDC);  // overridden to draw this view
    virtual BOOL PreCreateWindow(CREATESTRUCT& cs);
    protected:
    virtual BOOL OnPreparePrinting(CPrintInfo* pInfo);
    virtual void OnBeginPrinting(CDC* pDC, CPrintInfo* pInfo);
    virtual void OnEndPrinting(CDC* pDC, CPrintInfo* pInfo);
    //}}AFX_VIRTUAL

// Implementation
public:
    virtual ~CMultiviewView();
#ifdef _DEBUG
    virtual void AssertValid() const;
    virtual void Dump(CDumpContext& dc) const;
#endif

protected:

// Generated message map functions
protected:
    //{{AFX_MSG(CMultiviewView)
    afx_msg void OnChar(UINT nChar, UINT nRepCnt, UINT nFlags);
    //}}AFX_MSG
    DECLARE_MESSAGE_MAP()
};

#ifndef _DEBUG  // debug version in multiviewView.cpp
inline CMultiviewDoc* CMultiviewView::GetDocument()
   { return (CMultiviewDoc*)m_pDocument; }
#endif

/////////////////////////////////////////////////////////////////////////////

//{{AFX_INSERT_LOCATION}}
// Microsoft Developer Studio will insert additional declarations immediately
// before the previous line.
```

Skill 11

```
#endif //
!defined(AFX_MULTIVIEWVIEW_H__12808D11_94CF_11D0_8860_444553540000__INCLUDED_)

// multiviewView.cpp : implementation of the CMultiviewView class
//

#include "stdafx.h"
#include "multiview.h"

#include "multiviewDoc.h"
#include "multiviewView.h"

#ifdef _DEBUG
#define new DEBUG_NEW
#undef THIS_FILE
static char THIS_FILE[] = __FILE__;
#endif

/////////////////////////////////////////////////////////////////////////////
// CMultiviewView

IMPLEMENT_DYNCREATE(CMultiviewView, CView)

BEGIN_MESSAGE_MAP(CMultiviewView, CView)
    //{{AFX_MSG_MAP(CMultiviewView)
    ON_WM_CHAR()
    //}}AFX_MSG_MAP
    // Standard printing commands
    ON_COMMAND(ID_FILE_PRINT, CView::OnFilePrint)
    ON_COMMAND(ID_FILE_PRINT_DIRECT, CView::OnFilePrint)
    ON_COMMAND(ID_FILE_PRINT_PREVIEW, CView::OnFilePrintPreview)
END_MESSAGE_MAP()

/////////////////////////////////////////////////////////////////////////////
// CMultiviewView construction/destruction

CMultiviewView::CMultiviewView()
{
    // TODO: add construction code here

}

CMultiviewView::~CMultiviewView()
{
}

BOOL CMultiviewView::PreCreateWindow(CREATESTRUCT& cs)
{
```

```
    // TODO: Modify the Window class or styles here by modifying
    //   the CREATESTRUCT cs

    return CView::PreCreateWindow(cs);
}

/////////////////////////////////////////////////////////////////////////////
// CMultiviewView drawing

void CMultiviewView::OnDraw(CDC* pDC)
{
    CMultiviewDoc* pDoc = GetDocument();
    ASSERT_VALID(pDoc);

    pDC->TextOut(0, 0, pDoc->StringData);
    // TODO: add draw code for native data here
}

/////////////////////////////////////////////////////////////////////////////
// CMultiviewView printing

BOOL CMultiviewView::OnPreparePrinting(CPrintInfo* pInfo)
{
    // default preparation
    return DoPreparePrinting(pInfo);
}

void CMultiviewView::OnBeginPrinting(CDC* /*pDC*/, CPrintInfo* /*pInfo*/)
{
    // TODO: add extra initialization before printing
}

void CMultiviewView::OnEndPrinting(CDC* /*pDC*/, CPrintInfo* /*pInfo*/)
{
    // TODO: add cleanup after printing
}

/////////////////////////////////////////////////////////////////////////////
// CMultiviewView diagnostics

#ifdef _DEBUG
void CMultiviewView::AssertValid() const
{
    CView::AssertValid();
}

void CMultiviewView::Dump(CDumpContext& dc) const
{
    CView::Dump(dc);
```

```
}

CMultiviewDoc* CMultiviewView::GetDocument() // non-debug version is inline
{
    ASSERT(m_pDocument->IsKindOf(RUNTIME_CLASS(CMultiviewDoc)));
    return (CMultiviewDoc*)m_pDocument;
}
#endif //_DEBUG

/////////////////////////////////////////////////////////////////////////////
// CMultiviewView message handlers

void CMultiviewView::OnChar(UINT nChar, UINT nRepCnt, UINT nFlags)
{
    // TODO: Add your message handler code here and/or call default
    CMultiviewDoc* pDoc = GetDocument();
    ASSERT_VALID(pDoc);

    pDoc->StringData += nChar;
    Invalidate();
    pDoc->UpdateAllViews(this, OL, NULL);
    pDoc->SetModifiedFlag();

    CView::OnChar(nChar, nRepCnt, nFlags);
}
```

We've started seeing how to work with multiple views now, but multiple views don't mean much unless you let the user view different parts of the document in different views. So far, we've only seen exactly the same view in the document in our various view windows, but in our next example, we'll see how to let the user scroll around in our documents independently in different views.

Scrolling Independent Views Independently

Now that we're supporting multiple views, let's see how to start scrolling around in those views so the user can actually view different parts of the same document in different views.

To do that, create a new AppWizard MDI program named scroller. However, we will not use the standard MFC CView class as the base class for our view in this example—we'll use the MFC CScrollView class. This class will support scrolling for us (with a few additions on our part). To install this class as our base class for the view, select that class in the "AppWizard creates the following classes for you:" box in Step 6 of AppWizard now, as shown in Figure 11.3.

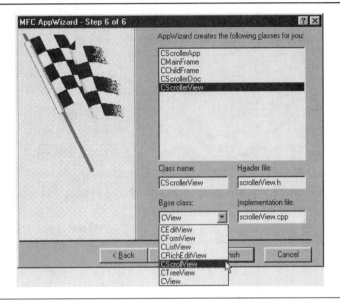

FIGURE 11.3: Selecting CScrollView as a our program's view class

Next, find `CScrollView` in the AppWizard Base class drop-down list box, as also shown in Figure 11.3, and select that class for our new program. Finally, click Finish and let AppWizard create the program.

This lets us use `CScrollView` as our view's base class, as you can see in the declaration of our view class in `scrollerView.h`:

```
// scrollerView.h : interface of the CScrollerView class
            .
            .
            .
→class CScrollerView : public CScrollView
  {
            .
            .
            .
  }
```

The `CScrollView` methods appear in Table 11.1.

T A B L E 1 1 . 1 : The CScrollView Class Methods

Method	Does This
CScrollView	Constructs a CScrollView object.
FillOutsideRect	Fills the area of a view outside the scrolling area.
GetDeviceScrollPosition	Gets the current scroll position in device units.
GetDeviceScrollSizes	Gets the current mapping mode, the total size, and the line and page sizes of the scrollable view.
GetScrollPosition	Gets the current scroll position in logical units.
GetTotalSize	Gets the total size of the scroll view in logical units.
ResizeParentToFit	Causes the size of the view to dictate the size of its frame.
ScrollToPosition	Scrolls the view to a given point, specified in logical units.
SetScaleToFitSize	Puts the scroll view into scale-to-fit mode.
SetScrollSizes	Sets the scroll view's mapping mode, total size, and horizontal and vertical scroll amounts.

Now we add the code we've used in the previous example, multiview, to let the user type text into our program. That is, we set up storage for that text in a CString object named StringData in the document, and place the characters the user types into that string in the view's OnChar() method:

```
void CScrollerView::OnChar(UINT nChar, UINT nRepCnt, UINT nFlags)
{
    CScrollerDoc* pDoc = GetDocument();
    ASSERT_VALID(pDoc);

    pDoc->StringData += nChar;
    Invalidate();

    pDoc->UpdateAllViews(this, 0L, NULL);
    pDoc->SetModifiedFlag();

    CScrollView::OnChar(nChar, nRepCnt, nFlags);
}
```

Everything's the same as it was in multiview, then—the user can create and work with multiple documents at the same time, as well as open multiple views in those documents. Now it's time to add the capability that makes scroller unique: view scrolling.

Making a View "Scrollable"

There are a few steps to making a view "scrollable," and we'll get a guided tour of the process here. The first step is determining what the size of the entire document is in screen pixels if it were all viewed on the screen at once. To be able to scroll through the data in the document, we have to give the CScrollView class some idea of the extent of the document. Each view will then act as a window into that document, and we'll be able to scroll around at will in the document (both horizontally and vertically). The CScrollView class will take care of the details for us when the user works with the scrollbars.

Giving a Document a Size

To give the whole document a size, we add a new object to the document of class CSize, which we name m_size:

```
// scrollerDoc.h : interface of the CScrollerDoc class
            .
            .
            .
class CScrollerDoc : public CDocument
{
protected: // create from serialization only
     CScrollerDoc();
     DECLARE_DYNCREATE(CScrollerDoc)
➔    CSize m_size;
            .
            .
            .
}
```

This new member is protected in our document, so we add a new method to return that size, GetDocSize():

```
// scrollerDoc.h : interface of the CScrollerDoc class
            .
            .
            .
class CScrollerDoc : public CDocument
{
protected: // create from serialization only
     CScrollerDoc();
     DECLARE_DYNCREATE(CScrollerDoc)
     CSize m_size;
```

// Attributes

Skill 11

```
public:
     CString StringData;
// Operations
public:
     CSize GetDocSize() {return m_size;}
             .
             .
             .
}
```

In addition, we initialize the size of our document to, say, 1000 x 1000 pixels this way in the document's constructor:

```
CScrollerDoc::CScrollerDoc()
{
     m_size = CSize(1000, 1000);
     StringData = "";
}
```

TIP   Although we use an arbitrary size for our document in this example—1000 x 1000 pixels—you can get the actual extent of the text in your document using methods like GetTextExtent() and GetTextMetrics(), so set the size of your document exactly.

Now we've given the document a size in screen pixels, but so far, CScrollView has no idea what that size is. We will inform our view what the document's size is with the SetScrollSizes() method.

In fact, AppWizard has already placed a call to SetScrollSizes() in our view's OnInitialUpdate() method, although here it has set our document's size to the default 100 x 100 pixels:

```
void CScrollerView::OnInitialUpdate()
{
     CScrollView::OnInitialUpdate();
     CSize sizeTotal;
     // TODO: calculate the total size of this view
     sizeTotal.cx = sizeTotal.cy = 100;

     SetScrollSizes(MM_TEXT, sizeTotal);
}
```

The MM_TEXT parameter in the SetScrollSizes() call indicates that we are using screen pixels as our dimensions. We change that code now so that we pass the actual dimensions of our document (which we get with our new `GetDocSize()` method) to `SetScrollSizes()` like this:

```
void CScrollerView::OnInitialUpdate()
{
    CScrollView::OnInitialUpdate();
    CSize sizeTotal;

    CScrollerDoc* pDoc = GetDocument();
    ASSERT_VALID(pDoc);

    sizeTotal.cx = pDoc->GetDocSize().cx;
    sizeTotal.cy = pDoc->GetDocSize().cy;

    SetScrollSizes(MM_TEXT, sizeTotal);
}
```

 NOTE If your document changes in size while the user works on it, call `SetScrollSizes()` again to make sure the view keeps track of the document's new size and can scroll it accordingly.

Now we're free to display the string the user has typed in `OnDraw()`:

```
void CScrollerView::OnDraw(CDC* pDC)
{
    CScrollerDoc* pDoc = GetDocument();
    ASSERT_VALID(pDoc);

    pDC->TextOut(0, 0, pDoc->StringData);
}
```

When the user scrolls the view, the `CScrollView` internal methods will actually change the location of the `OnDraw()` device context's origin, moving it in the direction opposite to what the user has scrolled. This means that all we have to do is to display our text in the device context passed to us. `CScrollView` has already prepared that device context for us, scrolling it automatically to match the user's scroll bar actions.

Adjusting a Scrolled Device Context

It is important to note that taking the user's scrolling actions into account only prepares the `OnDraw ()` device context for us. If we were to set up our own device context using the `CClientDC` class and display the text string in it, then there would be a problem:

```
CClientDC(this);
dc.TextOut(0, 0, StringData);
```

The problem is that the device context we've set up ourselves has not been scrolled properly by the `CScrollView` class to match the user's scroll bar actions. We can fix that, however, by preparing our own device context (that is, a device context that was not passed to us in `OnDraw()`) so that it passes a pointer to that device context on to the view method `OnPrepareDC()`:

```
  CClientDC(this);
➔OnPrepareDC(&dc);
  dc.TextOut(0, 0, StringData);
```

Now the new device context is prepared properly, and we can display our text as before, scrolled automatically to the proper position.

Run scroller now, as shown in Figure 11.4. As you can see in that figure, we're able to scroll view independently into the same document.

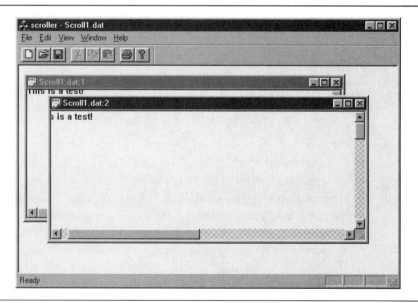

FIGURE 11.4: The scroller program lets us scroll our data.

The code for this program appears in `scrollerDoc.h`/`scrollerDoc.cpp` and `scrollView.h`/`scrollView.cpp`.

scrollerDoc.h and scrollerDoc.cpp

```
// scrollerDoc.h : interface of the CScrollerDoc class
//
/////////////////////////////////////////////////////////////////////

#if !defined(AFX_SCROLLERDOC_H__12808CF3_94CF_11D0_8860_444553540000__INCLUDED_)
#define AFX_SCROLLERDOC_H__12808CF3_94CF_11D0_8860_444553540000__INCLUDED_

#if _MSC_VER >= 1000
#pragma once
#endif // _MSC_VER >= 1000


class CScrollerDoc : public CDocument
{
protected: // create from serialization only
    CScrollerDoc();
    DECLARE_DYNCREATE(CScrollerDoc)
    CSize m_size;

// Attributes
public:
    CString StringData;
// Operations
public:
    CSize GetDocSize() {return m_size;}
// Overrides
    // ClassWizard generated virtual function overrides
    //{{AFX_VIRTUAL(CScrollerDoc)
    public:
    virtual BOOL OnNewDocument();
    virtual void Serialize(CArchive& ar);
    //}}AFX_VIRTUAL

// Implementation
public:
    virtual ~CScrollerDoc();
#ifdef _DEBUG
    virtual void AssertValid() const;
    virtual void Dump(CDumpContext& dc) const;
#endif

protected:

// Generated message map functions
protected:
    //{{AFX_MSG(CScrollerDoc)
```

```
            // NOTE - the ClassWizard will add and remove member functions here.
            //    DO NOT EDIT what you see in these blocks of generated code !
        //}}AFX_MSG
        DECLARE_MESSAGE_MAP()
};

//////////////////////////////////////////////////////////////////////////////

//{{AFX_INSERT_LOCATION}}
// Microsoft Developer Studio will insert additional declarations immediately
// before the previous line.

#endif //
!defined(AFX_SCROLLERDOC_H__12808CF3_94CF_11D0_8860_444553540000__INCLUDED_)



// scrollerDoc.cpp : implementation of the CScrollerDoc class
//

#include "stdafx.h"
#include "scroller.h"

#include "scrollerDoc.h"

#ifdef _DEBUG
#define new DEBUG_NEW
#undef THIS_FILE
static char THIS_FILE[] = __FILE__;
#endif

//////////////////////////////////////////////////////////////////////////////
// CScrollerDoc

IMPLEMENT_DYNCREATE(CScrollerDoc, CDocument)

BEGIN_MESSAGE_MAP(CScrollerDoc, CDocument)
    //{{AFX_MSG_MAP(CScrollerDoc)
        // NOTE - the ClassWizard will add and remove mapping macros here.
        //    DO NOT EDIT what you see in these blocks of generated code!
    //}}AFX_MSG_MAP
END_MESSAGE_MAP()

//////////////////////////////////////////////////////////////////////////////
// CScrollerDoc construction/destruction

CScrollerDoc::CScrollerDoc()
{
```

```
        // TODO: add one-time construction code here
        m_size = CSize(1000, 1000);
        StringData = "";
}

CScrollerDoc::~CScrollerDoc()
{
}

BOOL CScrollerDoc::OnNewDocument()
{
    if (!CDocument::OnNewDocument())
        return FALSE;

    // TODO: add reinitialization code here
    // (SDI documents will reuse this document)

    return TRUE;
}


/////////////////////////////////////////////////////////////////////////
// CScrollerDoc serialization

void CScrollerDoc::Serialize(CArchive& ar)
{
    if (ar.IsStoring())
    {
        ar << StringData;
    }
    else
    {
        ar >> StringData;
    }
}

/////////////////////////////////////////////////////////////////////////
// CScrollerDoc diagnostics

#ifdef _DEBUG
void CScrollerDoc::AssertValid() const
{
    CDocument::AssertValid();
}

void CScrollerDoc::Dump(CDumpContext& dc) const
{
```

```
        CDocument::Dump(dc);
}
#endif //_DEBUG


/////////////////////////////////////////////////////////////////////
// CScrollerDoc commands
```

scrollerView.h and *scrollerView.cpp*

```
// scrollerView.h : interface of the CScrollerView class
//
/////////////////////////////////////////////////////////////////////

#if !defined(AFX_SCROLLERVIEW_H__12808CF5_94CF_11D0_8860_444553540000__INCLUDED_)
#define AFX_SCROLLERVIEW_H__12808CF5_94CF_11D0_8860_444553540000__INCLUDED_

#if _MSC_VER >= 1000
#pragma once
#endif // _MSC_VER >= 1000

class CScrollerView : public CScrollView
{
protected: // create from serialization only
    CScrollerView();
    DECLARE_DYNCREATE(CScrollerView)

// Attributes
public:
    CScrollerDoc* GetDocument();

// Operations
public:

// Overrides
    // ClassWizard generated virtual function overrides
    //{{AFX_VIRTUAL(CScrollerView)
    public:
    virtual void OnDraw(CDC* pDC);  // overridden to draw this view
    virtual BOOL PreCreateWindow(CREATESTRUCT& cs);
    protected:
    virtual void OnInitialUpdate(); // called first time after construct
    virtual BOOL OnPreparePrinting(CPrintInfo* pInfo);
    virtual void OnBeginPrinting(CDC* pDC, CPrintInfo* pInfo);
    virtual void OnEndPrinting(CDC* pDC, CPrintInfo* pInfo);
    //}}AFX_VIRTUAL

// Implementation
public:
```

```
        virtual ~CScrollerView();
#ifdef _DEBUG
        virtual void AssertValid() const;
        virtual void Dump(CDumpContext& dc) const;
#endif

protected:

// Generated message map functions
protected:
        //{{AFX_MSG(CScrollerView)
        afx_msg void OnChar(UINT nChar, UINT nRepCnt, UINT nFlags);
        //}}AFX_MSG
        DECLARE_MESSAGE_MAP()
};

#ifndef _DEBUG  // debug version in scrollerView.cpp
inline CScrollerDoc* CScrollerView::GetDocument()
    { return (CScrollerDoc*)m_pDocument; }
#endif

/////////////////////////////////////////////////////////////////////////

//{{AFX_INSERT_LOCATION}}
// Microsoft Developer Studio will insert additional declarations immediately
// before the previous line.

#endif // !defined(AFX_SCROLLERVIEW_H__12808CF5_94CF_11D0_8860_444553540000__
➥INCLUDED_)



// scrollerView.cpp : implementation of the CScrollerView class
//

#include "stdafx.h"
#include "scroller.h"

#include "scrollerDoc.h"
#include "scrollerView.h"

#ifdef _DEBUG
#define new DEBUG_NEW
#undef THIS_FILE
static char THIS_FILE[] = __FILE__;
#endif

/////////////////////////////////////////////////////////////////////////
// CScrollerView
```

Skill 11

```
IMPLEMENT_DYNCREATE(CScrollerView, CScrollView)

BEGIN_MESSAGE_MAP(CScrollerView, CScrollView)
    //{{AFX_MSG_MAP(CScrollerView)
    ON_WM_CHAR()
    //}}AFX_MSG_MAP
    // Standard printing commands
    ON_COMMAND(ID_FILE_PRINT, CScrollView::OnFilePrint)
    ON_COMMAND(ID_FILE_PRINT_DIRECT, CScrollView::OnFilePrint)
    ON_COMMAND(ID_FILE_PRINT_PREVIEW, CScrollView::OnFilePrintPreview)
END_MESSAGE_MAP()

/////////////////////////////////////////////////////////////////////////////
// CScrollerView construction/destruction

CScrollerView::CScrollerView()
{
    // TODO: add construction code here

}

CScrollerView::~CScrollerView()
{
}

BOOL CScrollerView::PreCreateWindow(CREATESTRUCT& cs)
{
    // TODO: Modify the Window class or styles here by modifying
    //   the CREATESTRUCT cs

    return CScrollView::PreCreateWindow(cs);
}

/////////////////////////////////////////////////////////////////////////////
// CScrollerView drawing

void CScrollerView::OnDraw(CDC* pDC)
{
    CScrollerDoc* pDoc = GetDocument();
    ASSERT_VALID(pDoc);

    pDC->TextOut(0, 0, pDoc->StringData);
    // TODO: add draw code for native data here
}

void CScrollerView::OnInitialUpdate()
{
    CScrollView::OnInitialUpdate();
```

```
        CSize sizeTotal;
        // TODO: calculate the total size of this view
        //sizeTotal.cx = sizeTotal.cy = 100;
        CScrollerDoc* pDoc = GetDocument();
        ASSERT_VALID(pDoc);

        sizeTotal.cx = pDoc->GetDocSize().cx;
        sizeTotal.cy = pDoc->GetDocSize().cy;
        SetScrollSizes(MM_TEXT, sizeTotal);
}

/////////////////////////////////////////////////////////////////////////
// CScrollerView printing

BOOL CScrollerView::OnPreparePrinting(CPrintInfo* pInfo)
{
        // default preparation
        return DoPreparePrinting(pInfo);
}

void CScrollerView::OnBeginPrinting(CDC* /*pDC*/, CPrintInfo* /*pInfo*/)
{
        // TODO: add extra initialization before printing
}

void CScrollerView::OnEndPrinting(CDC* /*pDC*/, CPrintInfo* /*pInfo*/)
{
        // TODO: add cleanup after printing
}

/////////////////////////////////////////////////////////////////////////
// CScrollerView diagnostics

#ifdef _DEBUG
void CScrollerView::AssertValid() const
{
        CScrollView::AssertValid();
}

void CScrollerView::Dump(CDumpContext& dc) const
{
        CScrollView::Dump(dc);
}

CScrollerDoc* CScrollerView::GetDocument() // non-debug version is inline
{
        ASSERT(m_pDocument->IsKindOf(RUNTIME_CLASS(CScrollerDoc)));
        return (CScrollerDoc*)m_pDocument;
}
```

```
#endif //_DEBUG

//////////////////////////////////////////////////////////////////////
// CScrollerView message handlers

void CScrollerView::OnChar(UINT nChar, UINT nRepCnt, UINT nFlags)
{
    CScrollerDoc* pDoc = GetDocument();
    ASSERT_VALID(pDoc);

    pDoc->StringData += nChar;
    Invalidate();

    pDoc->UpdateAllViews(this, OL, NULL);
    pDoc->SetModifiedFlag();

    CScrollView::OnChar(nChar, nRepCnt, nFlags);
}
```

Now we've made our view scrollable, using the CScrollView class. You may have noticed that other view classes were available in AppWizard besides CScrollView. For example, you can use the CEditView class to base a view class on the text box class CEdit, or CFormView, to base a view class on forms. A form is much like a dialog box, except you usually use them as MDI child windows, as we'll see in the next skill. Here, however, we can take a look at the CEditView class, which lets us support windows that have all kinds of text-editing functions already built in.

Using a Text Box as a View

One of the most persistent problems in writing Windows programs is text handling. If you want to let the user type in multi-line text, edit it, scroll through it, and even copy or paste text to and from the clipboard, it always takes some work to write all the necessary code from scratch. However, the CEditView class can handle all this for us, including the cut and paste functions. This class creates a view class based on a text box, and it also enables the menu items in an MDI program like Cut and Paste. Let's see how to save a great deal of time and effort and add a lot of power to our programs using this new view class.

Create a new MDI program using AppWizard, naming it editor. In Step 6 of AppWizard, make sure you select CEditView as the base class of the program's view class, CEditorView. Then let AppWizard create the program for you. This installs CEditView as the base class of our new view class, as we see in `editorView.h`:

```
// editorView.h : interface of the CEditorView class
        .
        .
        .
→class CEditorView : public CEditView
  {
        .
        .
        .
  }
```

Amazingly, we really don't have to do anything more to have a fully functional editing program. As it stands now, the user can type in multi-line text, scroll through it, use the cut, paste, and copy functions in the menu or tool bar, save it to disk in the file they want, and read it back in from disk. In fact, they can even print the text out, using the built-in CEditView methods OnPreparePrinting(), OnBeginPrinting(), and OnEndPrinting(). With one easy step, we've created a multi-document, multiview fully featured word processor, as we see in Figure 11.5

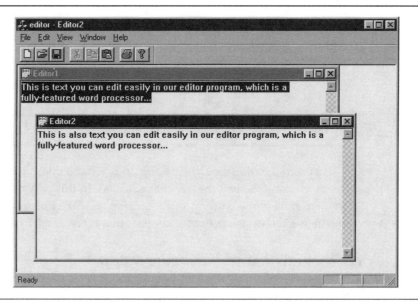

FIGURE 11.5: The editor program is a fully featured word processor.

But there does seem to be a snag—what if we want to work with the data in the text box ourselves? The editor program seems to do everything for us already. How do we break into the process and handle the text that the user has typed?

Reaching Editor's Internal Data

Let's say that we want to add a new item to the Edit menu in our editor program: Clear. This item will clear the selected text in the current document. How do we implement this new item? To do so, we need to be able to reach the data actually stored in the text box that covers our view. We can do that with the `CEditView` class's `GetEditCtrl()` method.

Let's see this at work. Add a new item to editor's Edit menu: Clear selected text. Now connect that menu item to an event-handler named `OnEditClear()`:

```
void CEditorView::OnEditClear()
{

}
```

To clear the text in the text box covering our view, we will simply call the `CEdit` class's `Clear()` method, and we do that like this:

```
    void CEditorView::OnEditClear()
    {
→       GetEditCtrl().Clear();

    }
```

TIP   The `CEdit` class's methods appear in Table 6.2.

That's all it took—now we are able to reach the internal data in our editor program, clearing the text the user has selected. In this way, we can gain access to the internal data in the editor program, using the `CEdit` class methods. The code for the view class of this program appears in `editorView.h/editorView.cpp`.

editorView.h and *editorView.cpp*

```
// editorView.h : interface of the CEditorView class
//
/////////////////////////////////////////////////////////////////////////////

#if !defined(AFX_EDITORVIEW_H__4D6E5447_94D7_11D0_8860_444553540000__INCLUDED_)
```

```
#define AFX_EDITORVIEW_H__4D6E5447_94D7_11D0_8860_444553540000__INCLUDED_

#if _MSC_VER >= 1000
#pragma once
#endif // _MSC_VER >= 1000

class CEditorView : public CEditView
{
protected: // create from serialization only
    CEditorView();
    DECLARE_DYNCREATE(CEditorView)

// Attributes
public:
    CEditorDoc* GetDocument();

// Operations
public:

// Overrides
    // ClassWizard generated virtual function overrides
    //{{AFX_VIRTUAL(CEditorView)
    public:
    virtual void OnDraw(CDC* pDC);  // overridden to draw this view
    virtual BOOL PreCreateWindow(CREATESTRUCT& cs);
    protected:
    virtual BOOL OnPreparePrinting(CPrintInfo* pInfo);
    virtual void OnBeginPrinting(CDC* pDC, CPrintInfo* pInfo);
    virtual void OnEndPrinting(CDC* pDC, CPrintInfo* pInfo);
    //}}AFX_VIRTUAL

// Implementation
public:
    virtual ~CEditorView();
#ifdef _DEBUG
    virtual void AssertValid() const;
    virtual void Dump(CDumpContext& dc) const;
#endif

protected:

// Generated message map functions
protected:
    //{{AFX_MSG(CEditorView)
    afx_msg void OnEditClear();
    afx_msg void OnUpdateEditClear(CCmdUI* pCmdUI);
    //}}AFX_MSG
    DECLARE_MESSAGE_MAP()
};
```

```
#ifndef _DEBUG  // debug version in editorView.cpp
inline CEditorDoc* CEditorView::GetDocument()
   { return (CEditorDoc*)m_pDocument; }
#endif

/////////////////////////////////////////////////////////////////////////////

//{{AFX_INSERT_LOCATION}}
// Microsoft Developer Studio will insert additional declarations immediately
// before the previous line.

#endif // !defined(AFX_EDITORVIEW_H__4D6E5447_94D7_11D0_8860_444553540000__
➡INCLUDED_)




// editorView.cpp : implementation of the CEditorView class
//

#include "stdafx.h"
#include "editor.h"

#include "editorDoc.h"
#include "editorView.h"

#ifdef _DEBUG
#define new DEBUG_NEW
#undef THIS_FILE
static char THIS_FILE[] = __FILE__;
#endif

/////////////////////////////////////////////////////////////////////////////
// CEditorView

IMPLEMENT_DYNCREATE(CEditorView, CEditView)

BEGIN_MESSAGE_MAP(CEditorView, CEditView)
    //{{AFX_MSG_MAP(CEditorView)
    ON_COMMAND(ID_EDIT_CLEAR, OnEditClear)
    ON_UPDATE_COMMAND_UI(ID_EDIT_CLEAR, OnUpdateEditClear)
    //}}AFX_MSG_MAP
    // Standard printing commands
    ON_COMMAND(ID_FILE_PRINT, CEditView::OnFilePrint)
    ON_COMMAND(ID_FILE_PRINT_DIRECT, CEditView::OnFilePrint)
    ON_COMMAND(ID_FILE_PRINT_PREVIEW, CEditView::OnFilePrintPreview)
END_MESSAGE_MAP()

/////////////////////////////////////////////////////////////////////////////
// CEditorView construction/destruction
```

```
CEditorView::CEditorView()
{
    // TODO: add construction code here

}

CEditorView::~CEditorView()
{
}

BOOL CEditorView::PreCreateWindow(CREATESTRUCT& cs)
{
    // TODO: Modify the Window class or styles here by modifying
    //   the CREATESTRUCT cs

    BOOL bPreCreated = CEditView::PreCreateWindow(cs);
    cs.style &= ~(ES_AUTOHSCROLL|WS_HSCROLL);     // Enable word-wrapping

    return bPreCreated;
}

/////////////////////////////////////////////////////////////////////////////
// CEditorView drawing

void CEditorView::OnDraw(CDC* pDC)
{
    CEditorDoc* pDoc = GetDocument();
    ASSERT_VALID(pDoc);

    // TODO: add draw code for native data here
}

/////////////////////////////////////////////////////////////////////////////
// CEditorView printing

BOOL CEditorView::OnPreparePrinting(CPrintInfo* pInfo)
{
    // default CEditView preparation
    return CEditView::OnPreparePrinting(pInfo);
}

void CEditorView::OnBeginPrinting(CDC* pDC, CPrintInfo* pInfo)
{
    // Default CEditView begin printing.
    CEditView::OnBeginPrinting(pDC, pInfo);
}

void CEditorView::OnEndPrinting(CDC* pDC, CPrintInfo* pInfo)
{
```

```
        // Default CEditView end printing
        CEditView::OnEndPrinting(pDC, pInfo);
}

//////////////////////////////////////////////////////////////////////////
// CEditorView diagnostics

#ifdef _DEBUG
void CEditorView::AssertValid() const
{
        CEditView::AssertValid();
}

void CEditorView::Dump(CDumpContext& dc) const
{
        CEditView::Dump(dc);
}

CEditorDoc* CEditorView::GetDocument() // non-debug version is inline
{
        ASSERT(m_pDocument->IsKindOf(RUNTIME_CLASS(CEditorDoc)));
        return (CEditorDoc*)m_pDocument;
}
#endif //_DEBUG

//////////////////////////////////////////////////////////////////////////
// CEditorView message handlers

void CEditorView::OnEditClear()
{
        GetEditCtrl().Clear();

}

void CEditorView::OnUpdateEditClear(CCmdUI* pCmdUI)
{
pCmdUI->Enable(true);
}
```

We've seen a great deal in this skill: from multiple documents to multiple views, from updating all views to using "smart" hints, from scrolling a view to creating a fully featured word processor that supports cutting, copying, pasting, printing, saving to disk, and more. As you can see, there's a lot going on in Visual C++ programs when it comes to working with multiple documents and views.

In the next skill, we're going to move on to a very exciting topic—reaching the Internet directly. In that skill, we'll see how to use the popular FTP and HTTP protocols to work with files directly from the Internet. In addition, we'll see that Visual C++ also makes working with databases easy, using the built-in support AppWizard gives us. Let's turn to that now.

Are You Experienced?

Now You Can...

- ☑ Create programs that handle mutiple documents
- ☑ Let the user open multiple views into a document
- ☑ Coordinate all views into a document so they are updated when the document's data changes
- ☑ Use new view classes to include added data-displaying functionality in a program
- ☑ Scroll a view using the CScrollView class
- ☑ Create a fully functional word processor with the CEditView class

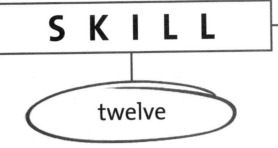

S K I L L

twelve

12

Creating Internet Programs—
Including a Web Browser

- ❑ Creating your own Web browser
- ❑ Exploring Visual C++ `WinInet`
- ❑ Using the FTP protocol
- ❑ Using the HTTP protocol
- ❑ Connecting a Visual C++ program to a database

In this skill, we are going to work with a very hot topic, the Internet, and see how to connect to the Internet in several ways.

First, we'll see how simple it is to create a new Web browser. It'll just take a few steps, and we'll have a fully functional Web browser; you'll be able to click hyperlinks, view graphics, download ActiveX controls, even run Java. All this power is built in because the Microsoft Internet Explorer actually comes packaged in a control, and we'll make use of that control ourselves.

Next, we'll see how to use the hypertext transfer protocol (HTTP) to download a Web page's raw HTML. In this case, we'll download the HTML of the Microsoft main page at http:www.microsoft.com.

Then we'll see how to use the Internet file transfer protocol (FTP) to download a file directly from ftp.microsoft.com. Transferring—that is, FTPing—files across the Internet is one of the Internet's most powerful techniques, and we'll see how to put it to work here.

Finally, we'll get a look at another aspect of how Visual C++ makes life easier— the AppWizard can now set up applications to let you work with databases very easily, and we'll take a look at that in this skill as well, because this adds yet more power to our skill set.

Let's start at once, seeing how to create and run our own Web browser.

Creating a Web Browser

Creating your own Web browser in Visual C++ is amazingly easy. It's easy because the Microsoft Internet Explorer, which comes with Visual C++ (the Internet Explorer is the foundation application of the InfoViewer in Visual C++, so you've already seen it at work if you've looked up any help topics), can be used as a control in our programs.

In fact, all we'll have to do to display the Microsoft home page in our Web browser will be to add a new Microsoft Web Browser control to our program, create a member object for it, and use its Navigate() method. Let's see this at work.

First, create a new dialog-based program called browser. Select Project ➤ Add to Project ➤ Components and Controls. This opens the Visual C++ Components and Controls Gallery. Now double-click the entry marked Registered ActiveX Controls to open the list of ActiveX controls in your system, as shown in Figure 12.1.

One of the controls in the components and controls gallery should be the Microsoft Web Browser Control, as shown in Figure 12.1. Click that, then click the

Insert button. Visual C++ asks you what class you want for this new control; accept the default suggestion: CWebBrowser. This adds the Web browser control to the dialog editor's toolbox.

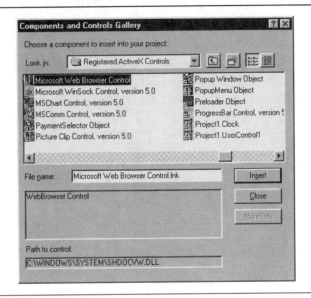

FIGURE 12.1: The Visual C++ Components and Controls Gallery

Open the main dialog window in the dialog editor now, as shown in Figure 12.2. The browser control appears at bottom in the toolbox; drag a new control of that type to the dialog window under design, sizing it as shown in Figure 12.2. This gives the new browser control the ID IDC_EXPLORER1.

Using ClassWizard, connect a member variable to this control now, naming that variable m_browser. In addition, add a button with the caption Browse to the dialog window and connect an event-handler method to that button, OnButton1().

When the user clicks the Browse button, we can navigate our Web browser to http://www.microsoft.com. We do that with the Web browser control method Navigate() (in this case, the last four parameters are flags that we set to 0 for our example):

```
void CBrowserDlg::OnButton1()
{
    m_browser.Navigate("http://www.microsoft.com", 0, 0, 0, 0);
}
```

Skill 12

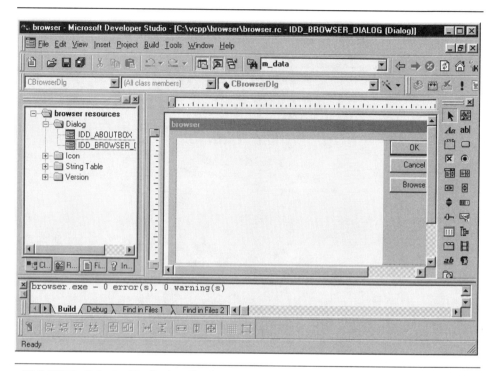

FIGURE 12.2: Designing Our Web Browser

This simple line is all it takes—now our browser is in business. Run the program, as shown in Figure 12.3, and click the Browse button.

 TIP   In a general version of this program, you can let the user enter the URL they want to navigate to in a combo box or text box—although you might not want to do that if you just want the user to be able to view your own Web page.

When you click that button, the Web browser navigates to the Microsoft home page, as also shown in Figure 12.3. That's it, now we've created our own functional Web browser. The hyperlinks work, as do the other aspects of the WWW the Internet Explorer supports.

 TIP   You can also use the other methods in the Microsoft Web Browser control, such as the GoHome() method or the GoBack() method, which implements browser "history."

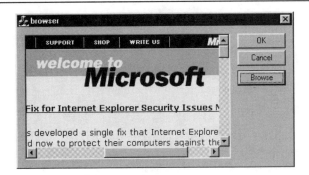

FIGURE 12.3: Our Web browser displays Microsoft's Web page.

The code for this example appears in browserDlg.h/BrowserDlg.cpp.

browserDlg.h and *browserDlg.cpp*

```
// browserDlg.h : header file
//
//{{AFX_INCLUDES()
#include "webbrowser.h"
//}}AFX_INCLUDES

#if !defined(AFX_BROWSERDLG_H__093DA507_9868_11D0_8860_444553540000__INCLUDED_)
#define AFX_BROWSERDLG_H__093DA507_9868_11D0_8860_444553540000__INCLUDED_

#if _MSC_VER >= 1000
#pragma once
#endif // _MSC_VER >= 1000

/////////////////////////////////////////////////////////////////////////
// CBrowserDlg dialog

class CBrowserDlg : public CDialog
{
// Construction
public:
    CBrowserDlg(CWnd* pParent = NULL);     // standard constructor

// Dialog Data
    //{{AFX_DATA(CBrowserDlg)
    enum { IDD = IDD_BROWSER_DIALOG };
    CWebBrowser      m_browser;
    //}}AFX_DATA
```

Skill 12

```
        // ClassWizard generated virtual function overrides
        //{{AFX_VIRTUAL(CBrowserDlg)
        protected:
        virtual void DoDataExchange(CDataExchange* pDX);        // DDX/DDV support
        //}}AFX_VIRTUAL

    // Implementation
    protected:
        HICON m_hIcon;

        // Generated message map functions
        //{{AFX_MSG(CBrowserDlg)
        virtual BOOL OnInitDialog();
        afx_msg void OnSysCommand(UINT nID, LPARAM lParam);
        afx_msg void OnPaint();
        afx_msg HCURSOR OnQueryDragIcon();
        afx_msg void OnButton1();
        //}}AFX_MSG
        DECLARE_MESSAGE_MAP()
    };

    //{{AFX_INSERT_LOCATION}}
    // Microsoft Developer Studio will insert additional declarations immediately
    // before the previous line.

    #endif // !defined(AFX_BROWSERDLG_H__093DA507_9868_11D0_8860_444553540000__
    ➥INCLUDED_)


    // browserDlg.cpp : implementation file
    //

    #include "stdafx.h"
    #include "browser.h"
    #include "browserDlg.h"

    #ifdef _DEBUG
    #define new DEBUG_NEW
    #undef THIS_FILE
    static char THIS_FILE[] = __FILE__;
    #endif

    /////////////////////////////////////////////////////////////////////////////
    // CAboutDlg dialog used for App About

    class CAboutDlg : public CDialog
    {
    public:
        CAboutDlg();
```

```
// Dialog Data
    //{{AFX_DATA(CAboutDlg)
    enum { IDD = IDD_ABOUTBOX };
    //}}AFX_DATA

    // ClassWizard generated virtual function overrides
    //{{AFX_VIRTUAL(CAboutDlg)
    protected:
    virtual void DoDataExchange(CDataExchange* pDX);    // DDX/DDV support
    //}}AFX_VIRTUAL

// Implementation
protected:
    //{{AFX_MSG(CAboutDlg)
    //}}AFX_MSG
    DECLARE_MESSAGE_MAP()
};

CAboutDlg::CAboutDlg() : CDialog(CAboutDlg::IDD)
{
    //{{AFX_DATA_INIT(CAboutDlg)
    //}}AFX_DATA_INIT
}

void CAboutDlg::DoDataExchange(CDataExchange* pDX)
{
    CDialog::DoDataExchange(pDX);
    //{{AFX_DATA_MAP(CAboutDlg)
    //}}AFX_DATA_MAP
}

BEGIN_MESSAGE_MAP(CAboutDlg, CDialog)
    //{{AFX_MSG_MAP(CAboutDlg)
        // No message handlers
    //}}AFX_MSG_MAP
END_MESSAGE_MAP()

/////////////////////////////////////////////////////////////////////////////
// CBrowserDlg dialog

CBrowserDlg::CBrowserDlg(CWnd* pParent /*=NULL*/)
    : CDialog(CBrowserDlg::IDD, pParent)
{
    //{{AFX_DATA_INIT(CBrowserDlg)
        // NOTE: the ClassWizard will add member initialization here
    //}}AFX_DATA_INIT
    // Note that LoadIcon does not require a subsequent DestroyIcon in Win32
    m_hIcon = AfxGetApp()->LoadIcon(IDR_MAINFRAME);
}
```

```
void CBrowserDlg::DoDataExchange(CDataExchange* pDX)
{
    CDialog::DoDataExchange(pDX);
    //{{AFX_DATA_MAP(CBrowserDlg)
    DDX_Control(pDX, IDC_EXPLORER1, m_browser);
    //}}AFX_DATA_MAP
}

BEGIN_MESSAGE_MAP(CBrowserDlg, CDialog)
    //{{AFX_MSG_MAP(CBrowserDlg)
    ON_WM_SYSCOMMAND()
    ON_WM_PAINT()
    ON_WM_QUERYDRAGICON()
    ON_BN_CLICKED(IDC_BUTTON1, OnButton1)
    //}}AFX_MSG_MAP
END_MESSAGE_MAP()

/////////////////////////////////////////////////////////////////////////////
// CBrowserDlg message handlers

BOOL CBrowserDlg::OnInitDialog()
{
    CDialog::OnInitDialog();

    // Add "About..." menu item to system menu.

    // IDM_ABOUTBOX must be in the system command range.
    ASSERT((IDM_ABOUTBOX & 0xFFF0) == IDM_ABOUTBOX);
    ASSERT(IDM_ABOUTBOX < 0xF000);

    CMenu* pSysMenu = GetSystemMenu(FALSE);
    if (pSysMenu != NULL)
    {
        CString strAboutMenu;
        strAboutMenu.LoadString(IDS_ABOUTBOX);
        if (!strAboutMenu.IsEmpty())
        {
            pSysMenu->AppendMenu(MF_SEPARATOR);
            pSysMenu->AppendMenu(MF_STRING, IDM_ABOUTBOX, strAboutMenu);
        }
    }

    // Set the icon for this dialog.  The framework does this automatically
    //  when the application's main window is not a dialog
    SetIcon(m_hIcon, TRUE);               // Set big icon
    SetIcon(m_hIcon, FALSE);          // Set small icon

    // TODO: Add extra initialization here

    return TRUE;  // return TRUE  unless you set the focus to a control
```

```
}

void CBrowserDlg::OnSysCommand(UINT nID, LPARAM lParam)
{
    if ((nID & 0xFFF0) == IDM_ABOUTBOX)
    {
        CAboutDlg dlgAbout;
        dlgAbout.DoModal();
    }
    else
    {
        CDialog::OnSysCommand(nID, lParam);
    }
}

// If you add a minimize button to your dialog, you will need the code below
//   to draw the icon.  For MFC applications using the document/view model,
//   this is automatically done for you by the framework.

void CBrowserDlg::OnPaint()
{
    if (IsIconic())
    {
        CPaintDC dc(this); // device context for painting

        SendMessage(WM_ICONERASEBKGND, (WPARAM) dc.GetSafeHdc(), 0);

        // Center icon in client rectangle
        int cxIcon = GetSystemMetrics(SM_CXICON);
        int cyIcon = GetSystemMetrics(SM_CYICON);
        CRect rect;
        GetClientRect(&rect);
        int x = (rect.Width() - cxIcon + 1) / 2;
        int y = (rect.Height() - cyIcon + 1) / 2;

        // Draw the icon
        dc.DrawIcon(x, y, m_hIcon);
    }
    else
    {
        CDialog::OnPaint();
    }
}

// The system calls this to obtain the cursor to display while the user drags
//   the minimized window.
HCURSOR CBrowserDlg::OnQueryDragIcon()
{
    return (HCURSOR) m_hIcon;
}
```

Skill 12

```
void CBrowserDlg::OnButton1()
{
    m_browser.Navigate("http://www.microsoft.com", 0, 0, 0, 0);
}
```

Using the Microsoft Web Browser control is a quick and easy way of support-ing a full Web browser, if your user has the Internet Explorer installed on their computer. There are other ways to work with the Internet in Visual C++, how-ever, and they don't use the Web Browser control at all. Instead, they use the WinInet support that is new to Visual C++ in version 5.0. We'll take a look at that now as we examine how to use the HTTP protocol from inside a program.

Reaching the Internet with HTTP

In this next example, we'll use HTTP, the WWW protocol, to actually download the raw HTML of the Microsoft home page. We'll do this with the built-in WinInet support in Visual C++.

Let's get started at once—our HTTP program will let the user click a button labeled "Download the Web page":

```
-------------------------------------------------------------
|HTTP                                                         |
|------------------------------------------------------------|
|                                              ---------      |
|    --------------------                     |   OK    |     |
|   |Download the Web page|                    ---------      |
|    --------------------                                     |
|                                                             |
|                                              ---------      |
|                                             | Cancel  |     |
|    Web page text:                            ---------      |
|    --------------------------------                         |
|   |                                |                        |
|   |                                |                        |
|   |                                |                        |
|   |                                |                        |
|   |                                |                        |
|   |                                |                        |
|   |                                |                        |
|    --------------------------------                         |
-------------------------------------------------------------
```

When they click that button, the program will download a section of the raw HTML of the Microsoft Web page—say the first 1000 bytes—and display it in the program's text box.

Create this new program, HTTP, as a dialog-based example now, and add a text box and a button with the "Download the Web page" caption now, as shown in Figure 12.4.

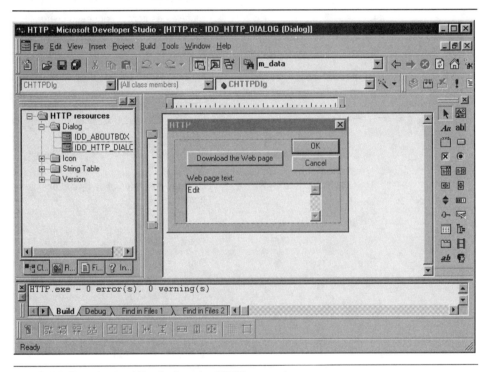

FIGURE 12.4: We design the HTTP example.

Now connect an event-handler, OnButton1(), to the button. In that method, we'll create a new *Internet session*. This Internet session is actually an object of the MFC CInternetSession class, and this class is the basis of Visual C++ Internet support:

```
void CHTTPDlg::OnButton1()
{
    CInternetSession* pInternetSession;
        .
        .
        .
}
```

The CInternetSession class supports HTTP, FTP, and Gopher sessions; the methods of this powerful class appear in Table 12.1.

TABLE 12.1: The CInternetSession Class Methods

Method	Does This
CinternetSession	Constructs a CInternetSession object.
Close	Closes the Internet connection when the Internet session is terminated.
EnableStatusCallback	Establishes a status callback routine.
GetContext	Gets the context value for an Internet or application session.
GetFtpConnection	Opens an FTP session with a server. Logs on the user.
GetGopherConnection	Opens a gopher server for an application that is trying to open a connection.
GetHttpConnection	Opens an HTTP server for an application that is trying to open a connection.
OnStatusCallback	Updates the status of an operation when status callback is enabled.
OpenURL	Parses and opens a URL.
operator HINTERNET	Holds a handle to the current Internet session.
QueryOption	Provides possible asserts for error-checking.
ServiceTypeFromHandle	Gets the type of service from the Internet handle.
SetOption	Sets options for the Internet session.

Now that we've set aside a pointer, pInternetSession, for our new Internet session, we create that session now:

```
void CHTTPDlg::OnButton1()
{
    CInternetSession* pInternetSession;

➜    pInternetSession = new CInternetSession();
        .
        .
        .
}
```

This starts a new Internet session, using the user's pre-configured Internet access method—that is, if the computer is not connected to the Internet, the program will display a connect box and make the connection. If the connection failed, we should terminate the program:

```
void CHTTPDlg::OnButton1()
{
    CInternetSession* pInternetSession;

    pInternetSession = new CInternetSession();
→   if (!pInternetSession)
    {
→       AfxMessageBox("Could not establish Internet session", MB_OK);
→       return;
    }
        .
        .
        .
}
```

On the other hand, if the connection to the Internet was successful, we want to download the HTML for the Microsoft main Web page.

Downloading through HTTP

We'll use the CInternetSession class's OpenURL() method to open a Web page for HTTP transfer. This returns a pointer to a file object of class CStdioFile (this class is derived from CFile, and it represents not a file on disk, but a C++ stream of the kind we discussed in Skill 1) and we save that pointer as pFile:

```
void CHTTPDlg::OnButton1()
{
    CInternetSession* pInternetSession;

    pInternetSession = new CInternetSession();

    if (!pInternetSession)
    {
        AfxMessageBox("Could not establish Internet session", MB_OK);
        return;
    }
→   CStdioFile* pFile = NULL;

→   pFile = pInternetSession->OpenURL( CString
    ➥("http://www.microsoft.com") );
```

Skill 12

```
             .
             .
             .
     }
```

Now we have a pointer to a file object representing the Web page we want to work with, and we can treat it just like a file. In this case, we want to download the file's first 1000 bytes, so we do that as we learned in our skill on file handling, by setting up a buffer for our data and using the Read( ) method:

```
void CHTTPDlg::OnButton1()
{
    CInternetSession* pInternetSession;

    pInternetSession = new CInternetSession();

    if (!pInternetSession)
    {
        AfxMessageBox("Could not establish Internet session", MB_OK);
        return;
    }

    CStdioFile* pFile = NULL;
➡    char* buffer;
➡    buffer = new char[1000];

    pFile = pInternetSession->OpenURL( CString
➡("http://www.microsoft.com") );

➡    pFile->Read(buffer,1000);
             .
             .
             .
}
```

This code reads in the first 1000 bytes of the Microsoft Web page and places it in the buffer.

TIP   Using Read( ) in this example is just like using it in our file-handling skill. For example, if you want to read the entire Web page, you could simply set up a loop, continually calling the Read( ) method until it returned a value of 0 for the number of bytes read.

Our last step is to display the data we received. We do that by connecting a member variable, m_text, to the text box in our program, and placing the downloaded text in that text box. We also close the file we've opened, as well as closing the Internet session this way:

```
void CHTTPDlg::OnButton1()
{
    CInternetSession* pInternetSession;

    pInternetSession = new CInternetSession();

    if (!pInternetSession)
    {
        AfxMessageBox("Could not establish Internet session", MB_OK);
        return;
    }

    CStdioFile* pFile = NULL;

    char* buffer;
    buffer = new char[1000];

    pFile = pInternetSession->OpenURL( CString
➡("http://www.microsoft.com") );

    pFile->Read(buffer,1000);

➜   m_text = CString(buffer, 1000);
➜   UpdateData(false);

➜   pFile->Close();
➜   pInternetSession->Close();
}
```

The program is complete. Run it, as shown in Figure 12.5, and click the Download the Web page button. This downloads the first 1000 characters of the Microsoft home Web page and displays them, as shown in Figure 12.5. Now we're using the HTTP protocol to download HTML across the Web.

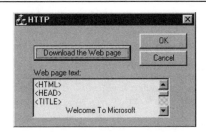

FIGURE 12.5: Using HTTP protocol, we download Microsoft's Web page.

As we've seen, the `OpenURL()` method provides a simple but powerful way to use the HTTP protocol by opening a file corresponding to an item on the Web so we can use standard file methods to work with that item.

If you're more experienced in HTTP, however, you might be more comfortable with the standard HTTP requests like Get, Put, or Post. Using HTTP requests is also easy in Visual C++; you just use the `CInternetSession` method `GetHttpConnection()` to create an object of the MFC `CHttpConnection` class. Then you use the `CHttpConnection` object's `OpenRequest()` method to execute HTTP requests, passing it "verb"constants like HTTP_VERB_GET, HTTP_VERB_PUT, or HTTP_VERB_POST.

 NOTE   The `CHttpConnection` **class only has two methods: a constructor, and the** `OpenRequest()` **method to execute HTTP requests.**

In this way, you can execute general HTTP requests in your programs in addition to using simpler methods like `OpenURL()`; with all this support, the MFC classes make it easy to use HTTP. That's it for our HTTP coverage for the moment. The code for the HTTP example program appears in `HTTPDlg.h/HTTPDlg/cpp`.

HTTPDlg.h and *HTTPDlg.cpp*

```
// HTTPDlg.h : header file
//

#if !defined(AFX_HTTPDLG_H__F4238337_9410_11D0_8860_444553540000__INCLUDED_)
#define AFX_HTTPDLG_H__F4238337_9410_11D0_8860_444553540000__INCLUDED_

#if _MSC_VER >= 1000
#pragma once
#endif // _MSC_VER >= 1000

/////////////////////////////////////////////////////////////////////////////
// CHTTPDlg dialog

class CHTTPDlg : public CDialog
{
// Construction
public:
    CHTTPDlg(CWnd* pParent = NULL);    // standard constructor

// Dialog Data
    //{{AFX_DATA(CHTTPDlg)
```

```
        enum { IDD = IDD_HTTP_DIALOG };
        CString     m_text;
        //}}AFX_DATA

        // ClassWizard generated virtual function overrides
        //{{AFX_VIRTUAL(CHTTPDlg)
        protected:
        virtual void DoDataExchange(CDataExchange* pDX);      // DDX/DDV support
        //}}AFX_VIRTUAL

// Implementation
protected:
        HICON m_hIcon;

        // Generated message map functions
        //{{AFX_MSG(CHTTPDlg)
        virtual BOOL OnInitDialog();
        afx_msg void OnSysCommand(UINT nID, LPARAM lParam);
        afx_msg void OnPaint();
        afx_msg HCURSOR OnQueryDragIcon();
        afx_msg void OnButton1();
        //}}AFX_MSG
        DECLARE_MESSAGE_MAP()
};

//{{AFX_INSERT_LOCATION}}
// Microsoft Developer Studio will insert additional declarations immediately
// before the previous line.

#endif // !defined(AFX_HTTPDLG_H__F4238337_9410_11D0_8860_444553540000__
➥INCLUDED_)


// HTTPDlg.cpp : implementation file
//

#include "stdafx.h"
#include "HTTP.h"
#include "HTTPDlg.h"
#include <afxinet.h>

#ifdef _DEBUG
#define new DEBUG_NEW
#undef THIS_FILE
static char THIS_FILE[] = __FILE__;
#endif

/////////////////////////////////////////////////////////////////////////////
// CAboutDlg dialog used for App About
```

```
class CAboutDlg : public CDialog
{
public:
    CAboutDlg();

// Dialog Data
    //{{AFX_DATA(CAboutDlg)
    enum { IDD = IDD_ABOUTBOX };
    //}}AFX_DATA

    // ClassWizard generated virtual function overrides
    //{{AFX_VIRTUAL(CAboutDlg)
    protected:
    virtual void DoDataExchange(CDataExchange* pDX);    // DDX/DDV support
    //}}AFX_VIRTUAL

// Implementation
protected:
    //{{AFX_MSG(CAboutDlg)
    //}}AFX_MSG
    DECLARE_MESSAGE_MAP()
};

CAboutDlg::CAboutDlg() : CDialog(CAboutDlg::IDD)
{
    //{{AFX_DATA_INIT(CAboutDlg)
    //}}AFX_DATA_INIT
}

void CAboutDlg::DoDataExchange(CDataExchange* pDX)
{
    CDialog::DoDataExchange(pDX);
    //{{AFX_DATA_MAP(CAboutDlg)
    //}}AFX_DATA_MAP
}

BEGIN_MESSAGE_MAP(CAboutDlg, CDialog)
    //{{AFX_MSG_MAP(CAboutDlg)
        // No message handlers
    //}}AFX_MSG_MAP
END_MESSAGE_MAP()

/////////////////////////////////////////////////////////////////////////////
// CHTTPDlg dialog

CHTTPDlg::CHTTPDlg(CWnd* pParent /*=NULL*/)
    : CDialog(CHTTPDlg::IDD, pParent)
{
```

```
    //{{AFX_DATA_INIT(CHTTPDlg)
    m_text = _T("");
    //}}AFX_DATA_INIT
    // Note that LoadIcon does not require a subsequent DestroyIcon in Win32
    m_hIcon = AfxGetApp()->LoadIcon(IDR_MAINFRAME);
}

void CHTTPDlg::DoDataExchange(CDataExchange* pDX)
{
    CDialog::DoDataExchange(pDX);
    //{{AFX_DATA_MAP(CHTTPDlg)
    DDX_Text(pDX, IDC_EDIT1, m_text);
    //}}AFX_DATA_MAP
}

BEGIN_MESSAGE_MAP(CHTTPDlg, CDialog)
    //{{AFX_MSG_MAP(CHTTPDlg)
    ON_WM_SYSCOMMAND()
    ON_WM_PAINT()
    ON_WM_QUERYDRAGICON()
    ON_BN_CLICKED(IDC_BUTTON1, OnButton1)
    //}}AFX_MSG_MAP
END_MESSAGE_MAP()

/////////////////////////////////////////////////////////////////////////
// CHTTPDlg message handlers

BOOL CHTTPDlg::OnInitDialog()
{
    CDialog::OnInitDialog();

    // Add "About..." menu item to system menu.

    // IDM_ABOUTBOX must be in the system command range.
    ASSERT((IDM_ABOUTBOX & 0xFFF0) == IDM_ABOUTBOX);
    ASSERT(IDM_ABOUTBOX < 0xF000);

    CMenu* pSysMenu = GetSystemMenu(FALSE);
    if (pSysMenu != NULL)
    {
        CString strAboutMenu;
        strAboutMenu.LoadString(IDS_ABOUTBOX);
        if (!strAboutMenu.IsEmpty())
        {
            pSysMenu->AppendMenu(MF_SEPARATOR);
            pSysMenu->AppendMenu(MF_STRING, IDM_ABOUTBOX, strAboutMenu);
        }
    }
```

```
    // Set the icon for this dialog.  The framework does this automatically
    //  when the application's main window is not a dialog
    SetIcon(m_hIcon, TRUE);              // Set big icon
    SetIcon(m_hIcon, FALSE);             // Set small icon

    // TODO: Add extra initialization here

    return TRUE;  // return TRUE  unless you set the focus to a control
}

void CHTTPDlg::OnSysCommand(UINT nID, LPARAM lParam)
{
    if ((nID & 0xFFF0) == IDM_ABOUTBOX)
    {
        CAboutDlg dlgAbout;
        dlgAbout.DoModal();
    }
    else
    {
        CDialog::OnSysCommand(nID, lParam);
    }
}

// If you add a minimize button to your dialog, you will need the code below
//  to draw the icon.  For MFC applications using the document/view model,
//  this is automatically done for you by the framework.

void CHTTPDlg::OnPaint()
{
    if (IsIconic())
    {
        CPaintDC dc(this); // device context for painting

        SendMessage(WM_ICONERASEBKGND, (WPARAM) dc.GetSafeHdc(), 0);

        // Center icon in client rectangle
        int cxIcon = GetSystemMetrics(SM_CXICON);
        int cyIcon = GetSystemMetrics(SM_CYICON);
        CRect rect;
        GetClientRect(&rect);
        int x = (rect.Width() - cxIcon + 1) / 2;
        int y = (rect.Height() - cyIcon + 1) / 2;

        // Draw the icon
        dc.DrawIcon(x, y, m_hIcon);
```

```
        }
        else
        {
            CDialog::OnPaint();
        }
    }

// The system calls this to obtain the cursor to display while the user drags
//  the minimized window.
HCURSOR CHTTPDlg::OnQueryDragIcon()
{
    return (HCURSOR) m_hIcon;
}

void CHTTPDlg::OnButton1()
{
    CInternetSession* pInternetSession;

    pInternetSession = new CInternetSession();

    if (!pInternetSession)
    {
        AfxMessageBox("Could not establish Internet session", MB_OK);
        return;
    }

    CStdioFile* pFile = NULL;

    char* buffer;
    buffer = new char[1000];

    pFile = pInternetSession->OpenURL( CString("http://www.microsoft.com") );

    pFile->Read(buffer,1000);

    m_text = CString(buffer, 1000);
    UpdateData(false);

    pFile->Close();
    pInternetSession->Close();
}
```

We've seen how to use the HTTP protocol to download a Web page's HTML now. We'll continue our WinInet exploration by looking at the FTP protocol next.

Using FTP on the Internet

In our next example, we'll see how to use the FTP protocol on the Internet. FTP is the file protocol on the Internet, so we'll download a file from the Microsoft FTP site in this example. Files come and go in the Microsoft FTP site, but one file seems eternal (it's been there for years now)—disclaimer.txt. In this file Microsoft explains that the files in their FTP site are provided "as is," without guarantees. We'll download disclaimer.txt in our program.

To download that file, we'll display a button with the text: "Download the file" and a text box in our program:

```
 ---------------------------------------------------------------
|FTP                                                            |
| ------------------------------------------------------------- |
|                                                 ---------      |
|   --------------------                         |    OK    |    |
|  |  Download the file  |                        ---------      |
|   --------------------                                         |
|                                                 ---------      |
|                                                |  Cancel  |    |
|   --------------------------------              ---------      |
|  |                                |                            |
|   --------------------------------                             |
|                                                               |
 ---------------------------------------------------------------
```

When the user clicks the button and we've started downloading the file to disk, we'll display the message "Downloading..." in a text box:

```
 ---------------------------------------------------------------
|FTP                                                            |
| ------------------------------------------------------------- |
|                                                 ---------      |
|   --------------------                         |    OK    |    |
|  |  Download the file  |                        ---------      |
|   --------------------                                         |
|                                                 ---------      |
|                                                |  Cancel  |    |
|   --------------------------------              ---------      |
|  |Downloading...                  |                            |
|   --------------------------------                             |
|                                                               |
 ---------------------------------------------------------------
```

For this example use AppWizard to create a dialog-based program named FTP. Next, add the button we'll need, with the caption "Download the file" and a text box to the main dialog window. Connect a member variable, m_text, to the text box's text, and an event-handler to the button, OnButton1(). Now let's connect to the Internet.

Connecting to the Internet with FTP

First, in OnButton1(), we start an Internet session, pInternetSession, as we did in the last example:

```
void CFTPDlg::OnButton1()
{
    CInternetSession* pInternetSession;

    pInternetSession = new CInternetSession();

    if (!pInternetSession)
    {
        AfxMessageBox("Could not establish Internet session", MB_OK);
        return;
    }
        .
        .
        .

}
```

Next, we create an object of class pFtpConnection named pFTPConnection. This class represents the FTP support in Visual C++, and to create this new object, we call the CInternetSession class's GetFtpConnection() method to make an anonymous FTP connection to the Microsoft site, passing that method the name of the FTP site we want to connect to, ftp.microsoft.com:

```
void CFTPDlg::OnButton1()
{
    CInternetSession* pInternetSession;
    CFtpConnection* pFTPConnection;

    pInternetSession = new CInternetSession();

    if (!pInternetSession)
    {
        AfxMessageBox("Could not establish Internet session", MB_OK);
        return;
    }
```

Skill 12

```
→     pFTPConnection = pInternetSession->GetFtpConnection( CString
  ⇥("ftp.microsoft.com") );
            .
            .
            .
  }
```

The CFtpConnection class lets us perform all the standard FTP actions like downloading a file, uploading a file, deleting a file, and so on. The CFtpConnection Class Methods appear in Table 12.2.

TABLE 12.2: The CFtpConnection Class Methods

Method	Does This
CFtpConnection	Constructs a CFtpConnection object.
Close	Closes the connection to the server.
CreateDirectory	Creates a directory on the server.
GetCurrentDirectory	Gets the current directory for this connection.
GetCurrentDirectoryAsURL	Gets the current directory for this connection as a URL.
GetFile	Gets a file from the connected server.
OpenFile	Opens a file on the connected server.
PutFile	Places a file on the server.
Remove	Removes a file from the server.
RemoveDirectory	Removes the specified directory from the server.
Rename	Renames a file on the server.
SetCurrentDirectory	Sets the current FTP directory.

TIP   If you don't want to or can't make an anonymous connection to an FTP site, you can specify a username and password in the call to GetFtpConnection().

If we were unsuccessful in connecting to the FTP site, we display an error message and finish up:

```
void CFTPDlg::OnButton1()
{
    CInternetSession* pInternetSession;
    CFtpConnection* pFTPConnection;

    pInternetSession = new CInternetSession();
```

```
      if (!pInternetSession)
      {
          AfxMessageBox("Could not establish Internet session", MB_OK);
          return;
      }

      pFTPConnection = pInternetSession->GetFtpConnection( CString
  ➥("ftp.microsoft.com") );

      if(!pFTPConnection){
➜         AfxMessageBox("Could not establish FTP connection.", MB_OK);
➜         return;
      }
                  .
                  .
                  .
  }
```

Otherwise, we indicate that we have started the downloading process by placing the message "Downloading..." in the text box:

```
  void CFTPDlg::OnButton1()
  {
      CInternetSession* pInternetSession;
      CFtpConnection* pFTPConnection;

      pInternetSession = new CInternetSession();
                  .
                  .
                  .
      if(!pFTPConnection){
          AfxMessageBox("Could not establish FTP connection.", MB_OK);
          return;
      }
➜     else{
➜         m_text = "Downloading...";
➜         UpdateData(false);
      }
                  .
                  .
                  .
  }
```

Getting the file itself is very easy, we just use the CFtpConnection class's
GetFile() method:

```
  void CFTPDlg::OnButton1()
  {
      CInternetSession* pInternetSession;
```

```
        CFtpConnection* pFTPConnection;

        pInternetSession = new CInternetSession();
                    .
                    .
                    .
→       pFTPConnection->GetFile(CString("disclaimer.txt"), CString
    ➡("disclaimer.txt"));

        pFTPConnection->Close();
        pInternetSession->Close();
    }
```

Note that we also close the FTP connection and the Internet session at the end of `OnButton1()`. The program is complete; run it as shown in Figure 12.6. Now click the "Download the file" button, to download the `disclaimer.txt` file.

After the FTP connection is made, the program displays the Downloading... message as also shown in Figure 12.6, and downloads `disclaimer.txt` to the directory in which we've placed the FTP project. Our program works just as we expected it to.

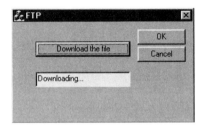

FIGURE 12.6: Using FTP protocol, we download a file.

The code for this example appears in `FTPDlg.h`/`FTPDlg.cpp`.

FTPDlg.h and *FTPDlg.cpp*

```
// FTPDlg.h : header file
//

#if !defined(AFX_FTPDLG_H__F4238327_9410_11D0_8860_444553540000__INCLUDED_)
#define AFX_FTPDLG_H__F4238327_9410_11D0_8860_444553540000__INCLUDED_

#if _MSC_VER >= 1000
```

```
#pragma once
#endif // _MSC_VER >= 1000

/////////////////////////////////////////////////////////////////////////////
// CFTPDlg dialog

class CFTPDlg : public CDialog
{
// Construction
public:
    CFTPDlg(CWnd* pParent = NULL);       // standard constructor

// Dialog Data
    //{{AFX_DATA(CFTPDlg)
    enum { IDD = IDD_FTP_DIALOG };
    CString     m_text;
    //}}AFX_DATA

    // ClassWizard generated virtual function overrides
    //{{AFX_VIRTUAL(CFTPDlg)
    protected:
    virtual void DoDataExchange(CDataExchange* pDX);      // DDX/DDV support
    //}}AFX_VIRTUAL

// Implementation
protected:
    HICON m_hIcon;

    // Generated message map functions
    //{{AFX_MSG(CFTPDlg)
    virtual BOOL OnInitDialog();
    afx_msg void OnSysCommand(UINT nID, LPARAM lParam);
    afx_msg void OnPaint();
    afx_msg HCURSOR OnQueryDragIcon();
    afx_msg void OnButton1();
    //}}AFX_MSG
    DECLARE_MESSAGE_MAP()
};

//{{AFX_INSERT_LOCATION}}
// Microsoft Developer Studio will insert additional declarations immediately
// before the previous line.

#endif // !defined(AFX_FTPDLG_H__F4238327_9410_11D0_8860_444553540000__INCLUDED_)


// FTPDlg.cpp : implementation file
//
```

Skill 12

```
#include "stdafx.h"
#include "FTP.h"
#include "FTPDlg.h"
#include <afxinet.h>

#ifdef _DEBUG
#define new DEBUG_NEW
#undef THIS_FILE
static char THIS_FILE[] = __FILE__;
#endif

/////////////////////////////////////////////////////////////////////////////
// CAboutDlg dialog used for App About

class CAboutDlg : public CDialog
{
public:
    CAboutDlg();

// Dialog Data
    //{{AFX_DATA(CAboutDlg)
    enum { IDD = IDD_ABOUTBOX };
    //}}AFX_DATA

    // ClassWizard generated virtual function overrides
    //{{AFX_VIRTUAL(CAboutDlg)
    protected:
    virtual void DoDataExchange(CDataExchange* pDX);    // DDX/DDV support
    //}}AFX_VIRTUAL

// Implementation
protected:
    //{{AFX_MSG(CAboutDlg)
    //}}AFX_MSG
    DECLARE_MESSAGE_MAP()
};

CAboutDlg::CAboutDlg() : CDialog(CAboutDlg::IDD)
{
    //{{AFX_DATA_INIT(CAboutDlg)
    //}}AFX_DATA_INIT
}

void CAboutDlg::DoDataExchange(CDataExchange* pDX)
{
    CDialog::DoDataExchange(pDX);
    //{{AFX_DATA_MAP(CAboutDlg)
    //}}AFX_DATA_MAP
}
```

```
BEGIN_MESSAGE_MAP(CAboutDlg, CDialog)
    //{{AFX_MSG_MAP(CAboutDlg)
        // No message handlers
    //}}AFX_MSG_MAP
END_MESSAGE_MAP()

/////////////////////////////////////////////////////////////////////////////
// CFTPDlg dialog

CFTPDlg::CFTPDlg(CWnd* pParent /*=NULL*/)
    : CDialog(CFTPDlg::IDD, pParent)
{
    //{{AFX_DATA_INIT(CFTPDlg)
    m_text = _T("");
    //}}AFX_DATA_INIT
    // Note that LoadIcon does not require a subsequent DestroyIcon in Win32
    m_hIcon = AfxGetApp()->LoadIcon(IDR_MAINFRAME);
}

void CFTPDlg::DoDataExchange(CDataExchange* pDX)
{
    CDialog::DoDataExchange(pDX);
    //{{AFX_DATA_MAP(CFTPDlg)
    DDX_Text(pDX, IDC_EDIT1, m_text);
    //}}AFX_DATA_MAP
}

BEGIN_MESSAGE_MAP(CFTPDlg, CDialog)
    //{{AFX_MSG_MAP(CFTPDlg)
    ON_WM_SYSCOMMAND()
    ON_WM_PAINT()
    ON_WM_QUERYDRAGICON()
    ON_BN_CLICKED(IDC_BUTTON1, OnButton1)
    //}}AFX_MSG_MAP
END_MESSAGE_MAP()

/////////////////////////////////////////////////////////////////////////////
// CFTPDlg message handlers

BOOL CFTPDlg::OnInitDialog()
{
    CDialog::OnInitDialog();

    // Add "About..." menu item to system menu.

    // IDM_ABOUTBOX must be in the system command range.
    ASSERT((IDM_ABOUTBOX & 0xFFF0) == IDM_ABOUTBOX);
    ASSERT(IDM_ABOUTBOX < 0xF000);
```

```
        CMenu* pSysMenu = GetSystemMenu(FALSE);
        if (pSysMenu != NULL)
        {
            CString strAboutMenu;
            strAboutMenu.LoadString(IDS_ABOUTBOX);
            if (!strAboutMenu.IsEmpty())
            {
                pSysMenu->AppendMenu(MF_SEPARATOR);
                pSysMenu->AppendMenu(MF_STRING, IDM_ABOUTBOX, strAboutMenu);
            }
        }

        // Set the icon for this dialog.  The framework does this automatically
        //  when the application's main window is not a dialog
        SetIcon(m_hIcon, TRUE);                  // Set big icon
        SetIcon(m_hIcon, FALSE);            // Set small icon

        // TODO: Add extra initialization here

        return TRUE;  // return TRUE  unless you set the focus to a control
}

void CFTPDlg::OnSysCommand(UINT nID, LPARAM lParam)
{
        if ((nID & 0xFFF0) == IDM_ABOUTBOX)
        {
            CAboutDlg dlgAbout;
            dlgAbout.DoModal();
        }
        else
        {
            CDialog::OnSysCommand(nID, lParam);
        }
}

// If you add a minimize button to your dialog, you will need the code below
//  to draw the icon.  For MFC applications using the document/view model,
//  this is automatically done for you by the framework.

void CFTPDlg::OnPaint()
{
        if (IsIconic())
        {
            CPaintDC dc(this); // device context for painting

            SendMessage(WM_ICONERASEBKGND, (WPARAM) dc.GetSafeHdc(), 0);

            // Center icon in client rectangle
```

```
        int cxIcon = GetSystemMetrics(SM_CXICON);
        int cyIcon = GetSystemMetrics(SM_CYICON);
        CRect rect;
        GetClientRect(&rect);
        int x = (rect.Width() - cxIcon + 1) / 2;
        int y = (rect.Height() - cyIcon + 1) / 2;

        // Draw the icon
        dc.DrawIcon(x, y, m_hIcon);
    }
    else
    {
        CDialog::OnPaint();
    }
}

// The system calls this to obtain the cursor to display while the user drags
//  the minimized window.
HCURSOR CFTPDlg::OnQueryDragIcon()
{
    return (HCURSOR) m_hIcon;
}

void CFTPDlg::OnButton1()
{
    CInternetSession* pInternetSession;
    CFtpConnection* pFTPConnection;

    pInternetSession = new CInternetSession();

    if (!pInternetSession)
    {
        AfxMessageBox("Could not establish Internet session", MB_OK);
        return;
    }

    pFTPConnection = pInternetSession->GetFtpConnection
➥(CString("ftp.microsoft.com"));

    if(!pFTPConnection){
        AfxMessageBox("Could not establish FTP connection.", MB_OK);
        return;
    }
    else{
        m_text = "Downloading...";
        UpdateData(false);
    }
```

```
    pFTPConnection->GetFile(CString("disclaimer.txt"), CString
➡("disclaimer.txt"));

    pFTPConnection->Close();
    pInternetSession->Close();
}
```

We've seen a lot of Internet power in this skill, and we've seen how Visual C++ is set up to make it easy to handle the Internet. In fact, in a similar way, Visual C++ makes it easy to handle another important aspect of programming—using databases. We'll take a look at that process next.

Handling Databases with Visual C++

We've seen how easy it was to create a Web browser using Visual C++, and it's easy to create another type of browser, too—a database browser, which we'll look at now. In this next example, we'll display the various fields in a database file, db.mdb. We will assume this file is used to keep track of student grades, and that it has a table named students with two fields in that table: Name and Grade. Each student will have a record in this file with their name and grade stored in that record.

 TIP   You can use the example db.mdb file on the CD or create your own with a database program.

Using AppWizard, we can tailor our program to the database file. When we run our new example program, we will see a new menu, Record, with the items First Record, Previous Record, Next Record, and Last Record in it to let the user move around in the database file. These menu items are also tied to arrow buttons in the toolbar. When the user uses these items, they set the *current record* in the program. Because we've named our fields Name and Grade, AppWizard will make the current record's fields available to us in the m_Name and m_Grade variables, and we can display those variables in our program.

Designing the db Program

Let's design our program now. We will place two text boxes and a button with the text: "Display the current record's fields" in our new program.

```
----------------------------------------------------------
|Untitled - db                                           |
|--------------------------------------------------------|
|File Edit Record View Help                              |
|--------------------------------------------------------|
|[ ] [ ] [ ] [ ] [ ] [ ] [|<] [<] [>] [>|]              |
|--------------------------------------------------------|
|                                                        |
|   ----------------------------------                   |
|   |Display the current record's fields |               |
|   ----------------------------------                   |
|                                                        |
|                                                        |
|   Name:          Grade:                                |
|   --------       ----------                            |
|   |       |      |          |                          |
|   --------       ----------                            |
|                                                        |
|                                                        |
----------------------------------------------------------
```

The user can use the arrow buttons or the Record menu's items to set the current record in the program, moving around in the database as they like. When the user clicks the "Display the current record's fields" button, we display those fields in the text boxes:

```
----------------------------------------------------------
|Untitled - db                                           |
|--------------------------------------------------------|
|File Edit Record View Help                              |
|--------------------------------------------------------|
|[ ] [ ] [ ] [ ] [ ] [ ] [|<] [<] [>] [>|]              |
|--------------------------------------------------------|
|                                                        |
|   ----------------------------------                   |
|   |Display the current record's fields |               |
|   ----------------------------------                   |
|                                                        |
|                                                        |
|   Name:          Grade:                                |
|   --------       ----------                            |
|   |Frank  |      |A         |                          |
|   --------       ----------                            |
|                                                        |
|                                                        |
----------------------------------------------------------
```

Let's put this example together now with AppWizard, naming this new program db. In Step 2 of AppWizard, in answer to the question "What database support would you like to include?", click the radio button labeled "Database view with file support". Next, click the button labeled Data Source to open the Database Options box, as shown in Figure 12.7.

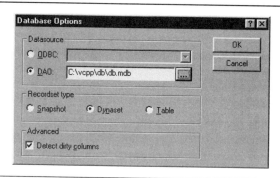

FIGURE 12.7: We set our db program's data source.

We select the DAO button, and we specify the db.mdb file as our data source, as shown in Figure 12.7. Now click the OK button and the Finish button in AppWizard, letting AppWizard create the new program.

This creates a program whose view class is based on the CDaoRecordView class, which in turn is based on the CFormView class. This class acts much like a dialog box—we can edit it in the dialog editor—except that it really is a standard view. We open the main view, IDD_DB_FORM, in the dialog editor, and add the controls we'll need: two text boxes and a button with the caption "Display the current record's fields", as shown in Figure 12.8.

TIP

You can select CFormView as the view class in your AppWizard programs in Step 6 of AppWizard. This allows you to place controls in your main window as though working with a dialog-based program, but also gives you the standard document and view classes in a normal Visual C++ program.

Using ClassWizard, we connect an event-handler, OnButton1(), to the button in our program, and two member variables, m_text and m_text2, to the text in the two text boxes.

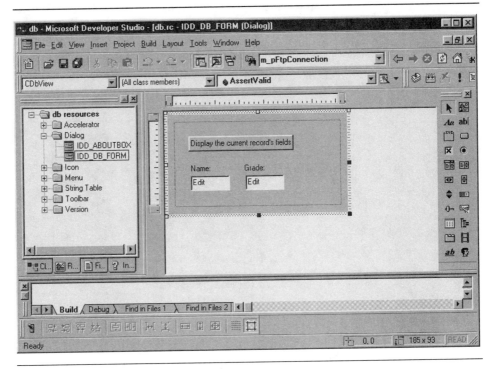

FIGURE 12.8: We design our db program.

Reaching the Current Record

When the user moves around in the database, the current record changes to match the current location in that database. The program provides us with a pointer to the current record set, m_pSet, so we can reach the Name field as m_pSet->m_Name and the Grade field as m_pSet->m_Grade. We'll display the values in those fields for the current record when the user clicks the "Display the current record's fields" button this way:

```
void CDbView::OnButton1()
{
→      m_text = m_pSet->m_Name;
→      UpdateData(false);

→      m_text2 = m_pSet->m_Grade;
→      UpdateData(false);
}
```

Skill 12

The program is ready—run it now, as shown in Figure 12.9. The user can click the arrow buttons or use the items in the Record menu to move around the database, setting the current record to a new record each time they move. When the user clicks the "Display the current record's fields" button, we can display the current record's fields in the two text boxes, as shown in Figure 12.9. Our db program is a success—now we've connected a program to a database file!

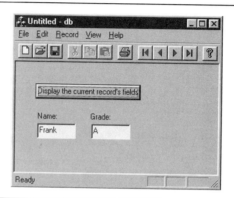

FIGURE 12.9: Our db program browses through a database.

The code for this program appears in dbView.h/dbView.cpp.

dbView.h and *dbView.cpp*

```
// dbView.h : interface of the CDbView class
//
/////////////////////////////////////////////////////////////////////

#if !defined(AFX_DBVIEW_H__ED6740A5_9309_11D0_8860_444553540000__INCLUDED_)
#define AFX_DBVIEW_H__ED6740A5_9309_11D0_8860_444553540000__INCLUDED_

#if _MSC_VER >= 1000
#pragma once
#endif // _MSC_VER >= 1000

class CDbSet;

class CDbView : public CDaoRecordView
{
protected: // create from serialization only
    CDbView();
```

```
    DECLARE_DYNCREATE(CDbView)
    boolean flag;

public:
    //{{AFX_DATA(CDbView)
    enum { IDD = IDD_DB_FORM };
    CDbSet* m_pSet;
    CString     m_text;
    CString     m_text2;
    //}}AFX_DATA


// Attributes
public:
    CDbDoc* GetDocument();


// Operations
public:


// Overrides
    // ClassWizard generated virtual function overrides
    //{{AFX_VIRTUAL(CDbView)
    public:
    virtual CDaoRecordset* OnGetRecordset();
    virtual BOOL PreCreateWindow(CREATESTRUCT& cs);
    protected:
    virtual void DoDataExchange(CDataExchange* pDX);     // DDX/DDV support
    virtual void OnInitialUpdate(); // called first time after construct
    virtual BOOL OnPreparePrinting(CPrintInfo* pInfo);
    virtual void OnBeginPrinting(CDC* pDC, CPrintInfo* pInfo);
    virtual void OnEndPrinting(CDC* pDC, CPrintInfo* pInfo);
    //}}AFX_VIRTUAL


// Implementation
public:
    virtual ~CDbView();
#ifdef _DEBUG
    virtual void AssertValid() const;
    virtual void Dump(CDumpContext& dc) const;
#endif


protected:


// Generated message map functions
protected:
    //{{AFX_MSG(CDbView)
    afx_msg void OnButton1();
    //}}AFX_MSG
    DECLARE_MESSAGE_MAP()
```

```
};

#ifndef _DEBUG  // debug version in dbView.cpp
inline CDbDoc* CDbView::GetDocument()
   { return (CDbDoc*)m_pDocument; }
#endif

//////////////////////////////////////////////////////////////////////////

//{{AFX_INSERT_LOCATION}}
// Microsoft Developer Studio will insert additional declarations immediately
// before the previous line.

#endif // !defined(AFX_DBVIEW_H__ED6740A5_9309_11D0_8860_444553540000__INCLUDED_)


// dbView.cpp : implementation of the CDbView class
//

#include "stdafx.h"
#include "db.h"

#include "dbSet.h"
#include "dbDoc.h"
#include "dbView.h"

#ifdef _DEBUG
#define new DEBUG_NEW
#undef THIS_FILE
static char THIS_FILE[] = __FILE__;
#endif

//////////////////////////////////////////////////////////////////////////
// CDbView

IMPLEMENT_DYNCREATE(CDbView, CDaoRecordView)

BEGIN_MESSAGE_MAP(CDbView, CDaoRecordView)
    //{{AFX_MSG_MAP(CDbView)
    ON_BN_CLICKED(IDC_BUTTON1, OnButton1)
    //}}AFX_MSG_MAP
    // Standard printing commands
    ON_COMMAND(ID_FILE_PRINT, CDaoRecordView::OnFilePrint)
    ON_COMMAND(ID_FILE_PRINT_DIRECT, CDaoRecordView::OnFilePrint)
    ON_COMMAND(ID_FILE_PRINT_PREVIEW, CDaoRecordView::OnFilePrintPreview)
END_MESSAGE_MAP()

//////////////////////////////////////////////////////////////////////////
```

```
// CDbView construction/destruction

CDbView::CDbView()
    : CDaoRecordView(CDbView::IDD)
{
    //{{AFX_DATA_INIT(CDbView)
    m_pSet = NULL;
    m_text = _T("");
    m_text2 = _T("");
    //}}AFX_DATA_INIT
    // TODO: add construction code here

}

CDbView::~CDbView()
{
}

void CDbView::DoDataExchange(CDataExchange* pDX)
{
    CDaoRecordView::DoDataExchange(pDX);
    //{{AFX_DATA_MAP(CDbView)
    DDX_Text(pDX, IDC_EDIT1, m_text);
    DDX_Text(pDX, IDC_EDIT2, m_text2);
    //}}AFX_DATA_MAP
}

BOOL CDbView::PreCreateWindow(CREATESTRUCT& cs)
{
    // TODO: Modify the Window class or styles here by modifying
    //   the CREATESTRUCT cs

    return CDaoRecordView::PreCreateWindow(cs);
}

void CDbView::OnInitialUpdate()
{
    m_pSet = &GetDocument()->m_dbSet;
    CDaoRecordView::OnInitialUpdate();
}

/////////////////////////////////////////////////////////////////////////
// CDbView printing

BOOL CDbView::OnPreparePrinting(CPrintInfo* pInfo)
{
    // default preparation
    return DoPreparePrinting(pInfo);
```

```
}

void CDbView::OnBeginPrinting(CDC* /*pDC*/, CPrintInfo* /*pInfo*/)
{
    // TODO: add extra initialization before printing
}

void CDbView::OnEndPrinting(CDC* /*pDC*/, CPrintInfo* /*pInfo*/)
{
    // TODO: add cleanup after printing
}

/////////////////////////////////////////////////////////////////////////////
// CDbView diagnostics

#ifdef _DEBUG
void CDbView::AssertValid() const
{
    CDaoRecordView::AssertValid();
}

void CDbView::Dump(CDumpContext& dc) const
{
    CDaoRecordView::Dump(dc);
}

CDbDoc* CDbView::GetDocument() // non-debug version is inline
{
    ASSERT(m_pDocument->IsKindOf(RUNTIME_CLASS(CDbDoc)));
    return (CDbDoc*)m_pDocument;
}
#endif //_DEBUG

/////////////////////////////////////////////////////////////////////////////
// CDbView database support
CDaoRecordset* CDbView::OnGetRecordset()
{
    return m_pSet;
}


/////////////////////////////////////////////////////////////////////////////
// CDbView message handlers

void CDbView::OnButton1()
{
    // TODO: Add your control notification handler code here
    m_text = m_pSet->m_Name;
```

```
        UpdateData(false);

        m_text2 = m_pSet->m_Grade;
        UpdateData(false);
}
```

That completes our database example, and completes this skill as well. We've seen how to create a full Web browser, establish an Internet session, download a Web page using the HTTP protocol, use the FTP protocol, even how to connect a database file to our programs. We've come very far in this skill, connecting to the Internet in a variety of ways and seeing some strong programming techniques. In the next skill, we'll start working with another very popular Visual C++ topic—ActiveX controls.

Are You Experienced?

Now You Can...

- ☑ **Create a Web browser in a few easy steps**
- ☑ **Connect to the Internet**
- ☑ **Use the HTTP protocol on the Internet to download Web pages**
- ☑ **Create programs that use the FTP protocol**
- ☑ **Connect a Visual C++ program to a database file**

Skill 12

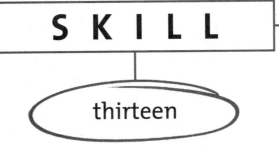

Creating ActiveX Controls

☐ Creating ActiveX controls

☐ Testing ActiveX controls

☐ Inserting ActiveX controls in Visual C++ programs

☐ Deriving ActiveX controls from standard controls

☐ Drawing your ActiveX control

☐ ActiveX Events, properties, and methods

In this skill, we are going to work with ActiveX controls, which are controls specially designed to be embedded in programs, and especially in Web pages that browsers can display. Creating ActiveX controls means we'll be able to place those controls in other programs, which is a very powerful technique. In fact, we'll even be able to add our ActiveX controls to the dialog editor's toolbox, and drag such controls directly into dialog boxes under design.

We'll see how to create ActiveX controls, and how to use them, both in the ActiveX test container program that comes with Visual C++ and in other Visual C++ programs that we write ourselves. We'll see how to draw the ActiveX control so it appears however we like.

We'll also see how to derive an ActiveX control from other, standard controls, such as buttons. If your ActiveX control is supposed to look like a standard control, this is a very helpful technique.

Finally, we'll see how to give ActiveX control methods that other programs can call, as well as properties (stored as internal variables) that other programs can set. And we'll see how to let an ActiveX control support its own custom events in this skill.

There's a lot coming up in this skill, so let's start now with our first ActiveX control—boxer.

The Boxer ActiveX Control

Our first ActiveX control will present the user with a small rectangle, divided into four sections; when the user clicks one of those sections, we will shade that section in black:

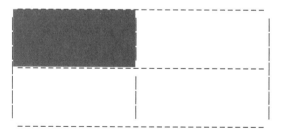

When the user clicks another section, we will switch the shading to that section:

This will be our first, full ActiveX control, which we will be able to embed in other programs, as we'll see.

Start Visual C++ now to create the boxer program. This time in the New dialog box, select the entry marked MFC ActiveX ControlWizard, as shown in Figure 13.1.

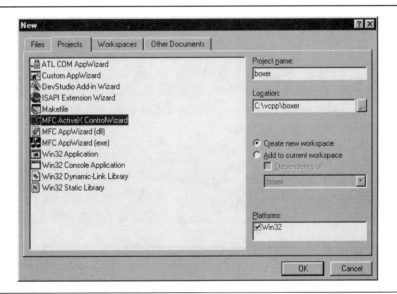

FIGURE 13.1: Creating a new ActiveX control

There are only two steps in the MFC ActiveX ControlWizard. Accept all the defaults by pressing the Finish button and allow the ControlWizard to create our new ActiveX control.

Now that we've created the control's project, the code for this new control appears in the files BoxerCtl.h and BoxerCtl.cpp. This new control is based on the C0leControl class, and the code in BoxerCtl.cpp resembles the code we'd find in a standard view class. For example, there is an OnDraw() method in which we'll draw our control. We'll draw our control now.

Drawing the ActiveX Control

Currently, our ActiveX control's OnDraw() method in BoxerCtl.cpp looks like this:

```
void CBoxerCtrl::OnDraw(CDC* pdc, const CRect& rcBounds, const CRect&
➥rcInvalid)
{
    // TODO: Replace the following code with your own drawing code.
    pdc->FillRect(rcBounds, CBrush::FromHandle((HBRUSH)GetStockObject
➥(WHITE_BRUSH)));
    pdc->Ellipse(rcBounds);

}
```

We are passed a rectangle in which to draw the control, rcBounds, and the code already in place simply colors in that rectangle white and draws a demo ellipse. We'll do our own drawing in Boxer, so remove the above line of code that draws the ellipse, pdc->Ellipse(rcBounds);.

Our job here is to start by dividing the control up into four rectangles, naming those rectangles box1 to box4, and declaring them this way in BoxerCtl.h:

```
class CBoxerCtrl : public C0leControl
{
                    .
                    .
                    .
// Implementation
protected:
    ~CBoxerCtrl();
➜    CRect box1;
➜    CRect box2;
➜    CRect box3;
➜    CRect box4;
```

Now we'll use those four rectangles to divide the control up in OnDraw(), placing the four boxes at upper left, upper right, lower left, and lower right:

```
void CBoxerCtrl::OnDraw(CDC* pdc, const CRect& rcBounds, const CRect&
➥rcInvalid)
{
    pdc->FillRect(rcBounds, CBrush::FromHandle((HBRUSH)
➥GetStockObject(WHITE_BRUSH)));
```

```
→       box1 = CRect(rcBounds.left, rcBounds.top, rcBounds.right/2,
➥rcBounds.bottom/2);                          ‹
→       box2 = CRect(rcBounds.left, rcBounds.bottom/2, rcBounds.right/2,
➥rcBounds.bottom);  ‹
        box3 = CRect(rcBounds.right/2, rcBounds.top, rcBounds.right,
➥rcBounds.bottom/2);                               ‹
        box4 = CRect(rcBounds.right/2, rcBounds.bottom/2, rcBounds.right,
rcBounds.bottom);   ‹

                .
                .
                .

}
```

Then we draw the four rectangles:

```
void CBoxerCtrl::OnDraw(CDC* pdc, const CRect& rcBounds, const CRect&
➥rcInvalid)
{
        pdc->FillRect(rcBounds,
CBrush::FromHandle((HBRUSH)GetStockObject(WHITE_BRUSH)));

        box1 = CRect(rcBounds.left, rcBounds.top, rcBounds.right/2,
➥rcBounds.bottom/2);
        box2 = CRect(rcBounds.left, rcBounds.bottom/2, rcBounds.right/2,
➥rcBounds.bottom);
        box3 = CRect(rcBounds.right/2, rcBounds.top, rcBounds.right,
rcBounds.bottom/2);
        box4 = CRect(rcBounds.right/2, rcBounds.bottom/2, rcBounds.right,
➥rcBounds.bottom);

→       pdc->Rectangle(&box1);
→       pdc->Rectangle(&box2);
→       pdc->Rectangle(&box3);
→       pdc->Rectangle(&box4);

}
```

Now our four rectangles appear on the screen. The next task is to enable mouse events so we can shade in the rectangle that the user clicks.

Adding an Event-Handler to an ActiveX Control

ActiveX controls support event-handlers just like other programs do—and in fact, we can use ClassWizard to connect the WM_LBUTTONDOWN message to our control so that we can handle mouse clicks. We do that with ClassWizard, as shown in Figure 13.2.

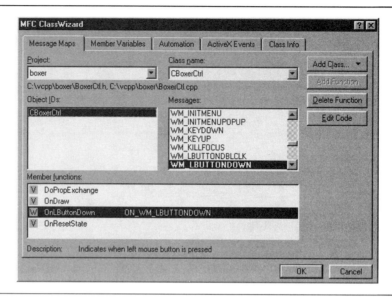

FIGURE 13.2: Adding mouse support to our ActiveX control

ClassWizard adds an OnLButtonDown() method to our ActiveX control this way:

```
void CBoxerCtrl::OnLButtonDown(UINT nFlags, CPoint point)
{
    // TODO: Add your message handler code here and/or call default
    COleControl::OnLButtonDown(nFlags, point);

}
```

Here we can record which of our four rectangles the user clicked, and thus which rectangle to fill with color—by setting up four new Boolean flags, fill1 to fill4 in the CBoxerCtl header:

```
class CBoxerCtrl : public COleControl
{
            .

            .

            .
// Implementation
protected:
    ~CBoxerCtrl();
    CRect box1;
    CRect box2;
    CRect box3;
```

```
        CRect box4;
→       boolean fill1;
→       boolean fill2;
→       boolean fill3;
→       boolean fill4;
            .
            .
            .
    }
```

And we set those flags to false in the control's constructor:

```
CBoxerCtrl::CBoxerCtrl()
{
    InitializeIIDs(&IID_DBoxer, &IID_DBoxerEvents);

→   fill1 = fill2 = fill3 = fill4 = false;
}
```

Then, in OnLButtonDown(), we can set the Boolean fill flags using the handy CRect method PtInRect(), which returns true if the point you pass to it is in a certain rectangle, such as our **box1** to **box4** objects:

```
void CBoxerCtrl::OnLButtonDown(UINT nFlags, CPoint point)
{
→   fill1 = box1.PtInRect(point);
→   fill2 = box2.PtInRect(point);
→   fill3 = box3.PtInRect(point);
→   fill4 = box4.PtInRect(point);
→   Invalidate();

    COleControl::OnLButtonDown(nFlags, point);
}
```

After setting the Boolean flags to indicate which rectangle the user clicked, we call Invalidate()to redraw the view. This calls OnDraw(), and there all we need to do is to check the four Boolean fill flags and fill the corresponding rectangle using the CDC method FillSolidRect():

```
void CBoxerCtrl::OnDraw(CDC* pdc, const CRect& rcBounds, const CRect&
➥rcInvalid)
{
    pdc->FillRect(rcBounds, CBrush::FromHandle((HBRUSH)
➥GetStockObject(WHITE_BRUSH)));

    box1 = CRect(rcBounds.left, rcBounds.top, rcBounds.right/2,
➥rcBounds.bottom/2);
    box2 = CRect(rcBounds.left, rcBounds.bottom/2, rcBounds.right/2,
➥rcBounds.bottom);
```

```
        box3 = CRect(rcBounds.right/2, rcBounds.top, rcBounds.right,
➥rcBounds.bottom/2);
        box4 = CRect(rcBounds.right/2, rcBounds.bottom/2, rcBounds.right,
➥rcBounds.bottom);

        pdc->Rectangle(&box1);
        pdc->Rectangle(&box2);
        pdc->Rectangle(&box3);
        pdc->Rectangle(&box4);

➜       if(fill1) pdc->FillSolidRect(&box1, RGB(0, 0, 0));
➜       if(fill2) pdc->FillSolidRect(&box2, RGB(0, 0, 0));
➜       if(fill3) pdc->FillSolidRect(&box3, RGB(0, 0, 0));
➜       if(fill4) pdc->FillSolidRect(&box4, RGB(0, 0, 0));
    }
```

Now our code is complete and the program is ready to test.

Testing an ActiveX Control

To test Boxer, start by selecting the Build Boxer.ocx menu item in the Build menu to create `Boxer.ocx` (ActiveX controls have the extension `.ocx`) and register that control with Windows. Next, select the ActiveX Control Test Container item in the Tools menu, which brings up the very useful test container tool as shown in Figure 13.3.

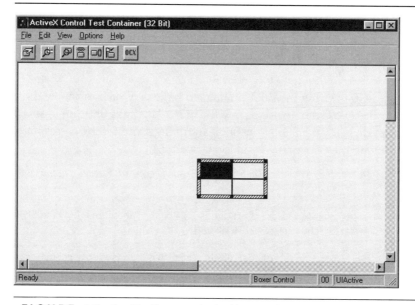

FIGURE 13.3: Testing our ActiveX control

Now select the Insert OLE control item in the test container's Edit menu, and double-click the Boxer control in the Insert OLE Control box that appears. This inserts our ActiveX control in the test container, as you can see in Figure 13.3.

You can click one of the boxes in the control now, shading it as shown in Figure 13.3. Clicking another rectangle shades that rectangle instead. Our ActiveX control works as planned; now it's time to embed it in a program.

Using an ActiveX Control in a Visual C++ Program

Let's see Boxer at work in a new Visual C++ program. Using AppWizard, create a new dialog-based program now named Boxerapp. We'll be able to insert a control of the Boxer type in this program. To do so, select Project ➤ Add To Project ➤ Components and Controls, opening the Components and Controls Gallery. Now double-click the Registered ActiveX Controls entry, displaying the available ActiveX controls, as shown in Figure 13.4.

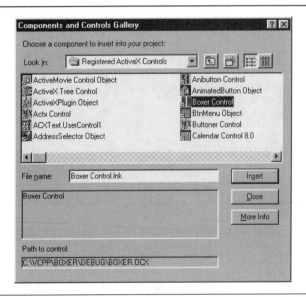

FIGURE 13.4: The Components and Controls Gallery

Select the Boxer Control entry, as also shown in Figure 13.4, and click the Insert button. A box pops up asking if you want to insert this control; click OK. Next, the Confirm Class box appears, indicating that a new class will be created for this control, CBoxer. Click OK, then close the Components and Controls Gallery. This inserts the Boxer control into the dialog editor's toolbox, as shown in Figure 13.5, where it has an icon displaying the letters OCX.

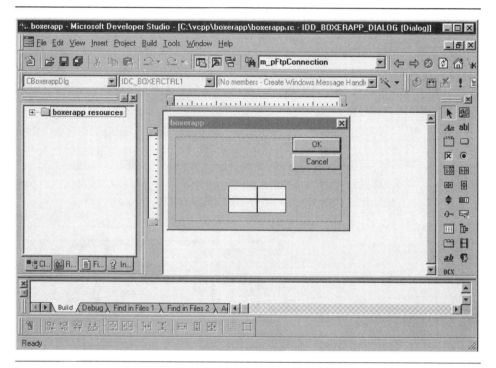

FIGURE 13.5: Our ActiveX control in the toolbox

 TIP   To change the toolbox icon for your ActiveX control, just double-click the IDB_BOXER bitmap resource in Visual C++, opening it in the bitmap editor. You can then customize it as you like.

As with any other control, we are now free to draw the Boxer control to the dialog window in the dialog editor, which you should do now, as shown in Figure 13.5. This installs our new Boxer control; run the program, as shown in Figure 13.6.

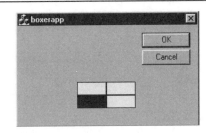

FIGURE 13.6: Our ActiveX control in a program

The Boxer control appears in our Visual C++ program, and it's active. You can click our ActiveX control as you like, shading the clicked rectangle, as shown in Figure 13.6. Our ActiveX control is working—now we're creating ActiveX controls! The code for this program appears in BoxerCtl.h/BoxerCtl.cpp.

BoxerCtl.h and *BoxerCtl.cpp*

```
#if !defined(AFX_BOXERCTL_H__00B2C1F4_95A2_11D0_8860_444553540000__INCLUDED_)
#define AFX_BOXERCTL_H__00B2C1F4_95A2_11D0_8860_444553540000__INCLUDED_

#if _MSC_VER >= 1000
#pragma once
#endif // _MSC_VER >= 1000

// BoxerCtl.h : Declaration of the CBoxerCtrl ActiveX Control class.

/////////////////////////////////////////////////////////////////////////////
// CBoxerCtrl : See BoxerCtl.cpp for implementation.

class CBoxerCtrl : public COleControl
{
    DECLARE_DYNCREATE(CBoxerCtrl)

// Constructor
public:
    CBoxerCtrl();

// Overrides
    // ClassWizard generated virtual function overrides
    //{{AFX_VIRTUAL(CBoxerCtrl)
    public:
    virtual void OnDraw(CDC* pdc, const CRect& rcBounds, const CRect&
rcInvalid);
```

```
          virtual void DoPropExchange(CPropExchange* pPX);
          virtual void OnResetState();
          //}}AFX_VIRTUAL

// Implementation
protected:
          ~CBoxerCtrl();
          CRect box1;
          CRect box2;
          CRect box3;
          CRect box4;
          boolean fill1;
          boolean fill2;
          boolean fill3;
          boolean fill4;

          DECLARE_OLECREATE_EX(CBoxerCtrl)      // Class factory and guid
          DECLARE_OLETYPELIB(CBoxerCtrl)        // GetTypeInfo
          DECLARE_PROPPAGEIDS(CBoxerCtrl)       // Property page IDs
          DECLARE_OLECTLTYPE(CBoxerCtrl)           // Type name and misc status

// Message maps
          //{{AFX_MSG(CBoxerCtrl)
          afx_msg void OnLButtonDown(UINT nFlags, CPoint point);
          //}}AFX_MSG
          DECLARE_MESSAGE_MAP()

// Dispatch maps
          //{{AFX_DISPATCH(CBoxerCtrl)
                // NOTE - ClassWizard will add and remove member functions here.
                //      DO NOT EDIT what you see in these blocks of generated code !
          //}}AFX_DISPATCH
          DECLARE_DISPATCH_MAP()

          afx_msg void AboutBox();

// Event maps
          //{{AFX_EVENT(CBoxerCtrl)
                // NOTE - ClassWizard will add and remove member functions here.
                //      DO NOT EDIT what you see in these blocks of generated code !
          //}}AFX_EVENT
          DECLARE_EVENT_MAP()

// Dispatch and event IDs
public:
          enum {
          //{{AFX_DISP_ID(CBoxerCtrl)
                // NOTE: ClassWizard will add and remove enumeration elements here.
```

```
            //    DO NOT EDIT what you see in these blocks of generated code !
      //}}AFX_DISP_ID
      };
};

//{{AFX_INSERT_LOCATION}}
// Microsoft Developer Studio will insert additional declarations immediately
// before the previous line.

#endif // !defined(AFX_BOXERCTL_H__00B2C1F4_95A2_11D0_8860_444553540000__
➡INCLUDED)




// BoxerCtl.cpp : Implementation of the CBoxerCtrl ActiveX Control class.

#include "stdafx.h"
#include "boxer.h"
#include "BoxerCtl.h"
#include "BoxerPpg.h"


#ifdef _DEBUG
#define new DEBUG_NEW
#undef THIS_FILE
static char THIS_FILE[] = __FILE__;
#endif


IMPLEMENT_DYNCREATE(CBoxerCtrl, COleControl)


/////////////////////////////////////////////////////////////////////////////
// Message map

BEGIN_MESSAGE_MAP(CBoxerCtrl, COleControl)
      //{{AFX_MSG_MAP(CBoxerCtrl)
      ON_WM_LBUTTONDOWN()
      //}}AFX_MSG_MAP
      ON_OLEVERB(AFX_IDS_VERB_PROPERTIES, OnProperties)
END_MESSAGE_MAP()


/////////////////////////////////////////////////////////////////////////////
// Dispatch map

BEGIN_DISPATCH_MAP(CBoxerCtrl, COleControl)
      //{{AFX_DISPATCH_MAP(CBoxerCtrl)
```

```
        // NOTE - ClassWizard will add and remove dispatch map entries
        //      DO NOT EDIT what you see in these blocks of generated code !
        //}}AFX_DISPATCH_MAP
        DISP_FUNCTION_ID(CBoxerCtrl, "AboutBox", DISPID_ABOUTBOX, AboutBox,
➥VT_EMPTY, VTS_NONE)
END_DISPATCH_MAP()


/////////////////////////////////////////////////////////////////////////
// Event map

BEGIN_EVENT_MAP(CBoxerCtrl, COleControl)
        //{{AFX_EVENT_MAP(CBoxerCtrl)
        // NOTE - ClassWizard will add and remove event map entries
        //      DO NOT EDIT what you see in these blocks of generated code !
        //}}AFX_EVENT_MAP
END_EVENT_MAP()


/////////////////////////////////////////////////////////////////////////
// Property pages

// TODO: Add more property pages as needed.  Remember to increase the count!
BEGIN_PROPPAGEIDS(CBoxerCtrl, 1)
    PROPPAGEID(CBoxerPropPage::guid)
END_PROPPAGEIDS(CBoxerCtrl)


/////////////////////////////////////////////////////////////////////////
// Initialize class factory and guid

IMPLEMENT_OLECREATE_EX(CBoxerCtrl, "BOXER.BoxerCtrl.1",
    0xb2c1e6, 0x95a2, 0x11d0, 0x88, 0x60, 0x44, 0x45, 0x53, 0x54, 0, 0)


/////////////////////////////////////////////////////////////////////////
// Type library ID and version

IMPLEMENT_OLETYPELIB(CBoxerCtrl, _tlid, _wVerMajor, _wVerMinor)


/////////////////////////////////////////////////////////////////////////
// Interface IDs

const IID BASED_CODE IID_DBoxer = { 0xb2c1e4, 0x95a2, 0x11d0, { 0x88, 0x60, 0x44,
➥0x45, 0x53, 0x54, 0, 0 } };
const IID BASED_CODE IID_DBoxerEvents = { 0xb2c1e5, 0x95a2, 0x11d0, { 0x88, 0x60,
➥0x44, 0x45, 0x53, 0x54, 0, 0 } };
```

```
//////////////////////////////////////////////////////////////////////
// Control type information

static const DWORD BASED_CODE _dwBoxerOleMisc =
    OLEMISC_ACTIVATEWHENVISIBLE |
    OLEMISC_SETCLIENTSITEFIRST |
    OLEMISC_INSIDEOUT |
    OLEMISC_CANTLINKINSIDE |
    OLEMISC_RECOMPOSEONRESIZE;

IMPLEMENT_OLECTLTYPE(CBoxerCtrl, IDS_BOXER, _dwBoxerOleMisc)


//////////////////////////////////////////////////////////////////////
// CBoxerCtrl::CBoxerCtrlFactory::UpdateRegistry -
// Adds or removes system registry entries for CBoxerCtrl

BOOL CBoxerCtrl::CBoxerCtrlFactory::UpdateRegistry(BOOL bRegister)
{
    // TODO: Verify that your control follows apartment-model threading rules.
    // Refer to MFC TechNote 64 for more information.
    // If your control does not conform to the apartment-model rules, then
    // you must modify the code below, changing the 6th parameter from
    // afxRegApartmentThreading to 0.

    if (bRegister)
        return AfxOleRegisterControlClass(
            AfxGetInstanceHandle(),
            m_clsid,
            m_lpszProgID,
            IDS_BOXER,
            IDB_BOXER,
            afxRegApartmentThreading,
            _dwBoxerOleMisc,
            _tlid,
            _wVerMajor,
            _wVerMinor);
    else
        return AfxOleUnregisterClass(m_clsid, m_lpszProgID);
}


//////////////////////////////////////////////////////////////////////
// CBoxerCtrl::CBoxerCtrl - Constructor

CBoxerCtrl::CBoxerCtrl()
{
    InitializeIIDs(&IID_DBoxer, &IID_DBoxerEvents);
```

```
        // TODO: Initialize your control's instance data here.
        fill1 = fill2 = fill3 = fill4 = false;
}


/////////////////////////////////////////////////////////////////////////
// CBoxerCtrl::~CBoxerCtrl - Destructor

CBoxerCtrl::~CBoxerCtrl()
{
        // TODO: Cleanup your control's instance data here.
}


/////////////////////////////////////////////////////////////////////////
// CBoxerCtrl::OnDraw - Drawing function

void CBoxerCtrl::OnDraw(
                CDC* pdc, const CRect& rcBounds, const CRect& rcInvalid)
{
        // TODO: Replace the following code with your own drawing code.
        pdc->FillRect(rcBounds,
CBrush::FromHandle((HBRUSH)GetStockObject(WHITE_BRUSH)));

        box1 = CRect(rcBounds.left, rcBounds.top, rcBounds.right/2,
➥rcBounds.bottom/2);
        box2 = CRect(rcBounds.left, rcBounds.bottom/2, rcBounds.right/2,
➥rcBounds.bottom);
        box3 = CRect(rcBounds.right/2, rcBounds.top, rcBounds.right,
➥rcBounds.bottom/2);
        box4 = CRect(rcBounds.right/2, rcBounds.bottom/2, rcBounds.right,
rcBounds.bottom);

        pdc->Rectangle(&box1);
        pdc->Rectangle(&box2);
        pdc->Rectangle(&box3);
        pdc->Rectangle(&box4);

        if(fill1) pdc->FillSolidRect(&box1, RGB(0, 0, 0));
        if(fill2) pdc->FillSolidRect(&box2, RGB(0, 0, 0));
        if(fill3) pdc->FillSolidRect(&box3, RGB(0, 0, 0));
        if(fill4) pdc->FillSolidRect(&box4, RGB(0, 0, 0));

}


/////////////////////////////////////////////////////////////////////////
```

```
// CBoxerCtrl::DoPropExchange - Persistence support

void CBoxerCtrl::DoPropExchange(CPropExchange* pPX)
{
    ExchangeVersion(pPX, MAKELONG(_wVerMinor, _wVerMajor));
    COleControl::DoPropExchange(pPX);

    // TODO: Call PX_ functions for each persistent custom property.

}


/////////////////////////////////////////////////////////////////////////
// CBoxerCtrl::OnResetState - Reset control to default state

void CBoxerCtrl::OnResetState()
{
    COleControl::OnResetState();   // Resets defaults found in DoPropExchange

    // TODO: Reset any other control state here.
}


/////////////////////////////////////////////////////////////////////////
// CBoxerCtrl::AboutBox - Display an "About" box to the user

void CBoxerCtrl::AboutBox()
{
    CDialog dlgAbout(IDD_ABOUTBOX_BOXER);
    dlgAbout.DoModal();
}


/////////////////////////////////////////////////////////////////////////
// CBoxerCtrl message handlers

void CBoxerCtrl::OnLButtonDown(UINT nFlags, CPoint point)
{
    // TODO: Add your message handler code here and/or call default
    fill1 = box1.PtInRect(point);
    fill2 = box2.PtInRect(point);
    fill3 = box3.PtInRect(point);
    fill4 = box4.PtInRect(point);
    Invalidate();
    COleControl::OnLButtonDown(nFlags, point);
}
```

We've seen how to create an ActiveX control now, and draw it ourselves. But there is much more to ActiveX controls—for example, ActiveX controls can also support events, methods, and properties. We'll look into those now.

Creating a Button-Based ActiveX Control

In our next ActiveX control example, we'll see quite a few new aspects of ActiveX control programming, such as how to derive an ActiveX control from a pre-existing standard control like a button. We'll also see how to support ActiveX events like a Click event so the programs you embed the control in can use that event, just like any other Windows event. In our case, our new control is going to be named Buttoner, and we will indeed support a Click event, which means that programs that use our control will be able to use event-handler methods like OnClickButtonerctrl1() which will be called when the control is clicked in their program.

In addition, we'll see how to support ActiveX control methods in this example. In particular, we'll add a method named Beep() to our Buttoner control. In other programs, you can use ClassWizard to create a member variable like m_buttoner for our ActiveX control, and you'll be able to call our Beep() method like this: m_buttoner.Beep().

Finally, we'll see how to support ActiveX properties. In our case, we'll support a property we'll name data, which will hold the number of times the button in our control has been clicked. There are two ways to let other programs reach the data property. We could simply let them refer to it as m_buttoner.data, letting those programs get and set values in the data property directly, or we could employ the safer technique of using member functions to let other programs reach the data property. In that case, code in other programs will call m_buttoner .SetData() to set the value in the data property, and m_buttoner.GetData() to get that value. Using member functions like this is safer because you can check the values placed in the data property before accepting them, and we'll use this member function technique in our example.

Start Buttoner now by creating that program using the ControlWizard. In Step 2 of ControlWizard, select the entry BUTTON in the drop-down list box under the question "Which window class, if any, should this control subclass?", as shown in Figure 13.7, and click Finish to let ControlWizard create the new control.

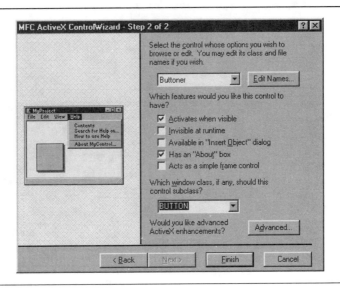

FIGURE 13.7: Basing our Buttoner control on a button

Now our Buttoner control is ready to be customized.

Customizing Buttoner

Our new ActiveX control simply appears as a blank button so far, but we can customize it by adding a caption to it, such as "Click Me!". We'll do that now in the constructor for our control in the ButtonerCtl.cpp file:

```
CButtonerCtrl::CButtonerCtrl()
{
    InitializeIIDs(&IID_DButtoner, &IID_DButtonerEvents);
    // TODO: Initialize your control's instance data here.

}
```

Like all ActiveX controls, Buttoner is based on the COleControl class, and we can use that class's SetText() method to set the ActiveX control's caption to Click Me!:

```
CButtonerCtrl::CButtonerCtrl()
{
    InitializeIIDs(&IID_DButtoner, &IID_DButtonerEvents);
    // TODO: Initialize your control's instance data here.
```

```
→        SetText("Click Me!");
    }
```

Now the Buttoner control will display that caption, as we see in the ActiveX Control Test Container in Figure 13.8.

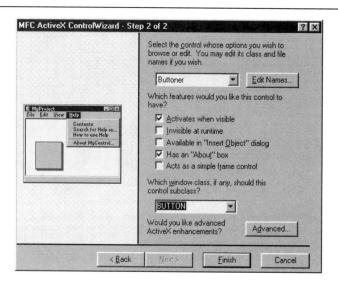

FIGURE 13.8: Customizing our Buttoner control

We're ready to dig into our ActiveX control's programming now. First, we'll see how to add an event to an ActiveX control. The code in other programs that make use of this ActiveX control will be able to add event-handling methods to handle this new event.

Adding ActiveX Control Events

Our new Buttoner event will be a Click event, which will occur when the user clicks the button. Causing an event to occur (and so to be reported to the program in which your ActiveX control is embedded) is called *firing* an event, and when the user clicks the button, we will fire the Click event. This causes the Click event-handler in the program our control is embedded in to be called. Let's see how this works now.

In ClassWizard, click the ActiveX Events tab, and click the button marked Add Event, opening the Add Event box, as shown in Figure 13.9.

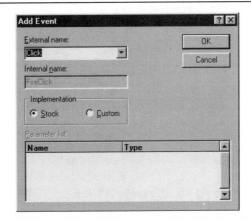

FIGURE 13.9: Adding an event to an ActiveX control

This is where we will add our Click event. To do that, find the Click entry in the External name drop-down list box, as shown in Figure 13.9. This adds the Click event to our control. To actually cause that event to occur, we will call the new method named FireClick(), which also appears in the Add Event box.

 NOTE   If you want to give your new event parameters (which will be passed to the event's handler in a program your control is embedded in), you can list those parameters and their types in the Parameter list box at the bottom of the Add Event box.

We will fire the Click event when the user clicks our button, so add an OnLButtonDown() event-handler to our ActiveX control now:

```
void CButtonerCtrl::OnLButtonDown(UINT nFlags, CPoint point)
{
    // TODO: Add your message handler code here and/or call default

    COleControl::OnLButtonDown(nFlags, point);
}
```

Here, we simply fire the Click event by calling the method ClassWizard set up for us: FireClick() (if your event passed parameters to event-handlers, you would simply pass those parameters to FireEvent(), where Event is the name of your event):

```
void CButtonerCtrl::OnLButtonDown(UINT nFlags, CPoint point)
{
```

```
→      FireClick();

       COleControl::OnLButtonDown(nFlags, point);
}
```

This code causes the control to fire a Click event each time the button is clicked, and programs that use this control will be able to set up a Click event-handler to handle such clicks.

Now we've seen how to fire an event from inside an ActiveX control. We will keep track of the number of times the user has clicked the button in the data property. We'll add that property now.

Adding ActiveX Control Properties

An ActiveX property is just a data member of our control's class. If a control has a property named data, other programs can reach that as m_buttoner.data or with Set and Get functions: m_buttoner.SetData() and m_buttoner.GetData(). An example of a property is the data property we'll add to our control now, which will hold the number of times the control has been clicked.

You add a property to an ActiveX control with ClassWizard. Open ClassWizard now, and click the Automation (named for OLE Automation) tab, then click the Add Property button, opening the Add Property box, as shown in Figure 13.10.

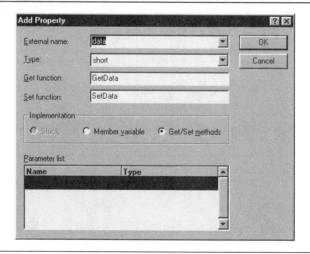

FIGURE 13.10: The Add Property box

Type **data** in the External name box to name the property, make it a short integer by selecting the "short" entry in the Type box, and click the Get/Set methods box as well, which means that programs will set the value in data with the method SetData() and get the value in data with GetData(). (If you click the Member Variable box instead, other programs can refer to the value in data simply by name like this: m_buttoner.data.) Now click OK to close the Add Property box and OK to close ClassWizard.

We can now refer to the value in the data property as m_data in our code, so we set that value to 0 in the control's constructor:

```
CButtonerCtrl::CButtonerCtrl()
{
    InitializeIIDs(&IID_DButtoner, &IID_DButtonerEvents);

    SetText("Click Me!");
→   m_data = 0;
}
```

We will store the number of times the user has clicked the button in this property, so we increment m_data in OnLButtonDown():

```
void CButtonerCtrl::OnLButtonDown(UINT nFlags, CPoint point)
{
    // TODO: Add your message handler code here and/or call default
    // FireClick();

→   m_data++;

    COleControl::OnLButtonDown(nFlags, point);
}
```

Now when other programs call our control's GetData() method, they'll get the value in m_data, which holds the number of buttons clicks that have occurred.

That's it—now we've added a new property to our control. So far, we've added an event, Click, and a property, data, to our control. Next, we will add a new method, Beep(), to our control, which can be called by other programs this way: m_buttoner.Beep().

Adding ActiveX Control Methods

To add a new method to our control, use ClassWizard and click the Automation tab. Next, click the Add Method button to open the Add Method box, as shown in Figure 13.11.

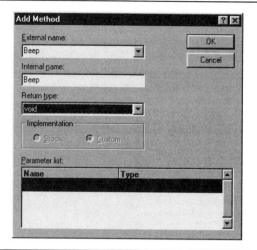

Give this new method the name Beep in the External name and Internal name boxes, and make its return type void, as shown in Figure 13.11. Now click OK to close the Add Method box, and click OK to close ClassWizard. This adds a new method to our control, Beep():

```
void CButtonerCtrl::Beep()
{
    // TODO: Add your dispatch handler code here
}
```

Our goal now is to have the computer beep, which we'll do with the MFC MessageBeep() method:

```
void CButtonerCtrl::Beep()
{
    MessageBeep(MB_OK);
}
```

And that's it—we've added a new method to our control which the code in other programs can make use of. Now they can call our control's Beep() method from inside their code.

In fact, let's see how Buttoner performs in other programs. We'll embed a Buttoner control in another program and see how to work with it in code.

Embedding the Buttoner Control in Other Programs

Create a new dialog-based program with AppWizard now, naming this new program Buttonerapp. Next, add the Buttoner control to the dialog editor's toolbox using the Components and Controls Gallery as we did in the previous example, accepting the default name that Visual C++ suggests for the new control's class name: CButtoner.

Now we add a Buttoner control to this new program using the dialog editor, as shown in Figure 13.12. The dialog editor gives this new control the ID ID_ BUTTONERCTRL1.

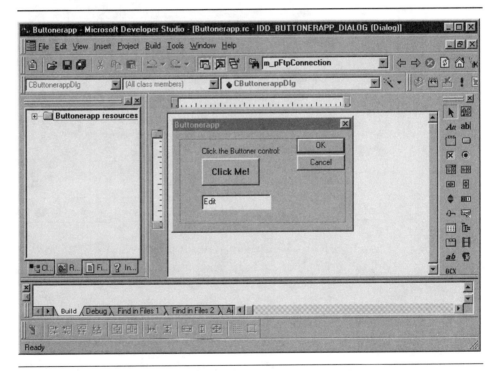

FIGURE 13.12: The Button Control in a new program

In this new program, we add a prompt label above the Buttoner control, "Click the Buttoner control:", and a text box in which we'll report the number of times the button was clicked, getting that value from the GetData() method, which returns the value of the data property.

Next, use ClassWizard to connect a member variable, m_buttoner, to the new Buttoner control, as shown in Figure 13.13. Note that the class of this new member variable is the class we just created: CButtoner. In addition, connect the text in the text box to the member variable m_text, as also shown in Figure 13.13.

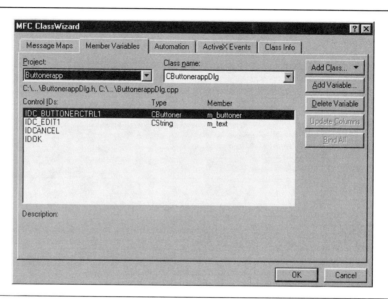

FIGURE 13.13: Adding a member variable for an ActiveX control

At this point, we've installed our Buttoner control in Buttonerapp, and we can call the methods of the Buttoner control like the Beep() method this way: m_buttoner.Beep().

Connecting the ActiveX Control to Code

We'll use ClassWizard to connect an event-handler to the Buttoner control's Click event. Find that event in ClassWizard, as shown in Figure 13.14, and add the new event-handler, which ClassWizard will name OnClickButtonerctrl1():

```
void CButtonerappDlg::OnClickButtonerctrl1()
{
    // TODO: Add your control notification handler code here

}
```

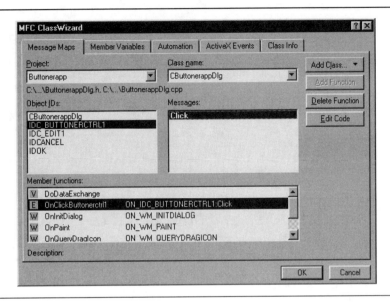

FIGURE 13.14: Adding a handler for an ActiveX control's event

This is the method that will be called when the user clicks the button control. We can display the number of times the user has clicked the button by reading the value in the control's `data` property, and we get that value with the control's `GetData()` method:

```
void CButtonerappDlg::OnClickButtonerctrl1()
{
    m_text.Format("data property = %ld", m_buttoner.GetData());
    UpdateData(false);
}
```

Now when the user clicks the button in our control, the Buttonerapp program will report the number of times the button has been clicked by displaying the value of the data property, as shown in Figure 13.15. Our program, including the ActiveX control, is working just as we want it to.

The Buttoner control has shown us how to derive an ActiveX control from a pre-existing Windows control, as well as how to support events, methods, and properties. All in all, a good deal of ActiveX power!

The code for this program appears in `ButtonerCtl.h`/`ButtonerCtl.cpp`, and the code for the Buttonerapp program appears in `ButtonerappDlg.h`/`ButtonerappDlg.cpp`.

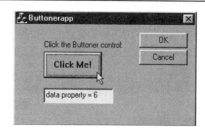

FIGURE 13.15: We use our ActiveX control's properties and methods

ButtonerCtl.h and *ButtonerCtl.cpp*

```
#if !defined(AFX_BUTTONERCTL_H__6AE5A16F_9584_11D0_8860_444553540000__INCLUDED_)
#define AFX_BUTTONERCTL_H__6AE5A16F_9584_11D0_8860_444553540000__INCLUDED_

#if _MSC_VER >= 1000
#pragma once
#endif // _MSC_VER >= 1000

// ButtonerCtl.h : Declaration of the CButtonerCtrl ActiveX Control class.

/////////////////////////////////////////////////////////////////////////////
// CButtonerCtrl : See ButtonerCtl.cpp for implementation.

class CButtonerCtrl : public COleControl
{
    DECLARE_DYNCREATE(CButtonerCtrl)

// Constructor
public:
    CButtonerCtrl();

// Overrides
    // ClassWizard generated virtual function overrides
    //{{AFX_VIRTUAL(CButtonerCtrl)
    public:
    virtual void OnDraw(CDC* pdc, const CRect& rcBounds, const CRect&
➥rcInvalid);
    virtual void DoPropExchange(CPropExchange* pPX);
    virtual void OnResetState();
    //}}AFX_VIRTUAL

// Implementation
protected:
    ~CButtonerCtrl();
```

```
        DECLARE_OLECREATE_EX(CButtonerCtrl)      // Class factory and guid
        DECLARE_OLETYPELIB(CButtonerCtrl)        // GetTypeInfo
        DECLARE_PROPPAGEIDS(CButtonerCtrl)       // Property page IDs
        DECLARE_OLECTLTYPE(CButtonerCtrl)          // Type name and misc status

        // Subclassed control support
        BOOL PreCreateWindow(CREATESTRUCT& cs);
        BOOL IsSubclassedControl();
        LRESULT OnOcmCommand(WPARAM wParam, LPARAM lParam);

// Message maps
    //{{AFX_MSG(CButtonerCtrl)
    afx_msg void OnLButtonDown(UINT nFlags, CPoint point);
    //}}AFX_MSG
    DECLARE_MESSAGE_MAP()

// Dispatch maps
    //{{AFX_DISPATCH(CButtonerCtrl)
    short m_data;
    afx_msg void OnDataChanged();
    afx_msg void Beep();
    //}}AFX_DISPATCH
    DECLARE_DISPATCH_MAP()

    afx_msg void AboutBox();

// Event maps
    //{{AFX_EVENT(CButtonerCtrl)
    //}}AFX_EVENT
    DECLARE_EVENT_MAP()

// Dispatch and event IDs
public:
    enum {
    //{{AFX_DISP_ID(CButtonerCtrl)
    dispidData = 1L,
    dispidBeep = 2L,
    //}}AFX_DISP_ID
    };
};

//{{AFX_INSERT_LOCATION}}
// Microsoft Developer Studio will insert additional declarations immediately
// before the previous line.

#endif // !defined(AFX_BUTTONERCTL_H__6AE5A16F_9584_11D0_8860_444553540000__
➥INCLUDED)
```

```
// ButtonerCtl.cpp : Implementation of the CButtonerCtrl ActiveX Control class.

#include "stdafx.h"
#include "Buttoner.h"
#include "ButtonerCtl.h"
#include "ButtonerPpg.h"


#ifdef _DEBUG
#define new DEBUG_NEW
#undef THIS_FILE
static char THIS_FILE[] = __FILE__;
#endif


IMPLEMENT_DYNCREATE(CButtonerCtrl, COleControl)


/////////////////////////////////////////////////////////////////////////////
// Message map

BEGIN_MESSAGE_MAP(CButtonerCtrl, COleControl)
    //{{AFX_MSG_MAP(CButtonerCtrl)
    ON_WM_LBUTTONDOWN()
    //}}AFX_MSG_MAP
    ON_MESSAGE(OCM_COMMAND, OnOcmCommand)
    ON_OLEVERB(AFX_IDS_VERB_PROPERTIES, OnProperties)
END_MESSAGE_MAP()


/////////////////////////////////////////////////////////////////////////////
// Dispatch map

BEGIN_DISPATCH_MAP(CButtonerCtrl, COleControl)
    //{{AFX_DISPATCH_MAP(CButtonerCtrl)
    DISP_PROPERTY_NOTIFY(CButtonerCtrl, "data", m_data, OnDataChanged, VT_I2)
    DISP_FUNCTION(CButtonerCtrl, "Beep", Beep, VT_EMPTY, VTS_NONE)
    //}}AFX_DISPATCH_MAP
    DISP_FUNCTION_ID(CButtonerCtrl, "AboutBox", DISPID_ABOUTBOX, AboutBox,
VT_EMPTY, VTS_NONE)
END_DISPATCH_MAP()


/////////////////////////////////////////////////////////////////////////////
// Event map

BEGIN_EVENT_MAP(CButtonerCtrl, COleControl)
    //{{AFX_EVENT_MAP(CButtonerCtrl)
    EVENT_STOCK_CLICK()
```

```
    //}}AFX_EVENT_MAP
END_EVENT_MAP()


/////////////////////////////////////////////////////////////////////
// Property pages

// TODO: Add more property pages as needed.  Remember to increase the count!
BEGIN_PROPPAGEIDS(CButtonerCtrl, 1)
    PROPPAGEID(CButtonerPropPage::guid)
END_PROPPAGEIDS(CButtonerCtrl)


/////////////////////////////////////////////////////////////////////
// Initialize class factory and guid

IMPLEMENT_OLECREATE_EX(CButtonerCtrl, "BUTTONER.ButtonerCtrl.1",
    0x6ae5a161, 0x9584, 0x11d0, 0x88, 0x60, 0x44, 0x45, 0x53, 0x54, 0, 0)


/////////////////////////////////////////////////////////////////////
// Type library ID and version

IMPLEMENT_OLETYPELIB(CButtonerCtrl, _tlid, _wVerMajor, _wVerMinor)


/////////////////////////////////////////////////////////////////////
// Interface IDs

const IID BASED_CODE IID_DButtoner = { 0x6ae5a15f, 0x9584, 0x11d0, { 0x88, 0x60,
➥0x44, 0x45, 0x53, 0x54, 0, 0 } };
const IID BASED_CODE IID_DButtonerEvents = { 0x6ae5a160, 0x9584, 0x11d0, { 0x88,
➥0x60, 0x44, 0x45, 0x53, 0x54, 0, 0 } };


/////////////////////////////////////////////////////////////////////
// Control type information

static const DWORD BASED_CODE _dwButtonerOleMisc =
    OLEMISC_ACTIVATEWHENVISIBLE |
    OLEMISC_SETCLIENTSITEFIRST |
    OLEMISC_INSIDEOUT |
    OLEMISC_CANTLINKINSIDE |
    OLEMISC_RECOMPOSEONRESIZE;

IMPLEMENT_OLECTLTYPE(CButtonerCtrl, IDS_BUTTONER, _dwButtonerOleMisc)


/////////////////////////////////////////////////////////////////////
```

```
// CButtonerCtrl::CButtonerCtrlFactory::UpdateRegistry -
// Adds or removes system registry entries for CButtonerCtrl

BOOL CButtonerCtrl::CButtonerCtrlFactory::UpdateRegistry(BOOL bRegister)
{
    // TODO: Verify that your control follows apartment-model threading rules.
    // Refer to MFC TechNote 64 for more information.
    // If your control does not conform to the apartment-model rules, then
    // you must modify the code below, changing the 6th parameter from
    // afxRegApartmentThreading to 0.

    if (bRegister)
        return AfxOleRegisterControlClass(
            AfxGetInstanceHandle(),
            m_clsid,
            m_lpszProgID,
            IDS_BUTTONER,
            IDB_BUTTONER,
            afxRegApartmentThreading,
            _dwButtonerOleMisc,
            _tlid,
            _wVerMajor,
            _wVerMinor);
    else
        return AfxOleUnregisterClass(m_clsid, m_lpszProgID);
}


/////////////////////////////////////////////////////////////////////////////
// CButtonerCtrl::CButtonerCtrl - Constructor

CButtonerCtrl::CButtonerCtrl()
{
    InitializeIIDs(&IID_DButtoner, &IID_DButtonerEvents);
    // TODO: Initialize your control's instance data here.

    SetText("Click Me!");
    m_data = 0;
}


/////////////////////////////////////////////////////////////////////////////
// CButtonerCtrl::~CButtonerCtrl - Destructor

CButtonerCtrl::~CButtonerCtrl()
{
    // TODO: Cleanup your control's instance data here.
}
```

```
/////////////////////////////////////////////////////////////////////////
// CButtonerCtrl::OnDraw - Drawing function

void CButtonerCtrl::OnDraw(CDC* pdc, const CRect& rcBounds, const CRect&
➥rcInvalid)
{
    DoSuperclassPaint(pdc, rcBounds);
}


/////////////////////////////////////////////////////////////////////////
// CButtonerCtrl::DoPropExchange - Persistence support

void CButtonerCtrl::DoPropExchange(CPropExchange* pPX)
{
    ExchangeVersion(pPX, MAKELONG(_wVerMinor, _wVerMajor));
    COleControl::DoPropExchange(pPX);

    // TODO: Call PX_ functions for each persistent custom property.

}


/////////////////////////////////////////////////////////////////////////
// CButtonerCtrl::OnResetState - Reset control to default state

void CButtonerCtrl::OnResetState()
{
    COleControl::OnResetState();  // Resets defaults found in DoPropExchange

    // TODO: Reset any other control state here.
}


/////////////////////////////////////////////////////////////////////////
// CButtonerCtrl::AboutBox - Display an "About" box to the user

void CButtonerCtrl::AboutBox()
{
    CDialog dlgAbout(IDD_ABOUTBOX_BUTTONER);
    dlgAbout.DoModal();
}


/////////////////////////////////////////////////////////////////////////
// CButtonerCtrl::PreCreateWindow - Modify parameters for CreateWindowEx

BOOL CButtonerCtrl::PreCreateWindow(CREATESTRUCT& cs)
{
```

```
        cs.lpszClass = _T("BUTTON");
        return COleControl::PreCreateWindow(cs);
}


/////////////////////////////////////////////////////////////////////////////
// CButtonerCtrl::IsSubclassedControl - This is a subclassed control

BOOL CButtonerCtrl::IsSubclassedControl()
{
        return TRUE;
}


/////////////////////////////////////////////////////////////////////////////
// CButtonerCtrl::OnOcmCommand - Handle command messages

LRESULT CButtonerCtrl::OnOcmCommand(WPARAM wParam, LPARAM lParam)
{
#ifdef _WIN32
        WORD wNotifyCode = HIWORD(wParam);
#else
        WORD wNotifyCode = HIWORD(lParam);
#endif

        // TODO: Switch on wNotifyCode here.

        return 0;
}


/////////////////////////////////////////////////////////////////////////////
// CButtonerCtrl message handlers


void CButtonerCtrl::OnLButtonDown(UINT nFlags, CPoint point)
{
        // TODO: Add your message handler code here and/or call default
        // FireClick();

        m_data++;

        COleControl::OnLButtonDown(nFlags, point);
}

void CButtonerCtrl::OnDataChanged()
{
        // TODO: Add notification handler code
```

```
        SetModifiedFlag();
}


void CButtonerCtrl::Beep()
{
        // TODO: Add your dispatch handler code here
        MessageBeep(MB_OK);
}
```

ButtonerappDlg.h and *ButtonerappDlg.cpp*

```
// ButtonerappDlg.h : header file
//
//{{AFX_INCLUDES()
#include "buttoner.h"
//}}AFX_INCLUDES

#if !defined(AFX_BUTTONERAPPDLG_H__9F6EEC67_988A_11D0_8860_444553540000__
➥INCLUDED_)
#define AFX_BUTTONERAPPDLG_H__9F6EEC67_988A_11D0_8860_444553540000__INCLUDED_

#if _MSC_VER >= 1000
#pragma once
#endif // _MSC_VER >= 1000


/////////////////////////////////////////////////////////////////////////
// CButtonerappDlg dialog

class CButtonerappDlg : public CDialog
{
// Construction
public:
    CButtonerappDlg(CWnd* pParent = NULL);    // standard constructor

// Dialog Data
    //{{AFX_DATA(CButtonerappDlg)
    enum { IDD = IDD_BUTTONERAPP_DIALOG };
    CString     m_text;
    CButtoner   m_buttoner;
    //}}AFX_DATA

    // ClassWizard generated virtual function overrides
    //{{AFX_VIRTUAL(CButtonerappDlg)
    protected:
    virtual void DoDataExchange(CDataExchange* pDX);    // DDX/DDV support
    //}}AFX_VIRTUAL
```

```
// Implementation
protected:
    HICON m_hIcon;

    // Generated message map functions
    //{{AFX_MSG(CButtonerappDlg)
    virtual BOOL OnInitDialog();
    afx_msg void OnSysCommand(UINT nID, LPARAM lParam);
    afx_msg void OnPaint();
    afx_msg HCURSOR OnQueryDragIcon();
    afx_msg void OnClickButtonerctrl1();
    DECLARE_EVENTSINK_MAP()
    //}}AFX_MSG
    DECLARE_MESSAGE_MAP()
};

//{{AFX_INSERT_LOCATION}}
// Microsoft Developer Studio will insert additional declarations immediately
// before the previous line.

#endif // !defined(AFX_BUTTONERAPPDLG_H__9F6EEC67_988A_11D0_8860_444553540000__
➡INCLUDED_)




// ButtonerappDlg.cpp : implementation file
//

#include "stdafx.h"
#include "Buttonerapp.h"
#include "ButtonerappDlg.h"

#ifdef _DEBUG
#define new DEBUG_NEW
#undef THIS_FILE
static char THIS_FILE[] = __FILE__;
#endif

/////////////////////////////////////////////////////////////////////////////
// CAboutDlg dialog used for App About

class CAboutDlg : public CDialog
{
public:
    CAboutDlg();

// Dialog Data
    //{{AFX_DATA(CAboutDlg)
```

```
    enum { IDD = IDD_ABOUTBOX };
    //}}AFX_DATA

    // ClassWizard generated virtual function overrides
    //{{AFX_VIRTUAL(CAboutDlg)
    protected:
    virtual void DoDataExchange(CDataExchange* pDX);    // DDX/DDV support
    //}}AFX_VIRTUAL

// Implementation
protected:
    //{{AFX_MSG(CAboutDlg)
    //}}AFX_MSG
    DECLARE_MESSAGE_MAP()
};

CAboutDlg::CAboutDlg() : CDialog(CAboutDlg::IDD)
{
    //{{AFX_DATA_INIT(CAboutDlg)
    //}}AFX_DATA_INIT
}

void CAboutDlg::DoDataExchange(CDataExchange* pDX)
{
    CDialog::DoDataExchange(pDX);
    //{{AFX_DATA_MAP(CAboutDlg)
    //}}AFX_DATA_MAP
}

BEGIN_MESSAGE_MAP(CAboutDlg, CDialog)
    //{{AFX_MSG_MAP(CAboutDlg)
        // No message handlers
    //}}AFX_MSG_MAP
END_MESSAGE_MAP()

/////////////////////////////////////////////////////////////////////////
// CButtonerappDlg dialog

CButtonerappDlg::CButtonerappDlg(CWnd* pParent /*=NULL*/)
    : CDialog(CButtonerappDlg::IDD, pParent)
{
    //{{AFX_DATA_INIT(CButtonerappDlg)
    m_text = _T("");
    //}}AFX_DATA_INIT
    // Note that LoadIcon does not require a subsequent DestroyIcon in Win32
    m_hIcon = AfxGetApp()->LoadIcon(IDR_MAINFRAME);
}

void CButtonerappDlg::DoDataExchange(CDataExchange* pDX)
{
```

```
        CDialog::DoDataExchange(pDX);
        //{{AFX_DATA_MAP(CButtonerappDlg)
        DDX_Text(pDX, IDC_EDIT1, m_text);
        DDX_Control(pDX, IDC_BUTTONERCTRL1, m_buttoner);
        //}}AFX_DATA_MAP
}

BEGIN_MESSAGE_MAP(CButtonerappDlg, CDialog)
        //{{AFX_MSG_MAP(CButtonerappDlg)
        ON_WM_SYSCOMMAND()
        ON_WM_PAINT()
        ON_WM_QUERYDRAGICON()
        //}}AFX_MSG_MAP
END_MESSAGE_MAP()

/////////////////////////////////////////////////////////////////////////
// CButtonerappDlg message handlers

BOOL CButtonerappDlg::OnInitDialog()
{
        CDialog::OnInitDialog();

        // Add "About..." menu item to system menu.

        // IDM_ABOUTBOX must be in the system command range.
        ASSERT((IDM_ABOUTBOX & 0xFFF0) == IDM_ABOUTBOX);
        ASSERT(IDM_ABOUTBOX < 0xF000);

        CMenu* pSysMenu = GetSystemMenu(FALSE);
        if (pSysMenu != NULL)
        {
            CString strAboutMenu;
            strAboutMenu.LoadString(IDS_ABOUTBOX);
            if (!strAboutMenu.IsEmpty())
            {
                pSysMenu->AppendMenu(MF_SEPARATOR);
                pSysMenu->AppendMenu(MF_STRING, IDM_ABOUTBOX, strAboutMenu);
            }
        }

        // Set the icon for this dialog.  The framework does this automatically
        //  when the application's main window is not a dialog
        SetIcon(m_hIcon, TRUE);                 // Set big icon
        SetIcon(m_hIcon, FALSE);                // Set small icon

        // TODO: Add extra initialization here

        return TRUE;  // return TRUE  unless you set the focus to a control
}
```

```
void CButtonerappDlg::OnSysCommand(UINT nID, LPARAM lParam)
{
    if ((nID & 0xFFF0) == IDM_ABOUTBOX)
    {
        CAboutDlg dlgAbout;
        dlgAbout.DoModal();
    }
    else
    {
        CDialog::OnSysCommand(nID, lParam);
    }
}

// If you add a minimize button to your dialog, you will need the code below
//  to draw the icon.  For MFC applications using the document/view model,
//  this is automatically done for you by the framework.

void CButtonerappDlg::OnPaint()
{
    if (IsIconic())
    {
        CPaintDC dc(this); // device context for painting

        SendMessage(WM_ICONERASEBKGND, (WPARAM) dc.GetSafeHdc(), 0);

        // Center icon in client rectangle
        int cxIcon = GetSystemMetrics(SM_CXICON);
        int cyIcon = GetSystemMetrics(SM_CYICON);
        CRect rect;
        GetClientRect(&rect);
        int x = (rect.Width() - cxIcon + 1) / 2;
        int y = (rect.Height() - cyIcon + 1) / 2;

        // Draw the icon
        dc.DrawIcon(x, y, m_hIcon);
    }
    else
    {
        CDialog::OnPaint();
    }
}

// The system calls this to obtain the cursor to display while the user drags
//  the minimized window.
HCURSOR CButtonerappDlg::OnQueryDragIcon()
{
    return (HCURSOR) m_hIcon;
}
```

```
BEGIN_EVENTSINK_MAP(CButtonerappDlg, CDialog)
    //{{AFX_EVENTSINK_MAP(CButtonerappDlg)
      ON_EVENT(CButtonerappDlg, IDC_BUTTONERCTRL1, -600 /* Click */,
➡OnClickButtonerctrl1, VTS_NONE)
    //}}AFX_EVENTSINK_MAP
END_EVENTSINK_MAP()

void CButtonerappDlg::OnClickButtonerctrl1()
{
    // TODO: Add your control notification handler code here
    m_text.Format("data property = %ld", m_buttoner.GetData());
    UpdateData(false);
}
```

We've come far in this skill, seeing how to create ActiveX controls, draw them, derive them from other Windows controls, and support ActiveX events, methods, and properties. Using these techniques, you can create your own powerful ActiveX controls and use them in your programs. In the next skill, we'll take a look at a topic befitting our last skill: debugging.

Are You Experienced?

Now You Can...

- ☑ Create an ActiveX control
- ☑ Draw an ActiveX control's appearance
- ☑ Derive an ActiveX control from a preexisting Windows control
- ☑ Support ActiveX events like mouse clicks
- ☑ Support ActiveX properties that other programs can read
- ☑ Support ActiveX methods that other programs can call

S K I L L

fourteen

Debugging Visual C++ Programs

- ❑ Using the Visual C++ debugger
- ❑ Single-stepping through a program
- ❑ Setting breakpoints
- ❑ Examining data in a running program
- ❑ Fixing bugs
- ❑ Stepping over, into, and out of code

In this skill, we are going to see how to debug our programs. Debugging is often a fact of life for programmers (most programs of any length have bugs that have to be fixed) and the debugging capabilities of Visual C++ help a great deal.

We'll start by creating a program with some bugs in it—in fact, the program will be named buggy—and then we'll see how to use the debugger to find and fix those bugs. In particular, we'll see how to set a *breakpoint* in a program, and execute the program up to that point. When we reach a breakpoint, program execution stops and the code we're debugging appears so that we can examine just what's going on.

You can then step through the code while it's running, a process called *single-stepping*. As we work through the code line by line, we'll be able to watch the values in the various variables in our program, and examining the values in those variables will tell us what's wrong with the program—when a variable holds an unexpected value, we should suspect a bug. After we've found the bugs, we can fix them and debug the program.

Let's start now by creating the buggy program, and then debugging it.

The Buggy Program

In the program for this skill, buggy, we'll just find the average of the first five positive integers: 1–5. The answer we expect is 3, but as we'll see, we'll get a variety of answers before debugging the program completely.

Create this program now using the AppWizard, and make it an SDI program. We'll store the first five integers in an array, data[], and we add that array to the document header now:

```
// buggyDoc.h : interface of the CBuggyDoc class
                         .
                         .
                         .
    public:
→       int data[5];
                         .
                         .
                         .
```

Next, we place the values we want to average in this array in the document's constructor:

```
CBuggyDoc::CBuggyDoc()
```

```
{
    data[0] = 1;
    data[1] = 2;
    data[2] = 3;
    data[3] = 4;
    data[4] = 5;
}
```

Now we're ready to do the calculation. Using the menu editor, add a new menu to the program, Calculate (we will place that menu between the File and Edit menus), with one item in it: "Calculate Average". Now use ClassWizard to add an event-handler to that menu item:

```
void CBuggyView::OnCalculateCalculateaverage()
{

}
```

In this method, we'll perform the calculation and display the results on the screen. We start by getting a pointer to our document, since the data to average is stored there:

```
      void CBuggyView::OnCalculateCalculateaverage()
      {
→         CBuggyDoc* pDoc = GetDocument();
→         ASSERT_VALID(pDoc);
                 .
                 .
                 .
      }
```

Next, we'll set up the variables we'll need. Finding an average involves summing up the values you want to average and dividing that sum by the number of items involved in finding the average, so we set up two variables, Sum and Average:

```
      void CBuggyView::OnCalculateCalculateaverage()
      {
          CBuggyDoc* pDoc = GetDocument();
          ASSERT_VALID(pDoc);

→         float Sum;
→         float Average;
                 .
                 .
                 .
      }
```

Now we set up a loop to calculate the sum of the five integers like this:

```
void CBuggyView::OnCalculateCalculateaverage()

{
    CBuggyDoc* pDoc = GetDocument();
    ASSERT_VALID(pDoc);

    float Sum;
    float Average;

    for(int loop_index = 1; loop_index < 5; loop_index++)
    {
        Sum += pDoc->data[loop_index];
    }
        .
        .
        .

}
```

Then we find the average we are looking for by dividing the sum by five:

```
void CBuggyView::OnCalculateCalculateaverage()
{
    CBuggyDoc* pDoc = GetDocument();
    ASSERT_VALID(pDoc);

    float Sum;
    float Average;

    for(int loop_index = 1; loop_index < 5; loop_index++)
    {
        Sum += pDoc->data[loop_index];
    }

    Average = Sum / (float) 5.0;
        .
        .
        .

}
```

Finally, we place the result in a string named OutputString and invalidate the view to display that string:

```
void CBuggyView::OnCalculateCalculateaverage()
{
    CBuggyDoc* pDoc = GetDocument();
    ASSERT_VALID(pDoc);

    float Sum;
```

```
    float Average;

    for(int loop_index = 1; loop_index < 5; loop_index++)
    {
        Sum += pDoc->data[loop_index];
    }

    Average = Sum / (float) 5.0;
```
→
```
    OutputString.Format("The average of the first five integers is:
➡%.3f", Average);
```
→
```
    Invalidate();
}
```

That completes the menu item handler. Next, we set up the OutputString object in the view's header:

```
// buggyView.h : interface of the CBuggyView class
        .
        .
        .
protected:
```
→
```
    CString OutputString;
        .
        .
        .
}
```

We place a prompt in that string inviting the user to select the Calculate Average item in the Calculate menu in the view's constructor (this prompt will be visible when the program first runs):

```
void CBuggyView::OnDraw(CDC* pDC)
{
    CBuggyDoc* pDoc = GetDocument();
    ASSERT_VALID(pDoc);

    pDC->TextOut(0, 0, OutputString);

}
```

Finally, we display OutputString in OnDraw():

```
CBuggyView::CBuggyView()
{
    OutputString = "Select the Calculate Average item in the Calculate
➡menu";
}
```

That finishes our code, so now we're set.

Run the program now and click the Calculate Average menu item. The program informs us that the average of the five integers 1–5 is 2818446765003793900.00, as shown in Figure 14.1.

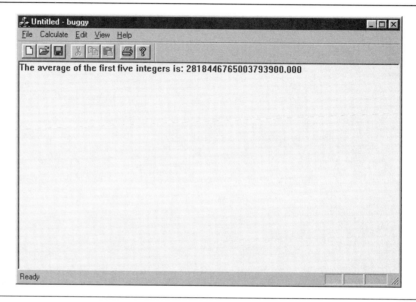

FIGURE 14.1: The buggy program: first attempt

We suspect a bug.

Setting a Breakpoint

It's time to debug the buggy program. The first step is to get into the program as it's running so we can start single-stepping through its lines of code; but we don't want to start from the beginning of the program, because that would mean executing interminable Visual C++ start-up code that we usually don't even see. Instead, we want to start debugging close to where we suspect the problem is—the code where we calculate the average.

To start debugging at a particular line of our code, we set a *breakpoint* there. Then, when we run our program, the program will stop at that breakpoint and we'll be able to look at our code, stepping through it as we want.

Let's see this in action. We can set a breakpoint at the beginning of our calculation code in the OnCalculateCalculateaverage() method, in particular, at the first line of the for loop:

```
void CBuggyView::OnCalculateCalculateaverage()
{
    CBuggyDoc* pDoc = GetDocument();
    ASSERT_VALID(pDoc);

    float Sum;
    float Average;

    for(int loop_index = 1; loop_index < 5; loop_index++)
    {
        Sum += pDoc->data[loop_index];
    }

    Average = Sum / (float) 5.0;

    OutputString.Format("The average of the first five integers is:
➥%.3f", Average);

    Invalidate();
}
```

Then we can single-step through our code one line at a time by pressing the F10 key; pressing that key once moves us to the next line of code:

```
void CBuggyView::OnCalculateCalculateaverage()
{
    CBuggyDoc* pDoc = GetDocument();
    ASSERT_VALID(pDoc);

    float Sum;
    float Average;

    for(int loop_index = 1; loop_index < 5; loop_index++)
    {
        Sum += pDoc->data[loop_index];
    }

    Average = Sum / (float) 5.0;

    OutputString.Format("The average of the first five integers is:
➥%.3f", Average);

    Invalidate();
}
```

Pressing F10 repeatedly allows us to move through our code as we like. We'll be able to examine the values in the various variables in our program as we move through it as well, so the practice of debugging is much like getting a window into our code as it executes. Because we know how the code is *supposed* to work, we can spot problems as they arise.

To set a breakpoint at the beginning of the for loop, place the insertion point caret (that is, the blinking cursor) at that line in Visual C++ and press the F9 key, or press the button in the toolbar with an upraised hand icon. This sets a breakpoint at that line (a program can have many breakpoints), as shown in Figure 14.2, where we see the breakpoint represented by a small stop sign symbol in the left margin.

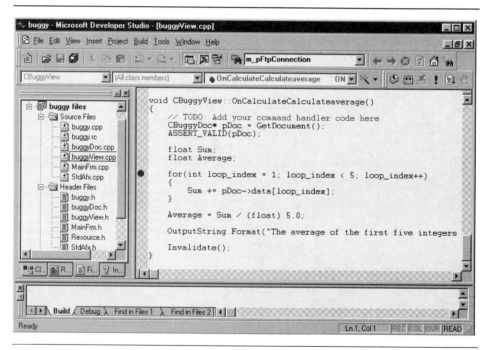

FIGURE 14.2: Setting a breakpoint

TIP   You can't set breakpoints at data declaration lines like Float Sum;.

Running to a Breakpoint

Now we run the program with the debugger. To do that, just select Build ≻ Start Debug ≻ Go. Our program appears on the screen, and you can select the Calculate ≻ Calculate Average item. This executes the code in OnCalculate-Calculateaverage(), until program execution reaches the line at which we've set the breakpoint. Then the program stops and displays the code in Visual C++, as shown in Figure 14.3. Notice the arrow in the left margin of Visual C++ in Figure 14.3; this arrow indicates the current line of execution in our program.

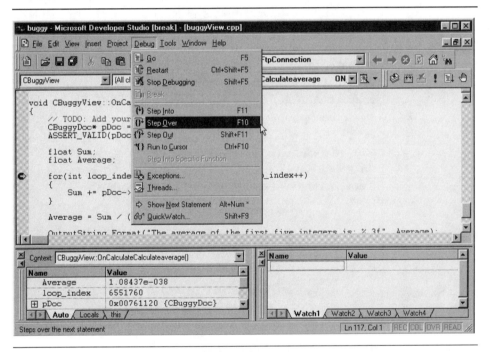

FIGURE 14.3: Stopped at a breakpoint

We note that Visual C++'s Build menu has now been replaced by the Debug menu, as shown in Figure 14.3. Note the selections there: Step Into (F11), Step Over (F10), Step Out (Shift+F11), and Run to Cursor (Ctrl+F10). These are the various ways we have of executing code now that we're in the Visual C++ debugger.

Single-Stepping through Code

When you are debugging Visual C++, you will encounter lines of code that call various methods (like this: `PerformWork(data);`), and if you just keep going line by line, you'll find yourself transported to that new method (for example, `PerformWork()`, which might be a long method). This means that you have to step through all the lines of code in that new method prior to getting back to the code you were debugging before the method call.

That's fine if you wanted to debug the called method, but what if you don't (for example, if the called method is a Visual C++ method)? In this case, you can step *over* method calls using the F10 key to single-step through your code.

If you do want to execute the code in called methods, use the F11 key to step *into* that code.

If you find yourself in a called method or block of code that you don't want to debug, you can step out of that code with the Shift+F11 key.

The other option is to place the insertion point at some location in the program past the current line of execution and press Ctrl+F10, which executes all the code up to the cursor.

In this case, we'll use F10 to single-step through our code. Press F10 once now to move us to the next line of code in our program:

```
void CBuggyView::OnCalculateCalculateaverage()
{
    CBuggyDoc* pDoc = GetDocument();
    ASSERT_VALID(pDoc);

    float Sum;
    float Average;

    for(int loop_index = 1; loop_index < 5; loop_index++)
    {
➜       Sum += pDoc->data[loop_index];
    }

    Average = Sum / (float) 5.0;

    OutputString.Format("The average of the first five integers is:
➥%.3f", Average);

    Invalidate();
}
```

Now we're at the next line of code, as shown in Figure 14.4. This is the line where we add values to our running sum in the Sum variable.

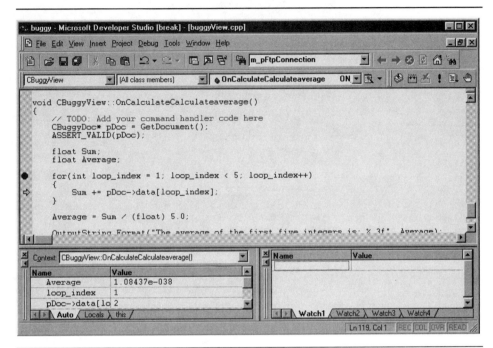

FIGURE 1 4 . 4 : Single-stepping through code

To execute the current line, where we update the running sum, press F10 again to move past that line, as shown in Figure 14.5. Now that we've added the first integer to the Sum variable, we can take a look at the value of that variable to make sure everything is OK.

Examining Variables as the Program Runs

To examine the value in the Sum variable—which should hold the first integer, 1—just rest the mouse cursor over that variable, as shown in Figure 14.5. A tool tip appears with the variable's value, which we see is 1.40922e+019, or 1.40922×10^{19}, rather more than we expected. We've found a problem.

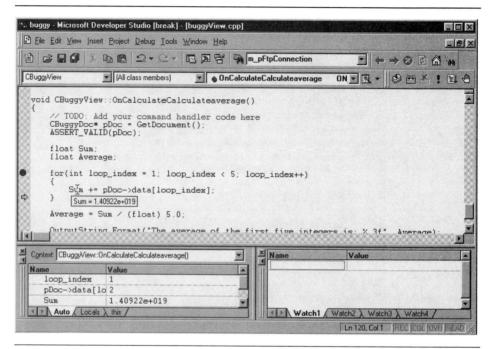

FIGURE 14.5: Examining the contents of a variable

The Auto and Locals Windows

Besides using a tool tip to determine the value in Sum, you can also see that variable and its value in the window at the bottom left of Figure 14.5, the Auto window (note the tab marked Auto in Figure 14.5). This window holds the most recent variables that Visual C++ has encountered, and we see our Sum variable there. In addition, if you switch to the Locals window by clicking the Locals tab, you'll see all the variables (including Sum) defined in the current method or code block.

> **TIP**   If you want to keep track of a specific variable at all times when debugging a program, type it into the Watch window at lower right in Visual C++.

Looking through our code, we can see that we forgot to initialize the running sum to 0, so we do that now. First, stop debugging by selecting the Stop Debugging item in the Debug menu, then edit the code to initialize our running sum to 0.

```
void CBuggyView::OnCalculateCalculateaverage()
{
    CBuggyDoc* pDoc = GetDocument();
    ASSERT_VALID(pDoc);

➼   float Sum = 0;
    float Average;

    for(int loop_index = 1; loop_index < 5; loop_index++)
    {
        Sum += pDoc->data[loop_index];
    }

    Average = Sum / (float) 5.0;

    OutputString.Format("The average of the first five integers is:
➼%.3f", Average);

    Invalidate();
}
```

Now that we've fixed the initialization bug, run the program again, as shown in Figure 14.6.

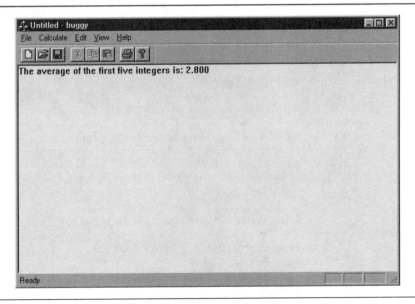

FIGURE 14.6: The buggy program: second attempt

Now we learn that the average of the first five integers is 2.800, which is certainly closer to the value of 3.000 that we expected, but not on target yet. It's time to go back to the debugger.

Start debugging by selecting Build ≻ Start Debug ≻ Go again, and run the program to the breakpoint. Next, press F10 to start the for loop, as shown in Figure 14.7. Place the mouse cursor over the Sum variable to see that the value there is indeed 0.

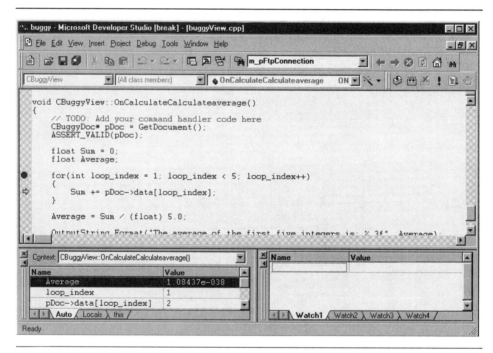

FIGURE 14.7: Debugging the buggy program's for loop

The Sum variable is fine, so let's look at the value we're adding to it, pDoc->data[loop_index]:

```cpp
void CBuggyView::OnCalculateCalculateaverage()
{
    CBuggyDoc* pDoc = GetDocument();
    ASSERT_VALID(pDoc);

    float Sum = 0;
    float Average;

    for(int loop_index = 1; loop_index < 5; loop_index++)
    {
```

```
→              Sum += pDoc->data[loop_index];
        }

        Average = Sum / (float) 5.0;

        OutputString.Format("The average of the first five integers is:
➥%.3f", Average);

        Invalidate();
}
```

To find the value of this expression, pDoc->data[loop_index], we can't just use the mouse cursor (because it's unclear what part of the expression we want to evaluate—just pDoc or the whole thing?), but we can find this expression's value in the Auto window at lower left. And there we see that the first integer we're about to add to the running sum is 2, not 1 as we expected.

Looking at our code, we see that we started the loop index with a value of 1, not 0 as it should be, so stop debugging and fix that now:

```
void CBuggyView::OnCalculateCalculateaverage()
{
        CBuggyDoc* pDoc = GetDocument();
        ASSERT_VALID(pDoc);

        float Sum = 0;
        float Average;

→       for(int loop_index = 0; loop_index < 5; loop_index++)
        {
                Sum += pDoc->data[loop_index];
        }

        Average = Sum / (float) 5.0;

        OutputString.Format("The average of the first five integers is:
➥%.3f", Average);

        Invalidate();
}
```

TIP   **To evaluate some expression while debugging a program, you can select the Debug menu's QuickWatch menu item and type that expression into the QuickWatch dialog box for Visual C++ to evaluate it.**

Now run the program, as shown in Figure 14.8; we've gotten the expected result: the average of 1-5 is 3. We've debugged our program, using the built-in debugging power of Visual C++.

To remove the breakpoint we set, place the insertion point caret on the breakpoint code line and press F9 again to toggle the breakpoint off.

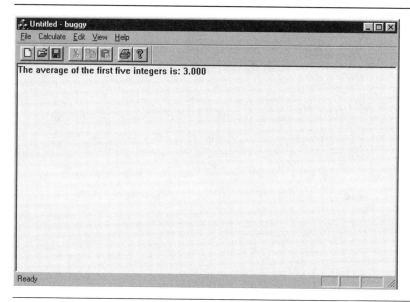

FIGURE 14.8: The debugged buggy program

 TIP   Now that the program is debugged, you can remove the debugging information from the .exe file. Select the Settings item in the Project and select Win32 Release instead of Win32 Debug in the drop-down list box in the Settings box (by default, Visual C++ programs are built to include a lot of information used by the debugger).

That finishes our tour of the Visual C++ debugger, and also finishes this book. All that remains now is to put all this power to work—happy programming!

Are You Experienced?

Now You Can...

☑ Use the Visual C++ debugger

☑ Single-step through a program

☑ Examine the value of variables in a running program using the mouse

☑ Use the Auto and Locals debug windows

☑ Step over, into, and out of code blocks while debugging

☑ Set and remove breakpoints

INDEX

Note to the Reader: Throughout this index **boldfaced** page numbers indicate primary discussions of a topic. *Italicized* page numbers indicate illustrations.

E

F

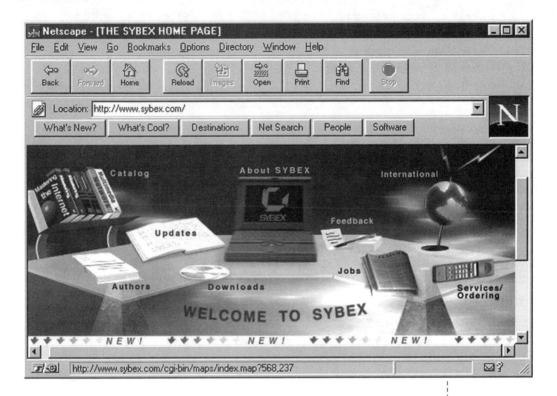

Visual C++ in Microsoft's Developer Studio 97

The Microsoft Visual Studio 97 is where you develop and test the Visual C++ programs. In this environment, you create and fine tune applications for the Internet, word processing, graphics manipulation, and more. Many Visual C++ tools and resources are labeled here, all of which are fully explained in the book.

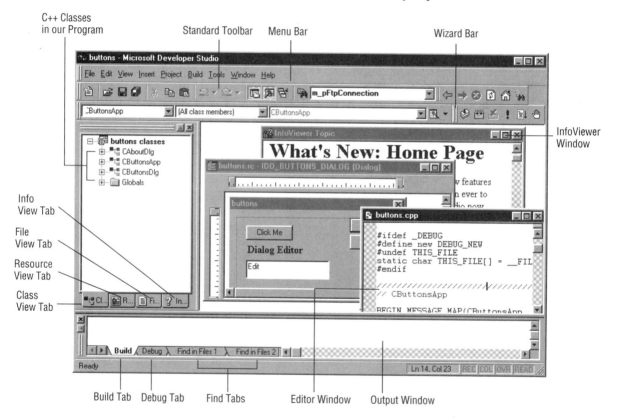